EUN YOUNG Ahn

Principles of Computer Science

CULLEN SCHAFFER

Rutgers University

PRENTICE HALL, Englewood Cliffs, New Jersey 07632

Library of Congress Cataloging-in-Publication Data

SCHAFFER, CULLEN, (date)
    Principles of computer science.

    Includes index.
    1. Computers.   2. Electronic data processing.
I. Title.
QA76.S345 1988   004   87-29061
ISBN 0-13-709759-X

Editorial/production supervision
and interior design: *Joan McCulley*
Cover design: *Photo Plus Art*
Manufacturing buyer: *Rick Washburn*

 © 1988 by Prentice-Hall, Inc.
A Division of Simon & Schuster
Englewood Cliffs, New Jersey 07632

Printed in the United States of America
10 9 8 7 6 5 4 3 2 1

ISBN   0-13-709759-X   025

PRENTICE-HALL INTERNATIONAL (UK) LIMITED, *London*
PRENTICE-HALL OF AUSTRALIA PTY. LIMITED, *Sydney*
PRENTICE-HALL CANADA INC., *Toronto*
PRENTICE-HALL HISPANOAMERICANA, S.A., *Mexico*
PRENTICE-HALL OF INDIA PRIVATE LIMITED, *New Delhi*
PRENTICE-HALL OF JAPAN, INC., *Tokyo*
SIMON & SCHUSTER ASIA PTE. LTD., *Singapore*
EDITORIA PRENTICE-HALL DO BRASIL, LTDA., *Rio de Janeiro*

For Guthrie and Cecily,
whom I admire

Contents

10. Translation   *299*

11. An Algorithmic Language   *334*

Preface

Frankly speaking, the volume at hand is an odd one—a kind of eccentric friend whom I am glad to have had as a companion these many months, but yet am rather apprehensive in introducing to a larger acquaintance.

The book opens with a detailed account of how to build a computer from transistors, and yet it relegates external memory and I/O devices to a few pages at the end. It introduces the halting problem and uncomputability; complexity analysis and recursion; and yet it presumes virtually no mathematics, not even algebra. Finally, as if it were not enough to treat computer science topics from Boolean logic to artificial intelligence, the narrative ranges off at times into biology, philosophy, psychology, and economics.

I think it is safe to say the approach is unique. The question, of course, is whether it has any *other* merits.

One, certainly, is that it concentrates on some of the most exciting, important ideas in the history of technology. These are implicit, of course, in other introductory texts, but all too often scintillating ideas are couched in inscrutable equations, with relevance and ramifications written only between the lines.

Furthermore, the first goal of most texts is to convey *practical* information, much of which is rather less than earthshaking. Most people appreciate the utility of a keyboard; few care to read about it.

The topics treated here are of practical value, but they have been chosen primarily on grounds of intellectual significance. I have asked myself what ideas we computer scientists have reason to be proud of and then attempted to present these at an introductory level.

The result is a knockout lineup. As the deep insights of our discipline are revealed, students ought to experience not just understanding, but awe; and if I occasionally overstep the usual bounds of textbook matter and prose, it is with the idea of exciting this reaction. I would hope the tenor of the presentation is so fitted to the brilliance of the material that students will be moved to burst out from time to time into unprintable, but appreciative, expletives. Certainly, if they do not, it is the writing and not the material to blame.

*   *   *   *   *

To get at the powerful ideas of computer science, a surprisingly simple model of the computer suffices. By paring the machine down to essentials, dispensing with everything but a serviceable processor and some internal memory, I have managed to say nearly everything about how it works in a few chapters.

I expect students will get a certain satisfaction from learning what makes a computer tick, from transistors to CPU; but the project of building a computer also provides a framework into which other topics may be introduced coherently: formal logic, through Boolean algebra; the central role of feedback in self-regulating systems; and the basis of arithmetic operations in the place-value scheme.

Moreover, the ascent from transistors to logic gates, from logic gates to flip-flops, and from flip-flops to memory systems and higher—this itself is an awesome and valuable introduction to the power of hierarchical design. Indeed, one of the deep lessons of the computer, and perhaps of technology as a whole, is that the agglomeration of simple, well-defined constituents may yield disproportionate power in the whole.

The intent of the first chapters, then, is not merely to explain computer architecture, but rather, as my title would suggest, to elucidate the principles underlying it.

Once the components of a model computer have been plausibly designed, a few elementary machine-language examples lead quickly and, I should hope, shockingly to the halting problem proof of uncomputability. This naturally raises important questions about the limits of mechanical information processing. But it is equally valuable here as a testament to the abstract approach which distinguishes computer science from computer programming.

This distinction is often drawn in textbook prefaces, but I think it is rarely impressed upon students in the chapters following. To my mind, the halting problem proof is the strongest and best medicine for adept programmers, who are all too apt to treat analysis as a kind of artificial complication.

To drive the point home, the text continues with an analytic look at algorithms and data structures, considering searching and sorting problems with an emphasis on efficiency. I expect students to leave this section with an intuitive appreciation of the enormous difference between functions of various orders—$\log n$, linear, $n \log n$, and n^2—as well as with a practical respect for what may be gained through the creative organization and handling of information.

Again, no mathematics is presumed. Rather than treating logarithms as a prerequisite to complexity analysis, I have used complexity examples to motivate logarithms, and, with apologies to the mathematics department, I think students will be grateful for the more concrete approach.

From a general consideration of data structures, the text focuses on the special role of stacks in subroutines and recursion. These are both of major importance: subroutines because they allow us to apply hierarchical design principles to software as well as to hardware; recursion because it provides an alternative, equally powerful model of computation.

Both also suggest ways of raising the machine to a higher level of understanding, a topic with which most of the rest of the book is concerned. Translation and bootstrapping are the principal topics, but I have also included a description of a high-level language, a simplified one designed to give programmers a fresh view of the essential algorithmic elements and nonprogrammers a feel for the ease of high-level programming, unclouded by the syntactic complexities of practical languages.

With the essence of the computer bared, then, from transistors to translators, the text finishes its tour where most begin, by introducing practical, auxiliary features such as disk drives, I/O devices, and operating systems, along with some of the jargon avoided elsewhere in the text. This ties together many otherwise disparate subjects and relates the sophisticated, abstract notion of a computer developed in the text to the pedestrian contraption with which many students are already quite familiar.

From these pragmatic concerns, however, the text turns for its conclusion to the question of artificial intelligence. If the preceding chapters are not wholly uninterpretive, this last one is frankly opinionated. It will have served its purpose well if it provokes a heated response.

                              *   *   *   *   *

It may be discerned from this description that what I have written is not simply a collection of related chapters. This text embodies a development, an organizing scheme. It aims to show students not only the ideas of our discipline, but how these are interwoven to *form* a discipline. Realizing that I cannot hope to include all the facts in a single volume, I have striven instead to provide an overview, a framework into which students may later fit details.

This makes the book a useful one, I think, for computer science majors, who will be bombarded with such details in other courses.

For two reasons, it should also find a place in the general introductory course, which constitutes a kind of invitation to the field. First, if we concentrate on Pascal in such classes, the ranks of our majors will swell with students who believe computer science is the study of programming. Second, conversely, if the introductory course does *not* offer a substantial taste of the best computer science has to offer, we risk losing the very brightest students, the ones we pine for in upper-level classes.

Finally, although it may seem odd to some, my own intent is to use the book in a Rutgers University course meant strictly for nonmajors. Existing literacy texts stress vocabulary, programming, and the use of applications packages. The fact is, however, that students who take a one-semester introductory course are extremely unlikely to have any use for programming skills after the course has concluded. They will, of course, have occasion to use word processing and spreadsheet programs, but these have been geared to the mass market and require little teaching.

This book gives substance to my deep conviction that technical subjects merit the respect and treatment normally reserved for works in the humanities. We teach literature not for any immediate, pragmatic benefit, but because of its inherent beauty and the difficulty, sometimes, of apprehending that beauty without guidance. In the same way, I would like to try to convey something of the feeling of computer science to nontechnical students.

*   *   *   *   *

With these words, then, I send my eccentric friend out to greet the world. The text is an odd one, admittedly, but it is written with a good deal of affection and respect for the material it treats. I entrust it to the consideration of my like-hearted colleagues.

Cullen Schaffer
New Brunswick, New Jersey

Introduction

Ten years ago, a book about computers might have begun with a definition. Today, most people already know more about the machine than a definition can tell. A hefty percentage have been taught to *use* a computer in some way—either to program it or to use a store-bought program like a word processor. Many own a computer or have considered buying one.

Computers are becoming as familiar as the family dog and, if we are to believe the advertising copy we read, nearly as friendly. Would a book called *Principles of Canine Science* begin with a definition? Nonsense. Everyone knows what a dog is, and most people know quite a bit more: what dogs eat, how to teach them tricks, what the difference is between a collie and a poodle, and so on.

But, for all this knowledge, how much *do* we know?

For one thing, a dog's internal workings are more complex, by far, than our most fabulous mechanical and electronic inventions. From intricate cells to major organs like the heart and stomach, the body of a dog is a miracle of design—a miracle few people appreciate in any depth.

Moreover, knowing how a dog digests food and pumps blood is only the beginning—it still leaves us with questions on a higher level. Why does the dog sleep? What kind of control system keeps all its parts functioning smoothly together? Despite the simplicity of these questions, it is fair to say that *no one*—neither scientist nor dog lover—knows the full answer.

On a third level, consider behavior. In part, this is based on instinct. We all know that dogs have a built-in tendency to chase cats and bury bones. Charting the full range of instinctual behavior, however, is a major scientific problem. Another is explaining why dogs have the instincts they do—how these contribute to its survival.

Behavior is more than instinct, however. Intelligence permits a dog to learn and to be trained. This fact leads to theoretical questions about *how* dogs learn. It also suggests practical questions about how to teach them—to perform tricks, guide blind people, or sniff out bombs.

Finally, all these points lead to questions on a yet higher level. How has evolution made the dog what it is? Through further evolution or breeding, what will it become? How far may a dog be trained? What is the limit of canine intelligence?

*   *   *   *   *

Understanding, it seems, is a matter of many levels. When we say that everyone knows about dogs, we really mean only that all people know a little about some of the middle levels. A scientist could fill a book with what most people do *not* know about the family dog.

Moreover, there would be good reasons for reading such a book. First, subjects like physiology, evolution, and animal behavior are fascinating in their own right. The fact of life grows all the more astounding and marvelous when we examine the details.

Second, a many-leveled understanding is important for practical purposes. To breed dogs efficiently, we need to know genetics. To train them, we ought to understand canine instinct and intelligence.

Last, and perhaps most important, much of what we might learn about dogs would apply beyond the canine world. Genetics, respiration, instinct—once we have learned about these things, we may apply our knowledge to animals in general, even to ourselves. Research into how dogs fight disease can lead to advances in human medicine.

Furthermore, beyond the applications in other parts of biology, knowledge about dogs might provide insight in unrelated fields. Engineers, for example, have a great deal to learn from the dog about design and control. They have yet to build a machine that walks and climbs as easily as the dog does over uneven surfaces.

Also, the dog is a marvel of planning and compromise. At any moment, it is bombarded with information and torn by conflicting desires. A hungry, tired dog may be called by its owner just as a cat runs by. Will the dog chase, eat, sleep, heed the call? Somehow, all the information and urges must be managed and coordinated so that the dog acts sensibly.

An understanding of the dog's decision process might well profit *people* who are bombarded with information and torn by conflicting pressures: people who manage and coordinate complex systems like factories and governments.

As a last example, consider evolution. Once we have the idea and understand how it applies to dogs, we may begin to consider the evolution of economies, peoples, or ideologies. Attempting to understand dogs may lead us to principles which are of general use, far beyond the original context.

This, in fact, is our main point: it is not only the dog we are interested in, but the *principles* behind it.

*   *   *   *   *

Naturally, all we have said is relevant to computers as well as canines. When we say that most people are familiar with computers, we mean that they know a little bit about the middle levels. This is as true of most programmers as it is of the English major who knows only how to write essays with a word processor.

Most of this book is an attempt to explain the other levels and to show how they are related. That is, we want to provide a broad understanding of what computers are and how they may be used.

We will begin by showing, in detail, how a computer is constructed. It is an odd fact that, although the computer is the most complex invention in the history of humankind, we can give a fairly complete explanation of its design in just a few chapters.

Part of the reason is that the computer is designed on many levels. By saying just a little about each level it is possible to show how the whole machine operates. At first, we will discuss the simple electronic parts that go into a computer. Then we will explain how the parts are assembled into components, how the components are used to build systems and, finally, how the systems go together to make a working computer.

All these lower levels concern the physiology of the computer, its inner workings. Once we have considered these thoroughly, we will move on to higher-level questions about the computer's behavior. In particular, we will want to ask what it can and cannot do.

Given that the computer can undertake quite a variety of useful projects, we will also need to consider *practical* questions of efficiency. As we will see, computers are information-handling machines. Efficiency depends on organizing and using information effectively.

Finally, on a still higher level, we will look into the peculiar fact that computers may be used to increase their own power. This leads to some exciting, perhaps crucial questions: How powerful can computers get? Can they match our own information-handling skills? Can they think?

The reasons for studying computers at all these levels are exactly those we gave a moment ago. First, the subject material is inherently intriguing. The computer is very nearly a miracle and it becomes all the more astounding and marvelous when we examine it closely.

Second, a many-leveled understanding is important for practical purposes. Knowing how the computer is constructed often aids efficient programming. Likewise, knowing the limits of what computers can do may keep us from attempting impossible projects.

Last, and perhaps most important, much of what we learn in studying computers applies in other fields as well. In part, this is because techniques for designing and controlling complex systems carry over into other kinds of engineering.

But, as we will see, the ideas behind computers also apply in many seemingly unrelated fields: biology, economics, and, especially, pyschology.

And now we come back, again, to our main point: It is not only the computer we are interested in, but the *principles* behind it. These are what make this book not a programming guide, but an introduction to computer science. It is the idea of the computer and the analysis of that idea which forms our subject of study.

1 Logic with Electricity

1.1 VALVES AND TRANSISTORS

The electronic digital computer is the crowning achievement and hallmark of our age. This book begins by explaining how it works.

Perhaps the first thing to say is that it is remarkable in itself that we can expect to explain the workings of such an intricate invention to someone without advanced training. Of course, the project is not an easy one. The first chapters of this book contain a flood of new ideas, and nearly anyone who reads them is likely to be overwhelmed for a time.

The fact is, however, that each of the ideas is quite simple. The computer is a marvel of power, but that power comes from simple things put together, just as the great power of factory production boils down to the simple tasks of the assembly line or as the complex workings of an anthill rest on the actions of many simple-minded ants.

Just as it would be natural to begin a study of anthills with the ants, we begin to explain computers by looking at the smallest part that goes into making one: a switch. We start with switches because computers work with information and, in a certain sense, a switch is the simplest thing that can store or control information.

A light switch on a wall, for example, can be used to leave a message. Two roommates might agree that, when the switch is left on, it means "Come meet me in the library."

Of course, a single light switch is not of much use in conveying meaning, since it can be left in only two positions, on or off. But what about a wall *covered* with switches? Each different pattern of switches on and off could be used for a different message.

The question of how to store information with switches turns out to be an essential one in building a computer. But, for now, the key point is that a switch stores information by having two different positions, or **states**, that it can assume: on and off.

The problem with a light switch is that the information it stores cannot be changed quickly. Even with fast reflexes, it is hard to flip a light switch up and down ten times in a second. If switches this slow were used in building computers, computers would take more than ten million times as long as they do to get work done. A computer would take roughly ten years, say, to alphabetize a list of a thousand names.

Luckily, computers use transistors.

A transistor works like a light switch in that it controls the flow of electricity. But, unlike a light switch, which uses metal parts that physically connect and disconnect, a transistor is a **solid-state** device; that is, it has no moving parts. A transistor uses electricity to turn electricity on and off.

If this sounds strange, it is only because electricity is somewhat abstract. To understand how it works, it is helpful to think first about how water flows through pipes.

One obvious point is that water in a pipe on flat ground will not flow at all unless something supplies water pressure. If we take a level section of pipe, fill it with water, and supply water pressure at one end with a pump, the water will flow through the pipe and out, as in Figure 1.1.

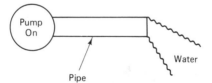

Figure 1.1 Water in a pipe.

Clearly, this arrangement has the disadvantage of wasting water. To fix the problem, we can attach a pressure meter to the other end of the pipe, as in Figure 1.2. When the pump is turned on, it will supply pressure, pushing the water to the right. The meter at the right will sense this pressure. But, since the meter blocks the end of the pipe, no water will flow.

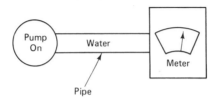

Figure 1.2 Testing water pressure.

Next, look at the valve in Figure 1.3. This is the key to what we will be discussing, so be sure to think carefully about how it operates. The valve consists of a spring, a plug, and two pipes, one vertical and the other horizontal. In the figure, the vertical pipe is free and clear. If we pump water in at the top, it will flow straight through to the bottom.

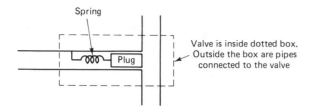

Figure 1.3 A cutoff valve.

Suppose, however, that we wanted to block up the vertical pipe. If we could somehow get the plug to slide to the right, that would do the job. The only problem is that the plug is held to the left by the spring.

One solution is to supply water pressure to the pipe on the left. When a pump is connected at the left and turned on, the water pressure pushes the plug to the right. That cuts off the flow of water through the vertical pipe.

If we attach a second pump at the top and a meter at the bottom, as in Figure 1.4., the meter will not show any pressure. There *is* pressure in the top half of the pipe, but that part of the pipe is cut off from the part attached to the meter.

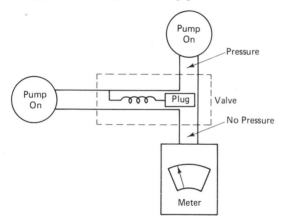

Figure 1.4 The cutoff valve: control pressure on.

If the pump on the left is turned off, the spring in the valve will pull the plug back out of the vertical pipe, as in Figure 1.5. Now the vertical pipe is clear again and the meter at the bottom will show pressure.

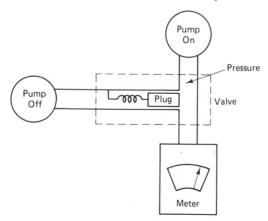

Figure 1.5 The cutoff valve: control pressure off.

A valve, then, may use water pressure to turn water pressure on and off. Perhaps now it will not seem so strange that a transistor uses electricity to turn electricity on and off.

In fact, electricity works very much like water. It is a flow of electrons through wires. The electrons in a piece of wire will not flow unless a kind of electrical pressure is applied. For example, a radio will not play unless we connect it to batteries or plug it into a wall outlet. The battery or the electric company's power plant supplies the necessary pressure.

Electrical pressure is called **voltage** and can be measured with a voltmeter. Just as with water, it is often convenient not to let the electricity flow.

Transistors do for electricity what valves do for water. For example, consider the transistor shown in Figure 1.6. Just as the horizontal pipe of our water valve controlled the flow of water through the vertical pipe, the horizontal wire in this picture controls the flow of electricity through the two vertical wires. If we apply voltage at the top of the vertical wire, as in Figure 1.6(a), the voltmeter will sense that voltage at the bottom. The path from top to bottom is free and clear. But if voltage is also applied at the left, as in Figure 1.6(b), it cuts off the flow of electricity in the vertical wire and the voltmeter will read zero. As we said before, the transistor uses electricity to turn electricity on and off.

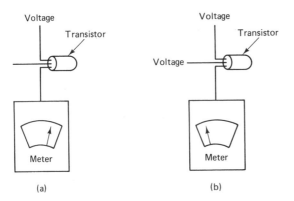

Figure 1.6 A transistor.

At this point it is reasonable to ask *how* transistors do what we say they do. It is clear from Figure 1.3. how we could build a water valve using some carefully designed pipes and a plug and spring. But how is it possible to build a transistor?

A complete answer will not be given here but may be found in many physics books. It has to do with the properties of certain materials called semiconductors, which take their name from the fact that they only partially conduct electricity (that is, allow it to flow). A transistor is a sandwich with one semiconductor material on the top and bottom and a different kind in the middle. Each of the three wires in Figure 1.6. is connected to a different layer of the sandwich.

With time, we could better explain the properties of the materials that make transistors work, but that explanation would lead to further questions about why the materials themselves behave so oddly. Instead of following this downward path of questions about smaller and smaller parts, we will work our way upward, asking what the parts can build.

Before we begin building, however, we are faced with a problem of notation. Complex connections between pipes are hard to draw and confusing to look at. Also, an engineer's standard picture of a transistor, shown in Figure 1.7, does not make clear what it does.

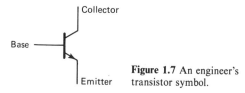

Figure 1.7 An engineer's transistor symbol.

We can solve two problems at once by drawing both valves and transistors as in Figure 1.8. The picture shows a main line—the vertical one—through which something flows, and a control line—coming in from the left—that can cut off flow in the main line. If we are talking about water, this is a picture of three pipes connected to a valve. If we are talking about electricity, it is a picture of three wires leading into a transistor.

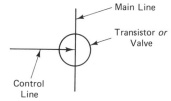

Figure 1.8 Transistor/Valve.

The only difference between a picture of a transistor circuit (several interconnected transistors) and a picture of pipes and valves is that one will have *voltage* written in certain places and the other will indicate *pressure*. From now on we will talk only about transistors, since they are what computers are really made of. Our diagrams, however, are just as good for pipes and pumps as they are for electronics.

If we wanted, we could build a very slow computer running completely on water pressure.

1.2 GATES

Now, suppose someone gives us a box, like the one in Figure 1.9, with two wires, labeled **In** and **Out**, running out of it. The question is, What is inside the box?

Testing the box with a battery and voltmeter, we find that the voltages at **In** and **Out** are always opposites. If we supply voltage to the wire at **In**, no voltage is measured at **Out**. If we do *not* put voltage in at **In**, voltage *does* come out at **Out**. What kind of circuit would work like this?

Figure 1.9 A mystery circuit.

The answer is shown in Figure 1.10. The box contains just a transistor and a voltage supply.

Here is how the circuit works. If voltage is supplied at **In**, the transistor will cut off the voltage in the vertical wire. The voltage from the supply inside the box will not get to **Out**. But if *no* voltage is supplied at **In**, the transistor does not cut off the vertical wire. The voltage from the inside voltage supply does get through to **Out**.

A box like this is not just a textbook example. It is possible to go into a real electronics store and buy one. It is usually called a **NOT gate**, because it puts voltage out only if we do *not* put voltage in.

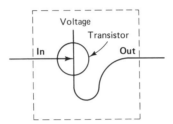

Figure 1.10 A NOT gate.

Now here is an easy question, but a slightly tricky one. What is the opposite of a NOT gate? That is, how can we design a box that puts out voltage exactly when voltage *is* put in? Think about it and then check the answer given in Figure 1.15 at the end of this section.

*   *   *   *   *

The NOT gate is one of only three gates needed to build a computer; and all three can be built with transistors.

An **OR gate**, the second of the three kinds, is a box with two wires coming in and one going out. Figure 1.11 shows one with the ingoing wires labeled **In-1** and **In-2** and the outgoing wire labeled **Out**.

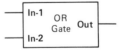

Figure 1.11 An OR gate.

The OR gate takes its name from a simple fact: It puts voltage out at **Out** when voltage is supplied at **In-1** *or* **In-2** *or* both.

Figure 1.12 shows how to build an OR gate using three transistors and a voltage supply. Incidentally, the figure shows voltage supplied in two places, but that does not mean we need two supplies. If we are using a battery, it could be hooked up to supply voltage in both places.

Notice that transistor 3 is turned on its side. The control wire runs vertically. If the voltage supplied at the top gets down to transistor 3, the transistor will cut off the horizontal wire at the bottom.

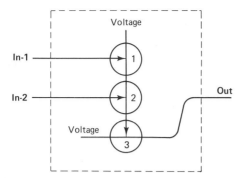

Figure 1.12 Design for an OR gate.

Now, here is how the OR gate works. Suppose voltage is supplied at **In-1** or **In-2** or both. Then the vertical wire will be cut off, by either transistor 1 or transistor 2 or both. In this case, no voltage will get to the control wire of transistor 3. Therefore transistor 3 will *not* cut off the horizontal wire at the bottom and the voltage supplied at the bottom left will register at **Out**.

In a nutshell, voltage in at either input—**In-1** or **In-2**—means the bottom wire will be free and clear. In that case, voltage supplied at the bottom left will get through to **Out**.

The only possibility we have not considered is when voltage is not supplied to either of the two inputs. In this case, neither transistor 1 nor transistor 2 cuts off the vertical wire. Voltage supplied at the top *does* get through to transistor 3, which cuts off the bottom wire. The end result is that the voltage supplied at the bottom left does not get through to the output.

*   *   *   *   *

OR and NOT gates do just what we would expect from their names. An OR gate puts out voltage if one *or* the other input is receiving voltage. A NOT gate puts out voltage if its input is *not* receiving voltage.

The third gate is a little harder to build, but what it does is still simple to understand. The **AND gate** in Figure 1.13 puts voltage out only if voltage is supplied to both **In-1** *and* **In-2**.

Figure 1.13 An AND gate.

Figure 1.14 shows the circuit design for an AND gate. A good way to analyze this circuit is to work backward. The only way for the voltage supplied at the lower left to reach **Out** is if neither transistor 3 nor transistor 4 cuts off the bottom wire. But the voltage supplied at the top *will* make these transistors cut off the bottom wire unless *it* is cut off somehow. Therefore the only way to get voltage at **Out** is if transistors 1 and 2 each cut off one of the vertical wires. This happens only if voltage is supplied at both **In-1** *and* **In-2**—exactly as we wanted.

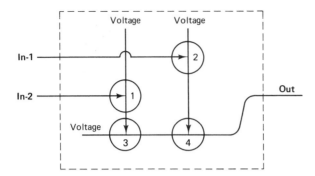

Figure 1.14 Design for an AND gate.

Now run the argument forward. If we supply voltage at both **In-1** and **In-2**, transistors 1 and 2 will cut off the vertical wires. That means that transistors 3 and 4 will *not* cut off the bottom wire. Thus the voltage supplied at the bottom left will reach **Out**.

If either **In-1** or **In-2** gets no voltage, then voltage will register all along one of the vertical wires. In that case, one of the transistors at the bottom will cut off the bottom wire and no voltage will register at **Out**.

*   *   *   *   *

By now, it may seem that computers will be almost impossible to understand. If a circuit using only four transistors is this confusing, how will we fare with circuits containing thousands or millions of transistors?

The comforting answer is that no one, not even an expert, attempts to understand computer circuits transistor by transistor. Now that we know how to build gates, we can put transistors completely out of mind.

Just as the human body is made of cells put together into organs like the stomach, which in turn form systems like the digestive tract, computers are made of transistors put together into gates which in turn form larger units.

It would be silly to study how people digest food by looking one at a time at each of the millions of cells in the stomach. Likewise, now that we understand the smallest part that goes into making a computer, it is best to think not of these parts, but of the more powerful ones they are used to build.

Before leaving transistors behind, however, take time to relish the principle that allows us to do so.

This way of grouping complicated things together and thinking of them as one simple system is part of what makes the human mind powerful. Psychologists and computer scientists who study thinking sometimes call it **chunking**. As a first step in understanding digestion, we mentally chunk millions of cells together and think of them simply as teeth. An executive mentally chunks together a chaos of people, boxes, forms, telephones, and procedures and thinks of it all simply as the shipping department. The idea of chunking will reappear many times in this book as we continue to put parts together into more and more powerful units.

Incidentally, noticing *how* we think, as we tackle the problem of building and using a computer, is part of finding the answer. After all, the machine we build is meant to do, at least in part, the things we do with our minds.

Chunking appears here for the first time as we begin to put the simplest possible parts together. It will figure in the last chapter when we consider the largest of computer science questions: the possibility of a thinking machine.

*   *   *   *   *

Figure 1.15 shows the answer to the question asked earlier in this section (What is the opposite of a NOT gate?).

Figure 1.15 Answer: The opposite of a NOT gate is just a wire.

1.3 A LOGIC PROBLEM

It is a long way from AND, OR, and NOT gates to thinking machines. But even these simple gates can be used to do a kind of thinking. Correctly connected, they can solve certain kinds of logic problems. In fact, they are normally called **logic gates**.

Here is one problem logic gates can be used to solve:

> Ed will go to a certain party only if Dan or Carol goes.
> Dan will go if Ann goes and Bob does not.
> Ann and Carol and Bob have decided not to go.
> **What will Ed do?**

Although this may sound confusing, it is not a difficult problem. If 20 or 100 people were setting such conditions for going to the party, however, the problem would be much more complicated. In that case, the best idea would be to use some kind of systematic way of solving it, a step-by-step approach guaranteed to get the right answer no matter how difficult the problem.

Anyone who has taken an algebra course has a hint about what kind of system we need. To solve hard logic problems we need a new kind of algebra: a system of rules for dealing with logic questions. In fact, however, this kind of algebra is not new at all. It was invented more than 100 years ago. Luckily, it is also quite simple, in many ways, compared with ordinary algebra.

But before explaining how the system works, we will take time to show how logic problems can be solved using logic gates. This makes sense because **Boolean algebra**—the algebra of logic—was all but forgotten before computers were invented. Today, it is mainly used not for solving logic problems, but for understanding *circuits* made with logic gates.

1.4 LOGIC CIRCUITS

One obvious point about the party problem of Section 1.3 is that it makes heavy use of the words *and*, *or*, and *not*. Are they used in the same sense as when we speak of AND gates, OR gates, and NOT gates?

Figure 1.16 helps us with the answer. The figure shows an ordinary OR gate with the input wires labeled **Dan goes** and **Carol goes** and the output wire labeled **Ed goes**. Naturally, we are free to label our diagrams any way we please, but does a picture like this make any sense?

Figure 1.16 Representing a statement: OR and *or.*

The answer is yes, in two ways.

One possibility is to think of the gate as representing the *word* or. In this case, Figure 1.16 is just a way of making a diagram of a fact from the party problem: Ed will go to the party if Dan *or* Carol goes.

But we may go further. Suppose we actually buy an OR gate and label it this way. Using a battery, we supply voltage to the wire labeled **Dan goes** if Dan is going to the party and to the wire labeled **Carol goes** if she is going. Will there be voltage on the output wire?

There will be, of course, if either of the inputs is receiving voltage. That is, voltage will be put out on the **Ed goes** wire if either Dan or Carol is going to the party—exactly the cases in which Ed will go.

Figure 1.16, then, can be interpreted as a plan for a circuit to *figure out* whether Ed will go to the party, based on information about Dan and Carol.

The idea of a circuit which can "figure out" the answer to a problem is really quite astounding, and before long, it will lead us to the more powerful circuit we call a computer. But while this simple OR gate is still before us, take a moment to think about an important point, one as true of the computer as it is of the OR gate: Words and ideas do not run through the wires as the circuit determines its answer.

We are beginning to think of logic gates and wires as having meanings. But wires simply conduct electricity, flowing under the pressure of voltage. It is *we* who interpret the meaning of conditions in the wires. In this case our interpretation is:

1. Each wire represents one person.
2. Voltage in the wire means that person is going to the party.

In general, we can let voltage in wires represent anything we like: numbers, words, ideas. For solving logic problems, however, we will stay with just one interpretation. Voltage in a wire means that a certain statement labeling that wire is true. If there is no voltage in the wire, the statement is false.

In using the OR gate of Figure 1.16, it was up to us to supply voltage to the **Dan goes** and **Carol goes** wires, if those statements were true. The voltage in the **Ed goes** wire was determined automatically. Our idea in building a logic circuit to solve the party problem is to have as many of the voltages figured automatically as possible.

Before we continue, though, we should say that the picture of the OR gate in Figure 1.16 is not the one most computer scientists use. Instead, the three basic gates are normally drawn as in Figure 1.17. We will use these standard symbols from here on.

AND Gate   OR Gate   NOT Gate

Figure 1.17 Standard logic gate symbols.

Figure 1.18, then, is just Figure 1.16 as a computer scientist would draw it. It shows an OR gate with the input wires labeled **Dan goes** and **Carol goes** and the output wire labeled **Ed goes**.

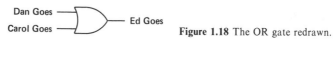

Dan Goes

Carol Goes   Ed Goes

Figure 1.18 The OR gate redrawn.

*   *   *   *   *

We have been using an OR gate to represent the first statement of our party problem. The second statement—Dan will go if Ann goes and Bob does not—uses two of our logic words: *and* and *not*. As a first step in thinking about how to represent the statement, consider the NOT gate shown in Figure 1.19. How should the output wire be labeled?

Bob Goes   ?   **Figure 1.19** A labeling problem.

The question really boils down to just this: When will there be voltage in the output wire? The answer is, The NOT gate will put out voltage when no voltage is received at the input, that is, when Bob is not going to the party. Since there is voltage in the output wire when Bob does not go, it makes sense to label the wire as shown in Figure 1.20. Notice that there will be voltage in the output wire just when the statement labeling it—**Bob does not go**—is true. Just as the voltages on the two wires of a NOT gate are always opposites, the statements labeling them are also opposites. Each is true when the other is false.

Bob Goes   Bob Does Not Go   **Figure 1.20** Answer to the labeling problem.

*   *   *   *   *

The next circuit, in Figure 1.21, uses an AND gate to determine whether Dan will go to the party. Remember that, according to the problem, Dan will go if Ann goes and Bob does *not* go.

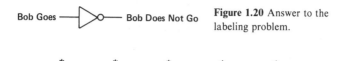

Ann Goes

Bob Does Not Go   Dan Goes

Figure 1.21 Circuit to answer for Dan.

The only way for the AND gate to put out voltage is if both input wires receive voltage. According to the labels, this should happen only if Ann goes to the party and Bob does not—exactly as stated in the problem. The AND gate does just what we want, if it is labeled this way.

So far, we have done a great deal of work and gained very little. Each of our three gates figures out something about the party problem, but this figuring is only of the simplest possible kind. The gain appears when we *connect* the gates.

For example, look back at the OR gate in Figure 1.18. This gate tells us whether Ed goes to the party, so long as we tell *it* whether Dan or Carol is going. If we use this gate by itself, it is *our* job to decide whether or not to supply voltage to each of the two input wires.

Of course, if we wanted, we could find out whether Dan is going by checking the output wire of the AND gate in Figure 1.21. But a better idea is just to connect the **Dan goes** output of the AND gate to the **Dan goes** input of the OR gate as in Figure 1.22. Now the voltage on the **Dan goes** wire is determined automatically. The AND gate will put out voltage only when it is true that Dan is going—just the same case in which voltage should be supplied to the OR gate input.

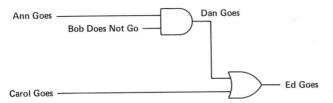

Figure 1.22 AND gives OR its answer.

The next step is obvious. We connect the **Bob does not go** output of the NOT gate in Figure 1.20 to the **Bob does not go** input of the AND gate. This saves us the work of figuring the voltage at that input.

The result is the logic circuit pictured in Figure 1.23. This circuit solves the problem we posed. It tells us whether Ed will attend the party, depending on what Ann, Bob, and Carol do. To use this circuit, we supply voltage at the three main inputs—**Ann goes**, **Bob goes**, and **Carol goes**—depending on whether Ann, Bob, and Carol will attend the party. All the other voltages, including the one which tells us what Ed will do, are figured automatically.

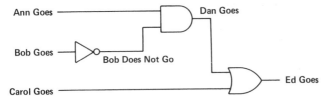

Figure 1.23 A logic circuit for the party problem.

The problem says that Ann, Bob, and Carol all decide not to go to the party. That means none of the three inputs should receive voltage. In this case:

1. The NOT gate receives no voltage, so it puts voltage out.

2. Only one input of the AND gate receives voltage, so it does not put voltage out.

3. The OR gate does not receive voltage at either input, so it does not put voltage out.

But the output wire of the OR gate represents the sentence *Ed goes*. No voltage in that wire means the sentence is false. Ed will *not* go, and that, of course, is the correct answer to the problem.

1.5 LOGIC FUNCTIONS

Two important points follow from our solution of the party problem.

First, although we could easily have solved this particular problem without the help of electronics, the *method* allows us to tackle harder ones. A party problem involving hundreds of people, each with complicated ways of deciding whether or not to attend, would simply use more gates and more connections.

Second, we can get more than one answer from each logic circuit we build. For example, the logic circuit for the party problem tells us what Ed will do, based on information about what Ann, Bob, and Carol do. In the last section, we supplied no voltage to the inputs, because all three had decided not to go to the party. But what if they had all decided they *would* go?

The same circuit will give us the answer. All we need to do is supply voltage at all three inputs. In fact, for any combination of decisions Ann, Bob, and Carol might make, the circuit correctly figures what Ed will do. We say that the circuit performs a **logic function**.

In mathematics, a function is just a rule that tells us how to take one or more numbers and turn them into another number. For example, x^2 is a function. It takes in the number 4 and turns it into 16. The rule is, Take the given number and multiply it by itself.

Ordinary addition is another function. It takes in the two numbers 5 and 6 and turns them into the number 11.

A logic function uses a rule to turn one or more logic values (**true** or **false**) into a single logic value. A simple logic function like AND takes two values in and puts one out. The rule is, Put out a **true** only when both inputs are **true**.

Our party problem logic circuit takes three inputs and uses a slightly more complicated rule to find the answer, but it still puts out just one answer.

In general, mathematical functions can be useful in day-to-day life. People buy calculators because they need to compute functions like addition and multiplication. But what about logic functions? Apparently, we are now in a position to design circuits which will calculate them. Is it conceivable that people would find an everyday use for such circuits?

Conceivable or not, the fact is that logic functions are even *more* useful than mathematical functions. In part, the reason is that complicated logic functions can be used in surprising ways. As we will see, they make possible the main work of a computer, storing and processing information.

Some people might argue, though, that the mathematics of the calculator is more important or fundamental than the logic involved in computer processing.

Here is perhaps the biggest surprise: The mathematical functions performed by a calculator are all based on logic functions. Calculators are built with logic gates.

1.6 BOOLEAN ALGEBRA

In order to design circuits powerful enough for useful work, we need a systematic way of dealing with logical relationships. As we have said, Boolean algebra provides just such a system.

As a first example of what Boolean algebra is for, look at the logic circuit in Figure 1.24. The input to the NOT gate is labeled **Peter is happy**. We already know that the output wire should be labeled **Peter is not happy**.

Peter Is Happy — Peter Is Not Happy   **Figure 1.24** A well-labeled NOT gate.

These labels make sense together because of how we designed the NOT gate. Voltage conditions are always opposite in the input and output wires, and the statements labeling the wires are also opposites. When one statement is true and voltage is on in the wire it labels, voltage will be off in the other wire, showing that its label is false.

Now suppose we add another NOT gate, as in Figure 1.25. How should the output of the second NOT gate be labeled? We can ask the same question another way: What sentence is the opposite of *Peter is not happy*?

Peter Is Happy — ?   **Figure 1.25** Another labeling problem.

There are two answers to the question and both are correct. One opposite is the sentence *Peter is not not happy*. Another is the more usual way of saying the same thing: *Peter is happy*.

Notice that we solved this labeling problem in two steps. First, we decided how to label the output of the left-hand NOT gate. Then we used this output as an input to the right-hand NOT gate and determined how to label its output.

A much better way to solve the labeling problem, however, is to see that the second NOT gate cancels the effect of the first. Whatever the voltage conditions in the original input, the first NOT gate's output will be the opposite. The second NOT gate's output will be the opposite of the opposite, just the same as the original input.

Here, then, is our first example of the kind of **axiom** or rule which forms the foundation of Boolean algebra: The opposite of the opposite of something is the same as the original. To put it another way, two NOT gates cancel.

1.7 LOGIC NOTATION

From this axiom, we see that Boolean algebra begins with some very obvious ideas. It does not take a system of logic to tell us that if a man is *not not* happy, he must be happy. The algebra will begin to be useful when we apply several simple axioms together. Meanwhile, it is nice to start with rules which we agree are simple and natural.

A second point about the first axiom is that, even if the idea is obvious, our way of saying it is confusing. The problem would be even worse if we continued to use ordinary English for the more complicated ideas we will soon see. So, before we continue, we need a better way of expressing logical statements and relationships.

In ordinary algebra, we use variables like x and y to represent quantities. For example, x might stand for the price in dollars of a gallon of gasoline and the value of x might be 0.93.

In Boolean algebra, variables represent sentences. The value of a variable is not a number, but a word: either **true** or **false**. For example, suppose the variable **R** stands for the sentence *It is raining today*. If it *is* raining today, the value of **R** is **true**, otherwise it is **false**.

We use the symbol $\sim$ to mean *opposite of*: $\sim$**R** means the opposite of the sentence represented by **R**. Thus, $\sim$**R** means it is *not* raining today. Usually we read $\sim$**R** as "not **R**."

Suppose **N** represents the sentence *It is not raining today*. Then we can write $\sim$**R** = **N**. The equals sign shows that $\sim$**R** and **N** have the same meaning. That is, they are either both true or both false.

Now we are ready to rewrite our first axiom. In words, the axiom says, The opposite of the opposite of something is the same as the original. In symbols, we write it this way: $\sim\sim$**Q** = **Q**. Notice that it does not matter what letter we use in the axiom. **Q** could represent any sentence at all. This way of writing the axiom means that it is true for *all* sentences.

Using symbolic notation to write logic statements makes them shorter and clearer. It also makes the meaning more exact.

The symbol $\sim$ does to logic variables what a NOT gate does to voltages. If we want our Boolean algebra to help with logic circuits, we also need symbols that do what AND and OR gates do.

We will use the plus sign (+) to mean *or* and the center point (·) to mean *and*. Thus, for example, **R** + **S** means, Either the sentence represented by **R** is true *or* the sentence represented by **S** is true.[1]

Notice that when we join sentences with a plus sign or a center point or when we add the symbol $\sim$, the result is a new sentence. If **R** represents *It is raining* and **S** represents *It is snowing*, then **R** + **S** represents the sentence *It is raining or it is snowing*.

This combined sentence is true if it is raining. It is true if it is snowing. It is also true if, by some chance, it is both raining and snowing. All this is just as it should be: it corresponds to our everyday idea of what the word *or* means and it is exactly the way our OR gate works. In the OR gate, voltage is put out when voltage is supplied at one input *or* the other input *or* both.

---

[1] Some people like to use the symbol + as an abbreviation for the word *and*. For example, they might write, "Would you + Ellen like to come over for dinner?" We use + for the word *or*. Be careful not to get confused.

To complete our notation, all we need are parentheses and a convention. Parentheses are used in ordinary algebra to tell us the correct order for adding, subtracting, and so on. Without them, it is not clear how to answer questions like, What is $5 - 3 - 1$? Should we first subtract the 1 from the 3? That gives us $5 - 2$, or 3, as a final answer. But if we first subtract the 3 from the 5, we get $2 - 1$, or 1, as a final answer.

To tell the difference, we put the subtraction that we mean to go first inside parentheses. If we write $5 - (3 - 1)$, the final answer is definitely 3.

Parentheses are used just the same way in Boolean algebra. They tell us what to do first.

Ordinary algebra also has a convention that tells us what to do when there are no parentheses. In Boolean algebra the convention is, First do all the *nots*, then the *ands* and finally the *ors*. But remember, anything in parentheses always comes first.

1.8 EVALUATING BOOLEAN EXPRESSIONS

To illustrate all the new notation, here is a Boolean algebra expression:

$$\sim\sim((P + \sim P) \cdot \sim\sim Q)$$

Since this expression is a combination of variables joined with our *and*, *or*, and *not* symbols, it must be a statement of some kind. Is it possible to say whether the statement is true or false?

The best answer is, Not yet.

This question is like asking for the value of the algebra expression $x + y$ without saying the value of x or y. If we know that x is 2 and y is 3, we can use those values in the expression to get $2 + 3$. Then we know the value of the expression is 5.

Likewise, before we can evaluate a Boolean expression, we need to know the values of the variables, to determine whether they are **true** or **false**.

Suppose, in our Boolean expression, **P** represents the sentence *Pears are purple* and **Q** represents *Quebec is in Canada*. Then the value of **P** is **false** and the value of **Q** is **true**. Now we can decide whether the expression that uses **P** and **Q** is true.

To evaluate the expression, we start with the innermost parentheses. Inside these we find $P + \sim P$. The value of **P**, we already know is, **false**. The value of $\sim P$ is the opposite of the value of **P**: **true**. Therefore $P + \sim P$ boils down to **false** + **true**. We have said that the value of a sentence made up of two parts joined by an *or* is true if either of its parts is true. Thus the value of $P + \sim P$ is **true**.[2]

Substituting the *value* of $P + \sim P$ in the original expression, we get:

$$\sim\sim(\textbf{true} \cdot \sim\sim Q)$$

---

[2] If this is confusing, think in terms of logic gates. **False** + **true** represents an OR gate with no voltage at one input and voltage at the other. The OR gate would put out voltage in this case, and voltage corresponds to the logical value **true**.

Looking at the right, we find ~~**Q**. **Q** has the value **true**, so that its opposite, ~**Q**, has the value **false**. Likewise, ~~**Q** is the opposite of ~**Q**, and so it has the value **true**. Substituting this value, we get:

$$\sim\sim(\textbf{true} \cdot \textbf{true})$$

We have not yet said how to figure the value of two sentences joined with an *and*, but the answer should be obvious. The combined sentence is true only if the first part is true *and* the second part is true. If a beggar says he makes a million dollars a year and lives in New York City, he is lying even if it is true that he lives in New York City.

In this case, both parts of the sentence are true, so the value of the expression inside the parentheses is **true** and we have:

$$\sim\sim\textbf{true}$$

~**true** is the opposite of **true**: **false**. ~~**true** is the opposite of the opposite of **true**, that is, the opposite of **false**, which is **true**. This is the value of the original expression.

What is it we are saying is true? The following:

> It is not the case that it is not the case that both
> 1. Pears are purple or they are not purple
>
> and
> 2. Quebec is not not in Canada

Now it should be clear why we use Boolean notation in place of English for complex logical relations.

1.9 APPLYING AXIOMS

Of course, the notation by itself is not enough. Its purpose is to make it easier to apply axioms.

For example, we could have saved a great deal of work in the example of the last section if we had applied our first axiom. Everywhere we found a pair of the ~ symbols, we should have realized that their effects would cancel. The first axiom tells us that the expression

$$\sim\sim((\textbf{P} + \sim\textbf{P}) \cdot \sim\sim\textbf{Q})$$

may be simplified to just:

$$(\textbf{P} + \sim\textbf{P}) \cdot \textbf{Q}$$

This new expression is true exactly when the original one is, and it is certainly easier to evaluate.

A second axiom will simplify matters even further.

The idea of this second axiom is that if we pick any sentence at all, we can make a true statement by saying the sentence is either true or false. For example, if the original sentence is *There is life on Mars*, we have no way of knowing if it is true or false. But if we say *There is life on Mars or there is not life on Mars*, then we are obviously saying something true.

Likewise, if we take any sentence **P**, the value of **P** may be **true** or **false**. But the value of **P** + ~**P** is certainly **true**. In symbols, we write this second axiom this way:

$$\mathbf{P} + \mathord{\sim}\mathbf{P} = \mathbf{true}$$

Really, all this says is that every sentence must be either true or false. Notice also that the **P** in the axiom stands for any sentence at all; if we changed the **P** to an **R**, the axiom would still mean the same thing.

We can apply this second axiom to simplify our expression again from

$$\mathbf{(P} + \mathord{\sim}\mathbf{P)} \cdot \mathbf{Q}$$

down to just

$$\mathbf{true} \cdot \mathbf{Q}$$

At this point, neither of our two axioms can help us. If we want to know the value of the original expression, we need to know the value of **Q**. But now, as soon as we know that the **Q** is true, it takes only one quick step to see that the value of the whole expression is **true**.

The two axioms we have looked at are so simple that sometimes it does not seem worth the trouble to say them. Certainly, we will need more powerful axioms before we will have a system worthy of being called an algebra. But keep in mind that our main aim in developing an algebra of logic is to use it in building a computer. Already, the little theory we have can help us.

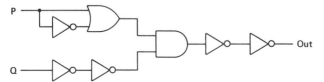

Figure 1.26 A logic circuit
for a computer.

Suppose, in building a computer, we have need of a circuit like the one in Figure 1.26. This circuit, we are supposing, is to be used hundreds of times in different parts of the machine. In essence, we want hundreds of boxes like the one in Figure 1.27, each of which contains the circuit shown in Figure 1.26.

Figure 1.27 A logic box:
What goes inside?

In fact, however, it does not matter to us what circuit goes inside the box, so long as it puts the correct voltage out for every possible combination of inputs. Maybe we can find a circuit that does just what we want using fewer gates. The first step is to analyze the original circuit, using our Boolean notation.

Figure 1.28 shows this analysis. This diagram looks complicated, but really, it is easy to understand. Just start at the left side and work gate by gate toward the right. For example, the two NOT gates at the very left take in **P** and **Q** and put out ~**P** and ~**Q**, that is, "not **P**" and "not **Q**." The OR gate takes in **P** and ~**P** and puts out **P** + ~**P**, that is, "**P** or ~**P**."

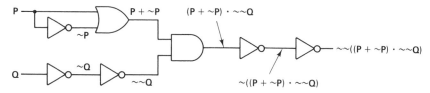

Figure 1.28 Analyzing the logic circuit.

When we get all the way to the right, we find something familiar. The final output is just the same as the Boolean expression we have simplified. The simplified answer, **true · Q**, can easily be turned into a logic circuit, as in Figure 1.29.

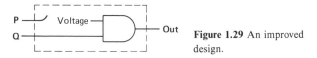

Figure 1.29 An improved design.

The point is that if we put this circuit inside the box, it will work the same way as the original circuit in Figure 1.26: for the same input values, it gives the same output.

Notice that, in this circuit, it clearly does not matter what value we use for **P**. The **P** input wire is disconnected. The value of **P** did not matter in the original circuit either, but that fact was hardly obvious.

Our improved design for the logic box saves six gates. But more than saving money for whoever is buying the gates, it saves space. In a real computer, transistors are crowded together on a chip of silicon that, for manufacturing reasons, cannot be made much larger than a thumbnail. The fewer transistor gates needed for each job, the more jobs the computer can do and the more powerful it will be.

Unfortunately, the gate-saving work of this section is of no practical consequence, since the circuit we designed has no use in a real computer. In just a few pages, however, we will work out circuits for a multiplexer and a majority organ— parts that really do go into making up a computer.

1.10 MORE AXIOMS

First, however, we need more axioms—a fairly long list of them. Here is the next one to consider:

$$\text{true} \cdot \text{P} = \text{P}$$

In general, when we want to show that a statement like this is correct, we can take two approaches. One is to use the axioms we already know to simplify the statement down to something obviously correct: **false** = **false**, for example.

We cannot take this approach with the third axiom, however, because neither of our first two axioms applies. In general, until we have a long list of basic axioms to work with, we will have to use a cruder approach: We will simply check to see whether the statement is correct for all possible values of its variables.

This method of proof is rarely used in ordinary algebra for the simple reason that there are nearly always too many values to check. Suppose we study the equation $x + 5 = 5 + x$. If we check to see what happens if x is 1, we get 6 on both sides of the equation. In this case, the equation is correct. If we try again using 2, 3, 4, or 5 for x, we also find that the equation is correct. But when can we stop checking? There are an infinite number of numbers that x might be, and we can never be sure, checking one number at a time, that the equation is true for all of them.

This is one way in which Boolean algebra is simple: Each variable can have only one of two values, **true** or **false**.

Our third axiom—**true** · **P** = **P**—has just one variable, and so there are only two cases to check. If the value of **P** is **true**, then the axiom claims that **true** · **true** = **true**. This is correct. If the value of **P** is **false**, the axiom claims that **true** · **false** = **false**. This is also correct. These are the only possible values for **P**, so the axiom is always correct.

We can use this axiom right away, because it applies to the expression we were simplifying in the last section. We had already simplified

$$\sim\sim((P + \sim P) \cdot \sim\sim\sim Q)$$

down to just

$$\text{true} \cdot Q$$

Now we apply our third axiom to get just **Q** for our final answer. The upshot is that the box that we were originally going to manufacture using seven logic gates and that we then simplified down to just one gate really does not need any gates at all. It does not even have to be a box. As Figure 1.30 shows, everywhere we would have used such a box, we could simply have connected the **Q** input wire to the output wire.

Figure 1.30 The final improvement.

The third axiom is just one of several related statements. Here are the others:

$$\text{false} \cdot P = \text{false}$$
$$\text{false} + P = P$$
$$\text{true} + P = \text{true}$$

All of these may be proved just by making sure they are correct both when the value of **P** is **true** and when it is **false**.

Incidentally, these axioms are very much like a similar group of algebra axioms that tell us about special properties of the numbers 1 and 0. Those axioms say that, for any number x,

$$0 \cdot \mathbf{x} = 0$$
$$0 + \mathbf{x} = \mathbf{x}$$
$$1 \cdot \mathbf{x} = \mathbf{x}$$

Many axioms from ordinary algebra carry over nicely to Boolean algebra. For example, one of the simplest ideas in algebra is that it does not matter in what order we add or multiply numbers: $4 + 5$ is the same as $5 + 4$. Likewise, when we join two sentences with *or* and *and*, it does not matter in what order we write the sentences: *I am a man and I am American* means the same as *I am American and I am a man.* If one combined sentence is true, so is the other.

Another idea from algebra is that if we have a *series* of additions or multiplications, it does not matter in what order we do them. If we have $3 + 6 + 8$, we get the same answer whether we first add the 3 and 6 to get $9 + 8$ or we first add the 6 and 8 to get $3 + 14$.

Likewise, if we start with the sentence *I am cold and I am hungry and I am tired* we can equally change it to

I am cold and hungry, and I am tired.

or

I am cold, and I am hungry and tired.

We can put these ideas into standard notation this way:

$$\mathbf{P} + \mathbf{Q} = \mathbf{Q} + \mathbf{P}$$
$$\mathbf{P} \cdot \mathbf{Q} = \mathbf{Q} \cdot \mathbf{P}$$
$$(\mathbf{P} + \mathbf{Q}) + \mathbf{R} = \mathbf{P} + (\mathbf{Q} + \mathbf{R})$$
$$(\mathbf{P} \cdot \mathbf{Q}) \cdot \mathbf{R} = \mathbf{P} \cdot (\mathbf{Q} \cdot \mathbf{R})$$

Notice that the first two of these tell us we can move our variables into a different order. The second two keep the order of the variables the same but group them differently.

So far, most of our axioms have come in pairs, one for *or* (+) and one for *and* ($\cdot$). Our second axiom, $\mathbf{P} + \sim\mathbf{P} = \textbf{true}$, is no exception. Here is the other half of the pair:

$$\mathbf{P} \cdot \sim\mathbf{P} = \textbf{false}$$

This can be checked by making sure it is correct for both possible values of $\mathbf{P}$. But common sense also tells us it is correct. All the axiom says is that if a sentence says something is true and also says that same thing is *not* true, the sentence must be false. For example, *It is raining and it is not raining* must be false, no matter what the weather is.

Common sense also tells us that a sentence like *It is Sunday or it is Sunday* is true just if the simple sentence *It is Sunday* is true. The same idea works if we use the word *and* in place of *or*. This gives us two more axioms:

$$\mathbf{P} + \mathbf{P} = \mathbf{P}$$
$$\mathbf{P} \cdot \mathbf{P} = \mathbf{P}$$

After all this, we are still not finished. Two of the most important axioms are yet to come, but we will take a break from theory now to put some of what we already know to use.

1.11 WIDER GATES

A few pages back, we said that any kind of logic problem like the party problem we worked on can be solved using a logic circuit. While that is true, someone who read only up to that point and then tried to design such circuits would quickly have run into trouble.

A sentence like

> Ann will make dinner only if
>   John promises to wash the dishes *and*
>   Mary sets the table.

translates neatly to an AND gate circuit, as in Figure 1.31.

Figure 1.31 Representing a sentence with one *and*.

But how can we handle a sentence like this one?

> Ann will make dinner only if
>   John promises to wash the dishes *and*
>   Mary sets the table *and*
>   there is food in the refrigerator.

What we want is a circuit that represents the expression $\mathbf{J} \cdot \mathbf{M} \cdot \mathbf{F}$, where $\mathbf{J}$ stands for *John promises to wash the dishes*, $\mathbf{M}$ for *Mary sets the table*, and $\mathbf{F}$ for *There is food in the refrigerator*. The problem is that our AND gate takes only two inputs and we need three.

Boolean algebra gives the answer.

One of our axioms tells us that we can group the variables any way we want. Thus we can add parentheses to the expression to get $(\mathbf{J} \cdot \mathbf{M}) \cdot \mathbf{F}$. This minor change solves the problem. The first *and*—the one inside the parentheses—has only two inputs, $\mathbf{J}$ and $\mathbf{M}$. The second *and* also has only two inputs: the single answer coming from inside the parentheses, and $\mathbf{F}$.

Figure 1.32 shows the circuit.

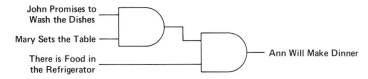

Figure 1.32 Representing a sentence with two *ands*.

This idea can be used to make AND gates and OR gates with any number of inputs, although there are electrical reasons why it is hard to make one with more than about eight. These wider AND and OR gates are so common that we usually draw them with just one symbol, as in Figure 1.33.

Figure 1.33 Three-input AND and OR gates.

Incidentally, someone trying to make a three-input AND gate might not immediately think of the design we have explained. It might seem more natural to use one AND gate for each *and* in the original sentence. That would give us two circuits, as in Figure 1.34. To get a final answer, maybe we should put the outputs through a third AND gate, as in Figure 1.35. Is this correct?

Figure 1.34 First step toward a different design.

The circuit in Figure 1.35 represents the expression $(\mathbf{J} \cdot \mathbf{M}) \cdot (\mathbf{M} \cdot \mathbf{F})$. By the regrouping axiom, we can move the parentheses to get $\mathbf{J} \cdot (\mathbf{M} \cdot \mathbf{M}) \cdot \mathbf{F}$. Now we have something familiar inside the parentheses: another of our axioms tells us that $\mathbf{M} \cdot \mathbf{M} = \mathbf{M}$. Therefore we can simplify the expression down to just

$$\mathbf{J} \cdot \mathbf{M} \cdot \mathbf{F}$$

But this is exactly what we wanted, and so the circuit in Figure 1.35 *is* correct. Boolean algebra proves it.

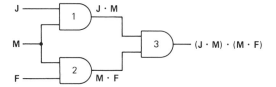

Figure 1.35 Another three-input AND: Does it work?

1.12 DE MORGAN'S LAWS

So far, all of our Boolean algebra axioms have expressed simple, obvious ideas. The circuit examples show that even these simple ideas can be powerful. Now we will look at two pairs of axioms that are much less obvious, and all the more useful. These axioms will complete the foundation of Boolean algebra.

The first pair is based on the idea that we may just as well describe a sentence by saying when it is false as by saying when it is true. For example, if a certain sentence **P** is false on Tuesdays (and only on Tuesdays), then the sentence must be true on the other days of the week. **P** might be the sentence *Today is Monday or Wednesday or Thursday or Friday or Saturday or Sunday.*

Notice that it is much easier in this case to say when the sentence is false than to say when it true. A much simpler way to express **P** is just to say *Today is not Tuesday.*

Sometimes it is useful to apply this idea in designing logic circuits. We design a circuit that does just the opposite of what we really want, one that puts out voltage exactly in the cases when it is not supposed to. Then we add a NOT gate at the end to set everything right.

For example, suppose we want a circuit that takes two inputs, **A** and **B**, and puts out voltage if either

1. Voltage is supplied to **A** and not **B** or
2. Voltage is supplied to **B** and not **A** or
3. No voltage is supplied to either input.

To design the circuit, we turn each of these statements into a Boolean expression:

1. $\mathbf{A} \cdot \sim\mathbf{B}$ or
2. $\mathbf{B} \cdot \sim\mathbf{A}$ or
3. $\sim\mathbf{A} \cdot \sim\mathbf{B}$

and then link them together into a single Boolean expression

$$(\mathbf{A} \cdot \sim\mathbf{B}) + (\mathbf{B} \cdot \sim\mathbf{A}) + (\sim\mathbf{A} \cdot \sim\mathbf{B}).$$

This expression gives us the logic circuit pictured in Figure 1.36. Notice that we designed the circuit by describing each of the three cases in which it puts out voltage. Each case yields one AND gate.

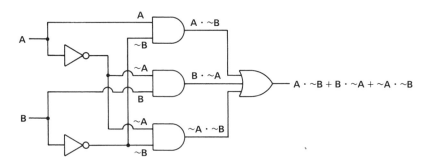

Figure 1.36 A logic circuit for the expression.

It takes just *one* statement, however, to say when the circuit will *not* put out voltage; this happens only when voltage is supplied at both inputs. The circuit that does just the opposite of what we want is one that puts out voltage when voltage is supplied at both inputs.

That circuit is simply an AND gate.

Check it. In any of the three cases when the circuit we want is supposed to put out voltage, at least one of the inputs has no voltage and so the AND gate puts out no voltage. If voltage is supplied to both inputs, the AND gate puts out voltage. The circuit we want does not.

Since the circuit we want does the opposite of an AND gate, we can build it as shown in Figure 1.37. This circuit does the same work as the more complicated circuit in Figure 1.36. It is called a NAND gate, because it has the effect of a NOT and an AND gate together.

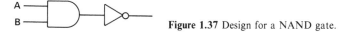

Figure 1.37 Design for a NAND gate.

Putting a NOT gate at the end of a circuit is the same as adding the symbol $\sim$ at the beginning of a Boolean expression to indicate a *not* operation. For example, the expression for the output of the circuit in Figure 1.37 is $\sim(\mathbf{A} \cdot \mathbf{B})$. In general, then, it will be useful to know what happens when we add the symbol $\sim$ at the beginning of an expression. We already have an axiom that tells us what happens if the next character is also the symbol $\sim$. In that case, the two *not*s cancel.

De Morgan's laws, our next-to-last axioms, tell us the effect of a *not* on sentences joined with an *or* or an *and*.[3]

When we write $\sim(\mathbf{P} \cdot \mathbf{Q})$, we are saying it is not the case that both $\mathbf{P}$ and $\mathbf{Q}$ are true. If $\mathbf{P}$ and $\mathbf{Q}$ are not both true, then one or both of them must be false: either $\mathbf{P}$ is false or $\mathbf{Q}$ is false. De Morgan's law says this in symbols:

$$\sim(\mathbf{P} \cdot \mathbf{Q}) = \sim\mathbf{P} + \sim\mathbf{Q}$$

De Morgan's law tells us that saying *The robber is not tall and thin* is the same as saying *Either the robber is not tall or he is not thin.*

The partner of this axiom tells us the effect of a *not* on sentences joined with an *or*. It says:

$$\sim(\mathbf{P} + \mathbf{Q}) = \sim\mathbf{P} \cdot \sim\mathbf{Q}$$

In other words, the opposite of saying one or the other of two things is true is to say that both of them are not true. If a woman claims to have seen something that was either a UFO or a ghost, a friend can tell her she is wrong in two ways. The friend can say, "It was not either a UFO or a ghost," or she can say, "It was not a UFO and it was not a ghost." De Morgan's law tells us the meaning is the same.

One interesting way to look at De Morgan's laws is to think of them as a way of turning *and* into *or* and vice versa. If we start with $\mathbf{P} \cdot \mathbf{Q}$, we know that adding a pair of *not*s does not change anything. That gives us:

$$\sim\sim(\mathbf{P} \cdot \mathbf{Q})$$

[3] The laws take their name from the English mathematician Augustus De Morgan.

Now we can apply De Morgan's law to everything but the leftmost *not* to get:

$$\sim(\sim P + \sim Q)$$

This last expression must mean the same as the original expression, $P \cdot Q$, since at each step the axioms tell us that we are replacing one thing with something else that means the same thing. Thus the expression tells us how to build an AND gate using only OR and NOT gates. (See Figure 1.38.)

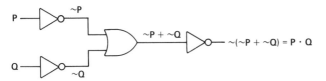

Figure 1.38 Building AND with OR and NOT.

It turns out, then, that we do not really need three basic gates. With just OR and NOT gates as raw material, we could manufacture AND gates whenever we needed them. Likewise, we could start with AND and NOT gates and use them to build OR gates.

If we value simplicity, we can do even better. All logic circuits can be built with just NAND gates like the one shown in Figure 1.37.[4]

1.13 DISTRIBUTIVE PROPERTIES

De Morgan's laws show one relationship between *and* and *or*. Our last pair of axioms shows another relationship.

These axioms take their name from the distributive property of multiplication. Algebra tells us that $x \cdot (y + z) = x \cdot y + x \cdot z$. For example, 3 times the sum 4 + 5 is 27, the same as the sum of 3 times 4 and 3 times 5.

The first distributive property in Boolean algebra tells us that

$$P \cdot (Q + R) = P \cdot Q + P \cdot R$$

This axiom looks exactly the same as the one for numbers. In fact, one reason we use addition and multiplication signs for logical functions is that it shows the similarity between logical and algebraic axioms. Keep in mind, however, that this is just for convenience. The second distributive property, for example, is correct for logical values, but not at all for numbers:

$$P + (Q \cdot R) = (P + Q) \cdot (P + R)$$

To see that the first Boolean distributive property is correct, we will use our crude method of checking all the possibilities. If every possible combination of values for P, Q, and R makes the left and right sides of the equation the same, the equation must be correct.

This time, however, there are so many possibilities to check that we will put them in a chart. Each row in Figure 1.39 shows one of the possible combinations

---

[4] We built the NAND gate using an AND gate and a NOT gate, but it could be designed from scratch using just transistors.

of values for **P**, **Q**, and **R** and the value of the left and right sides of the axiom using those values. This kind of chart is called a **truth table**.

P	Q	R	P · (Q + R)	P · Q + P · R
false	false	false	false	false
false	false	true	false	false
false	true	false	false	false
false	true	true	false	false
true	false	false	false	false
true	false	true	true	true
true	true	false	true	true
true	true	true	true	true

Figure 1.39 Truth table for the distributive property.

To see how the table was constructed, look at the first row. It tells us what happens when **P** and **Q** and **R** are all **false**. When we use these values in the left side of the equation—**P · (Q + R)**—we get **false · (false + false)**, or just simply **false**. This value is shown in the fourth column of the first row.

When we use the same values for **P**, **Q**, and **R** in the *right* side of the equation—**P · Q + P · R**—we get **false · false + false · false**, or simply **false**. This is shown in the last column of the first row.

In this case, the left and right sides of the equation were the same. The other rows of the truth table show that the left and right sides of the equation are *always* the same. That is, the first distributive property is correct.

Naturally, the second distributive property may be proved in just the same way. With it, our list of axioms is complete. Figure 1.40 lists all of them, along with their usual names.

1. Commutative	P + Q = Q + P	P · Q = Q · P
2. Associative	(P + Q) + R = P + (Q + R)	(P · Q) · R = P · (Q · R)
3. Distributive	P · (Q + R) = P · Q + P · R	P + (Q · R) = (P + Q) · (P + R)
4. De Morgan	~(P + Q) = ~P · ~Q	~(P · Q) = ~P + ~Q
5. Identity	true + P = true	true · P = P
	false + P = P	false · P = false
6. Complement	P + ~P = true	P · ~P = false
7. Idempotent	P + P = P	P · P = P
8. Involution	~~P = P	

Figure 1.40 Axioms of Boolean algebra.

1.14 MAJORITY ORGANS AND MULTIPLEXERS

Now, at last, Boolean algebra is at our service. We can put it to work designing two circuits that will be useful as we continue with our main project of building a computer.

The first of these is called either a **majority organ** or a **voting circuit**. It takes three inputs and tells us if there is voltage in at least two of them.

If three people decide to vote on some issue, it takes two votes to make a majority. Thus, if each of the people controls one input wire of the voting circuit and votes yes by supplying voltage, voltage in the output means that the issue has passed.

The best way to get a Boolean expression for this circuit is to think of a simple way to say when it puts out voltage. That is, When is the logical output **true**?

A good answer is that the output is **true** if any two inputs are **true**. Of course, this also means that the output is **true** if all three inputs are **true**.

Suppose we call the three inputs **A**, **B**, and **C**. Then the output of the voting circuit is **true** if **A** and **B** are **true** or **A** and **C** are **true** or **B** and **C** are **true**. This translates easily into the Boolean expression

$$A \cdot B + A \cdot C + B \cdot C.$$

A circuit for this expression would use three AND gates and two OR gates. But we can do slightly better by applying our first distributive axiom. This allows us to combine the last two terms, leaving just

$$A \cdot B + (A + B) \cdot C$$

The circuit for this, shown in Figure 1.41, uses only four logic gates.

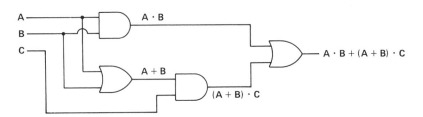

Figure 1.41 Design for a voting circuit.

Despite its name, the voting circuit is more often applied to arithmetic than elections. Exactly why is a subject reserved for Chapter 4, but the main idea is that majorities come up when we do addition.

Suppose we want to add two ordinary digits, like 6 and 7 or 1 and 9. We could use two groups of nine people to represent the digits. If the first digit is 6, six people in the first group raise their hands. If the second digit is 7, seven of the people in the second group raise their hands.

Sometimes, in adding two digits, we *carry* a 1. For example, when we add 6 and 7, we get "three with one carried"—13. When is it necessary to carry?

The answer is, When the sum is 10 or more. But another way of saying this is, When a *majority* of the people in the digit groups raise their hands. There are 18 people in all, so it takes 10 to make a majority.

*   *   *   *   *

To finish this section, we will build a kind of selection circuit called a **multi-plexer**. This circuit does roughly the same work that the receptionist in a large office does when there are two calls for the same person. The receptionist chooses which of the two calls to put through.

A single multiplexer takes two main inputs and a third input, which we will call a selector. If the selector input is **false**, whatever voltage is on the first input comes through the output. If the selector input is **true**, whatever voltage is on the second input comes through the output.

If we call the selector input **S** and the other inputs **In-1** and **In-2**, then we may use the following Boolean expression for the circuit:

$$\sim\!S \cdot In\text{-}1 + S \cdot In\text{-}2$$

To see why this is right, think about the two possible values for **S**. If **S** is **false**, the expression becomes

$$\sim\!\textbf{false} \cdot In\text{-}1 + \textbf{false} \cdot In\text{-}2$$

which simplifies to

$$\textbf{true} \cdot In\text{-}1 + \textbf{false} \cdot In\text{-}2$$

or, applying the identity axioms,

$$In\text{-}1 + \textbf{false}$$

or, finally, just

$$In\text{-}1$$

Therefore, when **S** is **false**, the output is the same as the input at **In-1**, just as we wanted. Likewise, when **S** is **true**, the expression simplifies to **In-2** and the output is the same as the second input.

Figure 1.42 shows the final circuit design.

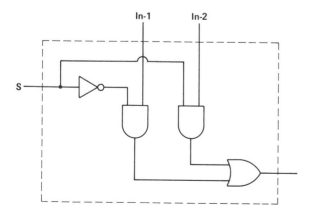

Figure 1.42 Design for a multiplexer.

Multiplexers will be useful in the next chapter when we build large groups of memory blocks for our computer. Each memory block will be like a numbered list of **trues** and **falses**. When we ask for list item 74, for example, each memory block will send us either a **true** or a **false**, depending on what the seventy-fourth item is in its particular list. Then we will use a multiplexer to choose just one of all these responses.

1.15 TAKING STOCK

At the beginning of this chapter, we promised to explain how computers work. We also promised that the ideas behind computers are quite simple. After the hard work of this chapter, it may seem that both promises are already broken.

Actually, we believe they can still be kept.

Think again about understanding the human body. If a man asked how it works and received in return a lecture about the organization of cells and how chemistry explains their functioning, he might well feel cheated. After all, these explanations do not begin to say why people act as they do. They do not even explain something as simple as chewing.

But cells are as complicated and interesting, in their own way, as the body itself. Moreover, from cells, it is only a few steps to organs, systems, and the operation of the whole body.

Boolean algebra is a little like chemistry. It is the basis for everything that goes on in a computer, even though many people who use computers may never have heard of it.

The algebra of logic is a fascinating subject in its own right, one that we have only touched on in this chapter. It also has a remarkable history. It is the invention of the English mathematician and logician George Boole, who was the son of a shoemaker, and a man with nearly no formal education: he completed only three grades of elementary school.

Boole published his system of algebraic logic in 1854 in a book called *An Investigation into the Laws of Thought*. Beginning with the Greeks, many people have tried to boil human reasoning down to a set of rules. They have called these rules of thinking logic. Boole's idea was to turn the rules into a kind of mathematics.

Today, research on thinking relies more and more on computers, which in turn are based on Boole's system. Ironically, though, it seems Boole was wrong. Modern research appears to show that the kind of thinking most people do in their everyday lives is not based on the rules of logic.

For us, Boolean algebra is a kind of digression. Our main interest is to see how computers work. The logic gates and logic circuits we have looked at are like cells in the body—interesting, but, for us, only building materials for a larger structure. Chapter 2 also talks about cells, cells for storing **true**s and **false**s, but by the end of that chapter we will have constructed our first system: the computer's main memory.

The circuits we have designed so far give outputs that depend on the inputs to them. As soon as we disconnect the inputs, the output changes. To make memory cells, we will need to design circuits that can tell us *now* what the inputs were *yesterday*, or even a thousandth of a second ago.

This is the next step.

As for our claim that the computer is based on simple ideas, we still hold to it. The transistor is just a switch. Our three basic logic gates are built with these switches and they do nothing more than apply the words *and, or,* and *not* to electricity. Logic circuits simply represent logical statements that use these three words in combinations.

Admittedly, it takes a good deal of concentration sometimes to work out the meaning of a complicated logical statement or to simplify a Boolean expression. But compare the ideas of this chapter with the confusion of chemistry and you will see why we call them simple. Everything is just a matter of connecting transistors.

Is it not remarkable that the most powerful invention of all human history can be built with just one part?

EXERCISES

1.1. The diagram for this exercise shows two transistors connected to form a circuit. The diagram also shows that voltage has been supplied at three places in the circuit. Should we expect to measure voltage at the point in the circuit marked **A**? What about at **B, C, D,** and **E**?

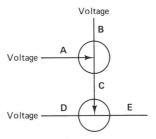

1.2. Say in one sentence how the voltage at **E** in the diagram depends on the voltages at **A, B, C,** and **D**.

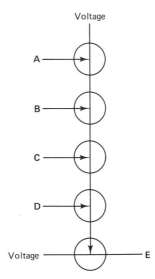

1.3. No voltage is measured at the output of the OR gate shown here. Has voltage been supplied at **In-1**? What about at **In-2**?

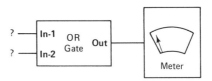

1.4. Will there be voltage at the output of the circuit in the diagram for this exercise?

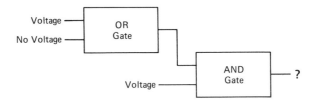

1.5. Give three examples of chunking, other than the ones discussed in the chapter. Try to make the three as different as possible from each other.

1.6. Label the output of the OR gate shown here. What would it mean about Fred if voltage were measured at the output?

1.7. Design a logic circuit like the one in Figure 1.23 to decide what Peter will do in the following problem.

> Peter will go to the bank only if Richard does the shopping
> and Sally sweeps up.
> Sally will sweep up if Tom or Victor makes the bed.
> Tom agrees to make the bed, but Richard refuses to go shopping.
> **What will Peter do?**

1.8. Suppose, in the party problem, that Ann does not go and Bob and Carol do. Copy Figure 1.23 and show
(a) Where voltage should be supplied.
(b) Where voltages will be present in all other parts of the circuit.

1.9. Suppose we know that garbage is collected every Tuesday (and never on other days). What should go inside a box labeled as in the diagram?

Today Is
Tuesday ————— [?] ————— Garbage Will Be
Collected Today

1.10. Taking Figure 1.28 as a model, label all the wires in the circuit shown here, using Boolean algebra notation.

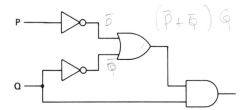

1.11. Relabel Figure 1.22 using only the names Ann, Bob, and Carol.

1.12. What Boolean algebra axiom backs up each of the following claims?
  (a) We know the earth is round, and so anyone who says that the earth and moon are *both* flat is obviously lying.
  (b) He says this is the answer and I say it's not. One of us has to be right.

1.13. Give an example of an everyday situation in which it is important to solve a logic problem.

1.14. Which of the following statements are true?
  (a) Either this book is about computers or the moon is made of green cheese.
  (b) Either this book is not about computers or the moon is not made of green cheese.
  (c) The statement *This book is about computers and the moon is not made of green cheese* is false.

1.15. Let **C** represent the statement *This book is about computers* and let **G** represent the statement *The moon is made of green cheese.* Use Boolean algrebra notation to represent the statements in Exercise 1.14.

1.16. Let **W** represent the statement *Today is a weekday* and let **C** represent the statement *It is cold out today.* Which of the following are true?
  (a) **W**
  (b) **C**
  (c) ~~~**W**
  (d) ~**C** + **W**
  (e) ~(**C** + **W**)
  (f) (**C** · **W**) + (**C** · ~**W**) + (~**C** · **W**) + (~**C** · ~**W**)
  (g) **W** · ~**W**
  (h) **C** + ~**C**

1.17. Write down any statement and call it **P**. Write down another and call it **Q**. Then translate the following into English:

$$\mathbf{P} \cdot \mathbf{Q} + (\sim\mathbf{P} + \sim\mathbf{Q})$$

In general, is this Boolean expression always true, is it always false, or does it depend on the statements chosen for **P** and **Q**?

1.18. Prove your answer to the last part of Exercise 1.17. Either use Boolean algebra, or show how to check all possible cases.

1.19. Show how to design a four-input OR gate using only ordinary, two-input OR gates.

1.20. Use De Morgan's laws to build an OR gate using just AND and NOT gates.

1.21. Will there be voltage at the output of the voting circuit in Figure 1.41 if we supply voltage to all three inputs (**A**, **B**, and **C**)?

1.22. Design a three-input circuit that puts out voltage only when voltage is supplied to *exactly* one input. You may want to use the first approach we employed in designing the NAND gate. That is, find all the cases in which voltage is put out, represent them separately with Boolean expressions using the symbols for *not* and *and* (∼ and ·), and then connect the expressions using *ors* (+).

1.23. What will the multiplexer from Section 1.14 put out if voltage is supplied to **S** and **In-1** but not to **In-2**? Will the output change if the voltage at **S** is then turned off?

1.24. Suppose we know that voltage is supplied to the multiplexer at both **In-1** and **In-2** but we do not know anything about the voltage at **S**. Can we tell what the voltage will be at **Out**?

1.25. Our multiplexer may be used as an OR gate. Explain how.

2 Memory

2.1 FEEDBACK AND THE STICKER

One of the interesting things about people is that they appear to control themselves. They decide what they will do and then they do it. It is as if a machine had been designed that could push its own buttons.

Actually, though, machines that control themselves are quite common. A furnace with a thermostat is a good example. The thermostat contains a switch that turns the furnace off when it gets too hot. In effect, the furnace turns itself on and off.

For something to control itself, it must have information about itself. With people, we generally call this information **consciousness**. A woman knows who she is, where she is—everything down to the position of her eyes and the contents of her stomach. She uses the information to decide between, say, eating and reading.

For the furnace, self-knowledge boils down to just one fact: It "knows" how hot it is. It uses the information to decide whether to be on or off.

When machines get information about their own operating conditions, we usually call the process **feedback**.

The idea is simple, but the more we look into complicated, interesting systems, the more it turns out that feedback is at the bottom of them. For example, feedback is what keeps our economic system largely self-controlled. If many people want to buy homes and there are only a few available, the price of houses goes up. When the price goes up, builders rush to build new houses.

In this case, prices serve the economic system as temperature serves a furnace. Without any dictators issuing economic commands, the system responds correctly to a housing shortage.

Feedback is also at the heart of the chemistry of cells. A single cell manufactures more kinds of chemicals than any factory in the world. It needs precise quantities of each chemical and it has no central management to issue production orders.

Instead, cells use special control chemicals called enzymes. Each enzyme causes a certain reaction to proceed more quickly, but the enzyme itself does not change during the reaction.

Here is how feedback may come into play. Often, the chemical produced in a reaction controlled by an enzyme interferes with the working of that same enzyme. Through this interaction, the chemical controls its own production.

If the supply of the chemical is low, the enzyme speeds up the reaction that produces it. But, as the reaction produces more and more of this chemical, it more and more blocks the enzyme from working and the reaction is slowed down. The more of the chemical there is, the less will be produced.

Later, if something uses up the chemical, the enzyme it has been blocking is freed and goes to work again spurring new production.

*   *   *   *   *

Of course, we are discussing feedback because it plays an important part in the workings of a computer. For one thing, feedback is what makes computers self-controlling. A computer is the best example we have of a man-made machine that pushes its own buttons. The details of how it does so are explained in Chapter 5.

But, in a much simpler way, feedback is what makes memory possible in a computer.

So far, none of our logic circuits has contained a loop. Some have been designed to send voltages along to be used by another circuit. But none has taken its own output as an input.

In a sense, the input wires of a logic circuit are the buttons that control it. None of our circuits so far pushes its own buttons.

Figure 2.1 shows our first example of a logic circuit with this kind of feedback. It is also the first example of what we promised to build at the end of Chapter 1: a circuit that will tell us *now* what the input was *yesterday*. We call this circuit a **sticker**, for reasons which will soon be clear.

Figure 2.1 A sticker.

To begin an analysis of the circuit, we will assume temporarily that there is no voltage at **In-1** or at the output of the OR gate. Since the output is connected to **In-2**, we know there is no voltage at that input either. Under our temporary assumption, then, the OR gate receives no voltage at either input and so it puts no voltage out. This condition is shown in Figure 2.2.

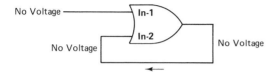

Figure 2.2 Analyzing the sticker (a).

Now, suppose we supply voltage to **In-1**. Since the OR gate has voltage coming in at one input, it will put voltage out. The voltage at the output circles back to **In-2**, as shown in Figure 2.3.

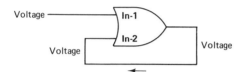

Figure 2.3 Analyzing the sticker (b).

Finally—and this is the key point—suppose we turn the voltage at **In-1** off again. The OR gate still receives voltage at **In-2** from its own output. With voltage coming in at one input, it continues to put voltage out. This situation is pictured in Figure 2.4.

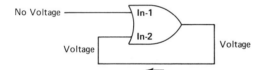

Figure 2.4 A stuck sticker.

The point is that the sticker is stuck. The voltage coming out of the OR gate supplies voltage coming in. The voltage coming in keeps the voltage coming out. No matter what we do with **In-1**, the OR gate will continue to put out voltage. When the output goes on, it stays on—forever.

It appears that the sticker is a kind of disposable circuit: we can use it only once. As such, it is not of much use except as an example. But it *is* a good example of how we can build a circuit with memory. By looking at the output of the sticker we can tell if voltage has *ever*—even for just a moment—been supplied to **In-1**. A sticker never forgets.

Of course, what we really want is a sticker that can be *made* to forget. We would like it to remember, as long as necessary, that voltage has been supplied. But it should also have an extra input that sets it back to its original state with all the voltages off.

A circuit that works like this is called a **flip-flop**. It can store one piece of logical information: voltage on in the output for **true**, voltage off for **false**. It is central to the functioning of a computer.

However, before we design a flip-flop, it is a good idea to look into some of the problems that can arise in circuits with feedback.

2.2 INSTABILITY AND INCONSISTENCY

When we design logic circuits without feedback, we can be sure of at least one thing. Whatever the inputs, the output must be either on or off.

Feedback creates new problems. For example, what about the circuit in Figure 2.5?

Figure 2.5 A feedback circuit.

Suppose that, when we begin to observe the circuit, there is no voltage at the NOT gate input. This causes the gate to put out voltage. But that voltage circles back to the input, and so, a moment later, there *will* be voltage at the input.

With voltage at the input, the NOT gate will stop putting voltage out. But, because of the loop, no voltage out means no voltage in. This brings the circuit back to its original state.

It appears that the circuit will flip continuously between the two states shown in Figure 2.6.

Figure 2.6 The circuit is unstable.

In general, there is nothing wrong with this kind of feedback. A furnace works the same way. It turns itself on and off, over and over again, as the temperature swings from cold to hot and back again. Unless it breaks or runs out of fuel, it never stops turning itself on and off.

The problem is that we want to use circuits for logic. Each wire in a logic circuit is supposed to represent a sentence. The voltage in the wire is supposed to tell us if the sentence is true or false. What does it mean if the voltage in a certain wire keeps flipping between on and off?

We can get the answer by labeling the looped NOT gate we have been studying. We know that the input and output of a NOT gate must be opposites, and so we can begin by choosing any sentence and its opposite as labels. In Figure 2.7, we use the labels **John is tall** and **John is not tall**.

John Is Tall ——————▷o—————— John Is Not Tall

Figure 2.7 Labeling a NOT gate.

When we connect the output wire of a gate to the input wire of another gate, we are saying, in effect, that the wires represent the same thing. In Chapter 1, we connected only wires that had the same label.

If we connect the output of a NOT gate to its input, as in Figure 2.8, we are saying that two opposite labels mean the same thing. Here, we are saying that **John is tall** means the same as **John is not tall**. No wonder the circuit has trouble making up its mind.

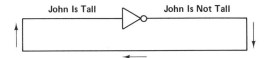

Figure 2.8 A labeled feedback circuit.

From a slightly different point of view, the problem is that we have only two logical values, neither of which makes the equation $J = \sim J$ correct. If we try **true** for J, the left side of the equation is **true**. To make the right side **true**, J would have to be **false**.

Likewise, if we try letting J be **false**, the left side of the equation will be **false**. To make the right side **false**, J would have to be **true**.

Logicians say that a statement like $J = \sim J$ is **inconsistent**. When we try to use feedback to turn an inconsistent statement into a logic circuit, we end up with a circuit that is **unstable**. That is, instead of settling into one pattern of voltages, it flips back and forth between two or more patterns.

In general, we do not want to design circuits that represent inconsistent statements. Most people agree that such statements are meaningless.

However, before we rule out inconsistency completely, we should point out that it leads to some strange and interesting questions. Take the statement *This sentence is false*. It *appears* to have meaning. Is it true or false?

If the sentence is true, then what it says is correct. It says it is false, and so, in fact, it must be false.

If the sentence is false, then what it says is wrong. It says it is false, and so, in fact, it must be true.

Either way we try to think about the sentence, we run into contradictions. The sentence is false if it is true and true if it is false. It is its own opposite.

But then what if we label our looped NOT gate as in Figure 2.9? Is this consistent or inconsistent?

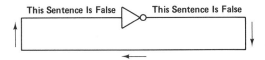

Figure 2.9 Is this labeling consistent?

This kind of paradox dates back to a statement by the Greek philosopher Epimenides, and after thousands of years, it still has not been resolved.[1]

---

[1] Epimenides, himself born on the island of Crete, is supposed to have said that all Cretans are liars. Was he lying when he made this claim?

Some people say that statements like *This sentence is false* are meaningless. Others say they should be assigned a *new* logical value, one that would correspond to a logic circuit voltage that flips on and off.[2]

For our purposes, however, it will not be necessary to represent inconsistent and paradoxical statements. Instead, we return to the problem of designing a flip-flop.

2.3 A SIMPLE FLIP-FLOP

The sticker is an example of a **bistable** circuit. That is, it is stable in *two* voltage patterns or states.

Bistable is a long way from unstable. The unstable looped NOT gate of Figure 2.8 flips continuously; it never settles into any state at all. By contrast, the bistable sticker stays quietly in one state—with its output voltage off—until someone supplies voltage to **In-1**. Then it flips once into its other state—with the output voltage on—and remains stably in that state forever after.

For a flip-flop, what we need is a bistable circuit that can be made to flip between its two states on command. One way is to add an AND gate and a NOT gate to the sticker, as in Figure 2.10.

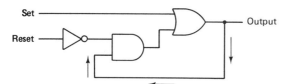

Figure 2.10 Design for a flip-flop.

To begin analysis of this circuit, suppose we do not supply voltage at the **Reset** input. In this case, the output of the NOT gate will supply voltage to one input of the AND gate.

But an AND gate with one input on serves no purpose. The voltage it puts out is exactly the same as the voltage at its other input.[3] If the **Reset** voltage is off, we might just as well connect the OR gate output directly to its own lower input, as in Figure 2.11. In this case, the circuit works exactly like a sticker. If anyone ever puts voltage into the **Set** input, the output goes on and it stays on. Voltage in the output feeds back into the OR gate input and keeps the output on.

To turn the sticker off again, all we need is a way to cut off this feedback loop. This is the function of the NOT and AND gates.

If voltage *is* supplied at **Reset**, the NOT gate will supply no voltage to the AND gate. With one input off, the AND gate will put out no voltage to the OR

---

[2] The argument is like the one that created the so-called imaginary number *i*. This number is supposed to be the square root of -1. It solves the equation $x^2 = -1$, which cannot be solved with any ordinary number. When *i* was first proposed, many people argued that it was meaningless. Now it is commonly accepted.

[3] This is just another way of expressing one of our Boolean identity axioms: **true** $\cdot$ **P** = **P**.

gate, no matter what voltage conditions are in the loop. With **Reset** turned on, we might as well cut the wire in the feedback loop, as shown in Figure 2.12.

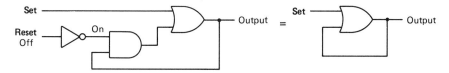

Figure 2.11 The flip-flop with **Reset** off is a sticker.**ticker**. *Note*: "Off" means no voltage "On" means voltage.

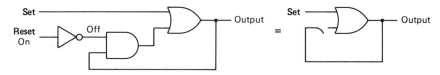

Figure 2.12 Cutting off the feedback resets the flip-flop.

Voltage to **Set** turns the sticker output on. Once on, it stays on, unless someone supplies voltage to **Reset** to turn it off again. Once off, it stays off, unless someone again supplies voltage to **Set**.

This flip-flop—a sticker with a cutoff switch—is bistable. If its inputs are disconnected, that is, if no voltage comes into either one, it will simply stay in one of the two voltage patterns shown in Figure 2.13.

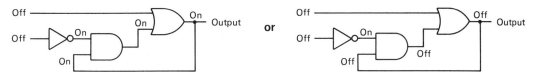

Figure 2.13 Stable states of the flip-flop. Inputs are off in both cases.

As we said earlier, we can use this kind of bistable circuit to store a logical value. If we want to store the logical value **true**, we "set" the flip-flop so that it puts out voltage. If we want to store **false**, we "reset" it so that it puts out no voltage. Either way, we can store a logical value today and then, by checking the output voltage, remember tomorrow what it was.

This simplest kind of memory circuit is usually called an **R-S flip-flop**, R-S being an abbreviation for *reset-set*. We will use it to build more sophisticated flip-flops, just as we used basic logic gates to build logic circuits. As usual, now that we know what goes into the R-S flip-flop, we will simplify matters by drawing it as just a labeled box, as in Figure 2.14.

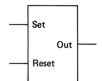

Figure 2.14 An R-S flip-flop.

2.4 CLOCKS

Most people know that computers process information. We are beginning to see, though, that this information is only a matter of voltages in wires. Also, it seems that computers will do their processing work by routing voltages through logic gates.

The electrical pressure of voltage moves along wires at nearly the speed of light, traveling about 300,000,000 meters every second. A battery hooked up to a wire three football fields long begins to make electrons flow at the other end after a delay of only a millionth of a second. Still, it *does* take time for the effect of voltage to be felt.

Also, transistors take a little time to adjust when we change the voltage in the control wire. This means that there is a brief delay between when we supply voltage at the input of a logic gate and when the output voltage is sure to be correct.

The upshot of all this is that there must be a controlled pause before each step that a computer takes. The pause must be long enough to allow electrical pressure fields to travel from one end of the computer to the other and for all the transistors to adjust.

Normally, we create this pause by running everything in the computer on a **clock**. The idea is that, inside the computer, a clock is ticking. Most of the steps that make up the computer's work are scheduled to happen exactly when the clock ticks. During the time between ticks, no work is performed. Voltages get a chance to race along the wires to their destinations, and the transistors adjust.

Of course, a real clock would be far too slow. Instead, we use an electronic device with an output that rapidly changes in voltage between on and off. Depending on the way our computer is set up, we consider the "tick" of this clock to be either the time when its output is on or the instant when its output is *changing* between on and off.

Incidentally, we have been claiming that a computer can be built using only transistors. What about the clock? It can be built with transistors too. The unstable circuit in Figure 2.15 could be used as a clock. We have already seen that it does what we want: it flips continuously between on and off.

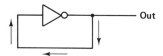

Figure 2.15 One way to build a clock.

2.5 CLOCKED FLIP-FLOPS AND D FLIP-FLOPS

The next step, then, is to put our R-S flip-flop on the clock. We want the flip-flop to be able to change only when the clock ticks. Otherwise, it should work just as it did before.

For now, we will consider the "tick" of the clock to be the time when it is putting out voltage.

To turn an ordinary R-S flip-flop into a clocked one, we need only make sure no voltage can get through to the **Set** and **Reset** inputs when the clock output is off. One way to do this is shown in Figure 2.16. The **Clock** input here is meant to be connected to the output of a clock. When the clock is putting out no voltage, one input of each AND gate is guaranteed to be off. AND gates put out no voltage unless both inputs are on; therefore, with the clock off, no voltage will be supplied to either **Set** or **Reset**.

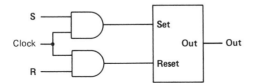

Figure 2.16 Putting the R-S flip-flop on the clock.

When the clock ticks, putting out voltage, the output of each AND gate depends entirely on the inputs **S** and **R**. It is as if we were putting these input voltages directly into **Set** and **Reset**.

The result is called a **clocked R-S flip-flop**. We will draw it as a labeled box, as shown in Figure 2.17.

Figure 2.17 A clocked R-S flip-flop.

*   *   *   *   *

One drawback of this R-S flip-flop is that it uses two input wires where just one would do. An improved circuit is shown in Figure 2.18a. If we supply voltage to the wire marked **D** when the clock is on, the flip-flop will be set. If no voltage is supplied to **D**, the NOT gate supplies voltage to **R** and the flip-flop will be reset. The logical value stored in the flip-flop is the same as the input on the **D**, or "data," wire.

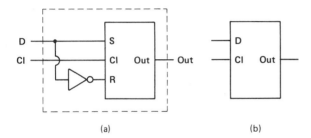

(a)   (b)

Figure 2.18 Circuit and symbol for a D flip-flop.

This kind of circuit—a clocked R-S flip-flop with a single wire controlling the **R** and **S** inputs—is called a **D flip-flop**. We will draw it as shown in Figure 2.18b.

2.6 MASTER-SLAVE FLIP-FLOPS

The R-S flip-flop and the D flip-flop both store a value during the time the clock is sending out voltage. As we said before, we may consider that time to be the "tick" of the clock. But it is often better to consider the tick to be the time when the clock is *changing* voltage.

One reason is that this time is more specific. If a scientist is keeping notes on weather conditions, she might check the sky at exactly the same time every day, say, at 1 P.M. If she were less precise and just noted down the conditions each day sometime between 1 and 2 P.M., she would run into trouble if a rainstorm happened to stop at 1:30 P.M. Should she write down that it was raining, or that it wasn't?

We have the same problem with flip-flops. Suppose the input to a D flip-flop changes between on and off during the time the clock is on. What should be stored?

Another problem with our simple flip-flops is that they are **transparent**. During the time the clock is on, the output of a D flip-flop is the same as its input. We say this kind of circuit is transparent because it is as if the output wire could see through the circuit to the input.

Because transistors take time to change states, the input to a flip-flop may waver between on and off for a short time before settling down to its correct value. While the input is wavering, the D flip-flop will put out a wavering voltage. Sometimes this will be confusing for whatever circuit uses the flip-flop's output.

Both problems can be solved by using a flip-flop that stores values precisely at the moment that the clock voltage changes.

We can build this kind of flip-flop beginning with two ordinary D flip-flops. The first one, as usual, changes values only when the clock is on. During the time the clock is on, this flip-flop may change from on to off a hundred times. But as soon as the clock goes off, it stops changing.

The last value, the one coming in at the precise instant the clock changes from on to off, is the one stored.

The second flip-flop is modified slightly so that it may change values only when the clock is *off*. Thus, while the clock is on and the first flip-flop is flipping and flopping, the second flip-flop stays steady. We use the output of this second flip-flop as the main output of our circuit.

While the clock is on, the main output cannot change.

At the moment the clock goes off, the second flip-flop is free to change. But we let it take its input from the *first* flip-flop. The first flip-flop cannot change during the time the clock is off, so it provides a steady input for the second flip-flop.

Thus the main output also stays steady while the clock is off. It changes only at the instant when the clock goes from on to off.

The circuit for this flip-flop is shown in Figure 2.19. It is normally called a **master-slave flip-flop**, because the first D flip-flop, the master, tells the second D flip-flop, the slave, what to store. Notice that, for the slave, we do not have to design a special D flip-flop that changes only when the clock is off. We just use an

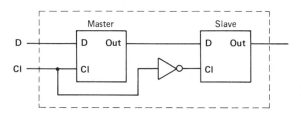

Figure 2.19 Design for a master-slave flip-flop.

ordinary D flip-flop and add a NOT gate at its clock input. When the main clock is off, the NOT gate turns the slave's clock input on.

2.7 A MEMORY BLOCK

Back before we began to build circuits, we pointed out that a wall covered with switches could be used to leave messages. Each switch can be placed in one of two states: on and off. Each *pattern* of switches on and off could stand for a different message.

The more switches on the wall, the more patterns we can make and the more different messages we can leave.

We are ready now to assemble our flip-flops into a memory unit. Each flip-flop in the unit will act like a switch, since its output can be either on or off. The information in our memory unit will be just a *pattern* of ons and offs, standing for logical **true**s and **false**s. As with the switches, the pattern has no meaning of its own. It is always up to us to supply an interpretation.

The simplest idea for a memory unit is just a large group of flip-flops. We might want to organize them into an array as in Figure 2.20. In a sense, this kind of array is very powerful. If we only make it large enough, we can store as much information as we like.

The problem is that the array is hard to use. For example, if we want to use the stored information as input to a logic circuit, it is up to *us* to find the flip-flop containing the **true** or **false** we want and then to connect the output of this flip-flop to the logic circuit.

This is a little like when it was up to us to decide what voltage to put into each logic gate. Unless the system is much more automatic, it will be easier to scrap the electronics and use paper and pencil.

We must automate the memory unit, then, and here is a plan for doing so.

The plan rests on referring to each flip-flop in the array by a name. To use the memory unit, we will first specify the name of one of the flip-flops and whether we want to put information in or get it out. If we want information out, the stored voltage will appear on a wire—the same wire no matter which flip-flop we name. If we want to store a logical value, we will put the corresponding voltage on a single input wire and the memory unit will use the given name to make sure it is stored in the correct flip-flop.

For names, we will use strings of logical values. For example, a certain flip-flop might have the name **true-false-false-true**.

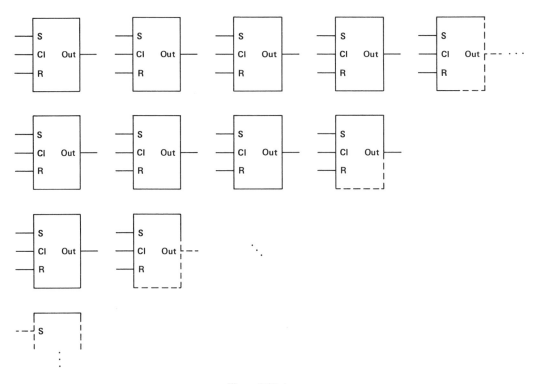

Figure 2.20 A memory array.

We will use any names we like so long as

1. Each flip-flop has a different name.
2. All names use the same total number of **true**s and **false**s.

In the sample name just shown, we used four logical values, but we could just as well have used six or twenty. The important thing is that we must use the same number in every name.

Figure 2.21 shows our plan for a memory unit. We call it a **memory block**, because we intend to use it as a building block for more complex memory systems.

The **Name** wires at the upper left of the memory block are used to specify one of the flip-flops in the array at the right. If the flip-flop we want is named **true-false-false-false**, we put the corresponding voltages into the **Name** wires, on for **true** and off for **false**.

The **Store/~Read** wire at the lower left is used to tell the block whether we are getting information out ("reading") or putting it in ("storing"). If we turn voltage off in this wire, to specify "read," and put the name of a flip-flop on the **Name** wires, the logical value stored in that flip-flop will come out on the **Data-Out** wire.

If we turn voltage on in the **Store/~Read** wire, to specify "store," the value on the **Data-In** wire will be stored in the named flip-flop.

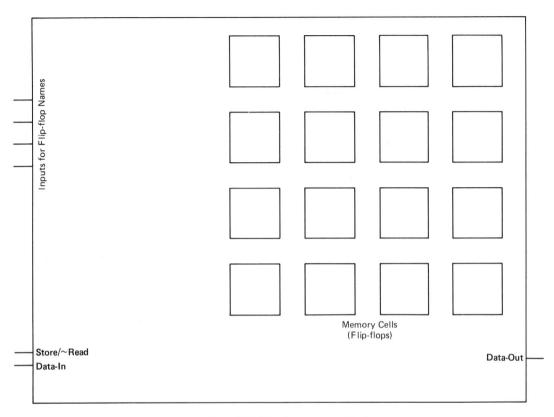

Figure 2.21 Plan for a memory block.

2.8 DECODING

Of course, it is easy to claim that the memory block will do these things, and quite another matter to show how.

The first job in putting our plan into action is to figure out a way for the **Name** wires to "pick out" single memory cells. What we need is a wire leading to each memory cell that will have voltage in it when that cell has been selected.

Suppose we take a cell with the name **true-false-false-true**. We can design a circuit to select it as shown in Figure 2.22. When the **Name** wires numbered 1 and 4 send out voltage and the two numbered 2 and 3 do not, the AND gate will

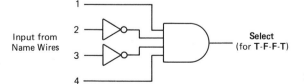

Figure 2.22 A selector circuit.

receive voltage at all four inputs. It is only in this case that the **Select** wire leading
into this memory cell will have voltage in it. That is, voltage in this wire will be on
just when we have chosen the flip-flop named **true-false-false-true**.

Clearly, we can use the same idea to design selector circuits for each of the
other memory cells. If each name uses four logical values, we can simply supply
each memory cell with a few NOT gates and a four-input AND gate hooked up to
put out voltage only when that cell has been selected.

In fact, we might think of collecting all these circuits together into one box,
as shown in Figure 2.23. The box, normally called a **decoder**, takes its four inputs
from the **Name** wires. Each output is determined by one selector circuit like the
one we have just designed.[4] If the inputs are **true-true-true-true**, the decoder puts
out voltage on just the top output. If the inputs are **true-true-true-false**, the
decoder puts out voltage on just the second wire.

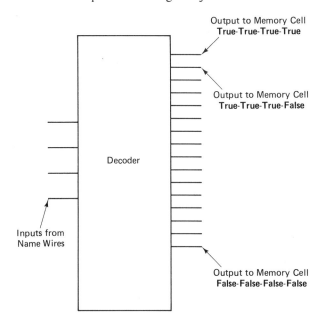

Figure 2.23 A decoder.

Each output wire corresponds to a single pattern of inputs, that is, to one possible name. Thus, for each name, exactly one output wire will be on.

As we are about to see, these wires will be employed to select memory cells,
so that only one is in use at any time.

---

[4] To build the decoder shown using 16 different selector circuits would take 48 two-input AND
gates. A better design uses only half as many. The trick is simply to allow one circuit which has determined that, say, the top two **Name** wires are on, to pass on the information to other circuits so that they
do not repeat the same figuring.

2.9 STORING AND READING

For memory cells, we will use D flip-flops. According to our plan for the block, we want the value stored in a memory cell to change only when

1. That cell has been selected, according to the voltages on the **Name** wires, and
2. The **Store/~Read** wire is on, meaning that we want to store a value rather than read one.

In this case, the clock input of the selected cell should go on. This is what allows a D flip-flop to change. At the same time, the voltage at its **D** input should be the same as the voltage at **Data-In**, since we use the **Data-In** wire to specify the logical value to be stored.

The necessary connections are shown, for a single cell, in Figure 2.24. Notice that voltage will go on in the flip-flop's **Cl** input only when voltage from the decoder indicates it has been selected *and* when voltage is on in the **Store/~Read** wire. In this case, since the **Data-In** wire is connected directly to the flip-flop's **D** input, the logical value on that wire will be stored.

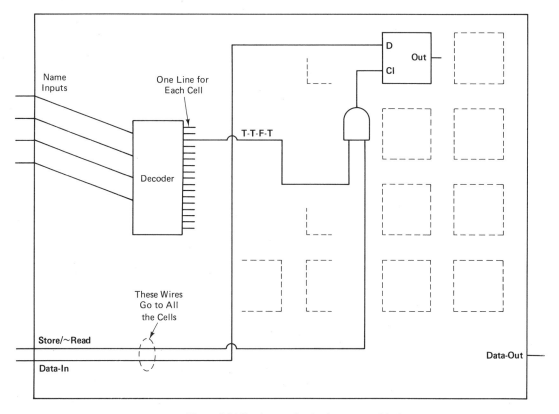

Figure 2.24 Storing a value in the memory block.

Incidentally, if we showed similar connections for each of the other memory cells, we would see **Data-In** running to the **D** input of each cell. The logical value on **Data-In** goes to all the cells, but *only the selected cell will receive voltage at its* **Cl** *input*. This cell alone will store the given value.

*   *   *   *   *

To complete our memory block design, we only need a way to get information out.

Remember that, to tell the memory block we want to read a logical value, we are supposed to supply no voltage to the **Store/~Read** wire. In this case, no voltage will get to the **Cl** input of any of the memory cells. That is, none of them can change values.

The upshot is that each cell will have a steady output: voltage on if it is storing a **true** and voltage off for a **false**. Our only problem is to choose the one of these outputs we want and channel it to the **Data-Out** wire.

As shown in Figure 2.25, the solution is to connect the output of each memory cell to an AND gate, with two additional inputs, and then run outputs from all the AND gates through a very wide OR. As before, the diagram shows connections for only a single memory cell.

Here is how the circuit works. The decoder sends out voltage over only one of its output wires—the one corresponding to the selected memory cell. The AND gates associated with all the other cells receive no voltage at the input connected to the decoder and so they all put out no voltage to the OR gate.

The OR gate will put out voltage if it is receiving voltage at any output. But we have just seen that it can receive voltage only from the selected cell. Therefore the final output of the memory block—the OR gate output we have called **Data-Out**—depends entirely on the voltage received from the AND gate at the selected memory cell.

This AND gate is receiving voltage from the decoder. It is also receiving voltage from the **Store/~Read** wire. That input wire is off, but it is run through a NOT gate.

We know, then, that the AND gate is receiving voltage at two of its three inputs. The third input will determine whether the AND gate puts out voltage. But this third input is just the output of the selected memory cell.

If the cell is storing a **true**, it will put out voltage. This causes the associated AND gate to put out voltage to the OR gate, which, in turn, puts out voltage over **Data-Out**.

If the cell is storing a **false**, it will put out no voltage. The associated AND gate then does not receive voltage at all of its inputs, and so it puts out no voltage to the OR gate. We have already seen that the OR gate does not receive voltage from any other cells. Therefore it receives no voltage at any input and puts out no voltage over **Data-Out**.

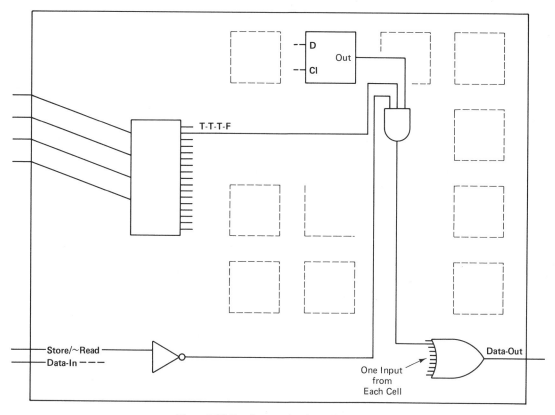

Figure 2.25 Reading a value from the memory block.

In either case the voltage on **Data-Out** is the same as the voltage put out by the selected memory cell, just as we wanted.

2.10 A MEMORY SYSTEM WITH FEEDBACK

We have shown, now, how it is possible to build a memory block that works according to our original plan. The unit is quite powerful and it is not hard to make it even more so, as we will soon show.

Still, as it stands, our memory block has a number of drawbacks.

For one thing, the more cells in our block, the more names we need. To get more names, we must use longer strings of logical values and, hence, more **Name** wires. After a while, all the wires coming out of the memory block will begin to look like a tangled web.

One solution to this problem is to use a single **Name** wire. Just as we may spell out a word letter by letter, we could put a name in over the single **Name** wire one logical value at a time. With this improvement, the memory block would have only four wires leading out of it—**Name**, **Store/~Read**, **Data-In**, and **Data-Out**—no matter how many cells it contains.

Another drawback of the memory block is of the opposite sort. No matter how large the block gets, the single **Data-Out** wire means we can get only one logical value out at a time. In this respect, we are *forced* to spell things out letter by letter.

It is precisely the desire to avoid this kind of spelling out that will lead us, later, to combine blocks into a larger **memory system**.

Still, even with its drawbacks, our memory block gives a good idea of how computers store information, and it leads us to quite an important point.

Consider again our first idea for a memory unit. It was just an array of memory cells with no connections at all. The problem with such an array is that it leaves us too much work. We added all the connections to make the system more automatic.

Even with the more sophisticated circuitry of the memory block, however, it is still up to us to get the voltages right on all the input wires—**Store/~Read**, **Data-In**, and the **Name** inputs.

This leads to an interesting question: Can we ever hope to make the system *completely* automatic?

In a certain sense, we can. We can let the memory unit output circle around and feed back into its own inputs. If we like, we might want to have some kind of logic circuit in the loop. That is, the memory output could filter through some AND, OR, and NOT gates before it was used as an input.

Probably, we would also want to use a clock so that voltages do not run helter-skelter around the feedback loop. On every tick of the clock, one output would circle around to be used as an input and a new output would appear. What we are proposing is shown in Figure 2.26.

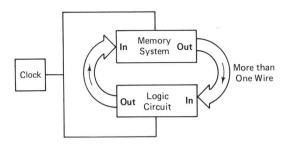

Figure 2.26 Plan for memory system with feedback.

Notice that the memory unit in this picture has several wires leading out, not just the single **Data-Out** wire of our simple memory block. We have not yet shown how to design this kind of system, but we have already hinted at how it might be built up from ordinary memory blocks. We will give the details in Section 2.12.

The system pictured in Figure 2.26 is designed to work automatically, but, of course, we would still be free to run it manually, if we wanted. We could store **true**s and **false**s, one at a time, in certain cells and then turn the system on automatic and watch to see what happens.

What would happen is simply this: On each tick of the clock, the pattern of **true**s and **false**s stored in the memory cells would change.

These changes would not be arbitrary. Each pattern—and the voltages on the input wires—would determine an output. This, in turn, would determine new input voltages and thus the next pattern.

The system we are imagining is a kind of combination checkerboard and Christmas tree, an array of flickering logic values. The obvious question to ask is why anyone would want to build one.

The odd answer is that what we are discussing can be a remarkably practical machine. The electronic digital computer, the crowning achievement and hallmark of our age, is a kind of combination checkerboard and Christmas tree: it is just a memory system with feedback.

The trick, of course, is in the logic circuit that works on the memory system output before it becomes the next input.

It is not too surprising that a computer turns out to be just a machine that changes information on the basis of information it already has. Its great power lies in the rules that say what to do next. These rules, and the logic circuits based on them, are the subject of Chapters 4 and 5.

Before we come to talk about rules and control circuits, however, we will need to discuss the problem of meaning. Of course, we are free to interpret the voltages stored in a memory system as we like. But a good interpretation will make it easier for us to get the computer to do useful work.

One especially useful interpretation is the subject of Chapter 3.

For now, however, we must get back to work on the memory unit itself, on which so much will depend.

2.11 SHIFT REGISTERS

At the beginning of Section 2.10, we suggested some possible changes in our basic memory system. The first was to design a unit with just a single **Name** input wire. The second was to design one that would allow us to put in or get out more than one logical value at a time.

Unfortunately, if we want to use the memory unit in a feedback loop, the simplicity of the first idea conflicts with the complexity of the second. Ideally, we would like the number of **Data-Out** wires to be the same as the number of **Name** wires. In this case, the **true**s and **false**s coming out of the memory unit would be just sufficient to serve as the name of the *next* memory location to be read.

In fact, this is exactly how we will proceed, beginning with Section 2.12. For a moment, however, it is useful to think about how we would carry out our first plan of using only a single **Name** input wire.

The idea we suggested was to send a name into the memory unit one logical value at a time. Naturally, however, the unit must not forget these values as quickly as we send them in. It must remember the entire string. For this purpose we need a small memory device—just large enough to hold a name.

A plan for such a device is shown in Figure 2.27. In general, a memory

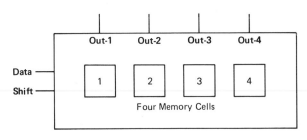

Figure 2.27 Plan for a shifting memory unit.

device designed to hold just a small chunk of logical information is called a **register**. The kind in the figure is called a **shift register**, for reasons we will soon explain.

A shift register may contain any number of memory cells, but the one we are considering would have just enough to hold the name of a flip-flop in our memory block.

The voltages corresponding to the logical values in this stored name are put out over the register's **Out** wires. These wires would be permanently connected to the inputs of the memory block decoder, in place of the **Name** wires.

Once a name was stored in the shift register, then, the corresponding flip-flop in the memory block would be selected. The only question is how to store a name.

For this, we need only use the two input wires **Data** and **Shift**. When voltage goes on at **Shift**, two things happen at the same time. First, the logical value on the **Data** wire is stored in the leftmost memory cell. Second, all the values already stored in the register are *shifted* one cell to the right.

To store a name, we put the logical values in one at a time. As each goes in, the others shift over to make room.

As planned, the shift register does just what we want. To turn the plan into a circuit, it would seem that we need only hook up a string of D flip-flops as shown in Figure 2.28. When the **Shift** wire goes on, each flip-flop will take a new value from the flip-flop on its left—that is, the values will shift to the right. And the leftmost flip-flop will take its value from the **Data** wire.

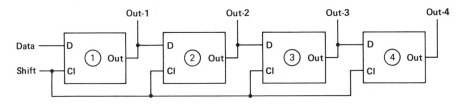

Figure 2.28 A trial design for the shift register.

Unfortunately, this circuit has a fatal flaw. Suppose all of the flip-flops are putting out no voltage when we start. That is, a **false** has somehow been stored in all of them. No voltage is coming in at the **Shift** input, so no voltage gets to the clock input of the flip-flops. The flip-flops stay steady.

Now we want to shift in a **true**. We put voltage on the **Data** wire, but nothing happens immediately, because the clock inputs are all still off.

When we turn on the **Shift** wire, the flip-flops go into action. Each flip-flop gets a new value from the flip-flop just to its left. Flip-flop 1 gets voltage coming in through the **Data** wire, so it stores a **true**.

A fraction of a second after the **shift** wire goes on, the situation is as pictured in Figure 2.29. So far, everything is working just as we want.

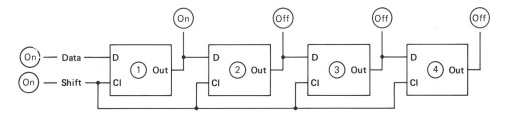

Figure 2.29 The shift register works at first. . . .

The problem is that, in the next fraction of a second, voltage is still coming in at all the clock inputs. Each flip-flop takes a new value from the flip-flop on its left. Flip-flop 2 takes a **true** from flip-flop 1 and flip-flop 1 takes a **true** from the **Data** wire.

The point is, before we get a chance to turn the voltage in the **Shift** wire off, the shift register will be *full* of **true**s. Four will have been shifted in, when we want just one. This is a good example of why transparency is sometimes a fault.

We can solve the problem simply by using master-slave flip-flops, as in Figure 2.30. To analyze the new circuit, we will start again with a **false** in each of the flip-flops. We put voltage on the **Data** wire, but nothing happens immediately, because the master flip-flops have no voltage coming in at the clock.

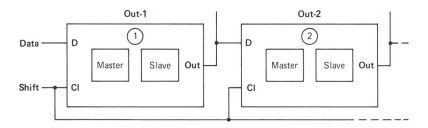

Figure 2.30 Final design for a shift register

When we put voltage on the **Shift** wire, master flip-flop 1 takes a **true** from the **Data** wire. Each of the other master flip-flops takes a new value from the slave flip-flop on its left. But, while the master flip-flops get their new values, none of the slave flip-flops change. The slaves change only when the clock—in this case the **Shift** wire—is off.

Thus the output of each master-slave flip-flop stays the same.

It is only when the **Shift** wire goes off that each slave takes on the new value stored in its master. But, while **Shift** is off, the master flip-flops cannot change, and so there is no way for the **true** to ripple along from cell to cell.

*   *   *   *   *

With this corrected design, we could put our shift register to use in the memory block. In fact, however, we have developed it for other purposes. Most of these are discussed in the next few chapters. But, for a hint, consider how shifting comes into play in multiplication.

When we multiply 123.456 by 10, for example, we get 1,234.56. The answer is the same as the original number except that all the digits have shifted over with respect to the decimal point. If we could somehow store numbers like these in a shift register, we could multiply them by 10 just by putting voltage into the **Shift** wire.

The details of how shifting can be used for multiplication, however, are reserved for Chapter 3.

2.12 MEMORY ORGANIZATION I

In Section 2.11, we considered how to make the memory unit *simpler* by using just one **Name** input. Now we will try to make it more *powerful*.

This is a large job, so we will tackle it in two parts. First, we will group memory blocks into "chunks." The result is a unit that, in one step, can take in or put out a whole "chunk" of logical values.

What we are suggesting is shown in Figure 2.31. Although the picture is complicated, the idea is simple. In essence, all we are proposing is to use the same wires as **Name** inputs to 20 memory blocks.

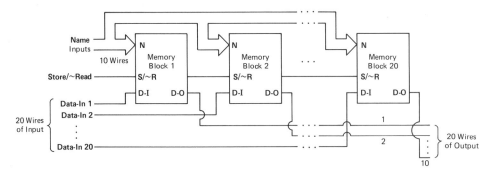

Figure 2.31 A "chunk" of memory blocks.

Until now, our examples have used strings of four logical values for names. With strings of just four logical values, however, it is possible to make up only a very few names—exactly 16, in fact.

To make a slightly more practical example, the figure shows memory blocks with ten **Name** wires. With strings of ten logical values it is possible to make up to 1,024 different names. Therefore each larger memory block contains an array of 1,024 memory cells and a much larger decoder to pick them out. Otherwise it is the same as the smaller memory block we originally designed.

As we said a moment ago, the same ten wires lead into the **Name** inputs of each of the 20 memory blocks in the figure. That means that the same flip-flop is selected in each block. Also, a single wire leads into the **Store/~Read** input of each block. Either all 20 blocks store at one time or all 20 are read.

Suppose, then, that we put the name of the flip-flop in the upper left corner of each block on the **Name** wires and use the common **Store/~Read** wire to indicate that we want information out. The 20 upper-left-corner flip-flops will each put out a logical value, and these values will emerge on the 20 **Data-Out** wires.

If we use the same name but put voltage on the **Store/~Read** wire, these 20 flip-flops will each receive a new logical value to store. The values to be stored come in over the 20 **Data-In** wires.

With this chunk of memory blocks, we have achieved our goal. Together they function as a memory unit that, in one step, takes in or puts out chunks of 20 logical values.

2.13 MEMORY ORGANIZATION II

The improved memory unit still has two problems, however. First, the number of **Data-Out** wires is not the same as the number of **Name** wires. Second, the unit is still too small. As it stands, it can store just 1,024 chunks of 20 logical values.

If we want to store more information, the obvious idea is simply to design memory blocks with more **Name** wires and cells. After all, we moved conceptually from four **Name** wires to ten in the last section. Why not use 20 or 100?

Of course, we could do just that. But one of the strongest lessons of all our previous design work is that we can go far by putting parts together. Instead of starting from scratch, we will show how to use the chunked memory blocks we have already designed to build up a larger system.

Figure 2.32 shows a picture of one of these chunks of 20 memory blocks. Note that this is just a simplified way of drawing the circuit shown in Figure 2.31.

Our idea is to use these chunked blocks just as we used memory cells before. That is, we will lay them out in an array and use names to pick them out one at a time.

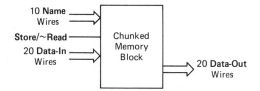

Figure 2.32 A "chunk" of memory blocks.

To keep things straight, we will make sure to call the chunked memory blocks that make up the array simply "blocks" and the array itself, the thing we are try-

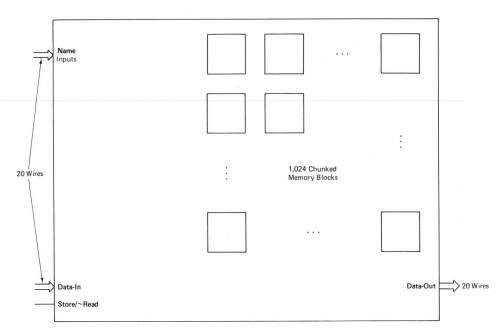

Figure 2.33 An array of memory blocks.

ing to design, the "memory system."

The plan begins, in Figure 2.33, much as it did with the original memory block, back in Figure 2.21. This time, however, there are two steps involved in specifying a position in the memory unit. First, we need to choose one of the 1,024 blocks in the array. But then, since the chosen block stores 1,024 chunks of logical values, we still need to say which chunk we want.

Notice that the figure shows 20 **Name** wires. Half of these wires are used in each stage of specifying a chunk.

The first ten run directly to the ten **Name** wires in each chunked memory block. They choose a single chunk within a block. The second ten are used to pick out just one of all the blocks.

From outside the memory system, though, this difference is not apparent. Someone using the system may consider all 20 wires to be used for specifying a long name. After all, each pattern of voltages on these wires picks out a different chunk of 20 flip-flops within the system. And once the chunk is chosen, new values to be stored may be sent in over the **Data-In** wires, or old values read out over the **Data-Out** wires.

For the user, the system behaves *as if* it were just a single chunk of memory blocks with 20 **Name** wires.

Incidentally, we have also arranged, now, to have the same number of **Name** and **Data-Out** wires. The planned memory system is nicely designed for feedback.

*   *   *   *   *

To turn the plan into a circuit is quite easy. From our work designing the original memory block, we already know how to use a decoder to pick out elements in an array and how to use a wide OR gate to choose one of many outputs. The details here are much the same.

One point, however, is worth considering. The decoder we are discussing would have 1,024 outputs. Likewise, the OR gate would have 1,024 inputs. Both of these are clumsier than they need to be.

A much better idea is to make use of an obvious fact about elements in an array: we can identify any element just by saying what row and column it is in. For example, it is perfectly precise to speak of the tenth memory block in the third row. There can be no mistaking which block we mean.

A square array of 1,024 memory blocks has only 32 rows and 32 columns. Rather than using a decoder with 1,024 outputs, then, we can use *two* decoders with just 32 outputs each—one to pick out rows and one to pick out columns.

To make sure new logical values are stored in the selected memory block, we allow voltage to get to the **Store/~Read** wire only if both the row decoder *and* the column decoder indicate that that memory block has been chosen.

The necessary circuits are shown in Figure 2.34. Notice that each decoder uses five of the ten **Name** inputs that go into choosing a memory block. It is no accident that we can supply voltage patterns to five wires in exactly 32 ways.

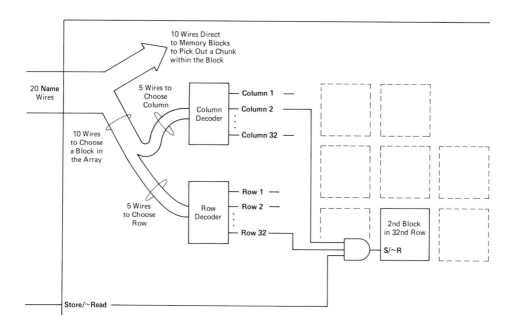

Figure 2.34 Choosing a block by row and column.

The same row-and-column idea eliminates the need for a 1,024-input-wide OR gate. Multiplexers do for output what decoders do for input. Of course, back in Chapter 1, we designed a very small multiplexer to select one of two inputs. Here we need the larger version pictured in Figure 2.35.

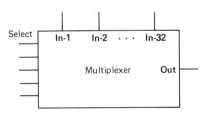

Figure 2.35 A 32-line multiplexer.

Notice that this multiplexer has five **Select** wires. As we said a moment ago, voltage may be supplied to five wires in 32 patterns. For each pattern, the voltage on a different one of the 32 inputs is channeled through to **Out**.

We are about to show how to use this multiplexer to choose a single output of the 1,024 coming from all the memory blocks. Of course, each block puts out a chunk of logical values over 20 wires. For a moment, however, it will be easier if we imagine each block putting out just a single value.

To choose one of these 1,024 values, we first use a multiplexer for each row. The 32 values on the row feed in at the top, and the five **Name** wires used to choose a column are connected to the **Select** wires. The result is that only the value from the block in the chosen column is channeled to the multiplexer output. The connections are shown in Figure 2.36.

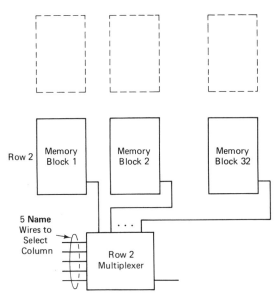

Figure 2.36 Choosing one value in each row.

The multiplexer on each of 32 rows, then, puts out the value from the block in the chosen column. Of course, the multiplexer in the chosen row is putting out just the value we want. To select it, we use one final multiplexer, as shown in Figure 2.37. This uses voltages on the remaining five **Name** wires to choose just one of the 32 row multiplexer outputs.

To complete our description of how to use the multiplexer, we have only to account for the fact that each chunked memory block puts out 20 values instead of the *one* we have been picturing. The solution is simple: just use the two-stage multiplexing system we have designed on each of the 20 output wires separately.

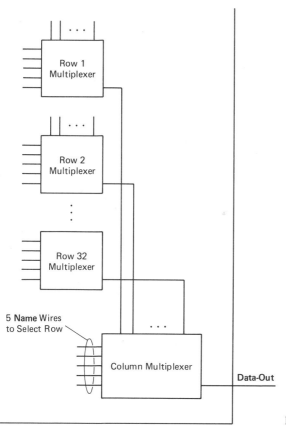

Figure 2.37 Choosing one of the row values.

2.14 HOW MANY TRANSISTORS?

With this last step, we have put the finishing touches on a memory system that uses 20 **Name** wires. With strings of 20 logical values, we can make up precisely 1,048,576 different names. This is the number of chunks of logical information the memory system can store.

The size of the number raises an interesting question. Since the first pages of this book, we have been chunking ideas together and trying to forget unnecessary details. For example, after we figured out how to build logic gates, we stopped thinking about the transistors that go into them.

As we have pointed out, it is this chunking principle that allows us to consider complicated ideas without letting details get in the way of our understanding.

By now, however, we have used transistors to build gates, gates to build flip-flops, flip-flops to build memory blocks, and memory blocks to build a memory system that can store more than 1 million chunks of logical information.

When we draw a rectangle and label it "Memory System," we are taking all of those smaller parts for granted. Stop for a moment now to see how many we have used.

A single memory system is built up from a few more than 1,000 memory blocks. Each block uses about 20,000 memory cells: 20 for each of 1,024 chunks. Therefore, one memory system uses roughly 20 million flip-flops.

Of course, it uses other things too, but we will not worry about those now. We are just trying to make a rough count. Each D flip-flop uses three AND gates, an OR gate, and two NOT gates. It takes one transistor to make a NOT gate, three to make an OR gate, and four to make an AND gate. In all, it takes 17 transistors to make a flip-flop.

Speaking of a memory system, then, is a very convenient way of forgetting about 340 million transistors. But how much space do that many transistors take up?

Consider, first, what would happen if we used water valves instead of transistors. A small water valve might be about as big as the last section of your thumb. 340 million valves that size would about fill a good-sized moving van.

In the first section of this book, we said computers use transistors because they switch on and off quickly. Another good reason is that they can be made very small. A million-chunk transistor memory system will fit easily in the palm of your hand.

As we mentioned briefly before, the transistors in such a system are not produced separately. Instead, they are etched onto a chip of silicon coated with semiconductor material. The result is called an **integrated circuit**.

In fairness, a real memory system is small, in part, because it is not built quite the way we have described. Professional circuit designers work hard to save transistors, whereas we just settled for the simplest design to understand. But even if we needed all 340 million transistors and more, the technology of integrated circuits would keep our memory system almost unbelievably compact.

2.15 COUNTING

In terms of storage capacity, our memory system is already quite practical. However, it still requires far too much manual work.

Eventually, as we have said, we want to make the system completely automatic. For now, however, it might be interesting to make it at least partially so.

Suppose, for example, that we have a memory system full of stored chunks and we want to get *all* of the information back out. As the system stands, we would have to put in voltages for each of a million different names.

Why not design a circuit to put in all those names automatically? It could be hooked up to a clock so that, on each tick, a different name would come out.

To begin, consider the looped master-slave flip-flop shown in Figure 2.38. Remember that a master-slave flip-flop takes on a new value at the instant voltage on its **Cl** input changes from on to off. Because of the loop and the NOT gate, the flip-flop in the figure will store the opposite of whatever it previously contained. On each tick of the clock, the flip-flop output switches.

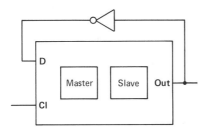

Figure 2.38 A flip-flop that "switches."

If we form a chain of these looped flip-flops, as in Figure 2.39, we get just the circuit we want. To analyze how this chain works, we will suppose that a **false** has been stored in each flip-flop. When the clock is set running, here is what happens.

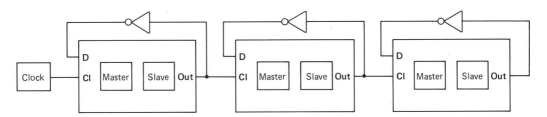

Figure 2.39 A chain of switching flip-flops.

Each flip-flop will switch states whenever the clock ticks. The trick is that each flip-flop has a different clock. The first runs on the main clock; the second gets its clock input from the output of the first flip-flop; and the third, from the output of the second. Each flip-flop switches values when its clock goes from on to off.

At first, the flip-flops are storing **false-false-false**. The main clock goes on; nothing happens.

As the main clock goes from on to off, the first flip-flop receives a "tick" and switches to **true**. Now the second flip-flop is receiving voltage at its clock input from the first flip-flop. The third flip-flop has no voltage coming in at the clock.

The stored pattern is **true-false-false**.

The main clock goes on; nothing happens. As it goes off again, the first flip-flop receives a tick and switches back to **false**.

But when the first flip-flop switches from **true** to **false**, the voltage it is sending to the second flip-flop's clock goes from on to off. Thus the second flip-flop receives a tick and switches to **true**.

Now the pattern is **false-true-false**.

We can explain what happens to the pattern this way:

1. At every tick of the main clock, the leftmost flip-flop switches.
2. Whenever any flip-flop switches from **true** to **false**, the flip-flop to its right receives a tick and switches.

According to these rules, the pattern changes as shown in Figure 2.40.

false-false-false
true-false-false
false-true-false
true-true-false
false-false-true
true-false-true
false-true-true
true-true-true   Figure 2.40 Patterns of a counter.

As the figure shows, the circuit produces every possible name that can be made with three flip-flops. If we had connected 20 flip-flops instead of just three, the pattern would change according to the same two rules. This would be just the circuit we set out to design.

Circuits like these are called **ripple counters**. The word ripple is used because of the way the effect of the main clock ripples across the circuit. It affects the leftmost flip-flop, which in turn affects the one on its right, and so on.

But why do we call it a "counter"?

If we watch the odometer of a car tick off miles, we are watching a machine that counts. But, as it goes from 00,000 miles to 99,999 miles, it makes every possible pattern of five digits. So, in a sense, counting is just a matter of making all possible patterns.

A ripple counter made with ten flip-flops runs through 1,024 patterns. If we wanted, we could assign each of these patterns a number from 0 to 1,023 so that the counter would count—that is, so that the first pattern it makes would be the one we have called 0, the next would be the one we have called 1 and so on up to 1,023.

But would this system of numbering make any sense, outside of giving a meaning to the patterns of the ripple counter? In fact, the system makes so much sense, and is so important, that we will spend all of the next chapter studying it.

2.16 TAKING STOCK

We are about to leave logic circuits behind for the space of a chapter. The reason, as we have said, is that it is time to think of a useful meaning for all the voltages our logic circuits produce.

The point is that we now have everything we will need to build a computer: a way to store information and an automatic way to apply rules to the information.

Unfortunately, the rules must be applied with logic circuits, and these are difficult to design. Also, our memory stores only a very limited kind of information—just strings of **true**s and **false**s.

That means we will need a way of representing information that is both compact and powerful. That is, our first goal is to store as much meaningful information as we can in the smallest possible space. Our second goal is to have a system in which simple rules do important work.

All this brings up an idea which is central to computer science, and really to science and human knowledge in general: Expression is a tool. To tackle a hard problem, we need a good way of talking about it. Just as it would be hard to saw a plank of wood with a butter knife, it would be hard to design logic circuits using words instead of diagrams and Boolean algebra symbols.

Part of the reason our own thinking is so powerful is that we seem to have a very good way of storing information in our brains. We can put in mathematical equations, pictures of people, songs, smells—nearly anything. And we can look most things up again in an instant.

Computer scientists spend a large part of their time inventing ways to express information about the world in terms of the **true**s and **false**s of computer memories. Making computers work depends heavily on having a good way to communicate with them.

The first step toward this communication is to decide on a meaning for patterns of **true**s and **false**s.

E X E R C I S E S

2.1. Give two examples of feedback in everyday life other than those discussed in the chapter.

2.2. The circuit in the diagram is just like the sticker in Figure 2.1 except that it is made with an AND gate. What happens in this circuit if we turn the voltage at **In-1** on and off several times? Does the circuit "remember"? Explain how it does or why it does not.

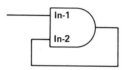

2.3. What happens to the flip-flop in Figure 2.10 if we supply voltage at *both* the wire labeled **Set** and the one labeled **Reset**?

2.4. Is it possible to design an unstable circuit using just AND gates? Using just OR gates? If so, show the circuits. If not, explain why.

2.5. **(a)** Consider the statement *This sentence is true.* Is it inconsistent? Explain why or why not.

    (b) What about the following pair of statements? Explain your answer.

        (i) Statement ii is true.

        (ii) Statement i is false.

2.6. What two things do we need to do to turn off the output of a D flip-flop?

2.7. What would determine the *rate* of the clock in Figure 2.15? That is, what affects how fast it ticks?

2.8. Suppose we begin with a clocked R-S flip-flop that is putting out no voltage and receiving no voltage at either input. What voltage will the flip-flop put out at the end of each of the following steps? (Note that the steps are taken in order.)

    (a) Voltage is supplied at **R**.

    (b) Voltage is supplied at **S**.

    (c) Voltage at **R** is turned off.

    (d) Voltage is supplied at **Clock**.

    (e) Voltage at **Clock** is turned off.

    (f) Voltage at **S** is turned off.

    (g) Voltage is supplied at **R**.

2.9. From the point of view of someone *using* flip-flops (rather than designing them), what is the main difference between a clocked R-S flip-flop and a master-slave flip-flop?

2.10. Design a circuit like the one in Figure 2.22 to select a cell labeled **true-false-true**.

2.11. How many different names may be formed using strings of three logical values? (**true-true-false** is one such string.) How many names may be formed using strings of four logical values? Using strings of five logical values? Without listing all the possibilities, can you say how many names six values long may be formed? 15 values long? 50 values long?

2.12. Use fewer than six ordinary two-input AND gates to design a circuit to select either **true-false-true-false** or **true-true-true-false**. The circuit should have four **Name** inputs and two outputs, one for each of the four-value names which may be selected. If a different name is put in over the **Name** wires, neither output should go on. Notice that simply using two circuits like the one shown in Figure 2.22 would require six ordinary AND gates, since a four-input AND gate is built with three ordinary ones. The best circuit uses only four two-input AND gates.

2.13. Design a two-input decoder, as shown in the diagram.

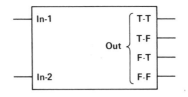

When voltage is supplied at both inputs, the circuit should put out voltage over the **true-true** wire. When voltage is supplied at the top input and not the bottom, it should put out voltage over the **true-false** wire, and so on.

2.14. Suppose a shift register built with four master-slave flip-flops happens to have a **false** stored in every flip-flop. We turn the voltage at the **Data** input on and, while leaving it on, turn the voltage at **Shift** on and then off and then on again. At this point, what will be the output of each flip-flop?

2.15. Figure 2.30 shows two master-slave flip-flops constructed from four R-S flip-flops. Assume that a **false** has been stored in each of the R-S flip-flops. What will be the output of each after the following steps? (Note that the steps are taken in order.)
   (a) Voltage is supplied to **Data**.
   (b) Voltage is supplied to **Shift**.
   (c) Voltage at **Shift** is turned off.
   (d) Voltage at **Data** is turned off.
   (e) Voltage is supplied to **Shift**.
   (f) Voltage at **Shift** is turned off.

2.16. What is the main difference between the memory device in Figure 2.21 and the one in Figure 2.33?

2.17. About how many transistors would be contained in a ripple counter made from 100 flip-flops? Explain how you got your answer.

2.18. Show the patterns that would be produced by a ripple counter made with two flip-flops. Be careful about the *order* in which the patterns would be produced.

2.19. How many **trues** and **falses** may be stored in the circuits pictured in each of the following figures?
   (a) 2.17
   (b) 2.19
   (c) 2.21
   (d) 2.27
   (e) 2.32
   (f) 2.33

3 Arithmetic

3.1 A STRANGER'S VIEW

Sometimes the hardest things to see clearly are the ones we look at every day. A familiar face takes only a glance to recognize, but just try to take a pencil and sketch it from memory. After years of glances, prominent features often go unnoticed.

Strangely enough, we carry out much of the business of our lives ignoring details. In fact, this seems to be a strength. Often, as we have already seen, details only get in the way.

Humans are designed for efficiency; in day-to-day life, it is simply more efficient to ignore everything but what we *need* to know. So long as we can recognize a face, the exact curve of the nose is not important.

Sometimes, however, it is essential to see things point by point. Here, efficiency can be a problem. Artists take years training themselves to notice details—to look at things as a stranger would, as if for the first time. To get this stranger's view of, say, a familiar face, an artist might resort to looking at it upside down.

In this chapter we will use a similar trick, taking a kind of upside down look at arithmetic. The idea is to see some of the details more clearly than we do in our day-to-day calculations.

3.2 AN ADDITION TABLE

Figure 3.1 shows an ordinary addition table. To use it to add 3 and 9, look across the third row and down the ninth column. The answer, 12, is at the intersection.

+	0	1	2	3	4	5	6	7	8	9
0	0	1	2	3	4	5	6	7	8	9
1	1	2	3	4	5	6	7	8	9	10
2	2	3	4	5	6	7	8	9	10	11
3	3	4	5	6	7	8	9	10	11	12
4	4	5	6	7	8	9	10	11	12	13
5	5	6	7	8	9	10	11	12	13	14
6	6	7	8	9	10	11	12	13	14	15
7	7	8	9	10	11	12	13	14	15	16
8	8	9	10	11	12	13	14	15	16	17
9	9	10	11	12	13	14	15	16	17	18

Figure 3.1 An addition table.

Most people have seen an addition table like this, but few use one. Anyone who has been through elementary school has memorized the information it contains. It is an interesting point, though, that we can use an addition table to add even if we have no idea what the symbols in it mean.

Consider Figure 3.2, for example. We can use this table to add up !&# and *!.

+	!	#	@	&	*
!	#	*	!	!@	&
#	*	&	#	!!	!@
@	!	#	@	&	*
&	!@	!!	&	!*	!#
*	&	!@	*	!#	!!

Figure 3.2 Another addition table.

We work the problem just as if we were dealing with ordinary numbers. First, we line the "digits" up into columns:

$$
\begin{array}{ccc}
! & \& & \# \\
  & * & ! \\
\hline
\end{array}
$$

Next, we add the two digits at the right using the table, as shown in Figure 3.3.

+	!	#	@	&	*
!	#	*	!	!@	&
#	*	&	#	!!	!@
@	!	#	@	&	*
&	!@	!!	&	!*	!#
*	&	!@	*	!#	!!

Figure 3.3. # + ! is *.

The addition table tells us that # plus ! is *, so we write this below.

```
    !    &    #
         *    !
    _____
              *
```

Moving on to the second column, we add & and *, using the table, and get !#. This is a two-digit answer, and we treat it just as we would in an ordinary arithmetic problem. If we were to add 3 and 9, getting 12 as an answer, we would put down the 2 and carry the 1. Here we have !# as an answer, so we put down # and carry the !:

```
         !
    !    &    #
         *    !
    _____
         #    *
```

As a last step in the calculation, we add ! and ! in the third column. Here is the final answer:

```
         !
    !    &    #
         *    !
    _____
    #    #    *
```

      *   *   *   *   *

The addition table with which we have been working is almost a kind of code puzzle. By now, it is natural to wonder what the symbols stand for. In fact, this is an easy question. But before we turn to decoding the table, there are other questions we ought to ask.

The main one is this: How do we know the table may really be used for addition? Perhaps there is no way at all to make sense of the symbols.

In general, a random table of symbols cannot be used for addition. The one in Figure 3.4, for example, is positively not an addition table.

+	X	H	U	I
X	H	U	I	X
H	I	H	X	H
U	U	X	HH	IU
I	X	I	UU	IX

Figure 3.4. An impossible addition table.

The reason is that addition is meant to describe what happens in the real world. If you have three boxes and get four more, you end up with seven boxes—just the same as if you had four boxes to begin with and got three more. It is a fact of life, when dealing with objects like boxes, that it makes no difference in which order we add: 3 + 4 is the same as 4 + 3.

Now look again at Figure 3.4. Here X + H is U, but H + X is I. If H and X represent numbers, we should get the same answer when we add them, no matter in what order. Thus Figure 3.4 cannot be an addition table.

In order to represent addition, a table must be **commutative**. That is, given any two symbols, the table should give the same answer, no matter in which order they are added.

It is easy to check a table to see whether it is commutative. For example, consider our previous addition table, shown again in Figure 3.5. Answers for the two sums * + & and & + * are just across the diagonal from each other. So are the answers for ! + & and & + !.

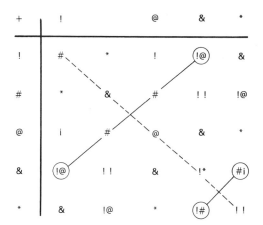

Figure 3.5. * + & = & + * and ! + & = & + !. The diagonal (dashed line) is like a mirror if the table is commutative.

We want answers for these pairs, and all other such pairs, to be the same. But then the upper right half of the table must be a mirror image of the lower left. Since this is true of the table we are considering, it must be commutative.

Figure 3.6 shows a third table. Is it possible that this is addition?

+	A	B	C
A	C	C	AB
B	C	B	A
C	AB	A	A

Figure 3.6 Another impossible addition table.

Using the mirror-image check, we see that the table *is* commutative. If we have two symbols, we get the same answer no matter in which order we add them.

This table has a different kind of problem. In Chapter 1 we pointed out that, in a series of additions, it does not matter which sum is calculated first. If we have 3 + 6 + 8, we can add the 3 and 6 first to get 9 and then add 8, or add the 6 and 8 first to get 14 and then add 3.

This is called **associativity**, and again, it is a property of the real world. If we have several piles of stones to combine together, it does not matter whether we combine the first two piles and then add in the third, or combine the second and third piles and then add in the first.

But the table in Figure 3.6 does not work this way. Suppose we have A + B + C. If we add the A and B first, we get C. So we have C + C, or A as a final answer. But if we add the B and C first, we get A. That leaves A + A, or C for a final answer.

3.3 MORE PROPERTIES OF ADDITION

There are plenty of other problems with this last table. An obvious one is that none of the symbols works like a zero.

The zero symbol, if it exists, should be easy to recognize in any table. No matter what symbol zero is added to, the answer is that same symbol. In our original table, it is easy to see that the symbol @ acts like a zero: @ + # = #, @ + ! = !, and so on. But the table in Figure 3.6 has no such symbol. Again, this is enough to prove it is not an addition table.

A third problem is that the table sometimes gives us two answers to a question that should have only one. In grade school, we learn to answer questions like this:

$$4 + ? = 7$$

It is an important property of addition that there are never two answers to such a question. But what about this question:

$$A + ? = C$$

According to Figure 3.6, both A and B are correct answers. This, too, is enough to show that the table does not represent addition.

*   *   *   *   *

So far, we have found four properties that must hold in any addition table. Such a table must be commutative, it must be associative, it must have a zero, and it must give distinct answers to certain questions. This is not a complete list, however. That is, it is not enough to *define* what we mean by addition.

It appears that simple addition is not so simple after all.

In fact, we have a great deal more to say about it in this chapter. But it is time to leave behind the basic properties we have been discussing. Instead, let us simply assume the table of Figure 3.2 represents addition and turn back to the problem of decoding it.

3.4 DECODING THE TABLE

We have already seen that @ is the zero of this addition table. The key to all the other symbols is to figure out which represents the number one. If we add this symbol to itself, the answer will be the symbol for two. If we add one to this, we will get the symbol for three, and so on.

In fact, this special property of the symbol for one allows us to find it. Suppose we guess, for example, that # means one. Then # + # should be two, # + # + # should be three and so on. When we perform the additions, however, we get following:

$$
\begin{array}{ll}
\# & = \# \\
\# + \# & = \& \\
\# + \# + \# & = \text{!!} \\
\end{array}
$$
and so on

The problem here is that, if we continue, we will get only answers of two digits or longer. That means we will never get the symbol * by itself. Apparently, if # is the symbol for one, * is not the symbol for any number.

The upshot is that our guess that # is the symbol for one must be wrong. In fact, if we test all the symbols in this way, we will find that only the symbol ! works like a one. Hence it must mean one.

When we add ! to itself repeatedly, we get the following results:

$$
\begin{array}{ll}
! & = ! \\
! + ! & = \# \\
! + ! + ! & = * \\
! + ! + ! + ! & = \& \\
\end{array}
$$
and so on

Thus # must stand for two, * for three, and & for four. Now that we know what the symbols stand for, it will make the table easier to work with if we rewrite it using ordinary numerals.[1]

---

[1] A numeral is a symbol used to represent a number. It is not the number itself; just a mark on paper to make us think of it.

Figure 3.7 shows the rewritten table twice—once with numerals in place of the symbols we have been using, and then again with the rows and columns put into a more convenient order. The information in both tables is exactly the same. For example, in both of them 4 + 1 is 10.

+	1	2	0	4	3
1	2	3	1	10	4
2	3	4	2	11	10
0	1	2	0	4	3
4	10	11	4	13	12
3	4	10	3	12	11

+	0	1	2	3	4
0	0	1	2	3	4
1	1	2	3	4	10
2	2	3	4	10	11
3	3	4	10	11	12
4	4	10	11	12	13

Figure 3.7 The addition table with familiar symbols.

3.5 PLACE VALUES

The fact that 4 + 1 is 10 gives us something new to puzzle out. Why is this not enough to convince us that the table does not represent addition?

We know from experience that if a man has four of something and gets one more, he will have five in all. The table claims he will have 10. Is the table wrong?

The odd answer, on the contrary, is that 10 is five.

Here, finally, is a good example of why we need to look at arithmetic upside down to understand it. Most of us, when we glance at a 1 and 0 next to each other, recognize a ten without noticing the separate symbols.

But why do a 1 and 0, side by side, mean ten? Why should they not mean five?

In fact, of course, we can let symbols represent anything we like. The real question is why the system we use is a good one.

The answer, to begin with, is that any system of writing down numbers can use only a limited set of symbols. In the system in our illustration, we have the five numerals 0, 1, 2, 3, and 4. By themselves, these five symbols can represent only five numbers—zero, one, two, three, and four.

Suppose we use these symbols to count coins. Figure 3.8 shows how they match up with any number of coins from zero to four. When we add one more coin, we have five, a number without a symbol. Let us temporarily call this number of coins a "stack." With this word and our five symbols, we can represent many new numbers.

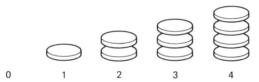

0   1   2   3   4   **Figure 3.8** The numbers zero to four.

As Figure 3.9 shows, five coins is 1 stack; seventeen coins is 3 stacks and 2; and twenty-four is 4 stacks and 4.

Figure 3.9 Five, seventeen and twenty-four.

When we add a coin to the twenty-four, however, we run into trouble again. This would be five stacks, but we have no symbol for the number five.

Or do we? If five coins is a stack, what would five stacks be? Why not a "stack-of-stacks," that is, five stacks of five coins?

With this idea, twenty-five coins is 1 stack-of-stacks; thirty-eight coins is 1 stack-of-stacks and 2 stacks and 3 (see Figure 3.10).

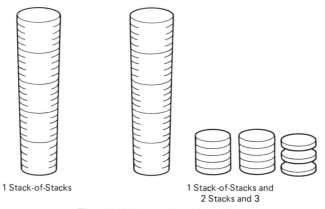

Figure 3.10 Twenty-five, thirty-eight.

Now how high can we go? The highest number we can represent is 4 stacks-of-stacks and 4 stacks and 4. Each stack-of-stacks is twenty-five coins, so that 4 stacks-of-stacks is a hundred coins. The 4 plain stacks each contain five coins, for a total of twenty; and there are 4 single coins. The grand total is one hundred twenty-four, as shown in Figure 3.11.

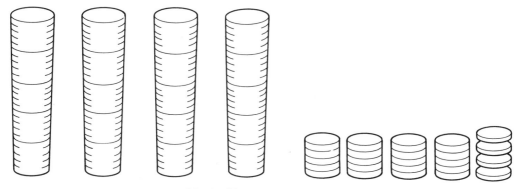

4 Stacks-of-Stacks and 4 Stacks and 4

Figure 3.11 One hundred twenty-four.

If we add one more coin, we get five stacks-of-stacks. Since we have no symbol for five, the best thing is to call this a stack-of-stacks-of-stacks.

By now it should be obvious that we can go on this way as long as we like. That is, we can represent numbers as large as we like using only the symbols 0, 1, 2, 3, and 4 and the word stack. The word stack is used as follows:

Stack	Five coins
Stack-of-stacks	Five stacks = twenty-five coins
Stack-of-stacks-of-stacks	Five stacks-of-stacks = one hundred twenty-five coins
Stack-of-stacks-of- stacks-of-stacks	Five stacks-of-stacks-of-stacks = six hundred twenty-five coins
(and so on)	

This system can be used to represent all numbers, but it is extremely awkward. We can improve it by agreeing on a convention. We will write the number of single coins at the right, the number of stacks just to the left, the number of stacks-of-stacks one position farther to the left, and so on.

This eliminates the need for the word stack. If we write 413, we mean 3 single coins, 1 stack of five coins, and 4 stacks-of-stacks, each containing twenty-five coins. Therefore 413 means one hundred eight.

This, finally, is how it is possible for 10 to mean five—the 1 means one stack of five coins. Notice that the 0 is an essential part of the written representation. It does not add any coins, but it puts the 1 in the proper position.

This idea of giving symbols different values that depend on where they are written and of using zeros to fill the empty positions is called the **place-value** system. It is one of the most important inventions of humankind, perhaps the single greatest step toward the technological brilliance of our modern world.

The importance of the place-value system is twofold.

First, it is compact. If two digits are written side by side, the one on the left counts whole stacks of what the one on the right counts individually. If a stack is five of something, then each step to the left, in effect, multiplies the amount counted by five.

A numeral in the tenth position from the right counts the number of stacks-of-stacks-of-stacks-of-stacks-of-stacks-of-stacks-of-stacks-of-stacks-of-stacks of coins, each of which contains five times five times five times five times five times five times five times five times five coins—just short of two million of them.

This means that with the numerals 0, 1, 2, 3, and 4 we can represent numbers up into the millions with a string of only ten symbols.

The compactness of the place-value system is something we tend to take for granted. But suppose an architect told you it takes five laborers to build a 3,000-square-foot building. How many do you guess it would take to build a 300,000-square-foot building? Fifty? Thirty?

Our place-value number system takes five digits to represent the number three thousand. But for three hundred thousand—a number a hundred times as big—it takes only three more, eight digits instead of fifty or even thirty.

3.6 WHY ADDITION WORKS

Even more important than compactness, though, is the power of the place-value system in calculation.

All through this chapter, we have added in the usual way—summing digits in columns according to an addition table and carrying extra digits to the next column. But this method depends on a system of place values.

In the Roman numeral system, which does not use place values, addition is much more complicated. Just try to apply the usual method to the following sum:

$$
\begin{array}{r}
X X X I V \\
+ \quad X V I \\
\hline
L
\end{array}
$$

If the usual method of addition using carrying and tables does not work for Roman numerals, why should it work at all? Here is another beauty of arithmetic that few people take time to appreciate.

Addition works, in part, because the addition table itself is correct, as far as it goes.

When the table shows that $3 + 4$ is 12, it is simply expressing something true about reality: four coins and three more make one stack of five and two left over.

This is the case with the other table entries as well. But even so, this only proves that our method of addition works when we add numbers smaller than five. Why should it work for larger numbers?

As it turns out, our method depends on the fact that the table is also correct for objects other than coins. Of course, it is no surprise that the table gives us the correct answer when we lump together four marbles and three more to get a "stack" of five marbles and two left over.

What matters is that the table still works even when the objects are *stacks*. If we lump together four stacks and three more, the table gives us the right answer—one stack-of-*stacks* and two (regular stacks) left over.

Likewise, the table will tell us correctly how to add four stacks-of-stacks and three more stacks-of-stacks or, in fact, four and three of any larger unit. To see the significance of all this for addition, consider the following problem, which has already been started.

$$
\begin{array}{r}
2\ 4\ 1 \\
3\ 3 \\
\hline
4
\end{array}
$$

When we add the second column, we are counting stacks. The addition table tells us that four of something plus three more makes one stack of those things and two left over. In this case, the things being added are stacks, so we have one stack-of-*stacks* and two *stacks* left over.

We put the two leftover stacks down as a 2 in the stacks position of the answer:

$$
\begin{array}{r}
2\ 4\ 1 \\
3\ 3 \\
\hline
2\ 4
\end{array}
$$

But we still have the stack-of-stacks to deal with. To represent this, we write a 1 in the stack-of-stacks column:

$$
\begin{array}{r}
1 \\
2\ 4\ 1 \\
3\ 3 \\
\hline
2\ 4
\end{array}
$$

Adding the 1 and 2 in this last column, we get a final answer of 324.

*   *   *   *   *

It turns out that the ordinary method of adding numbers, using an addition table and carrying, is just a systematic way to keep track of stacks, stacks-of-stacks, and larger units.

In a way, this number system is very much like our way of thinking about transistors, logic gates, and memory systems. A memory system contains many memory units, each of which contains many flip-flops, each of which contains many logic gates, and so on. Likewise, when we write 1000, the 1 stands for a stack of five 100s, each of which is a stack of five 10s, and so on.

We gain power when we talk and think about memory systems instead of about the millions of transistors inside. Using one simple concept to represent a complex system leaves room for other thoughts.

The place-value number system, too, is a way of chunking many small things into a manageable unit. It unclutters our minds.

3.7 STACK SIZE

The powerful, compact number system we have developed happens to use five symbols. It is no accident that our "stack" represents five units. Since the symbols start with zero, the number five is the first one for which there is no symbol. It is the first one we need two digits to represent.

The number system we learned in grade school works just the same way, except that it uses ten symbols: 0, 1, 2, 3, 4, 5, 6, 7, 8, and 9. The first number for which there is no symbol is ten. Therefore the stack size we normally use is ten.

If a stack is ten, then a stack-of-stacks is ten tens, or a hundred. When we write 537, we mean five stacks-of-stacks and three stacks and seven—that is, five hundreds and three tens and seven.

The stack size of a number system is called its **base**. The system we have developed in this chapter is called **base five**; the ordinary one is called **base ten**, or **decimal**.

The bigger the base, the more symbols the system uses and, thus, the more complex it gets. On the other hand, with a bigger base, numbers can be written more compactly. In base ten, the number six hundred twenty-five is written with three digits: 625. In base five it takes five: 10000.

If we made up a system with a thousand basic symbols, the symbols would stand for each of the numbers from zero to nine hundred ninety-nine. In this system, the number six hundred twenty-five would be written as a single symbol, say Λ. The number ΛΛ would be six hundred twenty-five stacks of a thousand and another six hundred twenty-five. That is, it would be the number we normally write much more clumsily as 625,625.

The more symbols we use, the less writing we need to do. But, as we said a moment ago, the more symbols, the more complex the system. For a system with a thousand symbols, the addition table would contain a thousand rows of a thousand entries each—a million entries in all.

To make the addition table as *simple* as possible, we can use just two symbols.[2] The table is shown in Figure 3.12.

+	F	T
F	F	T
T	T	TF

Figure 3.12 A base-two addition table.

We use T and F as symbols in this table for a reason that will soon be clear. Of course, any two symbols would work just as well.

From the table, it should be obvious that F acts as a zero. Since it is the only symbol left, T must be the one.

With only two symbols, it takes many digits to represent a large number. In base two, a stack is just two, the first number for which there is no symbol. A stack-of-stacks is two twos or four. A stack-of-stacks-of-stacks is two fours, still only eight.

---

[2] Base *one*, which uses just one symbol, is not really a place-value system. In this system, we write 111 for three, 1111111 for seven, and so on. Each 1 has the same value. Note also that the system gives us no way to represent zero.

The base-two number TTFT is one stack-of-stacks-of-stacks (eight) and one stack-of-stacks (four) and one. Therefore TTFT means thirteen. The number one thousand takes ten digits to represent—it is written as TTTTTFTFFF.

TTTTTFTFFF may seem like a long way to write one thousand, but base two is still quite a compact system for representing numbers. Although it takes ten digits to write one thousand, it does not take a hundred digits to write a number ten times as big. The number ten thousand is written in base two with 14 digits.

In fact, a number never takes more than $3\frac{1}{2}$ times as many digits to write in base two as it does in our usual decimal notation. The biggest number word we commonly use is "trillion," which takes 13 digits to write in base ten. Thus we can write most important numbers in base two in 50 digits or less.

Fifty digits strung together make a number that is hard to read, but the simplicity of the addition table is a real advantage, especially since we are hoping to turn the rules of arithmetic into logic circuits.

3.8 COUNTING IN BINARY

Usually we call the base-two number system **binary**. The prefix bi means two, just as it does in the word bicycle, a two-wheeled vehicle. For reference, here are the first six numbers in binary:

Zero	F
One	T
Two	T F
Three	T T
Four	T F F
Five	T F T

We can figure out these representations just by thinking of the place values. But, since adding is so simple in binary, it is even easier to "count" up to the next number by adding one.

For example, to figure out the representation for six, add one to five:

$$
\begin{array}{r}
\text{T F T} \\
+ \quad\ \ \text{T} \\
\hline
\end{array}
$$

According to the table, the two T's in the right-hand column sum to TF. Put down F and carry the T:

$$
\begin{array}{r}
\text{T} \\
\text{T F T} \\
+ \quad\ \ \text{T} \\
\hline
\text{F}
\end{array}
$$

In the second column, T and F sum to T. There is no carry, so in the leftmost column, we simply copy down the T. The final answer is TTF.

*   *   *   *   *

Actually, it is not necessary to use the addition table if we just want to add the number one. For example, suppose we want to add one to a very long number:

$$
\begin{array}{l}
\text{T T F T F F} \cdots \text{T T F T T T T T} \\
+ \underline{\hspace{7cm} \text{T}}
\end{array}
$$

The dots here stand for a long string of T's and F's.

As we carry out this addition, we will find a simple pattern. To start, we sum the two T's at the far right to get TF. We put down the F and carry T:

$$
\begin{array}{l}
\hspace{6.3cm} \text{T} \\
\text{T T F T F F} \cdots \text{T T F T T T T T} \\
+ \underline{\hspace{7cm} \text{T}} \\
\hspace{7cm} \text{F}
\end{array}
$$

Again we have to sum two T's, so we put down F and carry T:

$$
\begin{array}{l}
\hspace{6cm} \text{T T} \\
\text{T T F T F F} \cdots \text{T T F T T T T T} \\
+ \underline{\hspace{7cm} \text{T}} \\
\hspace{6.7cm} \text{F F}
\end{array}
$$

This continues as long as there are T's in the top row. After four more steps, we have:

$$
\begin{array}{l}
\hspace{5.3cm} \text{T T T T T} \\
\text{T T F T F F} \cdots \text{T T F T T T T T} \\
+ \underline{\hspace{7cm} \text{T}} \\
\hspace{5.7cm} \text{F F F F F}
\end{array}
$$

At the next step, however, we add a T and an F and get just a T. We put down the T, but there is nothing to carry. And since there is nothing left to add, we just copy down the rest of the long number. Our final answer looks like this:

```
        ┌─────────────────────────────────┐
        ↓ T T T T T                        The carries stop here, ┘
  T T F T F F · · · T T F T T T T T T      the first time we have an F
+                                   T      in the original number.
  ─────────────────────────────────────
  T T F T F F · · · T T T F F F F F F
```

To turn a binary number into the next higher number, then, it is only necessary to follow two rules:

1. Change all the T's at the right to F's.
2. Change the first F at the right to a T.

Notice that the rightmost digit changes in either case—if it is a T, it changes to F because of rule 1; if it is an F, it changes to T because of rule 2.

Also, if any digit changes from T to F, it must be one of the T's on the right affected by rule 1. If its neighbor on the left is a T, it too is one of the T's on the right and rule 1 says it must change. If its neighbor on the left is an F, it must be the *first* F on the right, so it changes because of rule 2. The upshot is this: If a digit changes from T to F, its left-hand neighbor also changes.

Having noticed these points, we can rewrite our rules in a different form. To add one to a number in binary:

A. Change the digit at the right.
B. If any digit changes from T to F, change its left-hand neighbor also.

3.9 A CONNECTION

To count, we add one; to add one, we follow rules A and B given at the end of Section 3.8. But these rules look oddly familiar. Compare them with the rules we gave in Chapter 2 for the ripple counter:

1. At every tick of the main clock, the leftmost flip-flop switches.
2. Whenever any flip-flop switches from **true** to **false**, the flip-flop to its right receives a tick and switches.

These rules use the word flip-flop instead of the word digit and they reverse the use of left and right, but otherwise they are much the same. It should not be surprising, then, that the patterns produced by the ripple counter are very much like the patterns we get by counting in binary. Here they are side by side:

false-false-false	F F F	Zero
true-false-false	F F T	One
false-true-false	F T F	Two
true-true-false	F T T	Three
false-false-true	T F F	Four
true-false-true	T F T	Five
false-true-true	T T F	Six
true-true-true	T T T	Seven

Notice that we have added F's at the left of any one- or two-digit binary numbers so that there are always the same number of digits as flip-flops. Adding an F to the left side of a binary number does not change its value, since F stands for zero. This is like writing 09 for nine in decimal.

With these zeros added on, the patterns are mirror images of each other. But remember that the ripple counter is a real, physical object made out of electronic parts. If we like, we can pick it up and turn it around. In this case, the patterns will be *exactly* the same.

It appears that the ripple counter lives up to its name—it counts in binary.

It also appears that we have answered the question posed at the end of Chapter 2. We have found a connection, between electronic circuits and the place-value number system, that gives us a powerful, compact way of representing information.

As we pointed out then, expression is a tool. The Roman numeral system is a poor tool, like a dull knife. By comparison, as we have already begun to see, the binary number system cuts through arithmetic like a laser.

3.10 TWO STATES FOR STORAGE

The number two is fundamental in representing information.

We can convey visual information with a black-and-white photograph, for example—a two-color picture. But a picture with one color would be the same as a blank page. It can tell us nothing.[3]

Likewise, as we pointed out in the first pages of this book, we can send messages using a wall of switches, each of which can be set in two positions—on or off. If the switches were stuck in just *one* position, they would be of no use in conveying information.

Flip-flops are ideal for storing information, because they have two states. Either they are on, putting out voltage, or they are off. We can call those states anything we like—on and off, true and false, T and F, or 1 and 0. The essential point is that there are two of them.

When we discussed switches, we said that the question of how to use them to store information is at the heart of computer science. This is the same as asking how to store information with flip-flops.

The answer to the question is simple. We use binary patterns to represent numbers and we use numbers to represent everything else.

For example, to store the number six in a computer, we find three flip-flops and set them to on, on, and off.

To store words, we turn the letters into numbers. One easy way is to let one stand for A, two for B, three for C and so on. If we want to represent the word CAB, we store the binary for three, followed by the binary for one, followed by the binary for two.

---

[3] Of course, we can use several *shades* of one color, or a single color on a white page, but in both cases we can see a picture only because there is a distinction, a difference between at least *two* elements.

If we want to store music, we break it up into fragments. Each fragment is the sound we hear in a very short interval of time, while the music is playing. The fragments are short enough that it takes, say, 20,000 of them to make up one second of music.

People can distinguish only a limited number of sounds. We assign each of these sounds a number. Then, to represent the music, we store the binary number for the sound in the first 20,000th of a second, then the binary number for the sound in the second 20,000th of a second, and so on.[4]

A similar method works if we want to store a color picture. We break the picture into squares so small that people cannot see where they begin and end. We assign a number to the color in each square, taking advantage of the fact that people can distinguish only a limited number of colors. Finally, we turn the numbers into binary and store them.

With enough two-state units—flip-flops, switches, even black-and-white dots in a photograph—we can store any information we like.

For now, however, we will restrict our attention to numbers and continue investigating binary arithmetic.

3.11 BINARY SUBTRACTION

We have been using the symbols T and F for binary digits to show the connection between arithmetic and logic. Now, since we will be concentrating on arithmetic, it will be easier to use the usual symbols 1 and 0 instead.

Figure 3.13 shows the binary addition table again, with these new symbols.

+	0	1
0	0	1
1	1	10

Figure 3.13 The binary addition table.

For reference, we will also give the place values of the first few positions in binary. The number 10010, written above these place values, represents the number eighteen, since it has a 1 in the sixteens place and a 1 in the twos place.

				1	0	0	1	0
256	128	64	32	16	8	4	2	1

We know how to represent numbers in binary and we know how to add them. What about subtracting?

One answer is that a subtraction problem can always be turned into an addition problem. The answer to 24 - 5, for example, is the number that can be added to 5 to make 24. That is,

---

[4] Farfetched as this may sound, it is the method actually used by the recording industry. It is called digital recording, since music is stored as digits.

```
    2 4    is the same        ? ?
  − 5      problem as      +   5
  ─────                    ─────
    ? ?                      2 4
```

This means that, if we are willing to work backwards, we can use an addition table for subtracting. Suppose we have the binary subtraction 10101 - 11. Converting this to an addition problem, we get

```
            ? ? ? ? ?
      +         1 1
         ─────────────
            1 0 1 0 1
```

Now, what could the rightmost question mark be? If it is a 1, the first column will have the sum 1 + 1. The addition table tells us this is 10, so we would put down a 0 and carry the 1. But we cannot put down a 0—the answer in the first column is a 1. Then the rightmost question mark must not be a 1. It must be a 0:

```
            ? ? ? ? 0
      +         1 1
         ─────────────
            1 0 1 0 1
```

Next we work on the second question mark. Could it also be a 0? If it were, the second column would sum to 1, but that does not match the given answer. Therefore this question mark must be a 1. Now, when we sum the second column, we get 10. We put down the 0 and carry the 1:

```
                1
            ? ? ? 1 0
      +         1 1
         ─────────────
            1 0 1 0 1
```

The next question mark must be a 0, so that the third column will sum to 1:

```
                1
            ? ? 0 1 0
      +         1 1
         ─────────────
            1 0 1 0 1
```

And now, there is nothing left to add. The two remaining question marks must be the same as the digits below them in the answer. Therefore the number we wanted is 10010.

We are saying $10101 - 11 = 10010$. Converting to decimal, as a check, we see that this means $21 - 3 = 18$.

*   *   *   *   *

This method of subtraction works, but it is not the only way. Another approach asks us to begin by memorizing four facts:

$$1 - 0 = 1 \qquad 1 - 1 = 0 \qquad 0 - 0 = 0 \qquad 10 - 1 = 1$$

Notice that, like the answers in the addition table, these are correct for any objects. For example, $10 - 1 = 1$ means that, if we have a stack of coins and take away one coin, we will have one left.[5] But this fact applies just as well to stacks as to coins. If we have a stack-of-*stacks* and take one *stack* away, we will have one *stack* left.

This means that the four basic subtraction facts apply in any column of a subtraction problem. Take the following problem as an example:

$$
\begin{array}{r}
1\ 0\ 0\ 1\ 0\ 1\ 1 \\
-\ \underline{\qquad\ \ 1\ 0\ 1} \\
\end{array}
$$

In the first two columns on the right, we can just use the answers we have memorized: $1 - 1 = 0$ and $1 - 0 = 1$:

$$
\begin{array}{r}
1\ 0\ 0\ 1\ 0\ 1\ 1 \\
-\ \underline{\qquad\ \ 1\ 0\ 1} \\
1\ 0
\end{array}
$$

In the third column, we want to subtract 1 from 0, but we have not memorized an answer for this. The third column counts stacks-of-stacks—we will call them SS's for short. The problem is that there are no SS's in the number 1001011.

However, in a sense, there *are* some SS's. The 1 in the fourth column means that there is a *stack* of SS's—two of them. That is,

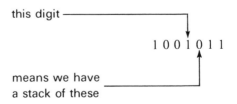

To show that we have a stack of SS's, we can rewrite the number this way:

$$
\begin{array}{r}
1\ 0\ 0\ 0\ 10\ 1\ 1 \\
-\ 1\ 0\ 1 \\
\hline
1\ 0
\end{array}
$$

Notice that we temporarily have two digits in a single column. Originally, we had 1 in the eights place. Now, we have 10, or two, in the fours place. Eight is the same as two fours, so the value of the number represented has not been changed.

This manipulation is what we learned in grade school as "borrowing." It is based on the fact that any digit counts whole stacks of what its neighbor on the right counts. The point of borrowing is that it allows us to use memorized subtraction rules. In our example, we can now apply the fact that $10 - 1 = 1$ to get

$$
\begin{array}{r}
1\ 0\ 0\ 0\ 10\ 1\ 1 \\
-\ 1\ 0\ 1 \\
\hline
1\ 1\ 0
\end{array}
$$

To finish the subtraction, we simply copy down the rest of the digits. The final answer is 1000110, or seventy. This is the correct answer when we subtract five from seventy-five.

3.12 A THIRD WAY TO SUBTRACT

We are about to show still another way to subtract binary numbers. It may seem strange, since we already have two methods, but we have good reasons.

This third method has some special advantages. For one, it is not just *based* on addition, like our first method; it *is* addition. We will show how to subtract by adding. Since we will soon build a logic circuit for addition, this means we will not need to design a separate circuit for subtraction.

Another advantage is that the method gives us a hint about extending our number system. If an item cost 20 dollars yesterday and costs 25 dollars today, the change in price is $25 - 20$, or 5 dollars. But what if it cost 25 dollars yesterday and 20 dollars today? What is the change in price?

The subtraction problem we are posing is $20 - 25$ and the usual way to write the answer is -5. We say the change is "negative" five dollars. But -5 uses a new symbol, the minus sign. As we will see in Chapter 4, the third method of subtraction suggests how to write negative numbers using just ordinary digits.

Finding systematic methods to solve problems is clearly at the heart of computer science. If we can give rules for how to solve a problem, we can build a circuit to get the answer automatically.

Finding a method that works is not enough, however. As a practical matter, we have only a limited number of parts to build circuits with and a limited amount of time before we need an answer. One of the great lessons of computer science is that it pays to look for alternative methods, and ways to compare them.

Here, a third method for subtraction saves us the trouble of designing a subtraction circuit. In Chapter 8, a similar comparison of methods will show us how to save years of working time on an extremely practical problem.

*   *   *   *   *

The third subtraction method is easiest to demonstrate on ordinary decimal numbers. Suppose, for example, that we have the subtraction problem 65 − 28. As a first step, we subtract 28 from *99* to get 71. Subtracting a number from 99 is always easy, because there is never any borrowing to do.

Next, we *add* 71 and the number we are subtracting from, 65. This gives 136. Finally, we cancel off the 1 at the left and add 1 to get 37. This is the correct answer: 65 − 28 = 37.

Here are the steps we used:

1. Subtract the second number from 9 · · · 9.

2. Add the answer to the first number.

3. Cancel the leftmost 1 and add 1.

Notice that, in step 1, we did not say how many 9s to string together. We should use as many as there are digits in the longer of the two numbers in the subtraction problem.

For example, to calculate 1,003 − 765, we first subtract 765 from 9,999 to get 9,234. Next, in step 2, we add 1,003 and 9,234 to get 10,237. If we cancel off the 1 at the left and add 1, we have 238: 1,003 − 765 = 238.

Why does this method work?

Look again at the last example. First we subtracted 765 from 9,999. So far we had

$$9,999 - 765$$

Then we added 1,003 to get

$$1,003 + 9,999 - 765$$

The next step was to cancel off the leftmost 1. In this case, that was the same as subtracting 10,000. So we had

$$1,003 + 9,999 - 765 - 10,000$$

Finally, we added 1 to get

$$1,003 + 9,999 - 765 - 10,000 + 1$$

If we rearrange this, everything becomes clear:

$$1,003 - 765 \quad + \quad 9,999 + 1 - 10,000$$

The subtraction we are really trying to carry out is on the left. At the right, we add in a total of 10,000 and subtract away the same amount. This has no effect on the answer.

*   *   *   *   *

A moment ago, we claimed that this new method would not use any subtraction. Apparently, however, we do need subtraction in step 1. The trick is that, in binary, we can use a simpler process.

For binary, step 1 reads

1. Subtract the second number from 1 · · · 1.

For example, if we want to calculate 10011 − 100, the first step is to subtract 100 from 11111. But look at this subtraction problem and its answer:

```
    1 1 1 1 1
 −  0 0 1 0 0   ◄──── Notice that we have added zeros at the left.
    ─────────
    1 1 0 1 1
```

To get the answer, we just switched all the digits in what we are subtracting—either from 1 to 0 or from 0 to 1. This is called **complementing** the digits. In fact, in binary we do *not* need to subtract. Instead we complement.

In the next chapter, we will show the details of how to do subtraction with circuits. But this part is obvious. To complement a digit, simply run it through a NOT gate.

To complete the problem we have started, we apply steps 2 and 3. We add 10011 and 11011:

```
    1     1 1
    1 1 0 1 1      In the second column we add 1 + 1 + 1.
 +    1 0 0 1 1    1 + 1 is 10. When we add 1 again, we get 11.
    ───────────    Therefore we put down 1 and carry 1.
  1 0 1 1 1 0
```

Then we cancel the leftmost 1—leaving 01110 or 1110—and add 1 to get the final answer, 1111. Our original problem, in decimal, was 19 − 4. The final answer is 15.

3.13 MULTIPLICATION

Multiplication is just repeated addition. When we say 23 times 415, we mean 415 added to itself 23 times.

We have already said that, if we build a circuit to do addition, it can be used for subtraction too. By using it over and over, the same circuit will do for multiplication as well. But adding a number to itself this way is a silly way to do multiplication. Instead, we can apply the efficient method we normally use in base ten.

We begin with a multiplication table like the one in Figure 3.14.

$$
\begin{array}{c|cc}
\times & 0 & 1 \\
\hline
0 & 0 & 0 \\
1 & 0 & 1
\end{array}
$$

Figure 3.14 A binary multiplication table.

Notice that, like the addition table, this one is correct as far as it goes. One times one is one and zero times anything is zero. We use the table just as we would use the ordinary one for base ten. Here is an example of a binary multiplication:

$$
\begin{array}{r}
1\,0\,0\,0\,0\,1 \\
\times \qquad 1\,0\,1 \\
\hline
1\,0\,0\,0\,0\,1 \\
0\,0\,0\,0\,0\,0 \\
+ \quad 1\,0\,0\,0\,0\,1 \\
\hline
1\,0\,1\,0\,0\,1\,0\,1
\end{array}
$$

If we check this in base ten, we see that we have multiplied 33 and 5 to get 165.

Why does the method work? A calculation in base ten provides the hint:

$$
\begin{array}{r}
2\,7\,4 \\
\times \quad 1\,1\,1 \\
\hline
2\,7\,4 \\
2\,7\,4 \\
+ \quad 2\,7\,4 \\
\hline
3\,0\,4\,1\,4
\end{array}
$$

We want to add up a hundred eleven 274s. But consider the meaning of 111 in base ten: the digits represent a hundred, a ten, and a unit. Thus we have one hundred 274s, ten 274s and a single 274—a stack-of-stacks of them, an ordinary stack, and one left over.

We have already seen how to make digits count stacks. Just shift them to the left. To count stacks-of-stacks, shift left twice.

Look again at the multiplication of 274 by 111. To show a stack-of-stacks of 274s, we shift the digits twice to the left. To show a plain stack, we shift left once. The one 274 left over is not shifted at all. We simply leave the digits in place.

The same logic applies to binary multiplication. We want to add up 101 —
five — 100001s. But the digits in 101 mean: one stack-of-stacks, zero stacks, and
one left over. This is how many 100001s we want.

To get a stack-of-stacks of 100001s, we shift those digits left twice. To get
the one left over, we leave the digits in place. As for the zero stacks, we do not
affect anything if we show them as a row of zeros. Here, again, is the result:

$$
\begin{array}{r}
1\,0\,0\,0\,0\,1 \\
\times \qquad 1\,0\,1 \\
\hline
1\,0\,0\,0\,0\,1 \\
0\,0\,0\,0\,0\,0 \\
+ \quad 1\,0\,0\,0\,0\,1 \\
\hline
1\,0\,1\,0\,0\,1\,0\,1
\end{array}
$$

⟵ one 100001 left over
⟵ zero stacks of 100001s
⟵ one stack-of-stacks of 100001s

*   *   *   *   *

Incidentally, all this explanation may disguise the real simplicity of binary
multiplication. To understand why it works may be difficult, but to do it is easy.

We multiply, as in base ten, by creating shifted rows to add up. We get each
row by multiplying the top number by a digit in the bottom one. In binary, if the
multiplying digit is 0, we write down a row of zeros. If the multiplying digit is 1,
we simply copy the number multiplied.

As we have already seen, the shifting part of multiplication is easy for logic
circuits. We can use a shift register.

3.14 A CONVERSION METHOD

Shifting a binary number left makes each digit count stacks of whatever it was
counting before. Since a stack in binary is two, the effect is to multiply the number
by two.

For example, seven is 111 in binary. Shifting left, we get 1110, which is
fourteen, two times seven.

Applying this backward, we can divide by two. Twenty-eight is 11100.
Shifting it right gives us 1110 or fourteen, which is twenty-eight divided by two.
Shifting right again gives 111, or seven — fourteen divided by two.

Notice that each time we shift right, we lose the rightmost digit. So far, this
lost digit has always been a zero, so we have not felt the effect. But what happens
if we shift 111 right?

When we divide seven by two, we get three with a remainder of one. That is,
if we want to divide seven things between two people, we can give three to each,
but we will have one remaining. Likewise, when we divide 111 by two by shifting
right, we get 11, or three. The lost 1 at the right is the remainder.

A moment ago, we divided 11100 by two to get 1110. In that case, the remainder was zero, since the rightmost digit was 0.

When we divide by two, then, the remainder is the rightmost digit. The upshot is that if we divide a number by two repeatedly, the remainders we get will be exactly the digits in the original number. For example,

1001101 divided by two is 100110 with a remainder of 1
100110 divided by two is 10011 with a remainder of 0
10011 divided by two is   1001 with a remainder of 1
1001 divided by two is   100 with a remainder of 1
100 divided by two is   10 with a remainder of 0
10 divided by two is   1 with a remainder of 0
1 divided by two is   0 with a remainder of 1

Reading the digits in the righthand column from bottom to top gives us 1001101, the number we started with.

Notice a key point: The remainders we get have nothing to do with what base we use for our number system. 1001101 is seventy-seven, and if we divide seventy-seven by two, we get two even parts of thirty-eight with one left over. We get this remainder of one whether we write seventy-seven as 77 or 1001101. It depends only on the fact that a group of seventy-seven things cannot be divided evenly into two parts.

Thus if we divide 77 by 2 repeatedly, using base ten notation, we will get the same string of remainders we got before. But these remainders are the digits of the numbers as represented in base two. It seems we have found an easy way to convert numbers from decimal to binary:

77 divided by two is 38 with a remainder of 1
38 divided by two is 19 with a remainder of 0
19 divided by two is 9 with a remainder of 1
9 divided by two is   4 with a remainder of 1
4 divided by two is   2 with a remainder of 0
2 divided by two is   1 with a remainder of 0
1 divided by two is   0 with a remainder of 1

Again, the righthand column, read bottom to top, gives us the binary for the number we started with, seventy-seven.

Incidentally, if we had divided by five, instead of two, the remainders would tell us how to write the number seventy-seven in base five.

3.15 TAKING STOCK

This chapter has been full of methods—systematic ways of solving problems. Here is a last example.

Our memory block in Chapter 2 used names made up of strings of ten logical values, **true** and **false**. One such name is

true-true-false-true-true-false-false-true-false-false.

In our circuit designs, we used the fact that there are exactly 1,024 different names that can be made with strings of **true**s and **false**s ten values long. But how did we know that there are 1,024 of them?

One way to get the answer—the mechanical, methodical way—is to list all the possibilities in some order and count them.

Every name must begin with either a **false** or a **true**. Therefore our list will contain two main parts, with headings as follows:

Names that begin with a **false**
> **false-false-false-false-false-false-false-false-false-false**
> **false-false-false-false-false-false-false-false-false-true**
> etc.

Names that begin with a **true**
> **true-true-true-true-true-true-true-true-true-true**
> **true-true-true-true-true-true-true-true-true-false**
> etc.

In each of these categories, some names will have **false** as the second value in the string and some will have **true** as the second value. We can add four subheadings, then, as follows:

Names that begin with a **false**

Names with second value **false**
> **false-false-false-false-false-false-false-false-false-false**
> etc.

Names with second value **true**
> **false-true-false-false-false-false-false-false-false-false**
> etc.

Names that begin with a **true**

Names with second value **false**
> **true-false-true-true-true-true-true-true-true-true**
> etc.

Names with second value **true**
> **true-true-true-true-true-true-true-true-true-true**
> etc.

Notice that every possible name must fall under one of the four subheadings.

If we continue this way, we will eventually have subheadings defining categories so specific that only one name fits the description. At this point, we can simply count up the number of categories and this will be the same as the number of possible names.

Obviously, though, there is a better way. Think again about how we formed the headings and subheadings. When we looked only at the first logical value, we had two categories. Looking at the second divides each of these categories into two parts, giving us four categories.

Each of these categories will be divided again into two parts when we consider the third logical value, since this can be either **true** or **false**. This gives us eight categories, and again, every name falls into exactly one category.

Each time we add a logical value, we have twice as many categories for the names. That means we can get the total number of names without counting. With one logical value, there are two possible categories. With names two values long there are twice as many, two times two, or four. With names three values long there are twice as many again, two times two times two, or eight.

With names ten values long, there are two times two times two times two times two times two times two times two times two times two, or 1,024.

Interestingly enough, someone familiar with binary numbers can get the answer without even counting categories. With ten binary digits, say, T and F, the highest number we can represent is TTTTTTTTTT, or 1,023 in base ten. Including zero, we can represent 1,024 numbers, which means there must be 1,024 possible patterns using ten T's and F's. The answer is obviously the same for patterns of **true**s and **false**s.

$$* \qquad * \qquad * \qquad * \qquad *$$

This example illustrates two points, an important one and a stupendously important one.

The important point has been made time and again through this chapter. It is possible to solve many problems with a step-by-step, methodical approach.

The importance of this fact is that purely methodical work can be carried out by machines. We can say this more strongly: If there are definite steps to take in solving a problem and definite rules for when to take each step, the problem can be solved by a machine.

Notice that this has nothing to do with arithmetic. If we could write down a step-by-step, sure-fire method for translating one language into another, a machine could do it. If we knew a completely systematic way to write good music, a machine could compose.

The question, then, is whether there are step-by-step methods for anything more interesting than arithmetic. This is the second point of our name-counting example.

Although it is possible to list out all possible names and count them, most people do not work that way. Many begin to make a list step by step and then, somehow, *leap* to the conclusion that there are twice as many names four values long as three values long, twice as many names five values long as four values long, and so on.

A few make an even longer leap to find the connection between the names and binary numbers.

This chapter is written for people, not machines. It is written to help them make unmethodical leaps of insight in dealing with numbers. For this reason, it concentrates on *why* arithmetic methods work.

People can make use of understanding.

The stupendously important question is this: Can we take the way people use insight and understanding and break it down into a step-by-step method? In essence, we want to know whether there is any difference between the kinds of thinking possible for people and machines.

The question takes part of its importance from the fact that many people believe the human body is a kind of machine. They would argue that people are made up of chemical and physical parts that follow definite rules like the parts of a mechanical or electronic machine.

If this is true, then machines can do anything people can do. Unfortunately, it also means people can do nothing more than machines.

Surprisingly, as we will see in Chapter 6, there are some simple things machines cannot do. If people are machines, then there are problems we cannot solve, cannot ever even hope to solve.

Of course, many people believe humans are not machines. For them the question is just as important. Where can we draw the line between things like arithmetic and poetry, things lifeless and things living?

In a nutshell, what exactly is human about humanity?

EXERCISES

3.1. Use the table in Figure 3.2 to add *!@ and !#&.

3.2. Use the table in Figure 3.2 to add &&& and ###.

3.3. Use the table in Figure 3.2 to add **&, #!&, and #&@.

3.4. Use the table in Figure 3.2 to subtract #!@ from *#&.

3.5. Use the table in Figure 3.2 to subtract ##& from &&#.

3.6. One reason the table in Figure 3.4 cannot represent addition is that it is not commutative. Give as many other reasons as you can.

3.7. Is the table in Figure 3.1 commutative? Is it associative?

3.8. In the number system discussed in Section 3.5, thirty-eight is 1 stack-of-stacks and 2 stacks and 3, or 123. How would the following be represented?
   (a) Thirty-seven
   (b) Thirty-nine
   (c) One hundred
   (d) One hundred ten
   (e) One hundred twenty-six
   (f) Two hundred
   (g) One thousand

3.9. In the number system discussed in Section 3.5, 123 represents the number thirty-eight. Write out in words what the following represent.

(a) 0

(b) 1

(c) 10

(d) 1000

(e) 33

(f) 132

(g) 243

(h) 4000

3.10. (a) For each of the numbers in Exercise 3.9, show how to represent a number five times as large.

(b) For each of the numbers in Exercise 3.9, show how to represent a number twenty-five times as large.

3.11. Give rules for adding any two numbers written in Roman numerals that use only the symbols I and V. The rules should enable someone who knows nothing about Roman numerals to add, say, VIII and IV. Try to make the rules as simple and compact as possible.

3.12. Use the table in Figure 3.12 to add TTFTT and TFTTT.

3.13. Add one to the following number: TFFTFFTTTTTTTTTTTTTTTTT.

3.14. Use T's and F's to write the numbers eight through thirty-five in binary.

3.15. Draw up an addition table for base three. Use the symbols 0, 1, and 2.

3.16. Add 212 and 220 in base three.

3.17. In Section 3.9 we pointed out that a turned-around ripple counter counts in binary. Assuming the ripple counter has three flip-flops, as in that section, what is the next number it will count to after seven?

3.18. Is there any kind of information that cannot be stored with two-state devices? Explain your answer.

3.19. Perform the following binary subtractions. Show your work and do *not* convert anything to base ten.

(a) $111 - 101$

(b) $10 - 1$

(c) $1000 - 11$

(d) $10110001 - 111$

3.20. Perform the following base-ten subtractions. Use the method of Section 3.12 and show your work.

(a) $23 - 7$

(b) $10,000 - 1$

(c) $2,130 - 862$

3.21. Multiply in binary:

(a) 1010×101

(b) 11011×1

(c) 110011×10000

3.22. Use the method of Section 3.14 to convert the following numbers to binary:
   (a)   1,024
   (b)   6,786
   (c)   1,000,000

3.23. Develop a method similar to the one described in Section 3.14 for converting base-ten numbers to base three. Explain your method and then demonstrate it by converting the base-ten number 9,362.

3.24. **(a)**   How many different names can be made by stringing together six logical values? **true-false-true-true-false-true** is one such name.
   (b)   How many names can be made by stringing together 11 logical values?
   (c)   How many names can be made by stringing together 15 logical values?

3.25. **(a)**   How many different two-letter "words" can be made by stringing together a combination of the letters A, B, and C? AA and CB are two examples of such "words."
   (b)   How many different three-letter words can be made with the same letters?
   (c)   How many different five-letter words can be made with the same letters?

4 An Arithmetic and Logic Unit

4.1 A CALCULATOR

We have compared the computer to the human body, since both are wonderfully complex structures built up from simpler parts. In some ways, though, building a computer from parts is less like surgery than it is like baking a cake.

All the time the cook is reading the recipe and shopping for ingredients and measuring them out, there is nothing to show—nothing to hint at the eventual product. Even when the batter is mixed, it is still more like a soup than a cake.

The icing, by contrast, has an air of reality to it. It looks and tastes practically the same in the bowl as it does on the cake. Also, it is the next-to-last step. When the batter is in the oven and the icing is mixed, we can just about taste fresh-baked cake.

In the beginning of this chapter, we still have some sifting and measuring to do. We have seen recipes for arithmetic, but we still need to cook up actual logic circuits for addition and subtraction.

By the end of the chapter, however, we will have combined together these new arithmetic circuits with the shifters and multiplexers of Chapter 2 to make something with an air of reality to it. This next-to-last step will bring success in building a computer just about close enough to taste.

The combined circuit is called an **arithmetic-logic unit**, because it can do both arithmetic and logic. But it is perfectly correct to think of it as a kind of calculator.

We have said that a computer is essentially a memory unit with feedback—a machine that changes information on the basis of information it already has. These *changes* will be simple matters of arithmetic or logic. We will want to take two numbers from the memory, add them, and then put back the answer, for example.

The calculator we will build in this chapter carries out these additions and other changes. Of course, a real calculator has buttons for a *person* to push. Ours will have control wires, since we eventually want the computer to push its own buttons.

4.2 A HALF-ADDER

The first step toward this calculator is a circuit for addition.

Circuits do not work with numbers, however. When we talk about the number 1101, we need to remember that it is stored in four flip-flops as TTFT, or **true-true-false-true**.

But even this is not quite the case. Circuits do not work with logical values either. In fact, the four flip-flops simply put out voltage or do not put out voltage.

The point, however, is that, while it is electricity and not logic that flows through the wires, we know that it makes sense to *interpret* conditions in wires as having meaning. In Chapters 1 and 2, we agreed to let voltage in a wire represent the logical value **true** and no voltage represent **false**.

In this chapter, it will make more sense to use a different interpretation. Since we will be dealing with numbers, we will let voltage represent the digit 1 and no voltage represent 0.

Figure 4.1, then, shows some familiar circuits working just as usual. The only difference is in our notation. The AND gate, for example, is putting out no voltage, because voltage has been supplied at only one input.

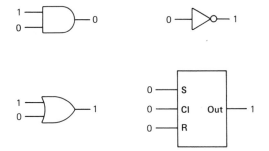

Figure 4.1 Voltages written as digits.

With this new notation, we are ready to design a circuit for addition. We would like to be able to add relatively long numbers: 10001011 and 1011010, for example. But, as we have seen, this can be accomplished by lining the numbers up into columns and then adding the digits in each column separately. In our example, we have

$$\begin{array}{r} 1\ 0\ 0\ 0\ 1\ 0\ 1\ 1 \\ +\quad\ \ 1\ 0\ 1\ 1\ 0\ 1\ 0 \\ \hline \end{array}$$

To begin, we first add the digits in the rightmost column, 1 and 0. Then, we add the pair in the second column, 1 and 1, and so on.

Notice that when we add a pair of digits, we want two pieces of information as the answer. One is the digit we should put down as part of the final sum. The other is whether or not there is a carry. We will design circuits for these two results separately.

The carry part is easy. The only way to get a carry is if both digits are 1 — that is, if the digit from the number on top is 1 *and* the digit from the number on the bottom is 1. Naturally, then, we can use an AND gate, as shown in Figure 4.2.

Figure 4.2 Generating a carry digit.

For the other part, Figure 4.3 gives a list of the results we want.

Top Digit	Bottom Digit	Sum Digit
0	0	0
0	1	1
1	0	1
1	1	0

Figure 4.3 Generating a digit in the sum.

Notice that the table tells us we get 0 in the sum if we add two 1s. This is correct. If we add two 1s in some column, we get 10. We put down a 0 and carry a 1.

According to the table, a circuit for the sum digit should put out a 1 in exactly two cases — if the top digit is 0 and the bottom is 1 *or* if the top digit is 1 and the bottom digit is 0. This means we can design the circuit as follows:

1. Use two subcircuits, each of which puts out a 1 in just one of these situations, and then
2. Connect them with an OR gate.

The first subcircuit should put out a 1 when the top digit is 0 *and* the bottom digit is 1. We build it with a NOT gate and an AND gate, as shown in Figure 4.4. The second subcircuit is nearly the same, but with the NOT gate applied to the bottom digit. If we run the output of both subcircuits through an OR gate, according to part 2 of our plan, we get the circuit shown in Figure 4.5.

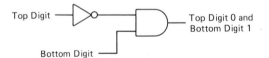

Figure 4.4 First step toward a sum-digit circuit.

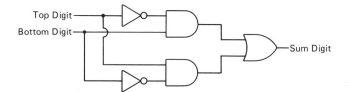

Figure 4.5 A circuit for the sum digit.

Together with the AND gate that tells whether there is a carry, this circuit tells us what we need to know in adding two binary digits. The combined circuit, shown in Figure 4.6, is called a **half-adder**. The figure also shows the simplified picture we will use to represent the circuit.

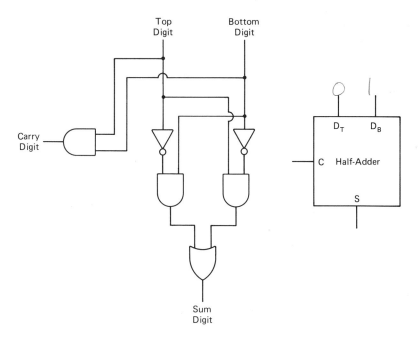

Figure 4.6 A half-adder.

4.3 A FULL ADDER

Using a half-adder, we can begin to carry out the problem we proposed earlier:

$$
\begin{array}{r}
1\,0\,0\,0\,1\,0\,1\,1 \\
+\quad 1\,0\,1\,1\,0\,1\,0 \\
\hline
0\,1
\end{array}
$$

In the first two columns, we let the circuit add the top and bottom digits and then write down the resulting sum digit it computes.

We run into trouble in the third column. Here, a half-adder would tell us correctly that 0 plus 0 is 0 with no carry, but we would be wrong to put down 0 in the answer. We need to account for the carry generated by the sum in the second column.

A half-adder adds two digits. Apparently, though, even if we are adding only two numbers, we will need to add three digits at a time: two from the numbers and a third carried over from the previous column.

A circuit designed to add three digits is called a **full adder**; it is shown, as we will draw it, in Figure 4.7. The circuit takes three digits as input: D_T and D_B, digits of the top and bottom numbers, and **Carry-In**, the digit carried over from the previous column. Of course, if there is no carry, the voltage on **Carry-In** is 0.

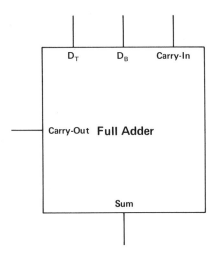

Figure 4.7 A full adder.

The circuit adds these three digits and puts out two answers: **Sum**, the digit to be written down as part of the final sum, and **Carry-Out**, the digit to be carried to the next column.

Figure 4.8 shows how the full adder may be built from two half-adders and an OR gate. The idea behind this circuit is simply that, if we want to add three digits, we can add two of them and then add the third to the result. The half-adder on top adds the two digits other than the carry.

The second half-adder takes the result of this addition and the carry digit and adds them. Its output, which is the full-adder's **Sum** wire, is the result of adding the three digits, so it is a digit of the final answer.

Of course, this does not show that our full-adder circuit produces the correct voltage on **Carry-Out**.

Here is the reasoning to show that **Carry-Out** is figured correctly. The full adder should produce a carry if the total sum of its three input digits is more than 1. We have already seen that the three digits are added in two stages. Therefore, if the total sum is more than one, either

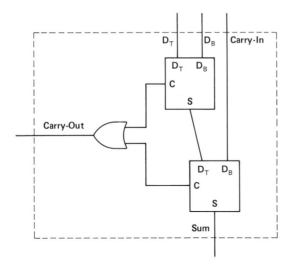

Figure 4.8 Circuit for a full adder.

1. The sum was more than one in the first stage, when the top and bottom digits were added, or
2. The sum got to be more than one in the second stage, when the carry digit was added in.

In the first case, the top half-adder will show a carry. In the second, the bottom half-adder will show a carry. The upshot is that we want to get a carry from the full adder if either the top *or* the bottom half-adder shows a carry. This is the function of the OR gate in Figure 4.8.

Of course, these arguments are meant to *explain* why the circuit works. If we want to *prove* that it works, we can just check that it does what we want for every possible combination of inputs.

In this case there are exactly eight possible input combinations, listed with the correct outputs in Figure 4.9. Figure 4.10 checks that our full-adder circuit works correctly in the fourth of these eight cases. A complete proof would check the other seven cases as well.

Top Digit	Bottom Digit	Carry In	Sum	Carry Out
0	0	0	0	0
0	0	1	1	0
0	1	0	1	0
0	1	1	0	1
1	0	0	1	0
1	0	1	0	1
1	1	0	0	1
1	1	1	1	1

Figure 4.9. Generating a digit of the sum.

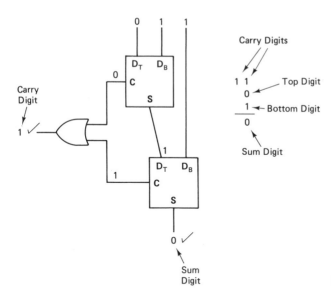

Figure 4.10 Checking the full-adder circuit.

Notice that we could design a full adder from scratch using the table in Figure 4.9, just as we did with the half-adder. In this case, we would not need to design a circuit for the carry output. Voltage is put out over **Carry-Out** if at least two of the three input digits are 1. Therefore, as we pointed out in Chapter 1, a voting circuit does just what we want. In fact, our full adder does the work of a voting circuit, along with addition.

4.4 USING THE FULL ADDER

We designed the full adder to sum up the digits in one column of an addition problem. But, from our study of arithmetic, we know that the rules for addition are the same in every column. This means we can use the same circuit for every column of the sum.

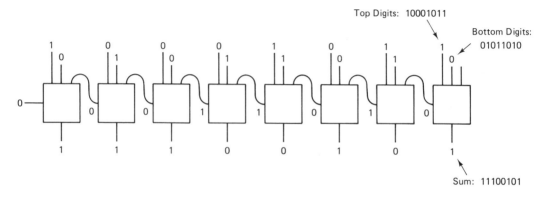

Figure 4.11 Circuit for adding 8-digit numbers.

If we want to add numbers of eight digits, we simply hook up a chain of eight full adders. Figure 4.11 shows how the combined circuit would work for the sample addition of Section 4.2. Notice that each full adder passes its carry digit to the **Carry-In** wire of the adder on its left.

Taken together, eight full adders form a circuit which takes in two numbers of eight binary digits each. The circuit puts out an answer, also eight binary digits long, and a leftmost carry, which acts like a ninth digit. Since **bit** is a common abbreviation for *binary digit*, the circuit is normally called an **8-bit adder**.

Just as full adders may be linked to make an 8-bit adder, two 8-bit adders may be linked to make a 16-bit adder. Figure 4.12 shows that we just need to use the ninth bit as a carry to the second adder. In fact, since each box contains a chain of eight full adders, the two together form a chain of 16 full adders.

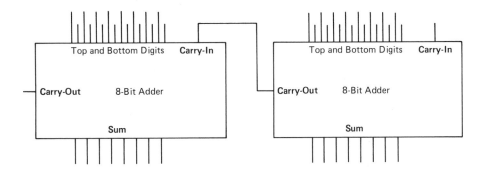

Figure 4.12 Circuit for adding 16-digit numbers.

The point is, once we know how to add two digits, we can add numbers as large as we like. The same addition table gives us correct answers for binary digits in any column, that is, whether we are adding coins or stacks of coins or stacks-of-stacks or larger units. Likewise, the same circuit works in any column. This again is the power of the place-value system.

*   *   *   *   *

The full adder has a hidden feature, however, that gives it even an extra bit of power. In fact, an extra bit is precisely the feature it has.

Take the 8-bit adder as an example. Figure 4.11 shows that the carry-in bit on the rightmost full adder is not used. There can never be a carry coming from the next column to the right because there is no such column.

Normally, this wire would not be connected, so that no voltage could ever be supplied to it. But what would happen if we *did* supply voltage to the wire?

In effect, we would be putting a 1 in the carry position of the first column. That is, we would be adding 1 to the final answer. Here is an example:

	normal addition		with an extra carry
			1

+	1 1 0 0 0 0 0 0
	    1 1 1 0 0 0
		+	1 1 0 0 0 0 0 0
			    1 1 1 0 0 0

	1 1 0 1 1 1 0 0 0		1 1 0 1 1 1 0 0 1
	correct answer		correct answer plus one

Putting voltage on the extra carry wire adds 1 to the final answer. This feature comes in handy when we want to subtract numbers, using the addition method of Chapter 3.

With this method, we subtract in three steps. If we are subtracting A from B, we first complement A. This gives the same answer as subtracting it from a long string of 1s. Next, we add the result to B. Finally, we *add an extra 1* to this complement and cancel the leftmost 1.

The first step is only a matter of passing each digit through a NOT gate. Figure 4.13 shows this step for the subtraction 111000 − 10110. Notice that we have added zeros on the left of 10110 to make the number of digits correct for an 8-bit adder.

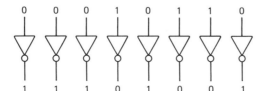

Figure 4.13 Complementing with NOT gates.

In the second step, we add this to 111000 using an 8-bit adder. At the same time, however, we put voltage in the extra carry wire to add in an additional 1, as shown in Figure 4.14. This takes care of part of the last step.

The last part of the third step is to cancel the leftmost 1. But this digit will always be on the adder's **Carry-Out** wire, the one on the far left. Therefore, we simply ignore this wire when we are subtracting.

The answer we want, then, is on the eight **Sum** wires. In this case it is 100010, or 34. This is correct for 111000 − 10110, or 56 − 22 in base ten.

At this point, it would be easy to show the circuit for a subtraction circuit. It would just be an 8-bit adder with NOT gates attached to the inputs for the bottom number, voltage supplied at the first carry-in, and the **Carry-Out** wire disconnected.

But we will do better than this before very long.

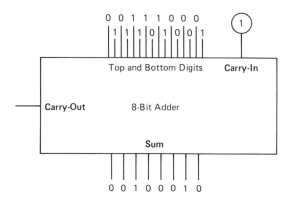

0 0 1 1 1 0 0 0

1 1 1 0 1 0 0 1   (1)

Top and Bottom Digits   Carry-In

Carry-Out   8-Bit Adder

Sum

0 0 1 0 0 0 1 0

Figure 4.14 Adding the complement and an extra 1.

Instead of designing a separate subtraction circuit, we will make one general-purpose circuit. It will add *or* subtract, depending on the voltage in a control wire. This will be a long step toward building a truly general-purpose circuit—the computer itself.

4.5 NEGATIVE NUMBERS

Before we continue designing circuits, we need to look a little more deeply into the numbers they will manipulate. The reason is that these numbers themselves appear to be severely limited.

With 8 bits, we can represent the decimal number 37 as 00100101 or the decimal number 98 as 01100010. But what about these numbers: -5, 638, 0.7? None of them can be represented in just 8 bits of the binary notation we have been using. The first and last cannot be represented at all, even with more bits.

The point, of course, is that it is no use designing a calculator that works on only a few numbers. Somehow we need to improve either the calculator or the number representations it works on.

*   *   *   *   *

In fact, the number system is by far the easier of the two to extend. As we are about to see, 8-bit binary numbers are quite enough for many practical purposes. The trick is to work out more sophisticated ways of interpreting them.

With these new interpretations, we can use an ordinary 8-bit adder and other simple arithmetic circuits in quite complex calculations.

The best place to start is with the hint we gave in Chapter 3. We said there that our peculiar third method of subtraction provides a clue about how to represent negative numbers.

These arise, of course, when we try to subtract larger numbers from smaller ones. As we pointed out in Chapter 3, if the price of an item goes up from 20 to 25 dollars, we say the change is $25 - 20$, or 5 dollars. If the price goes down from 25 to 20 dollars, we would like to say the change is $20 - 25$ dollars. This too is a change of 5 dollars, but in the opposite direction. To make the distinction clear, we call this a change of *negative* five dollars and write it as − 5.

We have already said that using a minus sign to indicate negative numbers causes problems for our adder. It also forces us to invent extra rules for addition and subtraction.

For example, if the price of an item goes from 15 to 19 dollars one day and from 19 to 22 dollars the next day, the two price changes are 4 dollars and 3 dollars. We can add them to get 7 dollars, the total change from 15 to 22 dollars.

But suppose the price goes from 15 to 13 dollars and then from 13 to 22 dollars. The changes are − 2 dollars and 9 dollars. The total change in price is just the same as before: 7 dollars, since the price has changed from 15 to 22 dollars. Therefore it must be that − 2 + 9 is 7.

In this case, the minus sign in − 2 seems to tell us to *subtract*. The answer to the problem − 2 + 9 is the same as the answer to the problem 9 − 2. But things do not always work this way.

Suppose the price falls by 2 dollars one day and 3 dollars the next. The changes are − 2 and − 3. The total change is a fall of five dollars, so it must be that − 2 + − 3 is − 5. In this case we seem to *add*.

Here is one last example.

If the price of an item is 30 dollars today and the change since yesterday is 5 dollars, it must have cost 30 − 5, or 25 dollars, yesterday. We subtract to get the answer.

But suppose the price is 30 dollars today and the change since yesterday is − 5 dollars. If the price fell five dollars and reached 30 dollars, it must have started at 35 dollars. So we see that 30 − − 5 is 35. Subtracting a negative number appears to be the same as adding a positive one.

All these extra rules are not particularly hard. But they spoil the simplicity of our binary system. If we stick with our usual way of representing numbers, our addition and subtraction circuits will have to be much more complicated.

*   *   *   *   *

The solution, as we have said, is to use the circuits as they stand and see what the consequences will be for our representation system.

As an example, suppose we use our circuits to subtract three from zero. The answer ought to be negative three. Thus, no matter what answer the circuit gives us, we will let that answer be the representation for negative three.

Applying our third subtraction method, the circuit will take three, written as 00000011, and complement it to get 11111100. Then it will add this, and an extra 1, to 00000000. Ignoring the carry digit, which in any case is 0, the final answer will be 11111101.

According to our usual way of understanding binary numbers, 11111101 means two hundred fifty-three. But we are *changing our interpretation*, as we are always free to do. From now on, 11111101 means negative three.

To see that this makes at least some degree of sense, consider *using* the new representation we have invented. For example, suppose we want to add negative three and seven. If we use our 8-bit adder, it will add 11111101 and 00000111 to get 100000100. Ignoring the ninth digit, the one on the **Carry-Out** wire, the answer is 100, or 4 in base ten. That is, $7 + -3$ is 4.

As a second example, if we add negative three to two, we should get negative one as an answer. If we use the adder circuit, it will put out 11111111. Is this negative one?

One way to check is to subtract 11111111 from zero. If it does represent negative one, then we are calculating $0 - -1$. The answer ought to be 1.

To subtract, with our 8-bit adder, we first pass each digit of the subtracted number through a NOT gate to get the complement. In this case, 11111111 complemented is 00000000, just zero. Next, we add this to the number we are subtracting from, 0, turning on the first carry-in wire to get an extra 1. The answer is $0 + 0 + 1$, or 1, exactly as we hoped.[1]

*   *   *   *   *

Apparently, odd as it may seem at first, using 11111101 to represent negative three is a good idea. The adder calculates correctly with that representation without any additional rules.

To find out how to represent other negative numbers, we can use the same approach: Subtract a positive number away from zero, using the 8-bit adder. Whatever the circuit gives as an answer must be the negative of that number.

4.6 THE LIMITS OF REPRESENTATION

This system works for a very good reason. In place of negative numbers, we are actually using positive numbers that are larger by two hundred fifty-six. For example, instead of the number negative three, we use 11111101—two hundred fifty-three—since $-3 + 256$ is 253.

The result is that when we add a negative number, we get an answer two hundred fifty-six bigger than it should be. But two hundred fifty-six, in binary, is 100000000, a nine-digit number. Since we ignore the ninth wire of the adder's output, this extra amount does not affect the answer.

When we subtract a negative number, we are subtracting an extra two hundred fifty-six. But, again, this affects only digits beyond the eight in our answer.

The system works, then, for every case. But it would seem to create even a bigger problem than the one it solves. If we see the number 11111101, for example, how can we tell if this means negative three or positive two hundred fifty-three?

---

[1] Remember that we do not have to cancel the leftmost 1. We simply ignore the ninth wire of the output.

To see how we *can* tell, look at following list of representations for the first few positive and negative numbers:

one	00000001	negative one	11111111
two	00000010	negative two	11111110
three	00000011	negative three	11111101
four	00000100	negative four	11111100

In the left-hand column, we are counting up in binary, beginning with one. In the right-hand column, we are counting down beginning with negative one. So far, no pattern of digits appears in both columns, so there is no problem telling positive numbers apart from negative ones. The question is, How far can we go?

To see the answer, recall our *old* interpretation of the binary patterns in the right-hand column. According to that interpretation, these numbers, in decimal, are 255, 254, 253, and 252. This is only natural, since these are the numbers two hundred fifty-six larger than the negative numbers they represent.

Apparently, the left-hand column counts up from one and the right-hand column counts down from two hundred fifty-five. The first number that would appear in both columns, then, is one hundred twenty-eight. The first hundred twenty-seven rows contain no duplicates.

The solution to our problem of distinguishing positive and negative numbers is simple, then. We will use only numbers in the first hundred twenty-seven rows of our list. In this case, every 8-bit binary pattern appears in the list exactly once.

Patterns in the right-hand column all begin with a 1 and patterns in the left-hand column with a 0. This digit tells us if a given pattern is negative or positive.

$$*\qquad*\qquad*\qquad*\qquad*$$

Of course, this plan has an obvious shortcoming. It allows us to represent only positive numbers up to one hundred twenty-seven and negative numbers down to negative one hundred twenty-eight.

The idea of only using numbers up to a certain limit is not as bad as it sounds, however. If we must use larger numbers, we can devise a similar system based on a 16-bit adder. This would allow us to represent numbers up to roughly positive and negative sixty-five thousand.

If this is still not enough, we can use an even larger adder. The point is, we very rarely use really huge numbers. Most of the time there is a workable limit.

Moreover, although we do not usually consider the fact, our number representation systems are *always* limited.

If a computer has three flip-flops in it, there are only eight possible on-off patterns using those flip-flops. No matter how we interpret the patterns, they cannot represent more than eight different numbers.

If the computer has a million flip-flops, there are still only a certain number of possible on-off patterns—a gigantic number, of course, but still limited. If each pattern represents a different number, then only a limited number of numbers may be represented.

Likewise, given a sheet of paper, there is a limit to the size of the number that can be written on it. Even if the written digits are so small that it takes a microscope to read them, after a certain point, no more will fit on the page.

In fact, we can go further. Even if all the resources of the world were turned into writing materials and digits were written as small as molecules, there would still be a limit to the number of digits that could be written. Still, only a limited number of numbers could be represented.

The fact is, although we understand perfectly how to write numbers, there are numbers too large to represent. We can discuss them—in fact, we have been doing just that—but we cannot write them down.

4.7 SCIENTIFIC NOTATION

No matter what representation system we use, then, we will be able to write only a limited number of numbers. Still, if the highest number we can write is one hundred twenty-seven, our system will not be of much practical use.

We have said we could increase the limit by using more bits, but we have also explained why we prefer to stay with just eight. Fortunately, there is a way out.

The trick is to represent each number by a pair of numbers. Each half of the pair uses 8 bits and is interpreted as a positive or negative number just as we explained in the previous section. Here is an example:

$$00000011 \quad 00000100$$

Taken separately, the numbers in this pair are three and four. In this representation, however, the second number is used to tell how many times to *double* the first. Since the second number is four, in this case, we double the first number in the pair four times. Doubling three four times, we get six, twelve, twenty-four and, finally, forty-eight.

Together, then, the pair of numbers represents forty-eight.

Incidentally, doubling a number is the same as multiplying it by two, and in binary, this is the same as shifting it to the left, adding a zero at the right. Doubling 11 four times yields 110000—11 with four extra zeros.

We can also think of the second number in the pair as specifying a multiplier for the first number. When the second number is 00000100, or four, the first number will be multiplied by two four times. In all, it will be multiplied by two times two times two times two, or sixteen. Thus 00000100 specifies the multiplier sixteen.

*   *   *   *   *

One advantage of the pair system is that it allows us to represent some very large numbers. The pair

00000001   01111111

stands for 1 shifted one hundred twenty-seven times to the left. This is the binary number

1000000000000000000000000000000000000000000000000000000000000000
0000000000000000000000000000000000000000000000000000000000000000

In base ten, this number is bigger than 100,000,000,000,000,000,000,000, 000,000,000,000,000 — a hundred trillion trillion trillion. Thus, with two 8-bit numbers, it seems we can represent numbers as large as we are ever likely to use.

This way of writing numbers in pairs is usually called **scientific notation**. Scientists use it because it is convenient for dealing with very large numbers.

4.8 SIGNIFICANT DIGITS

The fact that we can represent numbers as high as one hundred trillion trillion trillion with just 16 bits ought to seem somewhat strange. In fact, it amounts to a kind of paradox.

With 16 binary digits, we can make only a limited number of patterns. As we saw at the end of Chapter 3, we can make four patterns with two digits (00, 01, 10, and 11), twice as many with three digits (000, 001, 010, 011, 100, 101, 110, 111), twice as many again with four digits, and so on.

With 16 digits, there are

$$2 \times 2 \times 2 \times 2 \times 2 \times 2 \times 2 \times 2 \times 2 \times 2 \times 2 \times 2 \times 2 \times 2 \times 2 \times 2$$

possible patterns. To be precise, if each pattern represents a number, exactly 65,536 numbers can be represented.

We have invented a system that represents numbers up into the trillions of trillions of trillions with just 16 binary digits. But each of the possible patterns we can make with these digits stands for exactly one number, and there are only 65,536 possible patterns. The fact that we break the 16 digits into two groups of eight does not give us any extra patterns. Therefore our system must represent exactly 65,536 numbers.

Apparently, we must be leaving some numbers out.

Actually, the truth is much graver. We are leaving *practically all* the numbers out. We are representing only a few more than sixty-five thousand out of trillions and trillions.

Our system is a little like the following one for representing numbers up to one hundred with a single decimal digit:

0	means	one		5	means	ten
1	means	two		6	means	twenty
2	means	four		7	means	forty
3	means	six		8	means	sixty
4	means	eight		9	means	a hundred

The advantage of this system is that we can write large numbers like sixty with just one digit. The disadvantage is that we are leaving out ninety-one of the numbers between zero and a hundred. It is impossible, for example, to write the number three.

The system seems silly. Why would anyone want to use it?

One answer is that, in some cases, exact numbers are not important. For someone taking reservations at a restaurant, the ten numbers that *can* be represented might well be enough. If a reservation is made for a party of three, the maitre d' may as well set aside a table for four. And if the restaurant seats only a hundred people, it may as well close to the public if it is booked by a wedding party of anywhere from seventy to a hundred.

For practical purposes, three is the same as four and eighty-seven is the same as one hundred. It is not necessary to represent the numbers the system leaves out.

In fact, rough numbers are almost always good enough, so long as they are not *too* rough.

If we want to know the population of a large city, in most cases an approximate answer like seven million satisfies us. If we need a more exact number, we may get an answer like 7,543,000. This is still approximate, but it is probably good enough.

We can say more. For a city this large, a round answer like 7,543,000 is likely to be the most accurate one possible. If an official tells us that there are exactly 7,543,129 people living in a city, the answer is almost surely wrong. Does the official know about the baby just born ten minutes ago? Or about the lazy census taker who did not bother to knock on certain doors?

In this case, the digits 129 do not tell us anything, because we have no way of knowing if they are even close to correct. The other digits, 7543, do tell us something about the actual population. We say that we are willing to accept an answer correct to four **significant digits** and we write our answer as 7,543,000.

Since only four digits are meaningful, the best idea is to leave the others out. We can write 7,543,000, or, even better,

$$7{,}543 \ 3$$

where the 3 means to shift left three times, adding zeros.

This is the beauty of scientific notation. It reports only the digits that really have meaning, along with a number to show how many times the digits should be shifted.

Returning to binary, suppose someone tells us that 11010110101 people are expected to attend a dance party. We can break the number into two pieces:

	11010000000	(1,664 in base ten)
+	110101	(53 in base ten)

Then we can make the same kind of argument. Common sense tells us that no one knows exactly how many people will attend. A relatively small number like 110101 of them may change their minds at the last minute. These digits tell us nothing.

Although we have been told that 11010110101 people will come, it seems we are certain only that attendance will be roughly 11010000000. That is, only the first five digits of the original number are significant, and we might as well represent it as

$$00011010 \quad 00000110$$

which means 11010, the five meaningful digits, followed by 110, or six, zeros.

The original number, 11010110101, is one of the ones our system leaves out. When we write a number as a pair, the first number in the pair gives the significant digits. If we are writing a positive number, the first digit will be a 0. Only seven digits are left.

Thus the only numbers we can represent are those with up to seven digits followed by a number of zeros. 11010110101 is not this kind of number.

The point is, however, that we can represent a number *close* to this one — close enough to keep all of the important meaning of the number, in the case of the dance.

4.9 FRACTIONS

Scientific notation, it turns out, is only a matter of using round numbers. We get most numbers by measuring or guessing something and we are almost always at least a little bit wrong. This means it is not necessary to report the exact measurement or guess. Rounding it off to a simpler number gives just as much information.

This is one reason scientific notation is commonly used in computers. We can represent a huge range of numbers with only a few digits. Most numbers will be rounded off, but not changed significantly.

An equally good reason for using scientific notation is that it gives us a way to represent some new numbers. So far, in all our examples of scientific notation, the second number in the pair has been positive. What happens if it is negative?

Consider the following examples:

$$
\begin{array}{ll}
00000001 & 00000011 \\
00000001 & 00000010 \\
00000001 & 00000001 \\
00000001 & 00000000 \\
00000001 & 11111111
\end{array}
$$

The first number in each pair is just one. The second numbers are three, two, one, zero, and negative one.

The first few pairs, then, represent "one doubled three times," "one doubled two times," and "one doubled once" — eight, four, and two. In the fourth pair, we are supposed to double one zero times, that is, not at all. Therefore the represented number is just one.

But what about the fifth pair? 11111111 represents negative one. How can we double something negative one time? Figure 4.15 helps with the answer.

Second Number in the Pair	Double This Many Times	Or Multiply by
00000011	Three	Eight
00000010	Two	Four
00000001	One	Two
00000000	Zero	One
11111111	Negative One	???

Figure 4.15 Effect of the second number in binary scientific notation.

As the figure shows, doubling something three times is the same as multiplying by eight. Doubling two times is the same as multiplying by four.

The pattern in the table is simple. Each time we count down by one in the first and second columns, we halve the number to multiply by shown in the third column. The last number in the third column, then, ought to be one-half.

If we continue to count down, we will get multipliers of one-quarter and one-eighth when the second number in the pair is negative two and negative three. We can go on this way, as long as we like, to figure the multiplier corresponding to any negative number.

When we apply these multipliers, we get fractions, new numbers that we had no way to represent without scientific notation. For example,

$$00000101 \quad 11111111$$

is five times one-half, which we may write in base ten as $\frac{5}{2}$. Similarly,

$$00000011 \quad 11111110$$

is three times one-quarter, or $\frac{3}{4}$ in base ten.

Of course, it takes only a moment to see that not all fractions may be represented. The only possible denominators are two, four, eight, sixteen, and so on. Even the common fraction one-third cannot be represented.

Luckily, however, we can always represent a fraction close to the one we want. The point, again, is that we have space for a reasonable number of significant digits. But to show why this is so, we need to explain what significant digits mean when we are talking about fractions.

4.10 THE BINARY POINT

Look at the following numbers written in base-ten scientific notation:

1234	3	represents	1,234,000
1234	2	represents	123,400
1234	1	represents	12,340
1234	0	represents	1,234
1234	−1	represents	?

Each number is a tenth of the one above it. Therefore we can reason that the last number should be a tenth of 1,234.

It is correct to write this as 1,234/10, but a better way is 123.4. Writing fractions the first way makes it hard to calculate with them. It is better to write them using a **decimal point**. For example, which of the following problems is easier to solve?

$$\frac{1,234}{10} + \frac{42}{100} = \frac{12,382}{100} \quad \text{or} \quad \begin{array}{r} 123.4 \\ + \ \ 0.42 \\ \hline 123.82 \end{array}$$

The second is simpler, because we can just add up columns as we always have. Our usual addition rules apply.

In fact, we have just extended the place-value system. The position to the right of the decimal point counts tenths. The next position counts hundreths. This is consistent with values for the other positions. Look at a few of them:

| hundreds | tens | ones | . | tenths | hundredths |

Each position counts a stack, ten, of what the position to the right counts. It takes ten tens to make a hundred, for example. But, likewise, it takes ten tenths to make a one and ten hundredths to make a tenth.

Now we can see how significant digits come into play. Suppose we want to represent the fraction $\frac{1}{3}$. The number should be 0.33333333333333333, and so on, with an infinite number of 3s at the end. But we cannot write an infinite number of digits.

In the base-ten place-value system, there is no way to represent the number one-third.

For practical purposes, however, this is not a problem. If a clothing store is having a one-third-off sale, the cashier can calculate by using the number 0.333333. This means the prices will be slightly wrong, but only by a matter of a hundredth of a cent or so. This amount is not meaningful in the clothing business.

In this case, at most six digits are significant.

*   *   *   *   *

Everything we have just said about representing fractions applies as well to binary numbers. The only difference is that the dot that separates whole numbers from smaller parts is called a **binary point**.

The first few place values in binary are

| fours | twos | ones | . | halves | quarters |

It takes two twos to make a four. Likewise, it takes two quarters to make a half and two halves to make one.

The number one-third happens to be written in binary as .01010101010101, and so on—a binary point followed by an infinite number of 01s. But suppose we write just .01010101. The 1s here count a quarter, a sixteenth, a sixty-fourth, and a two-hundred-fifty-sixth. Together, the value is the number written in base ten as 0.332031.

This is close enough to one-third for many practical purposes, and .01010101 can be written in our binary scientific notation. It is

$$01010101 \quad 11111000$$

The second number in the pair is negative eight. If it were positive eight, we would shift the digits 1010101 to the left eight times, adding zeros. Since it is negative eight, we shift them to the *right* eight times, past the binary point, to get .01010101.

Shifting to the left is the same as doubling or multiplying by two. Shifting to the right is the same as halving or dividing by two.

Again, of all the possible fractions, only a very few can be represented using our scientific notation with pairs of 8-bit numbers. But we can get *close* to any fraction.

4.11 AN ADDER-SUBTRACTER

We began this chapter by designing a circuit to add 8-bit binary numbers. Without much additional work, we saw that a circuit could be designed to subtract 8-bit numbers. At that point, however, we stopped short, for a very compelling reason. It appeared that 8-bit, binary numbers were too limited for any useful work.

Now, we have quite a different perspective. Using just 8-bit numbers—a pair of them—we can represent negative numbers, fractions, and huge numbers up into the trillion trillion trillions.

Furthermore, since each half of the pair representing a number is just 8 bits long, it is tailor-made for our 8-bit adder and other, similar circuits. The details of how to calculate with numbers represented by pairs is somewhat complicated. But the upshot is that it comes down to adding, subtracting, and shifting the 8-bit components.

Circuits for manipulating ordinary 8-bit numbers are all we need for calculation with the more complex numbers we have been discussing. We can come back to designing such circuits, then, with a renewed purpose.

One circuit we promised to design is a general-purpose addition and subtraction unit. It will perform either function, depending on the voltage in a control wire. What we have in mind is shown in Figure 4.16. The numbers we are either adding or subtracting come in over the digit wires at the top. The wire labeled **Subtract/~Add** controls the action.

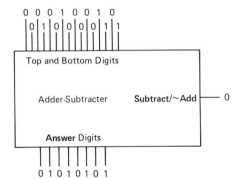

Figure 4.16 A combined adder-subtracter.

To perform an addition, we supply no voltage to the **Subtract/~Add** wire. The two input numbers are fed into an 8-bit adder and the sum comes out over the output wires.

To subtract, we do supply voltage to the **Subtract/~Add** wire. In this case, the top digits again go straight into the 8-bit adder. But the bottom digits are complemented before being fed into the adder and voltage is sent to the adder's first **Carry-In** wire. In this case, the number that comes out over the output wires is the difference of the two inputs.

The control wire, then, has two functions. It determines whether or not to complement the bottom digits and whether or not to supply voltage at the adder's carry-in.

For this second function, we simply connect the **Subtract/~Add** wire directly to the adder's **Carry-In** wire. If we are subtracting, the voltage we supply to the control wire will run straight to the carry-in.

For the first function, we need a logic circuit, but it turns out to be one we have already designed. Consider what happens to a digit of the bottom number. If there is a 0 on the **Subtract/~Add** wire, we are performing an addition and the bottom digit should not be changed. If it is 0, it stays 0; if it is 1, it stays 1.

If there is a 1 on the **Subtract/~Add** wire, we are subtracting and the bottom digit should be complemented. If it is a 0, it changes to 1; if it is a 1, it changes to 0. This is summarized in Figure 4.17.

Bottom digit	**Subtract/ ~Add**	Digit to go to adder
0	0	0
0	1	1
1	0	1
1	1	0

Figure 4.17 Effect of control voltage on the bottom digit.

The table in Figure 4.17 should look familiar. Apart from the headings, it is the same as the table in Figure 4.3, the one we used in designing a half-adder. That means we can use the circuit we built for that problem.

The circuit in Figure 4.18, then, is the same as the one in Figure 4.5, except for the labels. This circuit is called an **exclusive OR gate**. It puts out voltage when voltage is supplied *exclusively* at one input *or* the other—in other words, if voltage is supplied to one input but not both. The circuit is used so often that it has its

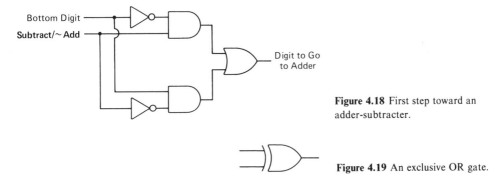

Figure 4.18 First step toward an adder-subtracter.

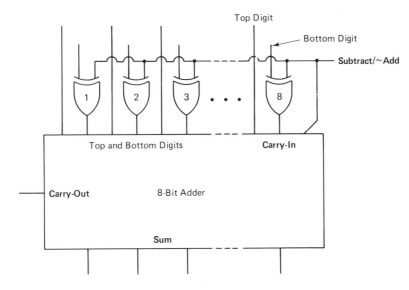

Figure 4.19 An exclusive OR gate.

own symbol, as shown in Figure 4.19. To build an adder-subtracter, all we need is an exclusive OR gate for each bottom digit, an 8-bit adder, and a control wire that goes to each of the exclusive OR gates and also to the adder's carry-in. The circuit is shown in Figure 4.20.

Figure 4.20 A circuit for the combined adder-subtracter.

4.12 MEMORY FOR THE CALCULATOR

This adder-subtracter unit is meant to be part of a calculator. But a calculator also needs memory to hold the numbers it is manipulating. For example, for a pocket calculator to add two numbers, it must be able to store the first while someone is punching in the second.

Our calculator will be able to store three 8-bit binary numbers: the two to be added, subtracted, or otherwise combined, and the calculated answer. For storage, we will use shift registers, like the ones we designed in Chapter 2, but slightly improved.

The shift register from Chapter 2 is pictured in Figure 4.21. Each of the memory cells is a master-slave flip-flop, but we can ignore that for now. The important point is that each cell is either putting out voltage or not; that is, it is storing a 1 or 0.

Notice that the output wires from all the cells are shown at the *bottom* of the register, a change from Chapter 2.

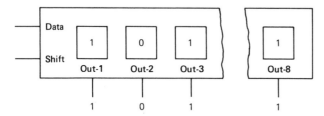

Figure 4.21 A shift register.

When we turn the **Shift** wire on and then off, each of these digits shifts one memory cell to the right. Whatever digit was on the **Data** wire goes into the left-most cell. The rightmost digit is lost. Figure 4.22 shows what happens if we shift the shift register in Figure 4.21.

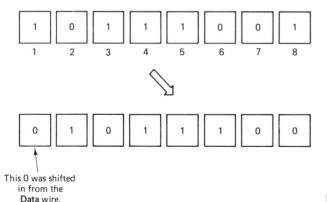

This 0 was shifted in from the **Data** wire.

Figure 4.22 Shifting the shift register.

To this basic shift register, we would like to add two features. The first is a **Clear** control wire. If we put voltage into this wire, all of the flip-flops are immediately reset to 0.

Also, we want to be able to put an 8-bit number into the register all at once, that is, without shifting it in one digit at a time. For this purpose, we add eight **Data-In** wires leading directly to the memory cells and an extra control wire, which we will call **Load**.

If we put voltage on the **Load** wire, the flip-flops will immediately be set or reset, according to the voltages on the **Data-In** wires. With the **Load** wire off, the **Data-In** wires have no effect; the only way to change what is in the cells is to use the **Shift** wire.

Figure 4.23 shows the modified shift register in use. In Figure 4.23a, we put a number on the **Data-In** wires. In Figure 4.23b, we put voltage on the **Load** wire and the number is stored in the register. In Figure 4.23c, the **Shift** wire is used to shift the number to the right.

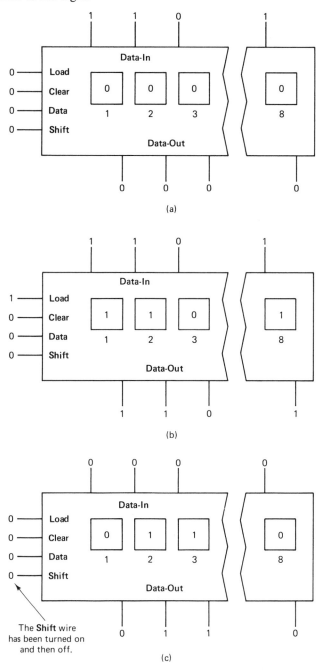

Figure 4.23 Using the improved shift register.

As a last point about the shift register, keep in mind that it is a real object. This means that if we want a shift register that shifts to the left, we do not need to design a new circuit. We can just pick up a shift register like the one we have designed . . . and turn it around.

4.13 OPERATIONS

Suppose, now, that we have numbers stored in two registers. We can connect the **Data-Out** wires to an adder-subtracter. Then, by using control wires on the adder-subtracter, we can add or subtract the numbers.

But our goal is to make the circuit as generally useful as possible. Why limit ourselves to addition and subtraction? Along with basic arithmetic operations, we might as well add some logical ones.

Figure 4.24 shows an example, a circuit that takes two 8-bit numbers and sends each pair of digits through an AND gate. The result is also an 8-bit number, and each digit is 1 only if the corresponding top digit *and* bottom digit are both 1.

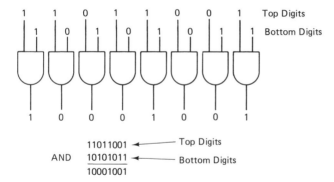

Figure 4.24 An 8-bit ANDing circuit.

We can obviously design a similar circuit with OR gates. It would put the numbers 11010101 and 01100110 together this way:

$$
\begin{array}{r}
1\ 1\ 0\ 1\ 0\ 1\ 0\ 1 \\
\text{OR} \quad 0\ 1\ 1\ 0\ 0\ 1\ 1\ 0 \\
\hline
1\ 1\ 1\ 1\ 0\ 1\ 1\ 1
\end{array}
$$

Each digit in the result is 1 if either the corresponding top digit *or* bottom digit *or* both are 1.

Now, just as we put addition and subtraction together in one circuit, we can combine these basic logical operations.[2] In this case, we use a multiplexer.

---

[2] Notice that we have omitted the NOT operation. We can get this using addition and subtraction. Subtracting a number from 0 has the effect of complementing it and adding 1. If we then subtract 1, we are left with just the complemented number, that is, the digits after they have each been run through a NOT gate.

Remember that a multiplexer chooses among the voltages on several wires. In Figure 4.25, we have shown how the multiplexer is used to get one of the eight digits. The top digit and bottom digit go through both an AND gate and an OR gate to give two separate answers. These answers are fed into the multiplexer. If there is no voltage in the **Select** wire, the multiplexer puts out the answer from the OR gate. If there *is* voltage on **Select**, it puts out the answer from the AND gate.

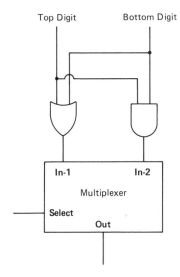

Figure 4.25 One digit of the combined logic circuit.

Eight circuits like this go into the general logic circuit shown in Figure 4.26. Notice that the single **And/~Or** control wire would be connected to the **Select** wires of all eight multiplexers. Either we OR together all eight pairs of digits or we AND them all together.

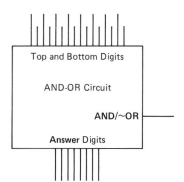

Figure 4.26 A combined logic circuit.

As a final step in designing a general operations circuit, we will combine the arithmetic and logic circuits. This can be done by using multiplexers, just as we combined the AND and OR circuits. Given two 8-bit numbers, we run them through both the arithmetic and logic circuits to get two separate 8-bit answers. Then we use eight multiplexers, one for each bit, to choose just one of the two answers.

What we get is the circuit shown in Figure 4.27. The **Subtract/~Add** and **And/~Or** separately control an adder-subtracter and a general logic circuit. According to these control wires, each performs an operation on the input numbers.

The **Logic/~Arithmetic** wire controls which answer we receive. If voltage is on in the wire, the result from the logic circuit comes out over the **Answer** wires. If it is off, the sum or difference from the arithmetic circuit comes out.

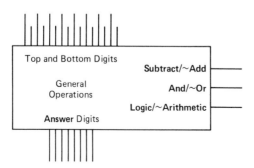

Figure 4.27 A general operations circuit.

*   *   *   *   *

With one more circuit, we will be ready to assemble our calculator. This circuit simply puts out voltage if the 8-bit number fed into it is zero. We will call it a **Zero?** circuit. The design is shown in Figure 4.28, along with a simplified way of representing it. The AND gate in the circuit puts out voltage only if all of its inputs are on. But since each input comes in through a NOT gate, the original inputs must all be off, or 0, for the circuit to put out voltage.

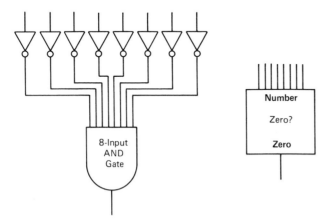

Figure 4.28 The Zero? circuit.

The circuit does what we want; it puts out voltage only if we put in the 8-bit number 00000000. If we connect the inputs of a Zero? circuit to the **Data-Out** wires of a register, the Zero? circuit will put out voltage only if the register is storing a zero.

4.14 THE ARITHMETIC AND LOGIC UNIT

Here, now, is our plan for a calculator. It is not at all like an ordinary pocket calculator, but we will see that it is still quite powerful.

The general plan is shown in Figure 4.29. The calculator contains three of our improved shift registers. These are labeled **Top**, **Bottom**, and **Answer**. **Top** shifts left and **Bottom** shifts right. **Answer** will never be shifted. The **Data** wire on all three is disconnected; if a register is shifted, a zero shifts in.

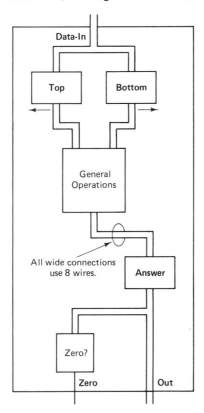

Figure 4.29 Plan for a calculator.

The same eight **Data-In** wires feed into the **Top** and **Bottom** registers. This means that the number on these wires is ready to be loaded into either register.

Data-Out wires from the **Top** and **Bottom** registers feed into our general operations circuit, so they may be added, subtracted, ANDed, or ORed. The result from the operations circuit feeds into the **Answer** register.

Finally, the **Answer** register is connected to a Zero? circuit that tells if it contains a zero.

From outside the box containing this calculator, all we can see are the wires that control the components inside. The view from outside is shown in Figure 4.30. At the top are the eight main **Data-In** wires, the ones leading to the **Top** and **Bottom** registers. These are something like the number buttons on a real calculator. We will use them to put 8-bit binary numbers into the calculator.

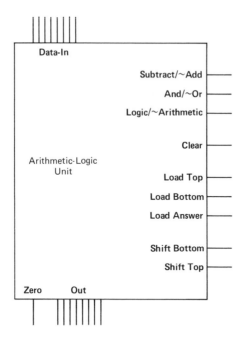

Figure 4.30 The arithmetic logic unit.

At the right of the box are the control wires. **Subtract/~Add**, **And/~Or**, and **Logic/~Arithmetic** are connected directly to the operations circuit. **Clear** is connected to the **Clear** input of all three registers. If we supply voltage to this control wire, all three will be reset to zero.

Load Top, **Load Bottom**, and **Load Answer** are connected to the **Load** inputs of the three registers. If we put voltage on the **Load Top** wire, for example, the number on the **Data-In** wires goes into the **Top** register. Voltage on **Load Answer** causes the number coming out of the general operations circuit to be stored in the **Answer** register.

Finally, **Shift Bottom** and **Shift Top** are connected to the **Shift** inputs of these two registers. Remember that **Top** shifts left and **Bottom** shifts right.

These wires at the top and right are what *we* control. We push the buttons by supplying voltages.

By contrast, the wires at the bottom are like the display of a real calculator. They tell us what the result is after the calculator has responded to our commands.

The eight **Out** wires show what number is stored in the **Answer** register. The **Zero** wire is the output of the Zero? circuit connected to the **Answer** register. It tells us whether the register contains the number zero.

4.15 USING THE ARITHMETIC-LOGIC UNIT

We are about to show how this arithmetic-logic unit, or calculator, may be used. Keep in mind, as we work, that the unit is not designed for people. For us, the many steps needed to solve even a simple problem make the calculator a poor tool. For a lightning-fast computer, it is quite a good one.

As an example, then, suppose we want to subtract 101 from 11010. Here are the steps we must take:

1. Put 00011010 on the **Data-In** wires and then 1 on the **Load Top** wire.[3] This puts the number 11010 into the **Top** register.
2. Put 00000101 on the **Data-In** wires and then 1 on the **Load Bottom** wire. This puts 101 into the **Bottom** register. Notice that it is essential to change the **Load Top** wire back to 0 before beginning this step. Otherwise 101 would be put into **Top** as well as into **Bottom**.
3. Put a 1 on the **Subtract/~Add** wire and make sure there is a 0 on the **Logic/~Arithmetic** wire. In this case, the general operations circuit will take the numbers in **Top** and **Bottom**, subtract them, and put the answer out over wires connected to the **Answer** register.
4. Next, without changing the voltages on the **Subtract/~Add** or **Logic/~Arithmetic** wires, we briefly put a 1 on the **Load Answer** wire. This causes the answer from the operations circuit, 00010101, to be stored in **Answer**.

We have explained what happens inside the calculator, but remember, all we have done is to supply voltages to labeled wires running out of a box. When we are finished, the answer we want is inside the box in the **Answer** register. But the important point, for us, is that the number in this register is also available outside the box.

The answer to our subtraction problem is now on the **Out** wires of the arithmetic logic unit.

*   *   *   *   *

Here is another example. Suppose there is a number in the **Top** register and we would like to know whether it is negative. All we really need to know is whether the first digit is a 1. If so, the number is negative.

To check, we begin by ANDing the number in **Top** together with 10000000. The operation will look like this:

$$
\begin{array}{r}
?????\,??? \qquad \longleftarrow \quad \text{The unknown number in } \textbf{Top} \\
\text{and} \quad \underline{10000000} \qquad\qquad\qquad\qquad\qquad\qquad \\
?0000000 \qquad\qquad\qquad\qquad\qquad\qquad
\end{array}
$$

We know the last seven digits of the answer must be zeros. Anything ANDed with 0 gives 0.

---

[3] Remember that "putting 1" on a wire is just another way of saying "supply voltage" to the wire.

The first digit will be 1 only if the first digit of the number in **Top** is 1. Therefore the answer will be 10000000 if the number in **Top** is negative and 00000000 if it is positive. This gives us a chance to use our zero detector.

Now, here are the steps for using the arithmetic-logic unit:

1. Put 10000000 on the **Data-In** wires and then 1 on the **Load Bottom** wire. This loads 10000000 into the **Bottom** register, where it is ready to be ANDed with the number in **Top**.

2. Put 1 on the **And/~Or** wire and on the **Logic/~Arithmetic** wire and then a 1 on the **Load Answer** wire.

At this point, the **Answer** register contains either 10000000 or 00000000, depending on whether the number in **Top** is negative or not. Thus, from outside the arithmetic-logic unit, all we must do is check the **Zero** wire. If this is putting out voltage, the number in **Answer** must be zero, implying that the number in **Top** is positive. If there is no voltage on **Zero**, the number in **Top** is negative.

Incidentally, we can use a similar approach to check whether the numbers in **Top** and **Bottom** are the *same*. We just subtract them and see whether the answer is zero. If it is, the numbers must be equal.

4.16 TAKING STOCK

By now, our picture of the computer is fairly complete.

Numbers are stored in a large memory system. From the memory system, they feed into an arithmetic-logic unit, which manipulates them in simple ways—it shifts them, adds them, ANDs them, and so on.

The results go back into the memory system.

What is missing from our picture is mainly the control. So far, it has been up to us to supply voltages to the memory system and the arithmetic-logic unit. But we have said many times that we would like to automate the process. This is where feedback comes into play.

Somehow, we would like the numbers coming out of the memory system to control how they themselves are manipulated. We want the numbers to say "add us" or "compare us to see if we are the same."

It seems almost impossible. But at the same time, it is extremely easy.

After all, a number coming out of the memory system is just a pattern of voltages on wires. If we connect those wires to the **Data-In** wires of the arithmetic-logic unit, the voltages will be treated as a number. That is, they will be added, ANDed, or something of the kind.

But voltages are just voltages, and there is nothing forcing us to use them as numbers. If we like, we can connect the wires running out of the memory system to the *control wires* of the arithmetic-logic unit. In this case, a number stored in the memory system is acting as a command. It controls what the arithmetic-logic unit will do.

In sum, voltages stored in the memory system can control what will happen to other voltages stored there. Numbers can act as instructions for manipulating numbers.

This simple idea of treating information and instructions for handling it in the same way is one of the most revolutionary ideas of the twentieth century—a world-altering contribution of computer science. We will put it into action in Chapter 5.

EXERCISES

4.1. What will be the output of the circuit shown in the diagram?

4.2. Consider the half-adder in Figure 4.6. What will be the output at **Carry** and **Sum** if we put in 0 at D_T and 1 at D_B? What about if we put in 1 at D_T and 1 at D_B?

4.3. Consider the full adder in Figure 4.7. What will be the output at **Carry-Out** and **Sum** if we put in
 (a) 0 at D_T, 0 at D_B and 1 at **Carry-In**?
 (b) 1 at D_T, 0 at D_B and 1 at **Carry-In**?
 (c) 1 at D_T, 1 at D_B and 1 at **Carry-In**?

4.4. Suppose that, in Figure 4.8, the D_T and D_B labels were reversed. Would the circuit still function correctly? What about if the D_B and **Carry-In** labels were reversed? Explain your answers.

4.5. What will be the output in the circuit pictured if we put in
 (a) 1 at D_T, 0 at D_B and 0 at **Carry-In**?
 (b) 0 at D_T, 1 at D_B and 1 at **Carry-In**?
 (c) 1 at D_T, 1 at D_B and 1 at **Carry-In**?

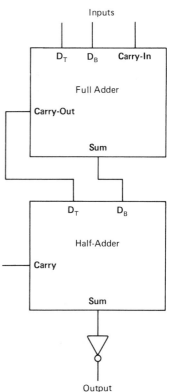

4.6. Describe in one sentence how the output of the circuit in Exercise 4.5 depends on the three inputs.

4.7. Redraw Figure 4.11 as it would look if the circuit were adding 1010011 and 10111.

4.8. Label Figure 4.12 with 1s and 0s to show it adding 111100001111 and 1111111111.

4.9. Label Figure 4.14 with 1s and 0s to show it subtracting 1110 from 101010. Remember that one of these numbers must first be complemented.

4.10. Use 8-bit numbers to represent what we would write in decimal as −4, −17, and −56.

4.11. The following positive and negative numbers are represented as described in Section 4.8. Convert them into base ten.
   (a) 00000000
   (b) 10000000
   (c) 01111111
   (d) 10101010

4.12. Someone asks how many people live in a certain city. Answer in decimal scientific notation, paying attention to the number of significant digits. Assume that the population is
   (a) 7,346,413, give or take a few hundred thousand
   (b) 7,346,413, give or take a few hundred
   (c) 7,346,413, give or take a few million

4.13. Write each of these in base ten:
   (a) 00001010 00000010
   (b) 00010101 11111101
   (c) 00000010 11111111
   (d) 00001111 11111011

4.14. Write each of these in base ten:
   (a) .1
   (b) 111.1
   (c) 101.01
   (d) .0001
   (e) .101
   (f) .111

4.15. Write each of these base-ten numbers in binary using binary point notation:
   (a) $\frac{5}{8}$
   (b) $7\frac{1}{4}$
   (c) 0.5
   (d) 31.75
   (e) 0.625

4.16. How would the answer digits change in Figure 4.16 if the 0 at **Subtract/∼Add** were changed to a 1?

4.17. Suppose the number 10101010 has been stored in a shift register like the one pictured in Figure 4.23. The **Data** input is set to 1, the **Data-In** inputs are set to 00001111 and all other inputs are set to 0. What number will be stored in the register after each of the following steps? (Note that the steps are taken in order.)

(a) Voltage at **Shift** is turned on and then off.

(b) Voltage at **Clear** is turned on and then off.

(c) Voltage at **Data** is turned on. Voltage at **Shift** is turned on and then off. Voltage at **Data** is turned off.

(d) Voltage at **Load** is turned on and then off.

(e) Voltage at **Shift** is turned on and then off.

4.18. What is the result when 11101110 and 11011010 are ANDed? When they are ORed?

4.19. What will be the output of the circuit in Figure 4.25 if the inputs are

(a) 1 at **Top**, 0 at **Bottom**, and 1 at **Select**?

(b) 1 at **Top**, 0 at **Bottom**, and 0 at **Select**?

(c) 1 at **Top**, 1 at **Bottom**, and 1 at **Select**?

4.20. Label Figure 4.27 with 1s and 0s to show it

(a) Adding 00011100 and 00001111

(b) ANDing 00011100 and 00001111

(c) Subtracting 00011100 from 00001111

4.21. In Section 4.15 we gave detailed instructions for using the arithmetic-logic unit to subtract two numbers. Give similar instructions for ORing 10101111 and 01010000.

4.22. Suppose numbers have been stored in **Top** and **Bottom**. How can we find out if they are the same? Give detailed instructions for what steps to take.

4.23. Suppose a number has been stored in **Top**. How can we find out what it is? Give detailed instructions for what steps to take. (*Hint*: Find a way to move the number from **Top** to **Answer**.)

4.24. Suppose a positive number has been stored in **Top**. We would like to check whether it is bigger than seven. Give detailed instructions that lead to the following result: If the number is smaller than or equal to seven, voltage will go on in the **Zero** wire; otherwise no voltage will be measured at **Zero**.

5 Control and Programming

5.1 A CONTROLLER CIRCUIT

Over the space of four chapters, we have gathered together the parts that go into making a computer. Now, we are about to give them life.

Our plan hinges on two different ways of using the numbers stored in a memory system. The numbers will serve both as information and as instructions for what to do with it.

We have already seen that this is possible. To use the numbers as information, we can feed them into the *registers* of an arithmetic-logic unit, where they will be subtracted, shifted, ORed, or otherwise manipulated. To use the numbers as instructions, we can feed them into the *control wires* of the arithmetic-logic unit. Since a memory system stores numbers as patterns of voltages, this is the same as supplying patterns of voltages to the control wires. Any such pattern of turned-on and turned-off wires determines what the unit will do with the numbers in its registers.

Numbers run into the arithmetic-logic unit to be processed. Numbers work the controls. Finally, the results, which are also numbers, run back into the memory system to be stored. In essence, this is our picture of a computer—it is a feedback loop of numbers controlling the way they themselves are manipulated.

The picture is simplified in some respects, however. For example, who is to decide what to do with a number emerging from the memory system? Should it go into a register of the arithmetic-logic unit, or into the control wires?

How do we know when an answer is ready to be stored back in the memory system? Who decides where in the memory system to put it?

132

At the very least, if we want to automate our computer, we will need a kind of traffic controller circuit to direct the flow of numbers.

In fact, practically speaking, we need more. Suppose a certain number, when interpreted as an instruction, means "subtract." It is not enough for the traffic controller simply to route this number to the control wires of the arithmetic-logic unit.

The problem, as we saw in Chapter 4, is that subtraction takes more than one step. A single pattern of voltages on the control wires is just one of these steps. When the number that means "subtract" emerges from the memory system, a whole series of steps should be carried out.

Because of this, our controller will never pass numbers directly from the memory system to the control wires.

Instead, it will be equipped with fixed plans, one for each instruction. If the number that means "subtract" emerges from the memory system, the controller will follow its subtraction plan. That is, it will send a *series* of voltage patterns to the control wires, one for each step of the subtraction.

The controller needs a few additional plans that do not directly involve the arithmetic-logic unit. One, for example, will include the steps necessary for storing a number in the memory system. Another will simply cause the flow of numbers to stop.

The controller also needs a clock to time the plans it oversees. At each tick of the clock, it will cause one step of a plan to be carried out.

But with these last additions, our computer will be complete. To use it, we will first store some numbers manually in the memory system. Then we will set the controller running. The numbers we have stored, working through the controller, will change themselves. Eventually, one number will cause the process to stop.

The question then will be: How can we make a machine that works like this do something useful? What information and instructions should we store before we set it on automatic?

5.2 COMPATIBILITY

Our immediate project, however, is to build the controller circuit.

Unfortunately, the two main components the circuit is supposed to control are badly matched. The memory system we designed in Chapter 2 uses names 20 values long to identify chunks of information. Our arithmetic-logic unit works with numbers eight values long.

In Chapter 2, we used long names because we wanted to show how large a memory system we could design. In Chapter 4, we used short numbers because we wanted to keep the arithmetic-logic unit simple.

Now, however, these different lengths make it hard to use the components together. Numbers coming out of the arithmetic-logic unit are too short to use as names in the memory system.

It is not impossible to work around this problem, but it would complicate our controller. Instead, we will simply use a smaller memory and a larger arithmetic-logic unit, both based on "chunks" of 16 values.

Our memory system, then, will contain flip-flops, or memory cells, arranged into chunks of 16, each chunk identified by a name 16 values long. In Chapter 2, we said each cell stores a logical value, **true** or **false**. Of course, the cells actually store voltages, which we are free to interpret as we like. In this chapter, it will be better to think of each cell as storing a binary digit, 0 or 1.

Each memory chunk, then, stores a single 16-bit number—one of the numbers that will flow through the feedback loop we are building.

Figure 5.1 shows the memory system we will use. The sixteen **Name** wires at the top left are used to pick out a chunk of memory cells. In Chapter 2, we thought of names as strings of logical values. But this too was just a way of interpreting voltages. A name that began **true-true-false-** identified the chunk selected by supplying voltage to the top two **Name** wires, not the third and so on.

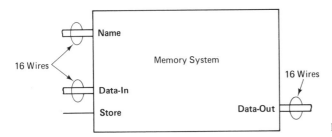

Figure 5.1 The computer's memory system.

In this chapter, it will be better to think of the names as numbers. The name 1100010100100101 means that voltage is supplied to the top two **Name** wires, not to the next three and so on.

Since there is always some pattern of voltages on the **Name** wires, one chunk of memory is always selected.[1] The number stored in this chunk comes out on the **Data-Out** wires.

To *store* a number in the selected chunk, we put the number on the **Data-In** wires and turn on the **Store** wire briefly.

The arithmetic-logic unit we will use is shown in Figure 5.2. It works exactly like the one we designed in Chapter 4, except that it calculates with 16-bit numbers.

5.3 THE CONTROLLER AT WORK I

Using numbers as chunk names in our memory system makes the names easier to talk about. For example, instead of saying "the number stored in the chunk identified by the name 0000000000000011," we can take advantage of the fact that this name is the number three. We can say "the number stored at Position three" or even just "the number at Position 3."

---

[1] If none of the name wires is connected to a voltage source, the chunk named 0000000000000000 is selected.

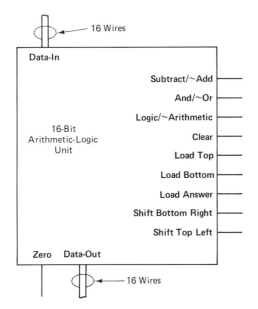

Figure 5.2 The computer's arithmetic-logic unit.

Likewise, if the number stored at Position 3 is 0000000000000111, we can take advantage of the fact that this is the number seven and say just "the number at Position 3 is 7."

It is important to remember that the actual names and stored numbers are patterns of voltages. These voltages must be interpreted as 1s and 0s in *binary* to make sense as numbers. But we can save space and keep things clear by using base ten in our discussion.

The memory system, then, boils down to a numbered series of positions, with one number stored at each position. We can picture it this way:

2	−4	17	11	300	−2		(stored number)
0	1	2	3	4	5	· · ·	(position)

In this example, the number stored at Position 2 is 17. The number at Position 1 is −4. Of course, most of the positions are not shown. They would run far off the right side of the page.

Notice also that the first position is Position 0. This is because the lowest-numbered name is 0000000000000000.

Using this picture of the memory, we can say more precisely what our controller will do.

When we set it running, it will read numbers from the memory one at a time beginning at Position 0. Although the memory puts out just one number at a time, the controller will often use numbers in pairs.

The first number the controller reads will always be interpreted as an instruction. For example, as an instruction, our controller will take the number 0 to mean "get the next number and load it into the **Top** register of the arithmetic-logic unit."

Suppose the first few positions of the memory look like this:

0	20	1	7	5	13	
0	1	2	3	4	5	...

Then the first thing the controller will do is put the number 20 into the **Top** register.

As an instruction, the number 1 means "take the next number and load it into the **Bottom** register of the arithmetic-logic unit." The number 5 means "add the numbers in the **Top** and **Bottom** registers."

Thus, in this example, the controller will continue by putting 7 in the **Bottom** register and then adding to get 27.

Note, at this point, that we have answered our earlier question about how to tell whether a number in the memory is an instruction. In our example, the number 0 was an instruction, because it was the first number read from memory. The number 20 was treated as a number, rather than an instruction, because it was *used* by the first instruction.

In general, the controller will read numbers one at a time from the memory, interpreting them as instructions. Sometimes the instructions will call for more numbers to be taken from memory and used somehow. After each instruction has been carried out, the next unused number will be interpreted as an instruction.

In the case of our example, the last instruction carried out was the 5 in Position 4. The next unused number is the 13 in Position 5, and so this will be interpreted as the next instruction.

5.4 THE CONTROLLER AT WORK II

So far, every number in the memory has either been interpreted as an instruction or used as an ordinary number. There is a third possibility: A number stored in the memory may serve as a name.

In the example from the last section, the controller had added 20 and 7, leaving 27 in the **Answer** register of the arithmetic-logic unit. The next instruction was the 13 in Position 5.

0	20	1	7	5	**13**	**1**	14	
0	1	2	3	4	5	6	7	...

The number 13, interpreted as an instruction, means "take the number in the **Answer** register of the arithmetic-logic unit and store it in the memory *using the next number as a name.*"

Thus the number 27 must be stored in the memory at some position. Which position? The one specified by the number following the instruction—that is, Position 1.

After the number 27 has been stored at Position 1, the memory will look like this:

0	**27**	1	7	5	13	1	**14**	
0	1	2	3	4	5	6	7	. . .

The controller continues with the next unused number, the 14 in Position 7. But 14, as an instruction, means simply "stop," and the controller does nothing further.

5.5 INSTRUCTIONS

Now that we have seen a little of what the controller is supposed to do, it may seem hard to believe that such a powerful circuit can be designed. In fact, however, we will show all the details of how to build it by the end of this chapter.

Before we begin designing, though, we must know everything the circuit will be able to do. To start, Figure 5.3 shows a complete list of the instructions it will be designed to carry out.

Instructions 2 through 8 simply make the arithmetic-logic unit do something. For example, we have already used Instruction 5 to make it add two numbers. Notice that there must already be numbers in the registers of the arithmetic-logic unit before we use most of these instructions.

To get numbers into the registers, we use Instruction 0, 1, 9 or 10. We have already seen the first two in action. With these, the number that goes into the register is just the one following the instruction.

For example, if the first part of the memory looks like this:

1	**4**	11	35	−7	0	
0	1	2	3	4	5	. . .

then the controller's first action will be to take the number 4 and put it into the **Bottom** register.

Instructions 9 and 10 also put numbers into the **Top** and **Bottom** registers. The difference is that they make the controller use the next number as a *name*.

As an example, suppose the memory begins like this:

10	**4**	11	35	−7	0	
0	1	2	3	4	5	. . .

Instruction Number	Instruction Name	Description
0	LOAD-TOP	Following number goes into **Top**.
1	LOAD-BOTTOM	Following number goes into **Bottom**.
2	SHIFT-BOTTOM-RIGHT	**Bottom** register is shifted right.
3	SHIFT-TOP-LEFT	**Top** register is shifted left.
4	SUBTRACT	Number in **Bottom** is subtracted from number in **Top**.
5	ADD	Numbers in **Top** and **Bottom** are added.
6	AND	Numbers in **Top** and **Bottom** are ANDed.
7	OR	Numbers in **Top** and **Bottom** are ORed.
8	CLEAR	**Top**, **Bottom**, and **Answer** registers are set to zero.
9	LOAD-TOP-FROM-POSITION	Following number gives the position in memory of a number to go into **Top**.
10	LOAD-BOTTOM-FROM-POSITION	Following number gives the position in memory of a number to go into **Bottom**.
11	JUMP-TO-POSITION	Following number gives the position of the next instruction.
12	JUMP-IF-ZERO-TO-POSITION	Following number gives the position of the next instruction if the number in **Answer** is zero; otherwise, no effect.
13	STORE-IN-POSITION	Number in **Answer** is stored in the position given by the next number following.
14	STOP	Processing halts.

Figure 5.3 Instruction list for the computer.

The controller's first action is to carry out Instruction 10, which puts a number into the **Bottom** register. But that number is not 4. The 4 gives the *position* of the number which should go into the register.

The number in Position 4 is −7. Therefore −7 goes into the **Bottom** register.

If this seems confusing, remember it this way: Instructions 0 and 1 tell us immediately *what* number to put into a register; Instructions 9 and 10 tell us *where to look* for the number to put in.

There are only four instructions remaining. Instructions 13 and 14 we have already seen—13 stores a number in the memory, using the next number as a name; 14 marks the end of a series of instructions.

*   *   *   *   *

The other instructions affect the controller itself, rather than telling it to use the arithmetic-logic unit or memory system.

As the controller reads numbers from the memory, it needs to keep track of what number is next. The simplest way is for it to remember the position of the next number in memory that should be read. When it reads this number, it increases the position number it is remembering by 1 to be ready for the next time.

For example, if the controller has just read the number from Position 8, the next number it should read is the one at Position 9. It remembers 9. When it reads the number at Position 9, it remembers 10, and so on.

We will call this remembered number the **Pointer**. It is as if the controller were browsing through the memory and keeping a finger pointed at the next number to read.

Instructions 11 and 12 change this **Pointer**. Consider the following example:

11	4	99	−1	0	42
0	1	2	3	4	5

. . .

The controller always begins by interpreting the number at Position 0 as an instruction. This means it must start with the pointer set at 0. In this case, it begins by reading the 11 at Position 0 from memory. Then it increases the pointer by 1, to show that the next number to be read is at Position 1.

The number 11, as an instruction, means to change the pointer. The number following the instruction tells what to change it to. It is easy for us to see that the pointer will be changed to 4, but let us follow the steps the controller will take.

When it has interpreted the 11, the controller sees that it needs to look at the next number. It reads this number, the 4, from the memory. Every time it reads a number from the memory, it increases the pointer by 1. The pointer was set at 1; now it is set at 2.

Finally, the controller has looked at the first two numbers in memory and is ready to carry out its first instruction. It sets the pointer to 4.

Now, since it is done with this instruction, it goes to the memory for its next instruction. But when the controller checks **Pointer**, it finds a 4 and it looks in Position 4 for its next instruction.

We can see that this instruction will cause the controller to put the number 42 into the **Top** register. But the important point is that the controller has skipped the numbers in Positions 2 and 3. These numbers are never read from the memory.

This is why Instruction 11 is called a "jump"—it makes the controller jump over part of the memory.

5.6 A LOOP

In the example we have just given, the controller jumps forward. This causes it to skip over some of the numbers in memory. If the controller jumps backward, something very different happens.

Here is an example:

0	0	1	1	5	13	1	11	0	...
0	1	2	3	4	5	6	7	8	

The first pair of numbers—the two 0s—will be interpreted as "load the number 0 into **Top**." Next, the pair of 1s will be interpreted as "load the number 1 into **Bottom**."

The third instruction to be carried out is the 5, which means "add." The controller causes the arithmetic-logic unit to add the 0 in **Top** to the 1 in **Bottom**. The sum, 1, goes into the **Answer** register.

Next, the controller looks at the 13 and the 1. These mean to take the number in the **Answer** register and store it at Position 1. After the number is stored, the memory looks like this:

0	**1**	1	1	5	13	1	11	0	...
0	1	2	3	4	5	6	7	8	

Now, the controller comes to the jump instruction. After reading the numbers in Positions 7 and 8, the controller sets **Pointer** to 0. But this means its next instruction will be taken from Position 0.

The jump causes the controller to start again from the beginning.

Notice, though, that the memory is slightly different from when we first started the controller running. Originally there was a 0 stored at Position 1; now that position contains a 1.

The controller continues, then, with the instruction at Position 0. This puts a 1 in **Top**. Next, the instruction at Position 2 causes the controller to put a 1 in **Bottom**. The instruction at Position 5 causes these two 1s to be added, and the instruction at Position 6 causes the answer, 2, to be stored in Position 1.

After the number is stored, the memory looks like this:

0	**2**	1	1	5	13	1	11	0	...
0	1	2	3	4	5	6	7	8	

At this point, the controller comes to the jump instruction again. This sets **Pointer** to 0, forcing the controller to begin at the beginning of these instructions for the third time.

Apparently, this backward jump creates a never-ending **loop** of instructions. Unless the power supply gives out, the controller will continue to carry out the same instructions over and over, looping back to the beginning each time it reaches the jump instruction.

Each time through the loop, the numbers in Positions 1 and 3 will be added and the result will be stored in Position 1. The number in Position 3 never changes; it is always 1. Thus we can sum up the instructions this way: They add 1 to the number in Position 1 and then put the answer back in Position 1.

In effect, each pass through the instructions increases the number at Position 1 by 1. We have already seen the number in this position change from 0 to 1 and then from 1 to 2. If we let the controller continue, it will change to 3, 4, 5, and so on.

We appear to have found a very roundabout way of counting.

More important, this example shows how it will be possible to string instructions together to do work that they cannot do individually. There is no "count" instruction, but we have shown we can count perfectly well with the instructions we have.

In effect, a list of numbers stored in the memory system spells out a program of action for the controller to follow. Usually, when we think of the list of numbers this way, we call it simply a **program**.

Incidentally, writing programs as a list of numbers makes them hard to read. As long as we are only *discussing* programs, and not actually putting numbers into a memory system, it will be easier to write them as in Figure 5.4. The figure shows our counting program rewritten. Notice that some lines take the place of a *pair* of numbers in the memory. For example, the first line combines the meaning of the pair of 0s originally stored in Positions 0 and 1.

```
0   LOAD-TOP 0
2   LOAD-BOTTOM 1
4   ADD
5   STORE-IN-POSITION 1
7   JUMP-TO-POSITION 0
```
Figure 5.4 A counting program.

The number at the left of each line is a position number that helps us keep track of where we are in memory. For example, the third line contains the instruction ADD with the position number 4. This tells us that the instruction is stored at Position 4 in the memory.

Keep in mind that this way of writing programs is only a convenience. The real program is always a list of numbers stored in the memory system as a pattern of voltages.

5.7 BREAKING THE LOOP

As we have seen, our counting program has a serious flaw. It counts perfectly well, but it never stops. A controller carrying out this program will never have time to do anything else.

Of course, we can always shut off the power. But it would be better to modify the program so that the controller will stop automatically after counting up to, say, 16. To do this, we need to use our last instruction.

Instruction 12 works very much like Instruction 11. It causes the controller to jump by changing the number called **Pointer**. The difference is that Instruction 12 changes **Pointer** only if the number in **Answer** is 0.

Our modified counting program will begin just like the original one. But instead of automatically jumping back to the beginning of the instructions when it comes to the end, it will first make a test.

The test is meant to see whether the number in Position 1 is 16. If it is, the controller has finished its work. Instead of jumping to the beginning, it will jump *forward* to a STOP instruction.

If the number in Position 1 is lower than 16, it will not pass the test. In this case, the controller will jump *backward* and continue carrying out the instructions that make it count.

The test itself is easy. Our program will take the number at Position 1 and subtract 16. If the answer is zero, the number at Position 1 must be 16 and the controller should jump forward to stop. Otherwise, it should jump backward and continue counting.

Notice that the first of these two jumps takes place only if the answer to a calculation is zero. This is suited perfectly to our JUMP-IF-ZERO-TO-POSITION instruction, Instruction 12.

The complete program, along with a picture of how it looks in memory, is shown in Figure 5.5. For convenience, we have labeled three parts of the program.

```
 0   LOAD-TOP 0
 2   LOAD-BOTTOM 1                         PART A
 4   ADD
 5   STORE-IN-POSITION 1

 7   LOAD-TOP-FROM-POSITION 1
 9   LOAD-BOTTOM 16                        PART B
11   SUBTRACT

12   JUMP-IF-ZERO-TO-POSITION 16
14   JUMP-TO-POSITION 0                    PART C
16   STOP
```

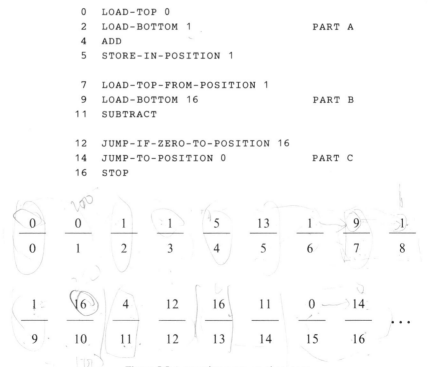

Figure 5.5 A counting program that stops.

Part A is exactly as in our original counting program. Carrying out these instructions has the effect of increasing the number at Position 1 by 1. Part B takes the number at Position 1, subtracts 16, and leaves the answer in the **Answer** register.[2]

Part C is the key to the program. If the number in Position 1 is 16, it makes the computer stop. Otherwise, it sends the controller back to Part A, where it will count up again to the next higher number.

To see how part C works, we can trace the controller's actions. Instead of watching it count up from zero, however, we will suppose the program has already gone as far as 14 and has just jumped back to the beginning of the instructions.

The controller continues, then, by carrying out the instructions in part A of the program. It takes the 14 stored at Position 1, adds 1, and puts the result, 15, back into Position 1.

Next, in part B, the controller takes this 15 from Position 1 and subtracts 16 to get −1. This −1 remains in the **Answer** register.

The next instruction, at the beginning of part C, is JUMP-IF-ZERO-TO-POSITION 16. This changes **Pointer** only if the number in **Answer** is zero. Since the number in **Answer** is −1, this instruction does nothing at all.

The following instruction is JUMP-TO-POSITION 0. It automatically sets **Pointer** to 0, forcing the controller to start again at part A. This is correct. The program has counted only up to 15, so it should continue.

Part A now increases the number at Position 1 to 16. Part B takes this 16 and subtracts 16, leaving 0 in **Answer**.

The next instruction is JUMP-IF-ZERO-TO-POSITION 16. Since the number in **Answer** *is* 0, the pointer is set to 16.

The controller takes its next instruction from Position 16. But this instruction is STOP. The program halts, just as we wanted.

*   *   *   *   *

Controlled loops like this are one reason computers are so powerful. Often a few simple steps can give us an important result if they are repeated many times. A program loop allows us to repeat the steps accurately.

As an example, suppose we are wondering how much money we would have in 150 years if we put 100 dollars in the bank today at 7 percent interest.

To find out how much money we will have *next* year is easy. We just multiply this year's balance by 1.07. We have 100 dollars now, so we will have 100 times 1.07, or 107 dollars, next year. In effect, we are multiplying by 1 to get the 100 dollars we have now, multiplying by 0.07 to get the 7 dollars of interest, and then adding.

---

[2] This is a good example of how the two different kinds of LOAD instructions are used. The 1 in LOAD-TOP-FROM-POSITION 1 is a name. The controller looks in *Position* 1 and puts the number it finds there into the **Top** register. The 16 in LOAD-BOTTOM 16 is an ordinary number. The controller will put 16 into the **Bottom** register. It will not look in Position 16.

To find out how much money we will have in two years, we take the balance after one year, $107, and multiply by 1.07 again. This gives us $114.49.

To find out how much money we will have in 150 years, we just need to carry out this simple step 150 times: Take the balance and multiply it by 1.07. But if we try to do this, what is the chance that we will get the right answer?

People are notoriously bad at this kind of work. More than likely, in the course of 150 multiplications, we will make a careless error or copy a number incorrectly. One error of this kind is enough to make the final answer worthless.

By contrast, the controller of a computer is extremely unlikely to make mistakes. We are far from knowing how to carry out even such a simple step as multiplying by 1.07 with our 15 basic instructions, but if we did know, it would be easy to get an accurate answer for this problem.

First, we would modify our counting program so that it counts up to 150. Second, we would add a few instructions at the beginning to store the number 100, our balance, at an unused position of the memory, say Position 999. Finally, we would add instructions in the middle of the counting program loop to multiply this number by 1.07 and put the result back in the same position.

When the controller executed this program, it would start by putting 100 into Position 999. Then it would go through a loop of instructions 150 times. Each time through, the number at Position 999 would be multiplied by 1.07. When the controller stopped, after exactly 150 times through the loop, the number at Position 999 would be the correct balance after 150 years.[3]

5.8 DISSECTING AN INSTRUCTION

It appears that, if we can only build a controller circuit that does what we have said it must do, we will have achieved our goal. Our combination memory system, arithmetic-logic unit and controller will be a useful, fully automatic machine for manipulating information.

We can begin by taking a careful look at the very first step of the counting program: the LOAD-TOP 0 instruction. To see exactly what the controller must do to carry out this instruction, we will break it into even smaller steps.

Keep in mind that, in the memory, the program begins like this:

$$
\begin{array}{cc}
0 & 0 \\
\hline
0 & 1
\end{array} \quad \cdots
$$

Now, here are the steps.

    A. When the controller begins its work, it does not know what the first instruction will be. *We* have looked at the numbers in the first two memory posi-

---

[3] Incidentally, after 150 years the balance would be a little more than $2.5 million. If we got this answer calculating by hand, we might well *think* we had made a mistake and start calculating all over again.

tions, but the controller has not. Therefore it needs to begin by reading the first number from the memory.

In general, when the controller reads a number from memory, it looks in the position remembered by **Pointer**. Since **Pointer** begins at 0, this is correct. However, even to get a number out of the memory takes more than one step.

The controller begins by telling the memory which number it wants. That is, it puts the number called **Pointer** into the memory system's **Name** wires. This is shown in Figure 5.6.

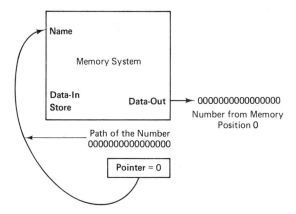

Name

Memory System

Data-In
Store   Data-Out   ► 0000000000000000
                                        Number from Memory
                                        Position 0

                Path of the Number
                0000000000000000

                  Pointer = 0

Figure 5.6 A. **Pointer** → **Name**.

B. After this is done, the number stored at Position 0 comes out on the memory system's **Data-Out** wires. The controller needs to remember this number. We will call it **Instruction**. Thus, after this second step, **Instruction** is the number just read from the memory—the 0 from Position 0.

C. When the controller reads a number from the memory using the pointer, it must always change the pointer. Otherwise, it would read the same number again the next time. In the third step, then, the controller increases the pointer to 1.

These first three steps are taken before the controller knows what instruction it is supposed to carry out. After they are completed, the controller has read the instruction number from memory and remembers it. It sees that the instruction is LOAD-TOP, and from this point on, it begins its fixed plan for carrying out LOAD-TOP.

D. As the first part of this plan, the controller needs to read the next number from memory—the one which is supposed to go into **Top**. It begins by putting the number called **Pointer** into the memory system's **Name** wires. As Figure 5.7 shows, the result is that the number in Position 1 comes out at the memory system's **Data-Out** wires.

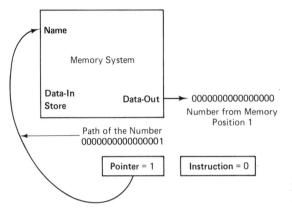

Figure 5.7 D. Number to load appears at **Data-Out**.

E. This number is the one that should go into the **Top** register, and the controller next puts this number into the arithmetic-logic unit's **Data-In** wires and turns on the **Load Top** control wire. The result, shown in Figure 5.8, is that the number 0 from Position 1 of the memory ends up in **Top**, as desired.

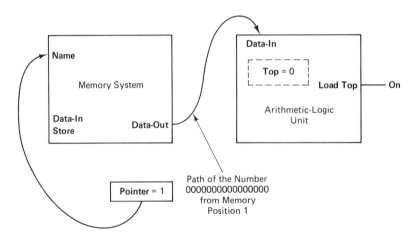

Figure 5.8 E. **Data-Out** → **Top**.

F. Finally, since a number has again been read from memory, the controller increases **Pointer** by 1.

After this first instruction has been carried out, the situation is as pictured in Figure 5.9. Notice that the pointer is now 2. The controller is set to read its next instruction from Position 2.

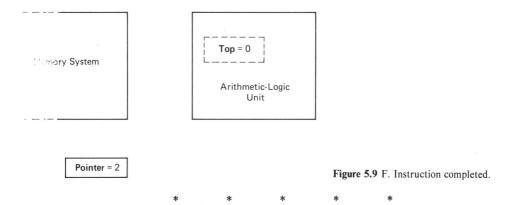

Pointer = 2

Figure 5.9 F. Instruction completed.

*   *   *   *   *

It may seem that we are making very little progress. First, we broke the simple problem of counting into a 5-instruction program. Now we have taken the first instruction of the program and broken it into six even smaller steps.

Fortunately, we have reached bottom. These smaller steps are as small as we need them.

The point is, each is only a matter of turning on certain control wires. We can design circuits to carry out this work—circuits that understand nothing about steps, instructions, or programs.

This point is important. Until now, we have been talking about the controller as if it were almost human. We have said, for example, that the controller "sees that the instruction is LOAD-TOP" or "carries out a plan." We are about to see how a circuit can do these things with no human understanding at all.

5.9 REGISTERS AND CONNECTIONS FOR THE CONTROLLER

A good place to start is with our statement that the controller "remembers" the numbers **Pointer** and **Instruction**. This is true in a mechanical sense. The controller stores these numbers in registers called **Pointer** and **Instruction**.

Instruction will be a 16-bit register exactly like the registers **Top**, **Bottom**, and **Answer**. It will never need to be shifted, but we will make use of the load wire. The register is shown in Figure 5.10.

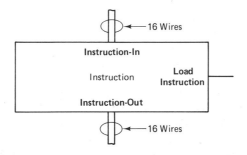

Figure 5.10 The **Instruction** register.

To avoid confusion, we have labeled the "load," "data-in," and "data-out" wires as **Load Instruction, Instruction-In**, and **Instruction-Out**. The other control wires are not shown, since they are not used.

Pointer will be a 16-bit ripple counter, like the 3-bit counter we designed in Chapter 2. We use a counter because it is so often necessary to increase **Pointer** by 1. That is, we will often want **Pointer** to *count* up to the next higher number.

To serve as a practical register, the counter must be modified slightly, just as we modified the shift register. The result is shown in Figure 5.11. The number stored in **Pointer** comes out on the **Pointer-Out** wires. The number on the **Pointer-In** wires normally has no effect, but if the **Load Pointer** wire is turned on, this number is stored in the register. Finally, if the **Count Pointer** wire is turned on and off, the number in the register increases by 1.[4]

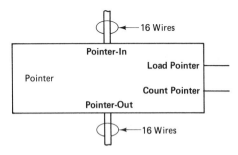

Figure 5.11 The **Pointer** register.

The controller will also use two other registers, **Position** and **Counter**.

Position is identical to the **Instruction** register. It simply holds a 16-bit number which may be stored using the **Position-In** and **Load Position** wires. The number stored in **Position** is always available for use on the **Position-Out** wires.

Position will hold the name of a memory chunk to be read from memory. Most of the time this is the same as the position name remembered by **Pointer**.

The last register, **Counter**, is a 4-bit ripple counter with a clock permanently attached to the input that makes it count. The clock is built with a **Stop Clock** control wire, and unless someone turns this wire on, it never stops ticking.

This little ticking clock is the beating heart of the whole complex structure we are building.

As the clock ticks, **Counter** counts off the steps of an instruction. The first few steps get the instruction number from the memory and put it into the **Instruction** register. The next steps carry it out.

The last step of each instruction will always be to set **Counter** back to 0 so that it will begin to count off steps of the *next* instruction.

*   *   *   *   *

In order for numbers to travel between these registers and the memory system and arithmetic-logic unit, certain connections must be made. These are shown in Figure 5.12. Notice that all the connections are made with bundles of 16 wires.

---

[4] This wire is the same as the **Clock** input in the ripple counter of Chapter 2.

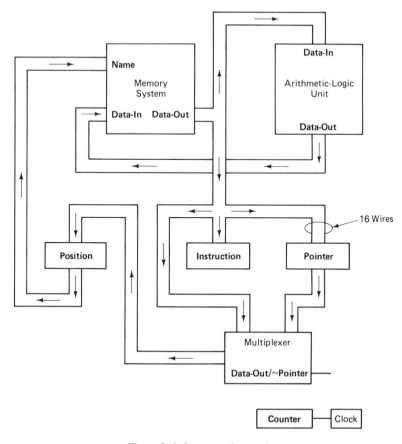

Figure 5.12 Computer data paths.

Although they may look confusing, these connections make good sense. Consider the connection from the **Data-Out** wires of the arithmetic-logic unit to the **Data-In** wires of the memory system, for example. This allows an answer calculated by the arithmetic-logic unit to get to the memory system to be stored.

As another example, notice that a number emerging from the memory system may go into the arithmetic-logic unit to be processed or into the **Instruction** register to direct the controller. In fact, a number put out by the memory goes to four different places where it might be used.

The reasons for all the other connections will be clear when we put the system to work. Take time now, though, to note the multiplexer at the bottom of the figure and its connection to the **Position** register.

As we have said, **Position** will be used to hold the name of a selected memory chunk. In fact, the figure shows that the number stored in **Position** will feed directly into the memory system's **Name** wires. This means the name stored in **Position** is the one the memory system will use to select a chunk.

The multiplexer determines what number will get to **Position** to be used as a name. Often, the number we want is the one stored in **Pointer**. If the multiplexer's control wire is off, the number in **Pointer** feeds through to **Position**.

But if the control wire is *on*, the number emerging from the *memory* feeds through to **Position**.

To see why this might be necessary, consider the instruction LOAD-TOP-FROM-POSITION 17. The number 17, here, is meant to be used as a name. It tells where to look in the memory for the number to put into **Top**. Thus when 17 emerges from the memory, it needs to be used as a name—that is, it needs to go to **Position**.

5.10 COUNTER CALLS THE SIGNALS

Now we can say exactly which control wires must receive voltage to carry out the steps of the LOAD-TOP instruction we dissected in Section 5.8.

In step A, we routed the number in **Pointer** to the memory system's **Name** wires. To do this, the controller must simply turn on the **Load Position** wire, making sure that the multiplexer's control wire **Data-Out/~Pointer** stays off.

As we have just seen, the **Position-Out** wires are permanently connected to the memory system's **Name** wires. Therefore, once the number from **Pointer** is loaded into **Position**, it automatically goes to the **Name** wires.

In step B, the number on the memory system's **Data-Out** wires was stored in the **Instruction** register. This is only a matter of turning on the **Load Instruction** wire, since the **Data-Out** wires are permanently connected to **Instruction-In**.

In step C, **Pointer** is increased by 1. To do this, the controller turns on the **Count Pointer** wire.

In step D, the controller begins to get another number from the memory by again routing the number in **Pointer** to **Position**. That is, it turns on the **Load Position** wire.

In step E, the controller puts the new number coming out on the memory's **Data-Out** wires into **Top**. Since these wires are connected to the arithmetic-logic unit's **Data-In** wires, this just means that it turns on the **Load Top** wire.

In step F, the controller again increases **Pointer** by 1 by turning on the **Count Pointer** wire.

The LOAD-TOP instruction, then, comes down to six simple steps. These are shown, with an additional seventh step, in Figure 5.13. We will come to the reason for the seventh step in just a moment.

1. Load Position
2. Load Instruction
3. Count Pointer
4. Load Position
5. Load Top
6. Count Pointer   **Figure 5.13** Steps for the LOAD-TOP
7. Clear Counter   instruction.

The figure shows just which wires must be turned on at each step. All other wires that the controller controls are off. Also, notice that we have numbered the steps instead of labeling them with letters. Our idea is that the controller's **Counter** will call signals like the quarterback on a football team.

The counter starts at 1. While it is 1, the controller turns on the **Load Position** wire, making sure all other control wires are off.

The little clock connected to **Counter** ticks and the number in **Counter** changes to 2.

While **Counter** is at 2, the controller turns on the **Load Instruction** wire, making sure all other control wires are off.

The clock ticks and the number in **Counter** changes to 3.

By the time **Counter** gets to 7, all six steps of the LOAD-TOP instruction have been completed. Then, when **Counter** is at 7, the controller turns on the **Clear Counter** wire. The counter is set to 0.

The next time the clock ticks, the number in **Counter** changes to 1, leaving it ready to call signals for the next instruction.[5]

This gives us our clearest picture yet of how our computer will operate. The ticking clock causes **Counter** to count. As it counts each number, a step of an instruction plan is carried out. The first step of each plan will be to read a number from memory to find out what instruction is to be carried out. The last step of each plan sets **Counter** back to zero, causing the next instruction to begin.

5.11 STEPS FOR OTHER INSTRUCTIONS

To design the controller, we need step-by-step plans for each of the 14 other basic instructions. Fortunately, most of the plans are quite similar to the one we developed in the last section.

The steps for the LOAD-BOTTOM instruction, for example, are exactly the same as for LOAD-TOP, except that in step 5 the **Load Bottom** wire is turned on instead of the **Load Top** wire.

Likewise, the SHIFT-BOTTOM-RIGHT, SHIFT-TOP-LEFT, SUBTRACT, ADD, AND, OR, and CLEAR instructions are almost identical. We will look at just one, SUBTRACT, which is broken into steps in Figure 5.14.

1. Load Position
2. Load Instruction
3. Count Pointer
4. Subtract/~Add
   Load Answer
5. Subtract/~Add   Figure 5.14 Steps for the SUBTRACT
6. Clear Counter   instruction.

The first three steps are the same as in the LOAD-TOP instruction. In fact, they will be the same for every instruction. These steps read from memory the number of the instruction to be carried out, put it in the **Instruction** register, and change **Pointer** to the next position in memory.

---

[5] Of course, with the **Clear Counter** wire on, we might have some difficulty getting the counter to count properly. This is not a serious design problem, however. We can easily arrange to let voltage get through to **Clear Counter** only until the clock goes on again.

In step 4, the controller must make the arithmetic-logic unit subtract. To do this, it needs to turn on the **Subtract/~Add** wire and turn off the **Logic/~Arithmetic** wire. The figure shows only the wires which must be turned on, and so it makes no reference to the **Logic/~Arithmetic** wire.

Also, during this step, the **Load Answer** wire is turned on so that the answer will be stored in the **Answer** register.

In step 5, **Subtract/~Add** remains on to keep the same number coming into **Answer**. If this number were to change before **Load Answer** was turned off, the changed number would be stored.

The last step is to set **Counter** back to 0 so it will be ready for the next instruction.

*   *   *   *   *

Figure 5.15 breaks the LOAD-TOP-FROM-POSITION instruction into steps. Naturally, the LOAD-BOTTOM-FROM-POSITION instruction is nearly identical.

1. **Load Position**
2. **Load Instruction**
3. **Count Pointer**
4. **Load Position**
5. **Data-Out/~Pointer**
   Load Position
   Count Pointer
6. **Load Top**
7. **Clear Counter**

Figure 5.15 Steps for the LOAD-TOP-FROM-POSITION instruction.

The first three steps, as usual, put the instruction number in the **Instruction** register and change **Pointer** to the next position in memory.

Now, since the instruction is LOAD-TOP-FROM-POSITION, the controller still needs to (a) read the next number from memory to use as a name, (b) take a third number from memory using this name, and (c) put this third number in **Top**. Here are the details:

(a). In step 4, the number in **Pointer** is routed to **Position** so that the next number from memory comes out over the memory system's **Data-Out** wires.

(b). This number needs to be used as a name, so it should go into the **Position** register. To get it there, in step 5, the controller switches on the multiplexer's control wire **Data-Out/~Pointer** and the **Load Position** wire.[6] At the same time, it increases **Pointer** by 1, since a number has been read from the memory.

Position now contains the name of the memory chunk we want to use—the

---

[6] If we are not careful, this new name will cause a new number to come out of the memory and to be routed to the **Position** register, causing a new number to come out of memory, and so on. **Position** must use the kind of trick we invented for the master-slave flip-flop to prevent this kind of transparency problem.

one with the third number. Since the correct name is in **Position**, this number comes out on the memory system's **Data-Out** wires.

(c). These wires are permanently connected to the arithmetic-logic unit's **Data-In** wires. Therefore, to get the number into **Top**, the controller just turns on **Load Top** in step 6.

The last step, as usual, resets **Counter** so it will begin to count signals for the next instruction.

*   *   *   *   *

Figure 5.16 shows the steps of the JUMP-IF-ZERO-TO-POSITION instruction. The steps for JUMP-TO-POSITION are nearly identical.

1. Load Position
2. Load Instruction
3. Count Pointer
4. Load Position
5. Count Pointer
6. Load Pointer (if Zero is on)
7. Clear Counter

Figure 5.16 Steps for the JUMP-IF-ZERO-TO-POSITION instruction.

The first three steps and the last step are the same as usual.

Step 4 routes the number in **Pointer** to **Position** so that the number following the instruction will come out over the memory system's **Data-Out** wires.

Step 5 increases **Pointer** by 1, since a number has just been read from the memory.

This number, now on the memory's **Data-Out** wires, is what **Pointer** should be changed to. But the change should be made only if the number in **Answer** is 0 — that is, if there is voltage on the arithmetic-logic unit's **Zero** wire.

Thus, in step 6, the controller turns on **Load Pointer** if the **Zero** wire is on. Otherwise, nothing happens during this step.

*   *   *   *   *

To complete our detailed look at the instructions, we need only to consider STORE-IN-POSITION and STOP. The first is shown in Figure 5.17.

1. Load Position
2. Load Instruction
3. Count Pointer
4. Load Position
5. Data-Out/~Pointer
   Load Position
   Count Pointer
6. Store
7. Clear Counter

Figure 5.17 Steps for the STORE-IN-POSITION instruction.

The first five steps are exactly as in LOAD-TOP-FROM-POSITION. They put the instruction number in **Instruction**, put the next number, the name of the memory chunk into which we are about to store something, in **Position**, and leave **Pointer** pointing to the number following the name.

Position now holds the name of the chunk in which we are supposed to store a number. The number to be stored is coming out on the arithmetic-logic unit's **Answer** wires, which are connected to the memory system's **Data-In** wires. All the controller needs to do, in step 6, is turn on the memory's **Store** wire.

Figure 5.18 shows the steps for STOP. Notice that this instruction does not have the usual **Clear Counter** ending. In fact, it ends much more dramatically. After the usual beginning, which brings the instruction number into the **Instruction** register, the controller turns on the **Stop Clock** wire.

1. Load Position
2. Load Instruction   **Figure 5.18** Steps for the STOP
3. Stop Clock   instruction.

This gives our computer the electronic equivalent of a heart attack. With voltage on this wire, the clock stops dead, the counter no longer calls signals, and the computer comes to a peaceful rest.

5.12 THE CONTROL NETWORK

Now we are within an ace of having a working computer.

All that remains is to build a circuit that will turn on and off all the control wires at the right times. Luckily, this circuit is simple to design.

The circuit has, as its inputs, the number in the counter, the number in the **Instruction** register, and the **Zero** wire of the arithmetic-logic unit. Using these, it decides whether or not to put out voltage on the control wires listed in Figure 5.19.

For example, suppose the **Instruction** register contains a 0 and the counter is at 5. In this case, the controller should carry out the fifth step of the LOAD-TOP instruction. Looking back to Figure 5.13, we can see that this step is simply to turn on the **Load Top** wire, leaving all the other control wires off.

As another example, suppose the counter is at 1. The first step of any instruction is the same: The controller should turn on the **Load Position** wire and nothing else.

To design the circuit we need, we consider one control wire at a time. Looking through all the steps of all the instructions, we make a complete list of the situations in which this control wire should be turned on. Then we use AND, OR, and NOT gates to design a circuit that puts out a 1 exactly at these times.

An easy example is the memory system's **Store** wire. This is turned on in only one case: step 6 of Instruction 13, STORE-IN-POSITION.

Memory System
> **Store**

Arithmetic-logic Unit
> **Subtract/~Add**
> **And/~Or**
> **Logic/~Arithmetic**
> **Clear**
> **Load Top**
> **Load Bottom**
> **Load Answer**
> **Shift Bottom**
> **Shift Top**

Controller
> **Load Pointer**
> **Count Pointer**
> **Load Position**
> **Load Instruction**
> **Clear Counter**
> **Stop Clock**   Figure 5.19 Control wires.

What we want, then, is a circuit that puts out voltage only when **Counter** contains 6 and the **Instruction** register contains 13. The circuit is shown in Figure 5.20. The AND gate on the left puts out voltage only if the number in the **Instruction** register is 0000000000001101, or 13 in base ten. The one on the right puts out voltage only if the number in **Counter** is 0110, or 6 in base ten.

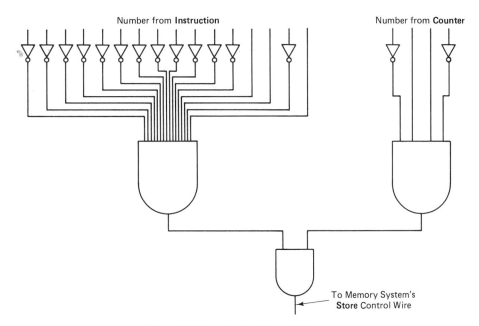

Figure 5.20 Control circuit for the **Store** wire.

Finally, the third AND gate puts out voltage only if the numbers in *both* **Counter** and the **Instruction** register are what we want. If we connect this output to the **Store** control wire, the wire will go on automatically at the correct times.

All of the other wires are controlled in exactly the same way.

The **Load Position** wire, for example, always goes on when **Counter** contains a 1. We have seen that it also goes on in step 4 of Instruction 12, JUMP-IF-ZERO-TO-POSITION, and in steps 4 and 5 of Instruction 9, LOAD-TOP-FROM-POSITION.

Of course, the wire goes on in steps of other instructions. The circuit to control it will be complex, but the idea of the design is still simple. We build a circuit for each individual situation—one that puts out voltage just when the counter contains a 1, one that puts out voltage just when the counter contains a 4 and the **Instruction** register contains a 12, and so on.

Then we connect all the separate outputs with a wide OR gate. The OR gate will put out voltage when we are at step 1 *or* when we are at the fourth step of Instruction 12 *or* whenever else the **Load Position** wire should be on.

If we connect the output of the OR gate to the **Load Position** wire, this wire, too, will be turned on and off automatically.

If we continue this way, building a control circuit for each control wire, we will end up with the **control network** pictured in Figure 5.21. This network, as we promised, takes in the numbers stored in **Counter** and the **Instruction** register and the voltage on the arithmetic-logic unit's **Zero** wire and puts out correct voltages over all the control wires.[7]

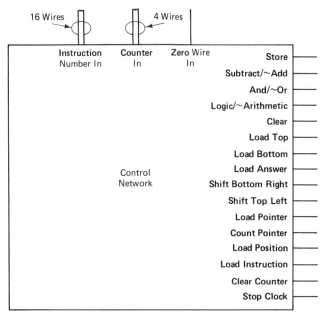

Figure 5.21 The control network.

---

[7] The **Zero** wire input is used to determine whether to send voltage to **Load Pointer** in step 6 of the JUMP-IF-ZERO-TO-POSITION instruction.

5.13 TAKING STOCK

The control network is the last link in the feedback loop we have been building. It takes information about the condition of the system and uses it to control the system.

With this step, our computer is complete.

Of course, the computer we have built is not up to the standards of what we can buy in a computer store for $100 or even less. In order to get the clearest idea of what a computer is, we have purposely left out nearly all of the conveniences that can make it easy to use.

It is as if we were to explain auto mechanics using a model of a car with no seats. Seats are not essential to the functioning of a car, but few people would buy a car without them. Chapter 12 will describe some of the features of real-life computers that are as convenient, comfortable, and common as seats in a car.

However, if our model computer is stripped down, make no mistake—even as it stands, it is an immensely powerful machine. Rather than outfitting it for comfort, we intend to take it out on the open road to see how it performs.

In a nutshell, we will continue to concentrate on essentials: what the machine is and what it can do. The chapters that follow, however, are as different from these first five as driving is from auto mechanics.

So far, we have studied the ideas that make it possible to *build* a computer. Nearly every page has referred to physical parts like transistors and arithmetic-logic units that we can walk into a store and buy.

As we connected these parts into more and more sophisticated circuits, we repeatedly took advantage of a mental ability we have called "chunking." Now that we have chunked transistors together into the almost unimaginably complex system we think of simply as a computer, it is time for another powerful mental maneuver: **abstraction**.

To abstract means to boil things down to essentials. It also means to consider an idea in general, rather than as it relates to a particular case.

We will do both. In the chapters that follow, we will consider the general idea of a computer, rather than the particular computer we have built. We will also boil this idea down to essentials.

A computer, as far as we are concerned from now on, is a machine that stores and processes an ordered list of numbers. It allows us to put in any numbers we like, manually, and then it processes them automatically.

For example, if the ordered list of numbers that we store manually is

0	34	1	43	5	13	0	14	
0	1	2	3	4	5	6	7	...

then the computer will process them automatically to get

77	34	1	43	5	13	0	14	
0	1	2	3	4	5	6	7	...

After five chapters of study, we understand quite a lot about this automatic process. We can say that the controller has loaded 34 into the **Top** register of the arithmetic-logic unit, has loaded 43 into the **Bottom** register, has had the unit add the two numbers, and has stored the result back in memory position 0.

If we like, we can go into much more detail. We can point out that the number 34 is actually represented in binary as 0000000000100010 and that this, in turn, is an interpretation of a pattern of voltages stored in flip-flops. We know that, to carry out an addition, the controller actually followed a multistep plan directed by a control network and timed by a clock.

We even know that the clock is an inconsistent feedback loop—an unstable circuit constructed by running the output of a NOT gate back into the gate's input. In fact, we can explain how the transistor inside the NOT gate causes it to reverse voltages, turning on to off and vice versa.

All this deep understanding, however, is not to the point. The questions we are about to consider apply to any machine that can process ordered lists of numbers in the manner we have discussed.

They apply to a computer built out of pipes and water valves that stores numbers as patterns of water pressures as well as to a mechanical computer made of gears and camshafts. They even apply to us, to human computers, so long as we simply process ordered lists of numbers accurately according to the same rules the other computers follow.

This is the power of abstraction. It gives us general answers that apply in many different, but related, situations.

What are these questions, then, to which we want general answers?

The first is a matter of levels. A computer, we know, is just a mass of carefully connected transistors and power supplies. But it would be next to impossible to understand such a complex transistor circuit. It is much easier to think of it as a circuit of interconnected logic gates.

This, we say, is a **higher-level** view of the organization.

The circuit is even easier to understand if we look at it at a much higher level, say, thinking of it as an interconnected memory system, arithmetic-logic unit, and controller.

At the highest level, so far, is our abstract picture of a list of numbers controlling the way the list itself is processed. At this level it is easy to see when two numbers will be added—something virtually impossible to tell from a circuit diagram marked with voltages.

On the other hand, even our highest-level view is still not very clear. Given a long program—say, an ordered list of a thousand numbers—figuring out the net effect of all the instructions would be a terrifically tedious project.

Our first question, then, is this: Is there an even higher-level way of understanding and controlling what a computer does?

This is an abstract question, but the answer is quite practical. If we can discover a high-level way of giving instructions to the computer, we will have an easier time getting it to do useful work.

A second question is also practical. Often, there are many different possible programs that will cause a computer to solve a problem. Sometimes a bad program will take a million years to get the same answer that a good one can get in minutes. We need some way to know about this before we set the computer running.

Since computer programs are just a way of expressing step-by-step methods for solving problems, we can ask our second question quite abstractly: Given any problem, which step-by-step method of solving it is the most efficient?

These two questions are large enough that an introduction to the answers fills up most of the rest of this book. But before we tackle them, we need to consider a more fundamental point: What problems can a computer solve? If we program it well enough and give it enough information, is there any limit to the questions it can answer?

We have already stated that computers can solve any problem, given step-by-step instructions for how to proceed. What we really want to know is this: Are there any problems so hard that we can never know how to solve them methodically?

This is a deep question, and it asks a great deal about human reasoning as well as about computer power. Surprisingly, the answer to the question is known. We will give it in the next chapter.

EXERCISES

5.1. In the memory picture given below,
  (a) What number is stored in memory position 4?
  (b) Is the number in memory position 0 an instruction? What about the one in Position 3?
  (c) After the controller carries out the instructions in this part of the memory, what will be stored in **Top**, **Bottom**, and **Answer**?

$$\frac{1}{0} \quad \frac{3}{1} \quad \frac{0}{2} \quad \frac{1}{3} \quad \frac{5}{4} \quad \cdots$$

5.2. Suppose the example of Section 5.4 is modified so that the computer begins with 5 stored in memory position 1. How will the memory look when the computer stops?

5.3. Suppose the example of Section 5.4 is modified so that the computer begins with 4 stored in memory position 6. How will the memory look when the computer stops?

5.4. The memory contains the numbers shown below when the computer begins its processing. How will the memory look when the computer stops?

$$\frac{9}{0} \quad \frac{8}{1} \quad \frac{1}{2} \quad \frac{4}{3} \quad \frac{5}{4} \quad \frac{13}{5} \quad \frac{3}{6} \quad \frac{14}{7} \quad \frac{11}{8} \quad \cdots$$

5.5. The memory contains the numbers shown below when the computer begins its processing. How will the memory look when the computer stops?

10	2	9	0	4	13	1	14	
0	1	2	3	4	5	6	7	...

5.6. The memory contains the numbers shown below when the computer begins its processing. How will the memory look when the computer stops?

0	5	1	6	5	13	0	9
0	1	2	3	4	5	6	7

0	1	7	5	13	1	14	
8	9	10	11	12	13	14	...

5.7. The memory contains the numbers shown below when the computer begins its processing. How will the memory look when the computer stops?

11	7	8	13	0	13	1	14	
0	1	2	3	4	5	6	7	...

5.8. Suppose we want the computer to subtract 34 from 98. How should the memory look when the computer begins? Where will the answer be when it is finished?

5.9. Suppose we want the computer to add 7, 4, and 13. How should the memory look when the computer begins? Where will the answer be when it is finished?

5.10. Suppose we want the computer to multiply 17 by 4. How should the memory look when the computer begins? Where will the answer be when it is finished? (*Hint:* Remember that multiplying a binary number by 4 is just the same as shifting it twice to the left.)

5.11. Describe in one sentence the effect of the following changes in the instructions discussed in Section 5.6:
  (a) The memory begins with 5 stored in Position 3 (instead of 1).
  (b) The memory begins with 4 stored in Position 4 (instead of 5).

5.12. Describe the effect of the following instructions:

11	4	13	1	11	0	
0	1	2	3	4	5	. . .

5.13. Translate the memory pictures given in Exercises 5.4, 5.5, and 5.6 into the form used in Figure 5.4.

5.14. The program in Figure 5.5 causes the computer to count from 0 to 16. Modify it so that the computer
   (a) Counts from 0 to 100
   (b) Counts from 6 to 16
   (c) Counts by fives from 0 to 200
   (d) Counts down from 10 to 1
   (e) Counts down from 200 to 0 by tens

5.15. Write a program to calculate 23 times 35. It should, first, store 0 in memory position 99 and, then, using a loop, increase the number in Position 99 by 23 thirty-five times.

5.16. Modify Figure 5.14 so that it shows the steps for the AND instruction.

5.17. Modify Figure 5.14 so that it shows the steps for the OR instruction.

5.18. Modify Figure 5.15 so that it shows the steps for the LOAD-BOTTOM-FROM-POSITION instruction.

5.19. Design the part of the control network that determines the voltage on the **Stop Clock** wire.

5.20. Modify Figure 5.14 so that it shows the steps for the CLEAR instruction. Then design the part of the control network that determines the voltage on the **Clear** wire.

5.21. As Figure 5.12 shows, a number emerging from the memory system is routed to four different places. For each of the paths, give one example of an instruction which uses it.

5.22. Look back at Figure 5.12 and give a complete list of instructions which
   (a) Use the connection between the arithmetic-logic unit's **Data-Out** wire and the memory system's **Data-In**
   (b) Use the connection between **Position-Out** and the memory system's **Name** wires
   (c) Turn on the multiplexer's **Data-Out/~Pointer** wire

5.23. What problems might arise if the controller's clock ticks too fast?

6 Programming and Unsolvability

6.1 PRACTICAL PROGRAMS

Now it is time to find out what we can do with the computer we have built.

As we have already said, it is not necessary to discuss transistors or memory cells or controller circuits when we tackle this question. As far as we are concerned, a computer is just a machine that processes a program, an ordered list of numbers.

In the first five chapters, we looked into *how* the machine does its processing. Now we want to know about the *effects* of the processing.

In fact, we are no longer asking about the computer so much as about the program. The machine only carries out instructions. What we want to know now is what the instructions can do.

Counting, we know, is one piece of practical work that boils down to following simple instructions. This is no great feat, of course, but, practically speaking, counting is quite important.

For example, suppose we have a list of the incomes of every United States citizen—a list of the sort the Internal Revenue Service might compile. We might want to use this list to find out how many people in the United States make more than $30,000 a year.

This is counting work. To perform it, we might write a computer program that checks each number in the list and counts up by 1 for every salary over $30,000. When it has finished checking all the numbers, it will have counted up to the number of people making more than $30,000.

The Internal Revenue Service is not the only government agency that undertakes immense counting jobs. In fact, one agency, the Census Bureau, is almost entirely concerned with this kind of work. Simple counting programs, not much different from the one we wrote in Chapter 5, are crucial to the bureau's functioning.

To see why computers are crucial, consider our income-list example again. A person who could look through 1,000 salaries every minute would still go through only about half a million in an eight-hour working day. Since there are about 100 million wage earners in the United States, checking all the incomes would take many months.

A computer, on the other hand, can count up to 100 million in a matter of minutes.

*   *   *   *   *

Counting is useful by itself, but it also forms the backbone of many other practical programs.

For example, suppose we have a list of instructions that make a computer add 5 to some position in memory. If we can get the computer to put 0 into this memory position and then carry out the "add 5" instructions 17 times, we will have multiplied 5 by 17. This is easy to do: Put the "add 5" instructions in the middle of a program loop that counts up to 17.

A similar approach allows us to divide. Suppose we have instructions that *subtract* 5 from some memory position. We can put 102, for example, into that position and then carry out the "subtract 5" instructions over and over, so long as the answer is not negative. If we arrange for the computer to count the subtractions as it performs them, it will tell us that exactly 20 are made before the answer is negative. This means that 102 ÷ 5 is 20. The remainder, 2, is left in the memory position that originally held 102.[1]

6.2 TOP-DOWN PROGRAMMING

These examples based on counting are only the merest beginning, of course. Before the end of this chapter, we will have considered some really intriguing programs— programs that truly put computer power to the test.

The first step toward these is a detailed look at a slightly more sophisticated example, a program to add up a list of numbers. Since it is often necessary to add up long lists of numbers and since people tend to make addition mistakes, this pro-

---

[1] These methods of multiplying and dividing get the right answer, but they are quite slow. Most computers are built with circuits that can multiply in one step. Others use a program that multiplies according to the method we discussed in Chapter 3, first getting several shifted rows of digits and then adding them. Virtually all computers divide according to the usual method taught in grade schools, although working in binary makes the process somewhat easier.

gram is quite useful. We study it, however, mainly to gain insight into the process of program writing.

As a first example of this kind of insight, take a moment to consider how easy it was for us to say what the program will do. It took just six words: "add up a list of numbers." This suggests an answer to a question we raised at the end of Chapter 5.

At the lowest level of a computer are the transistors. In theory, we can tell everything about what is happening in a computer if we know how the voltages are changing in each of the transistors. In practice, of course, it is easier to understand a computer in terms of what happens at a higher level, say, in terms of the voltages the controller circuit is receiving and sending out.

The highest level that we have considered so far is the program controlling the computer. In a sense, if we know the program, we know everything essential about what the computer is doing. At the end of Chapter 5, however, we wondered if there might be a still higher level for understanding and controlling a computer.

Now, as far as understanding is concerned, we have our answer.

The instruction numbers that make up a computer program are like words in a language, a language especially invented for explaining what the computer will do. But, as languages go, this one is extremely cumbersome. A better and higher-level language is plain English.

Most people take as little notice of the power of ordinary language as they do of the power of the place-value number system. But think, for a moment, how much information is contained in the single word *count*. It tells us just as much about what a computer is doing as a 5-instruction program.

Likewise, we are about to see how much information is contained in the six-word phrase *add up a list of numbers*.

Using English is nearly always the best way to explain and understand what we want a computer to do. It would be extremely convenient, then, if the computer could understand English. The question of how to raise a computer up to this higher level of understanding is a major topic, which we will take up in Chapters 10 and 13.

For now, however, the translation is up to us. In fact, this is the main work of programming. We know, in English, what we want the computer to do. Somehow we need to express the same idea in terms of computer instructions, to translate from a high-level to a lower-level language.

Our approach, roughly speaking, will be to work down one level at a time. We will begin by identifying the main tasks to be accomplished. Then we will break these into even smaller units of work. Eventually each unit will be a single, basic instruction and our translation will be complete.

This method of translating English into computer programs by describing tasks at lower and lower levels is called **top-down programming**.

6.3 ADDING A LIST

The first step downward from the top is to outline a general plan of attack. In rough form, the instructions for adding a list of numbers might look like this:

1. Keep a running total beginning at 0.

2. Go through the numbers in the list.

3. On coming to each number, add it to the total.

Notice that the phrase *add up a list of numbers* tells *what* we want to do. These instructions begin to say *how* we can do what we want.

We have a long way to go, however, before we will have instructions clear and simple enough for our computer. For one thing, we need to say what we mean by "the list." Obviously, it is a string of numbers stored in the computer's memory, but where does it begin and end?

Actually, we are free to choose where the list begins. Let us say the first number in the list is stored at Position 100, the second, at Position 101, and so on.

The other end of the list is slightly trickier. We cannot give the position of the last number, because we do not know how many numbers there are. We must have some way of marking the end of the list, however. Otherwise it would be impossible to tell when we had added the last number.

A simple solution is to use the number 0 as an endmarker. If the memory near Position 100 looks like this:

	51	65	17	44	0	32	
...	——	——	——	——	——	——	...
	99	100	101	102	103	104	

then the list contains just three numbers: 65, 17, and 44.

Now, here are the instructions again, at the next lower level:

1. Keep a running total beginning at 0.

2. Go through each of the numbers in memory from the one at Position 100 up to the first 0.

3. On coming to each number, add it to the total.

A "running total" is just a "total so far." In our example, the running total is 82 after the computer has added 65 and 17, but before it has added in 44. To keep a running total, then, the computer must simply remember a number. We will use Position 99 to store this number.

Our picture of the memory near Position 100 is now like this:

	Running total	First number	Second number	Third number	
...	——	——	——	——	...
	99	100	101	102	

Here is the next set of revised instructions:

1. Store a 0 at Position 99.

2. Go through each of the numbers in memory from the one at Position 100 up to the first 0.

3. On coming to each number, add it to the number at Position 99 and then store the result back at Position 99.

By now, steps 1 and 3 are very close to actual computer instructions. Step 2, however, is vague. How can the computer "go through" a list of numbers?

The answer is that we will use a **pointer**, just as we did in Chapter 5. There, the pointer was a register containing the position of the next number to be read from memory. Each time a number was read, we increased the pointer by one, so that it "pointed" to the next position in memory.

Here, the pointer will be just a number stored in the memory. It will begin at 100, to show that the first number in the list is at Position 100. When this number is added to the running total, we will increase the pointer by 1 to show that the next number to be added is at Position 101. When the number at Position 101 is added in, we will increase the pointer to 102, and so on.

The only tricky point about this new pointer is that we cannot yet say where in the memory it will be stored. Instead, we will have to give this storage position a temporary name: **Position-of-Pointer**. Here is a picture of how the pointer will look in the memory.

Pointer

· · · —————————————— · · ·

Position-of-Pointer

Notice that both the pointer and **Position-of-Pointer** are numbers. If **Position-of-Pointer** is, say, 37, then we should look in Position 37 to find the pointer. Suppose the number 105 is stored in Position 37. Then the pointer is 105.

Of course, if the pointer is 105, this number is not added to the running total. Instead, we look in *Position* 105 for the number to add. We say the pointer "points" to this number.

Using the pointer, we can further refine our outline. For clarity, we have added some comments in braces. These are not part of the outline being translated into a program, but they help us understand why it works.

1. Store a 0 at Position 99. {Start the running total at 0.}
2. Store 100 at **Position-of-Pointer**. {Start the pointer at 100, the position of the first number to be added.}

3. If the pointer now points to the number 0, then stop.
4. Otherwise, add the number to which the pointer is pointing to the number at Position 99 and store the result back at Position 99.
5. Increase the pointer by 1 and go back to step 3. {Change the pointer so that it points to the next number in the list.}

Notice that steps 3, 4 and 5 form a loop. After completing step 5, the computer is directed to go back to step 3. It will continue to carry out steps 3, 4, and 5 over and over, until it comes to the endmarker 0 in the list. Step 3 then causes the computer to stop.

Step 3 uses a number from the list—the one the pointer is pointing to—to decide what to do. Luckily, the decision is based on whether this number is zero, and so step 3 is perfectly compatible with our JUMP-IF-ZERO-TO-POSITION instruction.

On the other hand, JUMP-IF-ZERO-TO-POSITION looks only at the number in the **Answer** register of the arithmetic-logic unit. Therefore the first order of business in step 3 is to get the number the pointer is pointing to into the **Answer** register. The simplest way is to load it into the **Top** register and then add it to zero. The answer, which goes into the **Answer** register, will be the same as the original number.

If the number that ends up in **Answer** is zero, the program is supposed to stop. All we need, then, is a JUMP-IF-ZERO-TO-POSITION instruction that causes a jump to a STOP instruction. Here are the revised instructions:

1. Store a 0 at Position 99.   {Start the running total at 0.}
2. Store 100 at **Position-of-Pointer**.   {Start the pointer at 100, the
                                              position of the first number
                                              to be added.}

3. LOAD-TOP-FROM-POSITION pointer   {If the pointer now points
   LOAD-BOTTOM 0   to the number 0 then
   ADD   jump to a STOP instruction.}
   JUMP-IF-ZERO-TO-POSITION **Step 6**
4. Otherwise, add the number to which the
   pointer is pointing to the number at
   Position 99 and store the result back
   at Position 99.
5. Increase the pointer by 1 and   {Change the pointer so that it
   go back to step 3.   points to the next number in
                                              the list.}

6. STOP

Notice that we have introduced a new name, **Step 6**. When step 3 turns up the endmarker 0, we want the computer to jump to the STOP instruction, which will be represented as the instruction number 14, stored somewhere in memory. The problem is that we do not yet know where it will be stored. Temporarily, we call this unknown storage position **Step 6**.

To continue with our translation, consider step 4. Here, the computer is supposed to add a number in the list to the running total stored in Position 99. Fortunately, the number from the list is already in the **Top** register of the arithmetic-logic unit. We loaded it in as part of the work of step 3.

To perform the addition, then, we need only load the running total into **Bottom** and carry out the ADD instruction. The answer, the new running total, goes back into Position 99.

Here is the outline as it now stands:

1. Store a 0 at Position 99.   {Start the running total at 0.}
2. Store 100 at **Position-of-Pointer**.   {Start the pointer at 100, the
                                                      position of the first number
                                                      to be added.}

3. LOAD-TOP-FROM-POSITION pointer   {If the pointer now points
    LOAD-BOTTOM 0   to the number 0 then
    ADD   jump to a STOP instruction.}
    JUMP-IF-ZERO-TO-POSITION **Step 6**
4. LOAD-BOTTOM-FROM-POSITION 99   {Otherwise, add the number to which
    ADD   it points to the running total
    STORE-IN-POSITION 99   and store the sum back in memory
                                              as the new running total.}

5. Increase the pointer by 1 and   {Change the pointer so that it
    go back to step 3.   points to the next number in
                                              the list.}

6. STOP

By now, this is beginning to look like a program. Most of the main tasks of the original outline have been translated into basic instructions and the others are reduced to simple manipulations.

To finish, consider steps 1, 2, and 5.

The first asks us to store 0 in Position 99. To store any number, we first have to get it into the **Answer** register. In this case, all we need is a CLEAR instruction. This sets *all* the registers to 0. STORE-IN-POSITION 99 will put the 0 where we want it.

Step 2 calls for storing the number 100. To get 100 into **Answer**, we load it into **Top** and add. There is already a 0 in **Bottom** because of the CLEAR in step 1, and so the sum will be 100. STORE-IN-POSITION puts this 100 where we want it, in the memory location we have been calling **Position-of-Pointer**.

Finally, in step 5, we add 1 to a number in memory. This amounts to bringing the number into **Top**, putting 1 in **Bottom**, adding, and storing the answer back in the memory. To "go back to step 3," we simply use a JUMP-TO-POSITION instruction, although, again, we do not yet know where the instructions of this step will be stored in memory.

Here is the result:

1. CLEAR   {Start the running total at 0.}
    STORE-IN-POSITION 99
2. LOAD-TOP 100   {Start the pointer at 100, the
    ADD   position of the first number
    STORE-IN-POSITION **Position-of-Pointer** to be added.}

3. LOAD-TOP-FROM-POSITION pointer
   LOAD-BOTTOM 0
   ADD
   JUMP-IF-ZERO-TO-POSITION **Step 6**

{If the pointer now points
to the number 0 then
jump to a STOP instruction.}

4. LOAD-BOTTOM-FROM-POSITION 99
   ADD
   STORE-IN-POSITION 99

{Otherwise, add the number
to which it points to the
running total and store the
sum back in memory as the
new running total.}

5. LOAD-TOP-FROM-POSITION **Position-of-Pointer**
   LOAD-BOTTOM 1
   ADD
   STORE-IN-POSITION **Position-of-Pointer**
   JUMP-TO-POSITION **Step 3**
6. STOP

{Change the pointer so that it
points to the next list item . . .}

{. . . and go back to add it.}

The last detail of translation is to figure out what the temporary names **Step 3**, **Step 6**, and **Position-of-Pointer** stand for. Each of these is just a name for a position in the memory system. For example, **Step 3** is meant to be the position where the LOAD-TOP-FROM-POSITION instruction at the beginning of step 3 is stored.

Deciding what position that will be is now only a matter of counting. The CLEAR instruction is the first one in the program. It will be stored in Position 0. The following instruction, STORE-IN-POSITION, will be stored in the next higher storage location, Position 1. The 99 following this STORE-IN-POSITION will be in Position 2.

If we continue counting positions, we will eventually find that the LOAD-TOP-FROM-POSITION instruction at the beginning of step 3 is stored at Position 8. Thus **Step 3** stands for 8.

Checking the program again, we see that the very next memory position is the one that contains the pointer. Then **Position-of-Pointer** is Position 9.

Finally, counting all the way to the last instruction shows that the STOP instruction occupies Position 29. This, then, is our **Step 6**.

Here is the final translated program, with memory positions indicated at the left.

0 CLEAR   {Start the running total at 0.}
1 STORE-IN-POSITION 99

3 LOAD-TOP 100   {Start the pointer at 100, the
5 ADD   position of the first number
6 STORE-IN-POSITION 9   to be added.}
8 LOAD-TOP-FROM-POSITION —   {If the pointer now points
10 LOAD-BOTTOM 0   to the number 0 then
12 ADD   jump to a STOP instruction.}

13 JUMP-IF-ZERO-TO-POSITION 29

15 LOAD-BOTTOM-FROM-POSITION 99   {Otherwise, add the number to

17 ADD   which it points to the running

18 STORE-IN-POSITION 99   total and store the sum back in
memory as the new running
total.}

20 LOAD-TOP-FROM-POSITION 9   {Change the pointer so that it

22 LOAD-BOTTOM 1   points to the next number in

24 ADD   the list . . .}

25 STORE-IN-POSITION 9

27 JUMP-TO-POSITION 8   {. . . and go back to add it.}

29 STOP

Notice that we have left the pointer in Position 9 empty to start. The program begins by storing the number 100 in this position, so it does not matter what we put there.

We have reached the bottom level now. To use the program, we would still need to translate each instruction into its instruction number, but there is no question about how to do this.

6.4 SUBROUTINES

It has taken us a good deal of careful work to write a program to add up a list of numbers. To some people, programming may not seem worth the effort.

In fact, if we have a list of 50 numbers to add up, it is probably faster to use paper and pencil than a computer.

Keep in mind, though, that our program is designed so that it can add up a list of any length. Even if it takes hours to write the program, we will save time if our list contains, say, 100,000 numbers.

A second, even stronger point is that programs are rarely written to be used just once. If we plan to add up a list of 1,000 numbers every day for several years, spending one day writing a program is a kind of investment of time. It will pay off every day afterward when we use the computer instead of adding by hand.

This second point is especially important because *parts* of programs may be reused just as well as whole programs. This is another crucial insight into the nature of programming.

The list-adding program, for example, shows that we will often want to store a number in memory. This takes several steps, since, before the number can be stored, we need to get it into the arithmetic-logic unit's **Answer** register.

In general, here are the steps:

1. Put the number to be stored in **Top**.

2. Put 0 in **Bottom**.

3. Add, to get the number to be stored into **Answer**.

4. Store the number.

Translating into machine instructions, we get

> LOAD-TOP **Number**
> LOAD-BOTTOM 0
> ADD
> STORE-IN-POSITION **Position**

where **Number** is the number to be stored and **Position** is the position where it should be stored.

Figuring out how to store a number in memory is a little tricky. The point is, though, that we need to do the figuring only once. From now on, we can just *copy* these four instructions, thinking of them as a single unit for storing a number in the memory.

Using several instructions together as a unit is very much like combining transistors together into a logic gate. In both cases, it is easier to understand the function of the unit than the function of its parts. The unit is at a higher level than the parts that go into it.

Programming, it turns out, is often mainly a matter of collecting useful program parts and putting them together. A program is sometimes called a **routine**, since it puts the computer through its paces like a dancer in a dance routine. Program pieces, like the 4-instruction unit above, are called **subroutines**.

To demonstrate how subroutines can simplify programming, we will write a program which uses three of them. The first is the storing subroutine we have just completed.

The second is based on the fact that we will often want the computer to compare two numbers and *do* something if they are the same. The simplest approach is to subtract the numbers and then use JUMP-IF-ZERO-TO-POSITION. If the numbers are the same, the answer will be 0 and the computer will jump to a new part of the program. Here, we can write instructions for what to do when the numbers are the same.

This approach translates into four instructions:

> LOAD-TOP-FROM-POSITION **Position-of-First-Number**
> LOAD-BOTTOM-FROM-POSITION **Position-of-Second-Number**
> SUBTRACT
> JUMP-IF-ZERO-TO-POSITION **Where-to-Go-If-Same**

Again, now that we have written these instructions, we can use them any number of times. All we need to do is fill in the three position numbers.

Our third subroutine increases a number stored in the memory by 1. This will be useful any time a number in memory acts as a pointer holding the computer's place in a list.

The subroutine brings the pointer into the arithmetic-logic unit, adds 1, and then stores the answer back where the pointer came from. Here are the instructions:

> LOAD-TOP-FROM-POSITION **Position-of-Pointer**
> LOAD-BOTTOM 1
> ADD
> STORE-IN-POSITION **Position-of-Pointer**

6.5 A LETTER-SEARCHING PROGRAM

We will use these three subroutines to write a program that skims through text looking for a particular letter. For example, it might skim through this paragraph looking for a "c" and find that it appears for the first time in the middle of the word *particular*.

If it seems impossible for our computer to work with letters and words, check back in Section 3.10. We pointed out there that numbers can be used to represent nearly anything. In this case, we will let 1 stand for A, 2 for B, and so on. A partial table is given in Figure 6.1.

0 Space	10 J	20 T	30 ;
1 A	11 K	21 U	31 ?
2 B	12 L	22 V	32 -
3 C	13 M	23 W	33 :
4 D	14 N	24 X	.
5 E	15 O	25 Y	.
6 F	16 P	26 Z	.
7 G	17 Q	27 .	999 Endmarker
8 H	18 R	28 ,	
9 I	19 S	29 "	

Figure 6.1 Numbers for encoding text.

Notice that the table includes numbers to stand for punctuation marks like the period and quotation mark. The number 0 stands for a space between words. Finally, 999 is specially reserved to mark the end of the text.

The text the computer is supposed to skim through will be stored, then, as a list of numbers. Words will be separated by spaces, which in turn will be represented by 0s. The number 999 marks the end of the text to be searched.

We will store the text beginning in Position 101. Position 100 will contain the letter for which the computer is supposed to search. Here is an example of what the memory might look like:

1	9	0	1	13	27	999
100	101	102	103	104	105	106

The 1 in Position 100 means the computer should look for an A. The text runs from Position 101 to Position 105 and it reads: I AM. The 999 in Position 106 marks the end of the text.

We will also use three other memory positions for special purposes. Position 99 will be used to store individual letters taken from the text. Position 98 will contain 999.

As before, we will call the number that tells the computer where it is in the list the pointer. For example, the pointer will be 103 when the computer is checking the A in AM. This pointer, then, is just a number stored in memory. Since we cannot immediately say where it will be stored, we will call this third storage location **Position-of-Pointer**.

*   *   *   *   *

The general idea of the program is to look at letters from the text one at a time.

With each letter, the computer checks first to see whether it is the endmarker. If so, it must have gone through all the letters without finding the one it is searching for. In this case, it stops, leaving a special sign that the letter has not been found.

If the letter under scrutiny is *not* an endmarker, the computer checks whether it is the target letter, the one it is searching for. If so, it stops.

If the current letter is not an endmarker and it is not the target letter, the computer moves on to the next letter and checks it in the same fashion.

Here is an outline for the program:

1. Start the pointer at 101.

2. Take the number pointer points to and store it in Position 99.

3. Compare the numbers at Positions 98 and 99. If they are the same, go to step 7.

4. Compare the numbers at Positions 99 and 100. If they are the same, go to step 8.

5. Increase the pointer by 1.

6. Go back to step 2.

7. Set the pointer to 0.

8. Stop.

It is not easy to see why this outline corresponds to the plan we have laid out, so we will analyze it step by step. The pointer, as we have said, is supposed to be the position number of the current letter to be checked in the text. Since the text begins at Position 101, step 1 sets the pointer to 101.

Step 2 takes the letter to be scrutinized and puts it in Position 99. After this step, here is what the memory looks like near Position 99:

	999	letter taken from the text	letter we are looking for	
...	_____	_____	_____	...
	98	99	100	

Step 3 compares the numbers at Positions 98 and 99. That is, it checks to see whether the letter from the text is an endmarker. Likewise, step 4 checks to see if the letter from the text is the one the computer is looking for.

If the letter is neither an endmarker nor the target letter, steps 5 and 6 increase the pointer and send the computer back to step 2. This causes it to begin checking the *next* letter in text.

Steps 2 through 6 form a loop, then, and each time through the loop another letter in the text will be checked.

Eventually, the computer must come either to the letter it is looking for or to an endmarker. If it finds the target letter, it will be sent to step 8, where it will stop. Since the pointer is not changed, it will still point to the last letter checked.

If the computer comes to an endmarker, it will be sent to step 7. In this case, the pointer will be set to 0 before the computer stops.

The upshot is that when the computer stops, the pointer tells us the answer. If it is 0, the target letter has not been found. If the pointer is any number other than 0, the letter *has* been found and the pointer points to it.

*   *   *   *   *

Our program outline is easy to translate into instructions, because it has been designed with our subroutines in mind. Steps 1 and 7 call for the computer to store a number in memory. Steps 3 and 4 can make use of our compare-and-jump subroutine. Step 5 is tailor-made for the increase-pointer subroutine.

Using these subroutines, we get the following:

1. LOAD-TOP 101
   LOAD-BOTTOM 0
   ADD
   STORE-IN-POSITION **Position-of-Pointer**

2. Take the number the pointer is pointing to
   and store it in Position 99.

3. LOAD-TOP-FROM-POSITION 98
   LOAD-BOTTOM-FROM-POSITION 99
   SUBTRACT
   JUMP-IF-ZERO-TO-POSITION **Step 7**

4. LOAD-TOP-FROM-POSITION 99
   LOAD-BOTTOM-FROM-POSITION 100
   SUBTRACT
   JUMP-IF-ZERO-TO-POSITION **Step 8**

5. LOAD-TOP-FROM-POSITION **Position-of-Pointer**
   LOAD-BOTTOM 1
   ADD
   STORE-IN-POSITION **Position-of-Pointer**

6. Go back to step 2

      7. LOAD-TOP 0
          LOAD-BOTTOM 0
          ADD
          STORE-IN-POSITION **Position-of-Pointer**
      8. Stop.

The remaining steps are not difficult to translate.

    Step 6 clearly amounts to a JUMP-TO-POSITION instruction. Step 8 translates to STOP. For step 2, we can use a modified version of our storing subroutine. We simply substitute LOAD-TOP-FROM-POSITION for LOAD-TOP.

    Here is the program as it now stands. Notice that we have added position numbers in the left-hand column to show where each instruction will be stored.

    1.   0   LOAD-TOP 101
         2   LOAD-BOTTOM 0
         4   ADD
         5   STORE-IN-POSITION **Position-of-Pointer**

    2.   7   LOAD-TOP-FROM-POSITION pointer
         9   LOAD-BOTTOM 0
       11   ADD
       12   STORE-IN-POSITION 99

    3. 14   LOAD-TOP-FROM-POSITION 98
       16   LOAD-BOTTOM-FROM-POSITION 99
       18   SUBTRACT
       19   JUMP-IF-ZERO-TO-POSITION **Step 7**

    4. 21   LOAD-TOP-FROM-POSITION 99
       23   LOAD-BOTTOM-FROM-POSITION 100
       25   SUBTRACT
       26   JUMP-IF-ZERO-TO-POSITION **Step 8**

    5. 28   LOAD-TOP-FROM-POSITION **Position-of-Pointer**
       30   LOAD-BOTTOM 1
       32   ADD
       33   STORE-IN-POSITION **Position-of-Pointer**

    6. 35   JUMP-TO-POSITION **Step 2**

    7. 37   LOAD-TOP 0
       39   LOAD-BOTTOM 0
       41   ADD
       42   STORE-IN-POSITION **Position-of-Pointer**

    8. 44   STOP

The column of position numbers makes it easy to determine that **Step 2** stands for 7, **Step 7** for 37, and **Step 8** for 44. Also, the pointer is stored just after the LOAD-TOP-FROM-POSITION instruction of step 2. Therefore **Position-of-Pointer** must be Position 8.

Substituting these position numbers for the temporary names used in this latest listing of the program is the last task of the translation. Note that it does not matter what number is originally stored in Position 8. This position holds the pointer, which will be set to 101 in step 1.

6.6 SELF-ANALYSIS . . .

Our letter-searching example shows how easy it is to program with subroutines. Once we have an outline, translating to instructions is mainly a matter of copying.

Moreover, the program is of considerable interest in itself. For one thing, it is flexible. It can look through a text of any length. And by changing the number stored in Position 100, we can make it search for any letter.

Also, the text begins at Position 101 only because step 1 of our program sets the pointer to 101. If we modify the program very slightly, so that it begins by setting the pointer to 167, it will begin taking letters from *that* position.

To see why this might be useful, suppose the text to be searched is a book of poetry by Samuel Taylor Coleridge and we want to find the poem that begins

In Xanadu did Kubla Khan
A stately pleasure dome decree.

Assuming that the text has been stored in the computer beginning at Position 101, we can use our program to search through it looking for an X. Suppose the first X is found at Position 2,718. We manually check the next few positions to see whether we have found the word *Xanadu*.

If not, we modify the program so that it looks for an X beginning at Position 2,719. Continuing in this way, we will eventually find the word *Xanadu*, which marks the beginning of the poem.

Of course, an even better idea would be to make this process automatic by writing a more sophisticated program. The program would look for the letter X and then check to see whether the next five letters are a, n, a, d, and u. If so, it would stop. Otherwise it would move the pointer forward and begin searching for the next X.[2]

*   *   *   *   *

These examples show why the letter-searching program is useful in performing the work for which it was designed. But the program is actually more than a letter searcher. In fact, it searches through a list not of letters, but of numbers.

---

[2] Notice that this word-searching program would use the letter-searching program as a subroutine. This is a good example of how small pieces can be used to build large, powerful programs.

Of course, if the numbers stand for letters, we may as well say the program is looking through text. But the program will work just as well if the numbers have a different meaning.

If we have a list of salaries and we want to find the first one that is exactly $27,408, all we need to do is put the list in the computer beginning at Position 101 and store 27,408 in Position 100. Of course, we will still need to put the number 999 at the end of the list to serve as an endmarker.

Likewise, if we have a long computer program and we want to know whether it ever uses the SHIFT-TOP-LEFT instruction (Instruction 3 from the list of instructions in Section 5.5), our searching program can help. We put the program into the computer as a list of numbers, beginning at Position 101, and store the number 3 in Position 100.

If the number 3 never appears in the program, then Instruction 3, SHIFT-TOP-LEFT, is not used.[3]

It appears that our letter-searcher is also something that sounds nearly impossible—it is a program-analyzing program.

The fact that this *is* possible spotlights the two ways we have been using numbers stored in the memory. In the letter-searching example, the numbers stored in the first part of the memory were used as a program, instructions for the computer. Numbers stored near Position 100 were used as **data**, information for the program to use.

Our program-analyzing program is possible because all numbers are stored in the computer in exactly the same way. The same numbers that would control the computer, if they were put into the memory beginning in Position 0, are used as data by the analyzing program if they are put into memory beginning at Position 101.

This raises a peculiar question. Can the same numbers in memory be used *both* as instructions and as data?

For example, what about the program-analyzing program? Can it use itself as data? Can a program analyze itself?

6.7 . . . AND SELF-REFERENCE

The answer is yes.

Suppose we take our searching program and put it into memory beginning at Position 0. When we set the computer on automatic, this program will cause it to look through a list of numbers beginning at Position 101.

The program itself, however, is just a list of numbers. There is nothing to stop us from using this list again at Position 101, so long as we add an endmarker.

In other words, we can put one copy of the searching program into the memory beginning at Position 0 and another one into memory beginning at Position 101. The first copy will serve as instructions for the computer, telling it to look

---

[3] It is quite possible, of course, that the number 3 will be found even though the program does not use SHIFT-TOP-LEFT. It might contain the instruction LOAD-TOP 3, for example.

through a list. The second copy is the list to be scanned. But since the copies are the same, the program, in essence, will be looking through itself.

If we store a 3 in Position 100 and set the computer running, a moment later it will have stopped. Position 8, the pointer, will contain a 0. This means that the number 3 is not in the list.

In effect, the program is saying that it has analyzed itself and found that it does not contain a SHIFT-TOP-LEFT instruction.

*   *   *   *   *

A still easier way to have the searching program analyze itself is to use the modification we suggested earlier to change where the list begins.

As the program stands, it starts by setting the pointer to 101. When the program begins its search, it looks first at the number in Position 101. Then it increases the pointer to 102, looks at the number in *that* position, and so on. This, as we have said, is why the list begins at Position 101.

We have already considered the effect of setting the pointer forward to 167 or 2,719. But what about setting it backward?

Suppose the first step of the program set the pointer to 0. The program would begin its search with the number at Position 0. Then it would increase the pointer to 1 and look at the number in Position 1, and so on.

But think for a moment about what is stored in these memory positions. Oddly enough, the program would be looking at some of its own instructions—in fact, the very instructions that cause the computer to do this looking.

It is as if you were to turn your eyes inside out to have a look at your brain.

*   *   *   *   *

We have pointed out that the instruction numbers in a program are like words in a language. A program, then, is a statement expressing some kind of meaning.

A self-analyzing program is a peculiar kind of statement, but it is not unlike certain statements we can make in English. For example, the following is a self-analyzing sentence:

This sentence contains exactly four C's.

Statements of this kind are special members of a much larger class: those that refer to themselves. Statements in the larger class are said to use **self-reference**. Here are some examples:

This sentence is the first example.
This is a silly sentence, absolutely without purpose, and too long, to boot.
I am a much more serious sentence than the last one.

Each sentence talks about itself in some way.

As these example show, self-reference leads easily to word games. It can be put to more serious uses, however. In fact, strange as it may seem, self-reference is at the core of two of the most amazing discoveries of the twentieth century. One of these relates to computers, although its importance is far broader. It will be our subject for the remainder of this chapter.[4]

6.8 A STOP-ANALYZER

What we are about to study is called the **halting problem**. The problem is simply to find a systematic way of deciding whether computer programs will stop.

Our first counting program, for example, went on giving the computer instructions forever. So long as power is supplied, the computer keeps on counting.

By contrast, our second program controlled the computer for a fraction of a second—just long enough to count to 16—and then stopped the controller's clock.

These short programs are easy to analyze. The first counting program does not stop because it contains a loop of instructions and no way to get out of the loop. The second also contains a loop, but we can see that it will go through the loop only 16 times.

With long programs, however, analysis is much stickier. There may be many instruction loops or loops within loops. Sometimes it may be difficult to tell how many times the instructions in a loop will be executed.

By now, though, we are used to dealing with complexity. After our success with Boolean algebra and circuit design, it seems clear how to proceed. What we need is a system that begins by analyzing simple programs and then uses the results to build up to the analysis of harder ones. All we want is a step-by-step, sure-fire method for deciding whether a program will stop.

In fact, since any step-by-step method can be translated into a computer program, what we really want is a computer program that can analyze other computer programs to see whether they will stop. We will call this program a stop-analyzer.

Before we begin to talk about designing such a program, we should take a moment to stress its tremendous importance.

For one thing, as a purely practical matter, it is crucial to know whether programs will stop. Computers cost money, and as a result, it costs money to use them.

Suppose we write a program to solve an important problem. We set the computer running, but after three weeks, it still has not finished executing the program. Should we turn the machine off? If we do, we will have wasted three weeks of valuable computer time. If we do not, the computer may run for another three weeks or more.

A key consideration in our decision is this: Will the program *ever* be completed? This is an obvious use for our stop-analyzer.

A second practical point is that programs are difficult to write. In general, a programmer's first attempt contains errors which must be corrected.

---

[4] The other is a mathematical result, which is explained in an excellent, easy-to-read book called *Godel's Proof*, by Ernest Nagel and James R. Newman (New York University Press, 1958).

This suggests another important use for the stop-analyzer. A programmer could use it to test rough drafts of a program. Assuming the program is not meant to run forever, the stop-analyzer should indicate that it will stop. If it does not, the programmer would immediately know that there are errors to correct.

*   *   *   *   *

These examples show why it is useful to know whether a program will stop. But a stop-analyzer's *unexpected* power lies in its ability to answer other questions.

Consider an odd property of the number 6. The only numbers that divide it evenly, leaving no remainder, are 1, 2, and 3. But 1 + 2 + 3 is 6. The numbers that divide 6 evenly add up to 6. We can call numbers with this property **perfect numbers**.

Are there any other perfect numbers? In fact, there is a systematic way to check.

We begin with 7. The only number that divides 7 evenly is 1. But 1 does not add up to 7, so we move on to 8. The numbers that divide 8 evenly are 1, 2, and 4. But these add up to 7, so we move on to 9.

Continuing in this way, we will eventually find that 28 is a perfect number— it is 1 + 2 + 4 + 7 + 14.

If we check the next few hundred numbers past 28, however, we will not find any perfect numbers. Is there a perfect number larger than 28? Here is where our stop-analyzer comes in handy.

Since we know a systematic way to look for perfect numbers, we can write a program to look for them. Here is an outline of the program:

1. Let 29 be called the **Number-We-Are-Checking**.
2. Find all the numbers that divide this evenly.
3. If these add up to the **Number-We-Are-Checking**, go to step 6.
4. Add 1 to the **Number-We-Are-Checking**.
5. Go back to step 2.
6. Stop.

This outline contains a loop, steps 2 through 5. Each time through the loop, a different number is checked to see whether it is perfect. If a perfect number is found in step 3, the program jumps to step 6 and stops. On the other hand, if no number larger than 28 is perfect, the program will go on checking numbers forever.

The question *Is there a perfect number larger than 28?* can be as frustrating as a program that is still running after three weeks. Suppose we check all the numbers up to 400 and none of them is perfect. Should we keep checking? Maybe 401 is perfect. Or maybe we will check the next 400 numbers without finding a perfect one.

Luckily, we no longer have to worry about the original question. It is enough to know whether the checking program we just outlined will ever stop. If the program stops, that must be because there is a perfect number larger than 28; if it runs forever, there is no such number. The stop-analyzer can tell us whether the checking program will stop. Thus we can use it to find out whether there are any perfect numbers larger than 28.

This is why a stop-analyzer is so useful. Many questions that have nothing to do with computers amount to asking whether a certain program will ever stop.

Seeing how to answer our question about perfect numbers is like finding a nugget lying on top of a gold mine. Once we have the idea of this approach, the possibilities are, quite literally, endless.

6.9 UNSOLVABILITY

The stop-analyzing program, it turns out, is an amazingly powerful and versatile tool. Unfortunately, it does not exist. In fact, it will never be designed.

The halting problem cannot be solved.

Many people misunderstand this statement when they hear it for the first time, especially people who know something about programming. This is because programmers *can* often tell whether a complicated program will stop.

If a program appears to run forever, programmers have ways of tracing the effects of the instructions. They can often work backward to the source of the problem, like a sleuth following clues.

To an experienced programmer, it seems that these methods must always, eventually, lead to a solution. And, in fact, good programmers can analyze most programs they come across. Problems arise when the programmer tries to write down *systematic rules* for analyzing programs—rules that will *always* work.

Thinking of rules is easy.

For example, one might be to check for any instructions causing a backward jump. This is easy to do systematically with the help of our searching program. If no such jump instructions are used, we can say definitely that the program will stop.

However, if a program does include backward jumps, this does not necessarily mean that it runs forever. Our second counting program jumped backward, but it stopped almost immediately. The first rule, by itself, is not sufficient.

We can always add a second rule. But we will soon find an example of a program it does not help us with.

Now we can see what it means to say that the halting problem cannot be solved. No matter how many rules we add, there will always be exceptional programs that the rules do not cover.

Think again about our program that looks for perfect numbers larger than 28. Deciding whether it will stop is the same as figuring out the answer to a hard question of mathematics.

The point is, we can turn an infinite variety of other mathematical questions into similar programs. A stop-analyzer that could tell whether any given program will stop could also answer *all* of these mathematical questions. The same goes for a human programmer.

A programmer might, perhaps, aspire to this kind of almost magical genius. For the stop-analyzer, however, it is positively impossible.

6.10 THE HALTING PROBLEM PROOF

We have claimed that the halting problem is unsolvable. Now we will prove the claim.

As we mentioned in Section 6.7, the argument hinges on self-reference. In particular, it depends on inconsistent self-reference of a kind we studied in Chapter 2.

We looked then at a sentence called the Epimenides paradox: This sentence is false. The sentence is self-referential because it makes a statement about itself. It is inconsistent because there is no way to decide whether the statement is correct.

If the statement is true, then we must believe its claim that it is false. This is impossible because we are calling the sentence both true and false.

If the statement is false, then we must not believe its claim. The sentence claims to be false, but we must believe it is true. This is impossible, again, because we are calling the sentence both false and true.

Either way we reason, we reach a contradiction.

For our halting problem proof we are going to consider designing an inconsistent self-referential computer program that is like a translation of the Epimenides paradox. The outline of the program can be stated in a single sentence: This program will stop only if it will not stop.

There is an important difference, however, between the Epimenides paradox and any supposedly paradoxical program. We can never decide whether the paradoxical sentence is true. But we *can* decide about any program. All we need to do is load it into a computer and set the computer running.

When we do, there are only two possible results: Either it stops or it does not. In either case, the program has not done what it is supposed to do.

What we have just said is enough to show that a paradoxical program is impossible to write. If someone claims to have written it, we can always test the program and, whether it stops or not, we will have proved the claim wrong.

The last link in the proof is that a stop-analyzer—any stop analyzer—is just what we need to build a paradoxical program. That is, we will show that, if any stop-analyzing program could be written, we could easily modify it to get another program that stops only if it does not stop.

Since this second program is impossible, it must also be impossible to create the stop-analyzer.

This is the general idea of the proof. Now we turn to the details.

$$* \qquad * \qquad * \qquad * \qquad *$$

Suppose that, after years of work, a programmer has developed what appears to be a working stop-analyzer. It has been tested thousands of times and it has never failed to say correctly whether a given program will stop. The programmer calls the stop-analyzing program STOPTEST.

Since we have said stop-analyzers are impossible, it is up to us to prove STOPTEST a fraud.

STOPTEST must have *some* way of giving us an answer. For example, it might put a 1 in Position 123 of the memory if it concludes that the program it is analyzing will stop and a 0 in that position if it believes the program will run forever.

Since it does not matter to us how STOPTEST reports its answer, we may as well assume that this is the method. To repeat,

1 in Position 123 means YES, the program under analysis will stop.

0 in Position 123 means NO, the program under analysis will not stop.

We will use STOPTEST as a subroutine to write a slightly larger program. Here is the outline of our program:

1. Use STOPTEST to analyze the program stored in the memory beginning at Position 0.

2. If the number in Position 123 is 1, go to step 4.

3. Stop.

4. Go to step 4.

It is a very easy job to translate this outline into a working program.

Step 1 is just a matter of copying STOPTEST and making sure that it begins its analysis at the correct position. Step 2 is a kind of comparison-and-jump, like the subroutine we used in our letter-searching program. Step 3 translates to STOP, and step 4 translates to a JUMP-TO-POSITION instruction.

We will call our program PARADOX.

When we have translated PARADOX into instructions, we put it into the memory beginning at Position 0. Also, we put an endmarker after the last instruction. Then we set the computer running.

In step 1, PARADOX uses STOPTEST to analyze the program beginning at memory position 0. But the program beginning at that position is PARADOX itself.

Here we have our self-reference. PARADOX is using itself as data. It is performing a self-analysis to see whether it will stop, according to STOPTEST.

At the end of step 1, STOPTEST will have an answer. We have no way to know what answer it will give, so we will consider both possibilities.

Case 1. Suppose that, in step 1, STOPTEST decides PARADOX will stop. To report its answer, STOPTEST puts a 1 in Position 123.

In step 2, PARADOX checks the number at Position 123. Since it is a 1, it jumps to step 4.

But now PARADOX is stuck in a loop. Step 4 is a JUMP-TO-POSITION instruction. After it has been executed, the computer will be back at step 4. The computer is jumping in place; each time it completes the JUMP-TO-POSITION instruction it begins again with the same instruction. This means PARADOX will not stop.

It appears that, if STOPTEST says PARADOX will stop, it will be wrong. If it says so, PARADOX will run forever.

Case 2. STOPTEST must give an answer about PARADOX. If it says PARADOX will stop, we have seen, it will be giving the wrong answer. But, it will also be wrong if it says PARADOX will run forever.

In this case, step 1 of PARADOX will put a 0 in memory position 123. Step 2 will check this number, but, since it is not 1, the computer will not jump to step 4.

Instead, it will come to step 3 and stop.

*   *   *   *   *

It appears that STOPTEST cannot give a correct answer about PARADOX. If it says PARADOX will stop, PARADOX uses that information to decide to run forever. If it says PARADOX will run forever, PARADOX outsmarts it by stopping.

STOPTEST is claimed to be able to tell correctly whether any program will stop. But it cannot tell correctly whether PARADOX will stop. Therefore it is a fraud, just as we said it must be.

Any other would-be stop-analyzer can be debunked in the same manner. The upshot is that it must be impossible to build a stop-analyzer that always works correctly.

To see the argument in terms of inconsistency, consider this: The PARADOX program stops only if the stop-analyzer says it will not stop. If the stop-analyzer is always correct, then PARADOX stops only if it does not stop.

But we know paradoxical programs like this cannot be written. Therefore, correct stop-analyzers must not exist.

6.11 THE LIMITS OF METHOD

Most of our modern science and technology is built up on a foundation of method. Careful techniques of analysis and step-by-step, logical reasoning have given us tremendous knowledge and power — knowledge of everything from particles smaller than atoms to the great forces of the universe; power to build rockets, skyscrapers, and computers.

In fact, science and technology have gone so far that we tend to take it for granted that they rest on a solid foundation. We like to assume that any purely technical problem will eventually yield to the force of systematic thinking.

This is why the halting problem is so disturbing. It is a crack in the foundation — a problem systematic thinking cannot solve.

Of course, this is not the same as saying that people cannot solve the halting problem. It is possible that we have some kind of thinking power that goes beyond step-by-step reasoning. The point remains, however, that the thinking which has taken us so far will not help in this case.

If we attempt to write a stop-analyzing program, we are doomed to failure. It is not a matter of hard work or brilliant research. No matter how much we improve our program, it will always give some wrong answers.

Since a stop-analyzer would be extremely useful, this is disappointing. But why call the halting problem a "crack in the foundation"? It appears to be very much like the Epimenides paradox, just an interesting freak of self-reference.

Unfortunately, the computer halting problem is only the beginning of a long list of problems that step-by-step methods cannot solve.

For one thing, any system that can be used as a computer presents its own kind of halting problem.

It is possible to build a mechanical computer out of gears, rods, and a motor, for example. This means that there is no foolproof, step-by-step method for analyzing any machine and deciding if it will cause itself to stop.

It seems impossible. Any hookup of gears and rods works according to simple mechanical rules. Given time, we ought to be able to use these rules to figure out what the gears and rods will do. The fact is, though, that sometimes we cannot. Using rules to look at a problem leaves us with a blind spot.

*   *   *   *   *

Our list of unsolvable problems begins, then, with halting problems for various systems. It continues with other questions we cannot answer about programs.

For example, there is no surefire, never-fail method for deciding whether two programs do the same work.

It is not even possible, in general, to tell whether a program does the work it was designed to do. Of course, in many practical situations, we *can* check a program to see that it will function properly. Also, even if we cannot prove that it will always do what we want, we can usually *test* it so thoroughly that there is little room left for doubt.

The fact is, however, any method we develop for checking programs will always miss some that contain errors.

It takes a good deal of complicated reasoning to show that a computer cannot solve problems of this sort. But the idea behind the reasoning is simple.

It turns out that, if we could design a computer program to solve either problem, we could use it to build a stop-analyzer. Since stop-analyzers do not exist, we can say the same about programs to answer these other questions.

6.12 THE POST CORRESPONDENCE PROBLEM

So far, all the unsolvable problems on our list have something directly to do with computers. We can also add items that relate to computers only very indirectly.

For example, look at the four cards pictured in Figure 6.2. Suppose we have as many copies of each card as we like. Then we may lay out five cards as pictured in Figure 6.3.

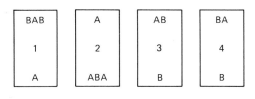

Figure 6.2 Cards for a Post correspondence puzzle.

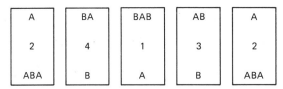

Figure 6.3 A "match" for the puzzle.

Notice that the letters across the top read A-BA-BAB-AB-A or ABABA-BABA. The letters across the bottom read ABA-B-A-B-ABA or ABABABABA. With this way of laying out the cards, the "word" spelled out across the top is the same as the one spelled out across the bottom.

This is called a **match**.

This kind of puzzle was invented by the logician Emil Post. The Post correspondence problem is this: Find a systematic way to decide, given certain cards, whether it is possible to find a match.

Before we say anything further about this problem, try out the two examples in Figure 6.4. If we want to work these puzzles out systematically, a good first question is how to begin. Naturally, when we find a match, the leftmost card will have the same first letter at the top and bottom. Otherwise the words spelled out along the top and bottom will not match at the beginning.

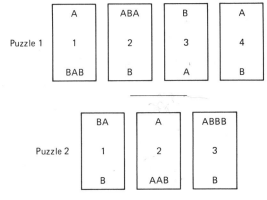

Figure 6.4 Two Post correspondence puzzles.

This immediately tells us there can be no match for puzzle 1. None of the four cards can serve as the leftmost.

As a first step toward solving the Post correspondence problem, we have invented a simple rule: If none of the cards have the same first letter at the top and bottom, there can be no match. This rule, however, tells us nothing about puzzle 2. Here cards 1 and 2 might both serve as the beginning of a match.

After a certain amount of reasoning and guesswork, we will find that this puzzle does have a match: If we lay out the cards in the order 2-2-1-3, they will spell AABAABBB on both top and bottom.

Having solved this puzzle, we may well be able to write additional rules to help us determine whether a set of cards has a match. In fact, with experience, we could write a long list of rules that would apply to thousands of puzzles.

The point, though, is that no list of rules would ever be complete. Either the rules would sometimes give us the wrong answer, or else there would be puzzles to which they would give us no answer at all.

Even such a simple kind of puzzle as the Post correspondence problem is too hard for a computer. In fact, as we have been saying all along, even a human expert cannot hope to be able to solve all such problems, unless with the aid of some power beyond methodical reasoning.

The Post correspondence problem is unsolvable because it is related to the halting problem. In fact, given a systematic way to find a match for any set of cards, we could decide systematically whether any program would stop.

The proof of this fact is complicated, but, again, the idea is simple.

Given any program, we can design special cards with information about the state of the computer written at the top and bottom. If we lay the cards out, the information across the top and bottom will spell out what happens to the computer as the program runs.

A match, in this case, would give us a complete picture of how the program proceeds, from start to finish. But this kind of complete picture is possible only if the program stops. On the other hand, if there is no match, no complete picture is possible. That is, the program will never stop.

A solution to the Post correspondence problem, then, would give us a systematic way to solve the halting problem. Since we know the halting problem is unsolvable, the Post correspondence problem must be also.

6.13 TAKING STOCK

A computer is a machine for carrying out simple instructions quickly and accurately. At the beginning of this chapter, we showed how these instructions could be combined into powerful, practical programs.

Later in the chapter we showed that the power of a computer can be turned inward. A program can be used as a lightning-fast way to analyze other programs, even to analyze itself.

This power of self-reference turns out to cause problems, however. In general, powerful languages that allow self-reference can be used to create paradoxes. Eventually we showed that, in the case of the computer, these paradoxes lead to the PARADOX program, a program impossible to design.

This, in turn, was enough to show that a particular, practical program—the stop-analyzer—is also impossible to design.

Finally, as the last part of the chapter has shown, the stop-analyzer is not alone. A remarkable variety of questions cannot be answered by methodical study. The halting problem is a serious crack, not only in the foundation of computer science, but in the foundation of systematic inquiry in general. It applies equally to computers and to many kinds of human reasoning.

Our main point is that the computer's powers are limited, possibly even that our own powers are limited. There are questions too hard to approach methodically, self-analyses too deep to undertake step by step.

Fortunately, however, the limited horizon bounds a domain which is still quite vast and curious. If computer power is not infinite, we must turn our attention to using it intelligently. This is the next subject we will take up.

EXERCISES

6.1. Modify the final version of the program developed in Section 6.3 so that

   (a) -1 marks the end of the list instead of 0.

   (b) The final answer will be in memory position 0 when the program stops.

   (c) The program does not use the CLEAR instruction.

6.2. How would it affect the program in Section 6.3 if the instruction at Position 22 were LOAD-BOTTOM 2? What if it were LOAD-BOTTOM -1?

6.3. Write a program to add up a list of numbers stored in memory positions 101 through 150, some of which may be zeros. Notice that, in this case, we know there are exactly 50 numbers to be added. It is not necessary to use a number in Position 151 as an endmarker. In fact, it is not possible to use an endmarker, since any number we choose to use as a marker might coincidentally appear in the list of numbers to be added. (*Hint*: Use a loop that counts from 101 to 150 and then stops.)

6.4. Write a general subroutine to subtract 3 from a number in memory position **Position-of-Number** and then store the answer back in this same position.

6.5. Write a general subroutine to check whether the number in memory position **Position-of-Number** is negative and to go to **Where-to-Go-Otherwise** if the number is *not* negative. (*Hint*: See Section 4.15 for an explanation of how to check whether a number is negative.)

6.6. Use the subroutines developed in Section 6.4 to store 7 in Position 32, store 8 in Position 35, increase the number at Position 32 by 1, and then jump to Position 99 if the numbers at Positions 32 and 35 are the same.

6.7. The program developed in Section 6.5 looks for a letter in a given text. Show how to set up the memory near Position 100 if we want the program to look for an "x" in the sentence *Put the sax in the box*. After the program is finished, what will the pointer be?

6.8. Modify the letter-searching program of Section 6.5 so that

   (a) It searches through text beginning in Position 150.

   (b) It leaves -1 in **Pointer**, instead of 0, if the given letter is not found.

   (c) It always looks for an A.

6.9. Write four self-referential sentences. Try to make them as different as possible, both from each other and from the examples given in the chapter.

6.10. The question *Is there a perfect number larger than 28?* boils down to asking whether a certain computer program will ever stop. Give another example of such a question, along with a rough outline for the corresponding program.

6.11. The program PARADOX uses STOPTEST. When PARADOX runs, is STOPTEST used as data, as instructions, or both? Explain your answer.

6.12. Is it possible to build a quasi stop-analyzer—one that always correctly gives one of the three answers *Yes, the program under analysis will stop*, *No, the program under analysis will not stop* or *I don't know*? If it *is* possible, explain how; otherwise, explain why not.

6.13. Suppose someone claims to have designed a nonstop stop-analyzer. This analyzer never makes a mistake, according to the claim. If it tells us the program under analysis will stop or will not stop, it is always correct. The only catch is that the analyzer itself is not guaranteed to stop. Sometimes we may have to wait years for an answer. Sometimes we may wait years and still not get an answer. Is it possible to prove this program a fraud by using it to build a PARADOX-type program? *Is* the program a fraud? Explain your answers.

6.14. In Section 6.10, we assumed it would be possible to modify STOPTEST to make it analyze the program beginning at Position 0. But what if this is not possible? Suppose STOPTEST always analyzes whatever program is stored beginning at Position 2000. Is it still possible to prove the program a fraud by constructing a PARADOX-type program? If so, how? If not, why not?

6.15. Find a match for the two Post correspondence puzzles shown.

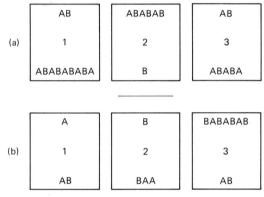

6.16. Design as difficult a Post correspondence puzzle as possible, using no more than four cards. The puzzle must have at least one possible match.

6.17. There is no match for either of the Post correspondence puzzles in the accompanying figure. Explain why.

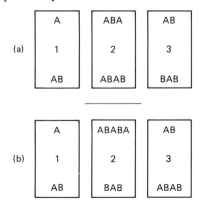

6.18. Exercises 6.15 and 6.17 call for you to solve Post correspondence puzzles. Assuming you can get the answers, does this prove that people can solve the Post correspondence problem? Does it contradict our statement that the problem is unsolvable? Explain your answer.

7 Searching and Sorting

7.1 EFFICIENCY

Computers process information. In particular, they perform simple operations on numbers stored in a memory system. Numbers are shifted, added, and moved from one position to another.

As simple as this may sound, it is all we need for an incredible variety of practical tasks. Information of nearly every kind may be represented with strings of numbers, and in this form, a few basic operations suffice to manipulate it.

In fact, the 15 instructions built into our model computer are enough to carry out *any* information processing work that may be reduced to a step-by-step procedure. In terms of what it can do, our computer is as powerful as any other that has been or will be built. It is limited only by the amount of information its rather small memory will hold.

Real working computers may use hundreds of basic instructions, instead of the 15 of our model. But these additional operations are nearly as simple-minded as those we have studied.

The fact is, no matter how large a computer gets, it always takes small steps. If computers work quickly, it is because of the amazing speed with which these steps are completed. A computer which can carry out 1 million basic operations in a second is not at all unusual.

With such small steps, however, 1 million basic operations often amounts to very little useful work. It is easy to find large or complex problems that would take a computer a century or more to solve, even operating at ten million or 100 million operations per second. Raw speed simply may not do the trick.

Instead, in many cases, it pays to *save* work, rather than just to do it faster. A clever, efficient approach may be worth more than brute computational force.

*   *   *   *   *

In the case of information processing, there are two main ways to gain efficiency. As an illustration, consider the monthly billing of a large law office.

One way the office manager can cut down on work is to simplify the *procedure* by which bills are sent out. Clerks perform a complicated series of steps—calculating, photocopying, and filling out forms—before each bill is mailed. If steps can be cut out or combined, a great deal of time may be saved.

The second main potential for efficiency is in the *organization* of information stored in the office. For example, since much of the billing work consists of looking up who owes what, it is extremely important to make that information easy to find. A better filing system is an important step toward streamlining the billing.

In general, all information processing tasks break down the same way. One part of the problem is finding a procedure that gets results in as few steps as possible. The other part is organizing the information to make the steps themselves easier to carry out.

As you would expect, how information is organized affects how it may be used. These two parts are rarely independent. In this chapter, we concentrate on problem-solving procedures—**algorithms**, as computer scientists call them. In the next, we will stress creative ways of organizing information. At many points, however, we will have to consider both together.

Our real focus throughout is on the spectacular results we can get by analyzing different approaches to a problem. Advertising campaigns have trained us to measure savings in percentage terms, a 50-percent-off sale being about the best we can hope for. We are about to discover efficiency savings so great, however, that percentages cannot measure them. With the right approach, we can eliminate nearly *all* of our work.

7.2 MEASURING AN ALGORITHM

As a first example, we will look a little more deeply into the problem we solved in Chapter 6—searching a list. The program we developed there was designed to skim through text looking for a letter, but we quickly realized it was more generally useful.

In fact, the program embodies a procedure or algorithm for finding a number in a list. Stripped of technicalities, here is the algorithm:

1. Consider the first number in the list.

2. If the number under consideration is the one wanted, report its position and stop.

3. Otherwise, move on to consider the number in the next position.

4. If this position is past the end of the list, report that the number was not found and stop.

5. Otherwise, go back to step 2.

In essence, the algorithm simply calls for the computer to check each of the numbers in the list, one at a time, to see if it is the one we are looking for.

We are beginning to concern ourselves with efficiency, so it is natural to ask now whether the algorithm can be improved. But before we talk of improvements, we need to have some idea of how good the algorithm is as it stands.

A good algorithm is one which takes as little time as possible to carry out. How long does ours take?

To make the question more specific, suppose we have a complete list of telephone numbers used in the United States. We want to know whether the number 936-771-1419 is in use. This is clearly the same as asking whether it is on the list.

Assume, now, that the number is *not* in use. In this case, the computer will check each of the numbers on the list before telling us that it cannot find 936-771-1419. There are well over 100 million phones in the United States, so this algorithm causes the computer to check more than 100 million numbers.

Exactly how fast a computer can look through numbers in a list depends on the make and model. But we will estimate that a fast computer can check 1 million numbers every second. At that rate, the computer would take about 100 seconds to tell us that 936-771-1419 is not in use.

This is not too long, by human standards. In most cases, we are willing to wait a minute and a half to get a piece of information. On the other hand, at this rate, the computer can check at most 864 numbers a day. This is less than the number of new telephones installed on an average day in the United States.

*   *   *   *   *

Now we have both a reason and a basis for finding improved algorithms. Looking one by one through all the numbers in a list may not be efficient enough for some purposes. How can we streamline the process?

One obvious idea is to have the computer search for more than one number at a time. For example, as it goes through the list, it could check each item against *two* target numbers, that is, numbers we are searching for. One pass through the list would give us the answer to two questions. This would appear to cut the work in half.

But does it?

Unfortunately, the answer is not simple. Our original algorithm makes twice as many passes through the list. On the other hand, it does less work on each pass. Each list item needs to be compared with only a single target number. Which is better, two easy passes or one harder one?

In fact, it is impossible for us to say which algorithm will take more time. To do so, we would need to know not only how each would be translated into instructions, but how long the individual instructions take to carry out. Since different computers use different instructions and work more or less quickly, our answer will depend on characteristics of the machine.

The real problem is in our way of assessing algorithms. Certainly, we want an algorithm that will take less time. But we cannot be *precise* about how long an algorithm will take without detailed information about the computer that carries it out. And details of the machine are exactly what we are trying to abstract away. We want to study the procedure alone, apart from any consideration of the computer with which it might be used.

The solution is to sidestep the question of time and, instead, to use a measure of the amount of *work* an algorithm requires the computer to do. Normally, of course, we may assume that less work means less time.

In the case of the telephone number problem, it is reasonable to say that the heart of any algorithm is the step in which the target number is compared with a number in the list. We will use the comparison, then, as our unit of work. The measure of any searching algorithm will be the number of comparisons it calls for.

Of course, this is not the only measure we could use. In fact, it is sometimes misleading. We will see, however, that it is precise enough to lead us to an algorithm that is good by nearly any standard.

Here, then, is how our search algorithms measure up when working on the telephone number list.

The original algorithm compares a target number with each of the 100 million numbers in the list, assuming the target is not in use. If we use it twice, to search for two different numbers, it will make a total of 200 million comparisons in two passes through the list, assuming, again, that the numbers are not in use.

The improved, check-two-numbers-at-a-time algorithm makes just one pass through the list to search for the same two numbers. Each number that it comes to in the list, however, must be compared with *both* target numbers. This algorithm, then, makes two comparisons for each of 100 million list items—200 million comparisons in all.

In terms of our new measure of work, the algorithms are comparable. We gain nothing by checking more than one number at a time.

*   *   *   *   *

The problem with both algorithms is that they call for checking every number in a 100-million-item list. An entirely different approach is based on the idea that it may not always be necessary to use the list at all.

Instead, suppose we keep a separate list of *area codes* which are in use. Since there are only 1,000 possible area codes, this list can never get very long.

Given the number 936-771-1419, the computer would first check this shorter list to see whether there are any telephone numbers at all in the 936 area. If not, it could tell us that 936-771-1419 is not being used after only 1,000 comparisons. This would be a tremendous saving of work.

Unfortunately, if the 936 area code *is* in use, this new algorithm might still need to compare the number it is looking for against all 100 million numbers in the main list.

This brings up another tricky point about comparing algorithms. Some do well only under special circumstances. For example, the algorithm we are discussing will do well if many of the numbers to be checked are from unused area codes.

In general, however, when we choose an algorithm, we will want it to perform well all the time. To be conservative, we will measure the work it does in the worst possible circumstances.[1] Again, this **worst-case analysis** is not the only way to compare two algorithms. But we will find it serves our purposes.

According to this way of measuring, the area code algorithm is even less efficient than our original one.

The unimproved algorithm makes at most 100 million comparisons per number checked. The new algorithm might look through the entire area code list before finding that the area code is in use. That is, at worst, it might make up to 1,000 *extra* comparisons before having to make 100 million comparisons with numbers on the main list.

7.3 A DEAD END AND A FRESH START

So far, we have made no progress. At worst, all of our searching algorithms will make at least 100 million comparisons before telling us that a telephone number is not in use.

In fact, we can show that *any* correct algorithm will in the worst case make at least this many comparisons. The argument is like the one we made against the possibility of a stop-analyzer. We suppose someone claims to have invented an algorithm that makes fewer than 100 million comparisons and then we set to work proving it a fraud.

For example, suppose someone tells us about an algorithm that makes only 50 million comparisons in checking whether a number is in the telephone list. We can prove it is a fraud by making at most two tests.

For the first test, we pick an unused telephone number and follow the steps of the algorithm. As we go along, we notice which numbers in the list are compared with the target.

Eventually, the algorithm will tell us whether this number is used or not. Since we are purposely testing an unused number, it had better tell us this number is not in the list. Otherwise, we can say immediately that the algorithm does not work.

Assuming the algorithm passes this first test, we conduct a second.

In the first test, the algorithm has compared the target number with at most 50 million numbers on the list. This means there are at least 50 million more which it has ignored. In particular, suppose we are looking for the number 936-771-1419 and we know it to be out of use and the algorithm has not compared this

---

[1] In fact, we have been considering the worst case all along, since we have calculated the number of comparisons which would be made in looking for a number which is *not* in the list. If the number happens to be in the list in the very first position, our original algorithm will find it using just one comparison.

with the fourth number on the list. Then, for the second test, we change the fourth number in the list to 936-771-1419 and use the algorithm to search again for this same number.

But if we follow the steps of the same algorithm, it will work precisely as it has already. The fact that the fourth number in the list is changed cannot affect an algorithm that never checks this number. Exactly the same comparisons will be made as in the first test, and the algorithm will lead us to the same conclusion, that 936-771-1419 is not in the list.

This time, however, the answer is wrong.

Of course, any algorithm that makes only 50 million comparisons can be tripped up in just the same way. Two tests are always enough to prove that it does not work correctly.

In fact, this kind of argument applies even to an algorithm that never makes more than 99,999,999 comparisons. We can fool it by changing the one number on the list which the algorithm ignores. Common sense leads us to the same conclusion: If we want to be sure that a telephone number is not on a list, we had better check every number in the list. If we check only half the list or three-quarters or even 99 percent, we will always be leaving some chance of error.

In the worst case, any algorithm to look for a number in a list will have to compare the number with every entry in the list.

*   *   *   *   *

This is not the end of the line, however. If it were, we would be in serious trouble.

Consider the number of names in an ordinary telephone book—perhaps there will be 100,000. An average person using a telephone book might be able to look through roughly 500 names in a minute. At that rate, we should expect that it would take about three hours to look up a number.

In fact, of course, we can usually look up a number in less than a minute. The obvious reason is that, since the names are in alphabetical order, it is not necessary to check every name in the book.

This is an excellent example of how the right system for organizing information can save time. If we find the entries

Lytwyn Alvin   94 Edison Road   362-456-1414
Lyzcen Nancy   24 Ardsaw Lane   182-987-1095

on page 277, we can be sure Kevin Lyver is not listed—even if we never check any of the other pages. If Kevin were listed, the alphabetical ordering guarantees we would find him between Alvin and Nancy.

We have said that any algorithm to find a number in a list must check each item in the list. This is true in general, when we know nothing about the organization of the list. If the list is ordered, however, we can find a much better way.

7.4 BINARY SEARCH

Suppose, for example, that our list of 100 million telephone numbers is in numerical order. The list begins with numbers close to 000-000-0000 and ends with numbers close to 999-999-9999. The number 936-771-1419, which we have been using as an example, will be near the end.

A natural way to begin searching for a number is to look roughly in the middle of the list. Suppose the number at this middle position is lower than the number we are looking for. Then the target number must be in the second half of the list, if it is in the list at all.

In this case, we can ignore the first half of the list. Notice that, with this one comparison, we have eliminated the necessity of checking 50 million numbers.

Now we need to search through the 50 million numbers in the second half of the original list. We look in the middle of this shorter list. Suppose the number at the middle position is too high. Then all the numbers after it must be too high also. We can ignore the second half of this shorter list. This leaves a list of 25 million numbers.

These first two steps are pictured in Figure 7.1.

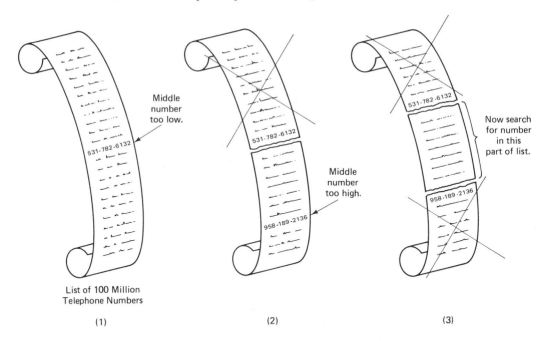

Figure 7.1 Searching for 936-771-1419

As the picture shows, two comparisons are enough to eliminate 75 million numbers from the list. If the number we are looking for is on the list at all, it is one of the 25 million remaining numbers.

How many comparisons will we need to find the number or to see that it is not in use?

The answer is easy, as soon as we notice what is happening to the list. Each time we make a comparison, we cut the list in half. Checking the middle number is enough to tell us whether the number we are looking for is in the top or bottom half of the list. Either way, the other half may be eliminated.

Our first comparison cuts the list down from 100 million to 50 million numbers. The second cuts it down from 50 million to 25 million. Figure 7.2 shows the effect of the following comparisons. The figure shows that, after 25 comparisons, the list will contain only two numbers. Either the number we are looking for is one of these two, or else it is not in the original list.

After this many comparisons	This many numbers will remain to be searched	After this many comparisons	This many numbers will remain to be searched
1	50,000,000	14	6,103
2	25,000,000	15	3,051
3	12,500,000	16	1,525
4	6,250,000	17	712
5	3,125,000	18	356
6	1,562,500	19	178
7	781,250	20	89
8	390,625	21	44
9	195,312	22	22
10	97,656	23	11
11	48,828	24	5
12	24,414	25	2
13	12,207		

Figure 7.2 Effect of comparisons.

It takes two comparisons to check our number against these last two. Therefore the total number of comparisons in the worst case is 27.

*   *   *   *   *

Our original searching algorithm worked through the list in a straight line, checking each number from beginning to end. For this reason, it is usually called **linear search**.

The new algorithm we have just developed is called **binary search**. As we have pointed out, the bi in binary means two. Binary search works by repeatedly breaking a list into two parts.

In a moment, we will see an even closer connection between binary search and binary numbers. For now, though, take time to appreciate the superiority of the new algorithm.

Earlier, we estimated that a computer might take 100 seconds to use linear search to look through a list of 100 million numbers. At this rate, the computer would be making 1 million comparisons every second.

Since our new algorithm makes only 27 comparisons to look up a number, 1 million comparisons would be enough for it to look up more than 37,000 numbers.

With linear search, the computer could look up fewer than 1,000 numbers in 24 hours of constant work. With binary search, it can look up more than 40 times as many in a single second.[2]

*   *   *   *   *

We have promised savings so great that they cannot be measured by fixed percentages. So far, we have cut the cost of looking through a certain list down from 100 million comparisons to just 27. This is a huge saving—99.999973 percent—but it is still a definite percentage.

The amazing fact about binary search, however, is that, the longer the list we use it with, the more it saves.

For example, if we start with a list of just three numbers, binary search may make as many as two comparisons. As Figure 7.3 shows, we begin by comparing the number in the middle with the one we are looking for. If we are lucky, this may be the one we want. But in the worst case, we will still need to check one other number.

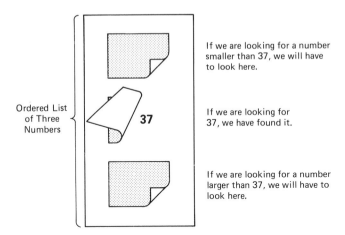

Ordered List of Three Numbers

If we are looking for a number smaller than 37, we will have to look here.

If we are looking for 37, we have found it.

If we are looking for a number larger than 37, we will have to look here.

Figure 7.3 First step in a binary search of three numbers.

Of course, we will never need to check all three. If the middle number is too low, we can ignore the one above it, since it must be even lower. If the middle number is too high, we can ignore the one below it.

In the worst case, then, a binary search of a list of three numbers takes two comparisons.

Now consider searching through a list of seven numbers. The first step is to check the middle number. If we are lucky, this will be the one we are looking for. But even if it is not, this first comparison leaves us only three numbers to check.

[2] This comparison is somewhat unfair, since binary search requires us to start with an ordered list. We are temporarily ignoring the work it takes to put the list in order.

For example, suppose the list is as in Figure 7.4. If we are looking for 73, we have found it in one comparison. If we are looking for a number smaller than 73, we need to check the list of three numbers above 73. If we are looking for a number larger than 73, we need to check the list of three numbers below.

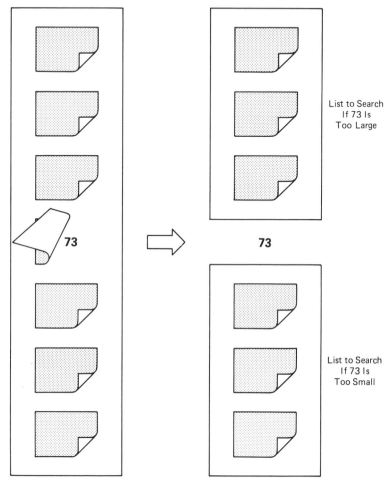

Figure 7.4 A list of seven is two lists of three and an extra number.

As the figure shows, a list of seven items is like two lists of three with an extra item in between. After a single comparison to check the middle number, we will be left with a list of three numbers to search.

But we already know it takes two comparisons to search a list of three items. In all, then, in the worst case, it takes three comparisons to search a list of seven items.

Now it is easy to see how to continue. A list of 15 numbers is like two lists of seven with an extra number in between. After one comparison, to check the middle number, we will be left with a list of seven numbers. We already know that it may take three comparisons to search this list. Thus, in all, it may take four comparisons to search a list of 15 numbers.

If we analyze a few longer lists this way, we may compile a table like the one shown in Figure 7.5.

Number of items in the list	Number of comparisons necessary for a binary search
3	2
7	3
15	4
31	5
63	6

Figure 7.5 Number of comparisons for a binary search.

The numbers in the lefthand column form a pattern. Each is one more than double the number before it, since we use two lists of the same length with an extra number in between. The pattern is even clearer if we convert the numbers in this column to binary. They are 11, 111, 1111, 11111, and 111111.

This simple pattern is no coincidence. Doubling a number is the same as multiplying it by 2. In binary, multiplying by two, or binary 10, is the same as adding a 0 at the end. For example, if we double 111, we get 1110. Adding 1 gives 1111. Thus, in binary, doubling a number and adding 1 is the same as adding a 1 at the right end of the number.

Now consider again what Figure 7.5 tells us. It takes four comparisons to search a list of 1111 numbers, five to look through a list of 11111 numbers, and so on. The number of comparisons is the same as the number of digits, so long as we write the length of the list in binary.

The upshot is that binary search is as efficient at looking through lists as the binary number system is efficient at representing numbers.

If a number takes nine digits to write in binary, a number twice as large does not take twice as many. It takes only ten digits to write. Likewise, if binary search requires nine comparisons to search a certain list, it does not take twice as many to search a list twice as long. It takes only ten comparisons.

By contrast, linear search *does* take twice as many comparisons to look through a list that is twice as long. This is why percentages are not enough to show how much better binary search is than linear search. The longer the list, the farther linear search falls behind.

The chart in Figure 7.6 shows the details. We can get virtually any percentage saving we like, just by comparing the two algorithms on a long enough list.

Number of items in list	Number of comparisons for a linear search	Number of comparisons for a binary search	Comparisons saved using binary search
100	100	7	93.00%
1,000	1,000	10	99.00%
10,000	10,000	14	99.86%
100,000	100,000	17	99.98%

Figure 7.6 Binary and linear search compared.

The superiority of binary search over linear search goes beyond percentages. The difference is in how each algorithm performs when the problem gets tougher.

Linear search does an amount of work directly related to the length of the list it is searching. Any algorithm of this sort—one for which the amount of work grows as fast as the problem—is called a **linear** algorithm.

By contrast, binary search does an amount of work that is related to how many *digits* it takes to write down the length of the list.

Roughly speaking, the number of digits it takes to write a number is called the **logarithm** of that number. For example, it takes seven digits to write the number 85 in binary. Therefore the logarithm of 85 is approximately seven.

We say "approximately," because we have not given the exact definition of a logarithm.[3] For our purposes, however, the approximate answer given by counting digits is good enough.

Binary search, then, does an amount of work that grows only as fast as the logarithm of the size of the problem. This makes it one of a class of algorithms termed **logarithmic**.

7.5 LINEAR VERSUS LOGARITHMIC

Back in Section 7.2, we said it would not matter if our measure of work was somewhat inaccurate. Now we can show why.

First, consider the details of the binary search algorithm. Our version will use three markers called **Low**, **High**, and **Middle**. These markers can be placed next to any number in the list to be searched.

High and **Low** mark off the part of the list that still remains to be searched. If the target number is in the list at all, then at any stage of our search it will be between the markers. After each comparison, half the list is eliminated and the markers are moved closer together.

In effect, **High** and **Low** are like walls closing in on the target number. If the number is in the list, eventually it will be in the middle position between **High** and **Low**. If the walls pass each other without catching the target number, it must not be in the list and the search should stop.

Here is an outline of the algorithm:

BINARY SEARCH

1. Put **Low** next to the first number in the list.
2. Put **High** next to the last number in the list.
3. Put **Middle** next to the number midway between **Low** and **High** (or as close to the middle as possible).

---

[3] The logarithm of 85 is actually closer to 6.4. If we put 2 to the power 6.4 on a pocket calculator, we will find that the answer is very close to 85. The power that would give exactly 85 is the logarithm of 85. Incidentally, notice that the number of digits it takes to write a number depends on the base of the number system used. In this book we use only *base-2* logarithms, since computer arithmetic and algorithms depend so heavily on binary.

4. Compare the number marked by **Middle** with the target number and
   (a) If it is the same, say that the number has been found and stop.
   (b) If it is smaller, move **Low** to the next number after **Middle** and go on to step 5.
   (c) If it is larger, move **High** to the number just before **Middle** and go on to step 5.

5. If **High** is now above **Low**, say that the number is not in the list and stop; otherwise go back to step 3.

Figure 7.7 shows the algorithm in action on a list of 15 numbers.

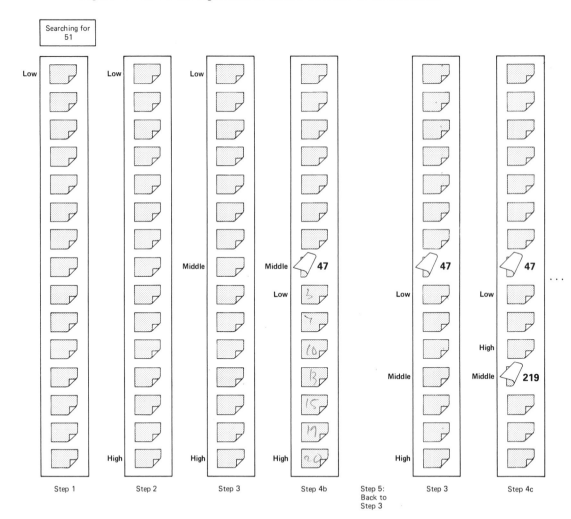

Figure 7.7 Applying the binary search algorithm.

As the figure shows, binary search does much more than make comparisons. The algorithm is more sophisticated than the linear search algorithm we outlined in Section 7.2. It would be harder to translate into a program and would almost certainly use more instructions. Even the comparison step is complex. In linear search, a comparison determined only whether two numbers were the same. Here, if they are not the same, it must also say which is larger.

All this might seem to suggest that measuring work by counting comparisons may be misleading. Both linear search and binary search go through a loop of steps each time they check a number, that is, each time a comparison is made. However, binary search may do much more work each time through the loop.

It may be that if linear search makes a certain number of comparisons and binary search makes many fewer, the linear algorithm will still be faster.

In fact, however, our measure of work is not misleading at all. Logarithmic algorithms are so much better than linear algorithms that a rough measure like counting comparisons is quite good enough. Once we see that binary search is logarithmic, it does not matter if each loop of steps takes 10, 50, or even *100* times longer than a loop of steps in linear search.

In fact, just to make the point stronger, we can analyze this last case. Suppose we find out that each comparison step in binary search really does take 100 times as long as a comparison step in linear search. Then if it takes one unit of time per comparison for linear search, it takes 100 units for binary search. In this case, Figure 7.8 shows how many units of time each algorithm will take to look for an unused number in lists of various lengths.

Number of items in list	Number of comparisons		Units of time	
	Linear search	Binary search	Linear search	Binary search
3	3	2	3	200
31	31	5	31	500
255	255	8	255	800
1,023	1,023	10	1,023	1,000
4,095	4,095	12	4,095	1,200
1,000,000	1,000,000	20	1,000,000	2,000
100,000,000	100,000,000	27	100,000,000	2,700

Figure 7.8 A handicap race between binary search and linear search.

The figure shows that linear search is faster than binary search for short lists, assuming binary search really takes 100 times as long for each comparison step. But, even with this tremendous handicap, binary search wins out for longer lists.

As the list grows, the time for a binary search increases according to the number of digits in the length of the list. This number changes very slowly.

In our hypothetical case, with a list of about 1,000 numbers, linear and binary search would take about the same amount of time. But for longer lists, binary search would be better. And for lists as long as our complete directory of telephone numbers, binary search would win by a huge percentage amount—it would take 99.9973 percent less time than linear search.

Of course, this example is exaggerated. A loop of steps in binary search would not really take 100 times as long as a loop of steps in linear search. In practice, binary search is superior even for very short lists.

Our point is simply that it does not matter how much more complicated binary search may be. Even if each of its comparison steps should require a thousand or a million times as much work, binary search would beat linear search for long lists.

This is just another way of saying that percentages cannot measure the difference between logarithmic and linear algorithms. Even if the linear algorithm is 50 percent or 99.99 percent faster on each loop, on a large enough problem the logarithmic algorithm will do so few loops that it will win.

7.6 EFFICIENCY VERSUS SPEED

This huge difference between algorithms can give us a good perspective on advances in computer operating speeds.

We have said several times that a fairly fast computer can do about 1 million operations per second. This was, in fact, the case in 1986 when these words were written. Computer technology progresses so quickly, however, that today's computers are probably substantially faster.

At this moment, a computer may be whizzing through 100 million or even 1 billion instructions every second. If it is not possible today, it will be soon.

These advances are breathtaking for anyone who works with computers. If today's computers are 10 times faster, work that used to take a year can be done in a little more than a month. If they are 100 times faster, work that took a year can now be finished in less than four days.

It is important to keep in mind, however, that these technology breakthroughs are only a matter of percentages. A computer that goes 10 times faster cuts working time by 90 percent; one that goes 100 times faster cuts it by 99 percent.

To the general public, percentages like these are overwhelmingly impressive. We are in a position to see, however, that faster computers may not be nearly as important as better algorithms. We know it is possible to go beyond percentage improvements.

Imagine, for example, a computer so slow that it can do only one loop of the binary search algorithm every second. Since binary search needs only 27 comparisons to comb a list of 100 million items, this computer could still find a number in our telephone number list in 27 seconds.

We have seen that, using linear search, a computer working almost 1 million times as fast would take 100 seconds to look through the same list—4 times longer.

Of course, a good algorithm works even better with a fast computer. Computing speed and algorithmic efficiency both help when we tackle difficult problems. The telephone number problem shows, however, that speed may be the less important of the two.

Perhaps the best example of what we are discussing is the human brain. Although we are far from understanding the details of how it operates, it is clear that the brain is built with components that are pitifully slow compared with transistors.

Apparently, it is the ingenious way these components are used that makes our thinking so fast. For many tasks, no computer can match it. What we are mainly lacking in the struggle to make computers as powerful as brains is, not the machinery, but the algorithms.

7.7 SELECTION SORTING

Binary search is of major importance because of the way computers are used. Of course, computers have an infinite number of applications, but many of these depend on an ability to store a massive quantity of information and then look through it quickly for some particular number or fact.

Binary search works, however, only when the information has been organized into an ordered list. This makes the problem of **sorting**—putting items in order— another major question for computer scientists.

We can start to consider the problem by looking at how we would ordinarily attack it. Suppose we are faced with a tall stack of, say, exam papers which must be sorted alphabetically according to students' last names. A natural first step toward sorting the papers is to lay them out in piles: papers from students with last names beginning with A, papers from students with last names beginning with B, and so on.

Usually, each of these piles will be small enough to sort easily. If not, the next step is to break the A pile into smaller piles, one each for every possible *second* letter in the last name.

The method works well in this case. One reason is that names tend to be fairly short. If we are extremely unlucky, when we go through the stack the first time, all the names might start with A. This means we would end up with only one pile—no better off than when we started. But, since most names are less than ten letters long, we cannot be unlucky this way more than ten times.

If names ran to a thousand letters long, the pile method might lead us into serious trouble.

An even more serious problem is that the method depends on our ability to pick names apart letter by letter. In general, we would like to be able to put items in order, given only an ability to compare any two and say which is bigger.

Consider, for example, the ten boxes in Figure 7.9. It is easy to compare any two boxes and see which is taller, and so we should be able to put the boxes in size

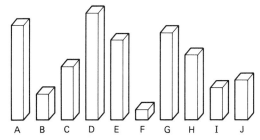

Figure 7.9 Boxes to be arranged in size order.

order. But we cannot break these heights up into components like the letters in a name. The pile method simply does not apply.

The upshot is that we need another approach.

One method that *would* work to put the boxes in order is just to repeatedly pick out the tallest box. That is, we find the tallest box and set it aside. Then we find the tallest remaining box—the second-tallest of the original ten—and set it down just to the left of the one we have previously removed. The tallest box remaining now is the third-tallest of the original ten. We remove it and set it down to the left of the two tallest boxes.

If we continue in this way, we will eventually end up with a row of boxes in size order.

This approach translates easily to a general method for sorting items in a list. Here is the outline of an algorithm we will call **selection sort**.

SELECTION SORT

1. Call the original list **Old** and start another list called **New**.

2. Remove the largest item in **Old**.

3. Put it at the top of **New**.

4. If **Old** is empty, stop; otherwise go back to step 2.

Notice that steps 2 through 4 create a loop. Each time through the loop, the algorithm instructs us to find the largest item remaining in the original list and put it at the top of a new list, just above all the larger items that have already been placed there. The algorithm finishes when all the items of the original list have been moved to the new list. At this point, the new list will be a sorted version of the original.

Figure 7.10 shows the first few steps of selection sort as it orders a list of ten numbers.

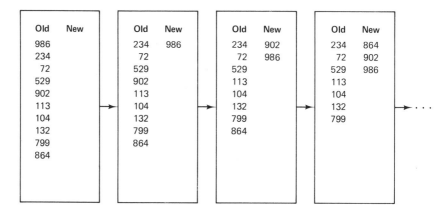

Figure 7.10 Selection sort of a list of numbers.

Actually, the outline for selection sort is incomplete, since we have not given detailed instructions for finding the largest item in a list. But before we go to work patching it up, take time to notice the algorithm's generality. We have said nothing at all about what kinds of items might be in the list.

If the items are numbers, the word *largest* in the algorithm has its usual meaning. But if the items are names, we can still use the algorithm to sort them. The "largest" name is the one that is last in alphabetical order. If the items are coins from around the world, the "largest" might be the one that is worth the most.

So long as we have a way to compare any two items, to say which is larger, we can always find the largest item in a list. In this case we can use selection sort.

*   *   *   *   *

To complete our description of selection sort, we need to give a step-by-step method for finding the largest element in a list.

A natural approach is simply to look through the list, always remembering the largest item so far. As we proceed, we ignore any items smaller than the one we are remembering. If we find an item larger than the one we are remembering, this new item is now the largest. We remember it and continue looking down the list.

When we reach the end of the list, the largest item so far—the one we are remembering—is the largest in the entire list.

Here is the outline of an algorithm that works this way. It uses a marker called **Largest** to mark the "largest item encountered so far."

1. Place the **Largest** marker next to the first item and look at the second item.

2. If this item is larger than the one marked by **Largest**, move the marker next to it.

3. If there are no more items in the list, stop; otherwise, look at the next item and go back to step 2.

When this algorithm begins, it places the **Largest** marker next to the first item. Since that item is the only one that has been encountered, it is automatically the largest so far. Each time the algorithm finds a larger item than the largest so far, it moves the **Largest** marker. When it stops, the marker will be next to the largest item in the entire list.

Figure 7.11 shows the algorithm at work.

7.8 ANALYZING SELECTION SORT

Now that we have a complete algorithm for sorting a list, we need to ask how good it is.

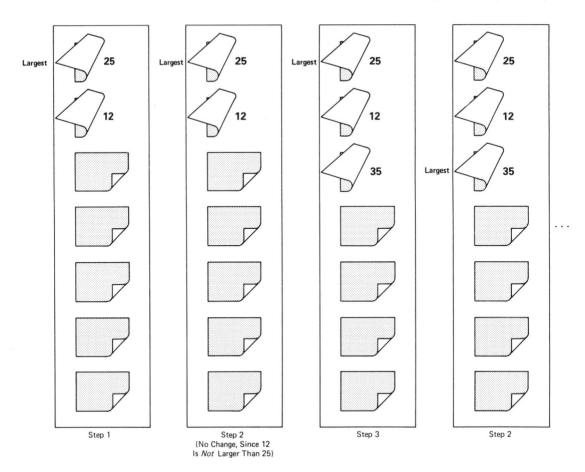

Figure 7.11 Finding the largest number in a list.

Before we can begin to answer this question, though, we need to decide again how we will measure work. Fortunately, simply counting comparisons is as good a way to judge sorting algorithms as it was to judge searching algorithms. This is especially true since we have already decided to look only at algorithms based on making comparisons between two items.

Of course, when we call the number of comparisons a good measure, we do not mean that it gives us a close approximation of the number of instructions a computer will actually carry out after the algorithm is translated to a program. We use the measure only to compare algorithms. When algorithms are as different as linear and logarithmic, even a very rough measure is enough to pick out the better one.

Analyzing selection sort, then, is just a matter of counting how many comparisons it calls for. The first step in the analysis is to look into our procedure for finding the largest item in a list.

The algorithm we have just described begins by calling the first element **Largest**. This does not use any comparisons at all. Then the algorithm looks at the other items in the list, one by one. Each of these items is compared with the number which is currently the one called **Largest**.

If the list contains ten items, all but the first will be compared once with the current largest number—nine comparisons will be made. In general, finding the largest item in a list takes one less comparison than the number of items in the list.

Now it is easy to count the number of comparisons used by selection sort.

Suppose we use the algorithm to put a list of eight items in order. To find the largest of all eight, the algorithm makes seven comparisons. It removes this item from the old list and puts it on the new list.

Next, it finds the largest item out of the seven remaining on **Old**. Finding the largest item on a list of seven items takes six comparisons. This item, too, is removed from **Old** and added to the top of **New**.

So far, selection sort has made seven comparisons and then six more. As it continues, it will make five comparisons to find the largest in a list of six, four comparisons to find the largest in a list of five, and so on.

Eventually, it will make one comparison to see which is the larger of two items remaining on **Old**. It will move this item to the top of **New**. The last remaining item in **Old** is automatically the largest in that list—it wins by default. Selection sort will move this to **New** without making any comparisons.

In all, the algorithm will have made seven comparisons and six comparisons and five comparisons and so on down to one; that is,

$$7 + 6 + 5 + 4 + 3 + 2 + 1$$

or 28 comparisons to sort a list of eight items.

$$* \qquad * \qquad * \qquad * \qquad *$$

This example gives us a pattern we can use to see how selection sort performs on longer lists. If we use the algorithm to put a list of 100 items in order, it will make this many comparisons:

$$99 + 98 + 97 + 96 + \cdots + 4 + 3 + 2 + 1$$

This sum is long—so long that we do not have space to write it down. Luckily, we can use a trick to calculate it. Instead of working on the sum we really want, we try to add up this one:

$$99 + 98 + 97 + 96 + \cdots + 4 + 3 + 2 + 1 +$$
$$1 + 2 + 3 + 4 + \cdots + 96 + 97 + 98 + 99$$

Here, we are adding each of the numbers from 1 to 99 twice, instead of just once. Therefore we will get an answer twice as big as the one we really want.

Now, suppose we group together the numbers in the new sum this way:

$$(99 + 1) + (98 + 2) + (97 + 3) + (96 + 4) + \cdots +$$
$$(4 + 96) + (3 + 97) + (2 + 98) + (1 + 99)$$

Suddenly, the answer is obvious. Inside each pair of parentheses we have two numbers that add up to 100. And how many pairs of parentheses are there? The numbers inside count them for us. In the first pair we add 1, in the next pair, 2, and so on up to the last pair, where we add 99. In all, then, there must be 99 pairs.

Thus we are adding up 99 small sums, each of which comes to exactly 100. The final answer is 99 times 100, or 9,900. Of course, this answer is twice as big as the one we really want. The answer to our original question is 9,900 ÷ 2, or 4,950.

To get the number of comparisons selection sort makes to put a list of 100 items in order, we multiply 99 by 100 and divide by 2—it makes 4,950 comparisons.

*   *   *   *   *

This trick works just as well for analyzing selection sort's performance on lists of other lengths. Adding the sum we want to the same sum listed backwards and collecting it into pairs yields the following form:

$$(\quad) + (\quad) + (\quad) + \cdots + (\quad) + (\quad) + (\quad)$$

Inside each pair of parentheses will be two numbers that add up to the number of items in our list. The *number* of pairs will be 1 less than the number of items.

To get the number of comparisons, we multiply 1 less than the number of items by the number of items and divide by 2. For example, for a list of eight items, we multiply 7 by 8 to get 56 and then divide by 2 to get 28 comparisons.

This is the same number we calculated earlier without using our new procedure.

7.9 AN *n*-SQUARED ALGORITHM

With linear search, the number of comparisons soared as we looked at larger and larger lists. Selection sort is even worse. Figure 7.12 shows how quickly we run into trouble. The table shows that a list of a 10,000 items takes about 50 million comparisons to sort. At 1 million comparisons per second, a computer would sort the list in under a minute.

But a list 10 times as long would take *more* than 10 minutes to sort. A list of 100,000 items requires nearly 5 *billion* comparisons. At 1 million per second, that would take well over an hour.

Number of items in list	Number of comparisons for selection sort
8	$(7 \cdot 8) \div 2 \ = \ 28$
100	$(99 \cdot 100) \div 2 \ = \ 4,950$
1,000	$(999 \cdot 1,000) \div 2 \ = \ 499,500$
10,000	$(9,999 \cdot 10,000) \div 2 \ = \ 49,995,000$
100,000	$(99,999 \cdot 100,000) \div 2 \ = \ 4,999,950,000$

Figure 7.12 Number of comparisons for selection sort.

Selection sort is even worse than linear. The work it calls for increases *faster* than the length of the list.

Another look at the telephone number list shows just how serious this problem can be. At 1 million comparisons per second, linear search could check for a number in the list in 100 seconds. Binary search could do it in a tiny fraction of a second, so long as we first put the list in order.

But how long would it take to put the list in order? If we use selection sort, we would need to make 99,999,999 times 100,000,000 divided by 2, or 4,999,999,950,000,000, comparisons—roughly 5 quadrillion. This means that, at 1 million comparisons per second, it would take about 5 billion seconds to sort the telephone number list—that is, roughly 160 years.

This is another good example of why fast computers cannot make up for poor algorithms. Even computers a hundred times faster than the ones we have been discussing will take more that a year and a half to sort the telephone number list if they use selection sort. By contrast, if we could only find a linear sorting algorithm, an ordinary computer would do the job in 100 seconds.

*   *   *   *   *

Selection sort is neither logarithmic nor linear. We call it an **n-squared** algorithm.

The *n* in *n*-squared stands for the length of the list. To square a number is just to multiply it by itself. Five squared is 5 · 5, or 25.

An *n*-squared sorting algorithm, then, is one that takes an amount of work roughly as large as the square of the length of the list. Figure 7.13 supports our claim that selection sort is an *n*-squared algorithm. In each case, the number of comparisons is very close to half of *n*-squared. This is not surprising. To find the number of comparisons, we first multiplied the number of items in the list, *n*, by a number smaller by 1. This is nearly the same as multiplying *n* by itself or calculating *n*-squared. Then, when we completed the calculation, dividing by 2, we got an answer of approximately half of *n*-squared.

n (number of items)	n-squared	Number of comparisons for selection sort
100	10,000	4,950
1,000	1,000,000	499,500
10,000	100,000,000	49,995,000
100,000	10,000,000,000	4,999,950,000

Figure 7.13 *n*-squared and the number of comparisons for selection sort.

When we call selection sort an *n*-squared algorithm, we are off by about 50 percent. As we have seen, however, percentage differences can be ignored when we are comparing algorithms of different classes.

If we can find a linear sorting algorithm, we will have saved more than 50 percent, more than 99 percent—in fact, more than any fixed percentage can measure.

7.10 A BETTER WAY TO SORT

One way to get a better sorting algorithm is to improve on what we have. Selection sort is not too bad at working with short lists. This suggests that we might save time by breaking a long list into shorter pieces.

For example, the algorithm uses nearly 5,000 comparisons to sort a list of 100 items. But, if the list is divided into two shorter lists of 50 items, each can be sorted with about 1,250 comparisons: for a total of only 2,500.

Figure 7.14 shows how we would begin to apply this observation to a list of eight items. Since the list items are words, we will attempt to put them in alphabetical order.

To start, the original eight-item list is split into two four-item lists: **List 1** and **List 2**. Each of these is then sorted using selection sort.

		List 1		**List 1**		
		Marble		Antelope		
Marble		Antelope		Freezer		
Antelope		Freezer		Grass		
Freezer		Grass		Marble		
Grass	→		→			
Bulb		**List 2**		**List 2**		
Slide						
Hammer		Bulb		Bulb		
Potato		Slide		Hammer		
		Hammer		Potato		
		Potato		Slide		
(1)	Split	(2)	Sort	(3)	???	(4)

Figure 7.14 Idea for a new way to sort.

Notice that sorting the shorter lists does not immediately give us what we want. We still need to merge these together somehow into a sorted list of all eight items. The best idea is to proceed as we did in selection sort. To put eight items in order, we first look for the largest item and use it to begin a new list. Then we find the largest remaining item—the second-largest of all—put it at the top of the new list, and so on.

The main work here is in finding the largest remaining item. Fortunately, since we are beginning with two sorted lists, this can always be done with just a single comparison.

For example, the largest item out of all eight must be either the item at the bottom of **List 1** or the one at the bottom of **List 2**. We can decide which by comparing the two.

After we remove this, the largest remaining item will again be at the bottom of one of the two lists. One comparison will tell us which.

Figure 7.15 shows the first two steps of this merging method. Notice that one item moves to **New** after each comparison. After seven comparisons, seven items will have been moved. There is nothing to compare the last item with, so it can be moved to the top of **New** without any additional comparisons. In all, then, merging two lists of four items takes seven comparisons.

List 1			List 1	
Antelope			Antelope	
Freezer			Freezer	
Grass	New		Grass	New
Marble	———		Marble	———
				Slide
List 2			List 2	
Bulb			Bulb	
Hammer			Hammer	
Potato			Potato	
Slide				

(1) Compare **Marble** and **Slide**; **Slide** is "larger"; move it to **New**.

List 1			List 1	
Antelope			Antelope	
Freezer			Freezer	
Grass	New		Grass	New
Marble	———		Marble	———
	Slide			Potato
List 2				Slide
Bulb			List 2	
Hammer			Bulb	
Potato			Hammer	

(2) Compare **Marble** and **Potato**; **Potato** is "larger"; move it to **New**.

Figure 7.15 Merging two sorted lists.

To sort a list of four items using selection sort takes $(3 \cdot 4) \div 2$, or six comparisons. The new algorithm, then, uses 12 comparisons to sort two lists of four items and then an additional seven to merge them together, 19 in all.

Our earlier work showed that an ordinary selection sort of eight items would use 28 comparisons. This new algorithm is definitely an improvement.

         *   *   *   *   *

This improvement however is only a matter of percentages. We have analyzed the performance of the new algorithm in sorting a list of eight items. A similar analysis for longer lists yields the results shown in Figure 7.16.

Number of items in list	Number of comparisons for selection sort	Number of comparisons for the improved selection sort
100	4,950	2,549
1,000	499,500	250,499
10,000	49,995,000	25,004,999
100,000	4,999,950,000	2,500,049,999

Figure 7.16 Comparing the original and improved selection sort.

Our improved algorithm cuts the number of comparisons by about 50 percent, but that still makes it an *n*-squared algorithm. It does not help much to know that we can now sort our telephone number list in 80 years instead of 160.

Moreover, if we try to extend the list-splitting idea, new problems arise.

For example, what happens if we split a list of eight items into four pieces instead of two? Each of the shorter lists will contain two items. To sort a two-item list takes just one comparison; we simply compare the two numbers and put the larger one on the bottom.

But when we attempt to merge four sorted lists into one, we find we have taken a step backward. With *two* sorted lists, we needed just one comparison to find the largest number. It had to be one of two numbers, the one at the bottom of **List 1** or the one at the bottom of **List 2**.

Now, with four sorted lists, the largest number might be in any of four places—at the bottom of **List 1**, **List 2**, **List 3**, or **List 4**. We have to find the largest of four numbers, and this, as we know, requires three comparisons.

We have made it easier to sort the lists, but harder to merge them together. A careful analysis shows that, in the worst case, the split-into-four method might take 22 comparisons to sort a list of eight items—three more than the split-into-two method.

In fact, if we carry the splitting idea to its logical conclusion, we will get eight lists of one item each. These one-item lists do not need to be sorted at all. But what about trying to merge them?

Figure 7.17 shows that splitting the list up into eight pieces just amounts to turning it on its side. In this case, finding the largest item takes seven comparisons. After it is removed, finding the next-largest item takes six comparisons, and so on. We have come full circle now back to selection sort.

7.11 MERGE SORTING

Fortunately, our work has not been wasted. The real lesson so far is that it is easy to merge a pair of sorted lists. In fact, in this case our merging algorithm is linear.

Here is the argument again, in a slightly more general form.

Suppose we have two sorted lists, **List 1** and **List 2**. To merge them, we repeatedly remove the larger of the two bottom items and put it at the top of a list called **New**.

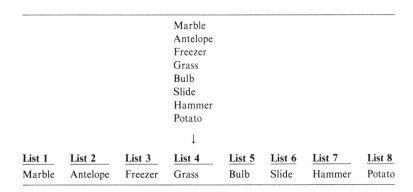

Figure 7.17 Splitting the list into eight pieces.

After each comparison, we move one item to **New**. That means we make as many comparisons as there are items in the final sorted list. If **List 1** contains seven items and **List 2** contains four items, it will take 11 comparisons to merge them.

Actually, this answer is slightly wrong in two respects.

For one thing, the final item moved to **New** does not need to be compared with anything. Therefore only ten comparisons are necessary to merge lists of seven and four items.

Also, if we are lucky, even fewer comparisons will be made. To see why, consider the example shown in Figure 7.18. After five comparisons, five numbers have been moved to **New**. At this point, however, **List 2** is empty. The rest of the numbers from **List 1** can be moved to **New** without additional comparisons. In this case, lists of seven and four items can be merged with only five comparisons.

List 1	List 2	New	List 1	List 2	New	List 1	List 2	New
23	72		23	72	90	23	72	85
35	75		35	75		35	75	90
36	85		36	85		36		
41	90		41			41		
59			59			59		
70			70			70		
81			81			81		
(Initial situation)			(After 1 comparison)			(After 2 comparisons)		

List 1	List 2	New	List 1	List 2	New	List 1	List 2	New
23	72	81	23	72	75	23		72
35	75	85	35		81	35		75
36		90	36		85	36		81
41			41		90	41		85
59			59			59		90
70			70			70		
(After 3 comparisons)			(After 4 comparisons)			(After 5 comparisons)		

Figure 7.18 Merging lists of seven and four items with five comparisons.

To be perfectly precise, then, we should say that ten comparisons are necessary *in the worst case* to merge lists containing four and seven items. If neither list is emptied early—before both are down to just one item—exactly ten comparisons will be made.

These points apply in general. To be precise, then, we should say that merging two lists takes at most one less comparison than the total number of items in the lists. The number of comparisons goes up just as fast as the total number of items. That is, the algorithm is linear.

*   *   *   *   *

Of course, this linear algorithm does not sort lists—it just puts them together. If we use selection sort to get sorted lists and then merge them together, we save only a percentage of our work.

Selection sort is an *n*-squared algorithm; merging is linear. We would be much better off if we could eliminate selection sort altogether and put lists in order just by merging.

Fortunately, this is possible. Suppose we look back to our example of a list of eight items. We begin by splitting this, again, into eight lists of just one item each, as in Figure 7.19.

List 1	List 2	List 3	List 4	List 5	List 6	List 7	List 8
Marble	Antelope	Freezer	Grass	Bulb	Slide	Hammer	Potato

Figure 7.19 Eight one-item lists.

A list of one item is obviously in order, since it takes at least two reversed items for a list to be out of order. Since the lists are in order, we can use our merging method to put any two of them together. Figure 7.20 shows what happens if we merge the two lists on the left.

List 1'	List 3	List 4	List 5	List 6	List 7	List 8
Antelope	Freezer	Grass	Bulb	Slide	Hammer	Potato
Marble						

Figure 7.20 Merging the left-hand pair of lists.

Continuing in the same way, we pair off the remaining one-item lists and merge each pair. As a result, we get the four sorted lists shown in Figure 7.21.

List 1'	List 2'	List 3'	List 4'
Antelope	Freezer	Bulb	Hammer
Marble	Grass	Slide	Potato

Figure 7.21 Four two-item lists.

Now we are beginning to make headway. Sorted lists are just what our merging method calls for. The next step is to pair off these lists and, again, merge the pairs. The result is shown in Figure 7.22.

List 1"	List 2"
Antelope	Bulb
Freezer	Hammer
Grass	Potato
Marble	Slide

Figure 7.22 Four two-item lists.

Finally, if we merge these two four-item lists, we will get the result we want—a sorted list of eight items.

*   *   *   *   *

The question, of course, is how many comparisons we have used.

We began by merging four pairs of one-item lists. The number of comparisons needed for any merge is one less than the number of items in the resulting list. In this step, each merge resulted in a two-item list, so at most one comparison was made. One comparison each for four merges makes four comparisons.

The second step was to merge two pairs of two-item lists. Each resulting list contained four items, so the merges used three comparisons. Three comparisons each for two merges makes six comparisons.

Finally, the third step merged two lists of four items. This used seven comparisons.

In all, we sorted an eight-item list with just 17 comparisons, two less than with the split-into-two method and 11 less than with selection sort.

7.12 ANALYZING MERGE SORT

The real test, however, is to see how the new algorithm performs on long lists. We are hoping that the number of comparisons grows less quickly than the square of the number of items in the list.

Here is the merge sorting algorithm we are attempting to analyze:

MERGE SORT

1. Break the list to be sorted into separate one-item lists.

2. Group the lists into pairs.

3. Merge the two lists in each pair.

4. If there is now just one list, stop; otherwise, go back to step 2.

Notice that steps 1, 2, and 4 do not call for any comparisons. If we want to count comparisons, all we need to know is how many are made in step 3 and how many times step 3 is carried out.

Incidentally, step 3 does not mention the word *comparison*, but we have seen that merging a pair of lists does require comparisons. In fact, as we have shown, it requires at most one less than the total number of items in the two original lists. In analyzing merge sort, however, we will be slightly less precise. We will say that merging two lists takes *exactly* as many comparisons as the total number of items.

This means our analysis will overestimate the number of comparisons made by merge sort. Keep in mind that the algorithm is even better than our calculations will show.

Now let us look into a typical step 3. We will imagine that we have caught merge sort in the middle of its work. It has already gone as far as producing sorted lists of four items and it is about to pair these off and merge them. The situation is as pictured in Figure 7.23.

List 1"	List 2"	List 3"	List 4"	List 5"	
71	13	92	51	60	
75	77	94	57	71	· · ·
79	91	96	93	84	
80	99	98	95	87	

Figure 7.23 Four-item lists about to be merged.

According to our slightly imprecise way of counting, merging the first pair of lists requires eight comparisons, since the lists contain a total of eight items.[4] Naturally, merging the second pair of lists also requires eight comparisons.

Merging each pair takes eight comparisons, one per item in the resulting list. But then, since step 3 merges *all* the pairs and each item ends up in one of the merged lists, the total number of comparisons must be the same as the total number of items.

This argument works just as well if we begin with a row of 16-item lists. Merging each pair takes 32 comparisons, according to our slight overestimate—one comparison per item. At this rate, the total number of comparisons to merge every pair in the row will be the same as the total number of items.

Apparently, every time step 3 is carried out, the algorithm makes a number of comparisons equal to the total number of items to be sorted. If there are 100 million items to be sorted, step 3 will require 100 million comparisons.

*   *   *   *   *

To complete our analysis of merge sort, we only need to know how many times step 3 will be carried out.

When merge sort begins, it creates a row of one-item lists. The first time step 3 is carried out, it merges these into two-item lists. The second time step 3 is carried out, it merges pairs of two-item lists into four-item lists.

Each execution of step 3 doubles the size of the lists in the row. Figure 7.24 shows how quickly they grow. If the original list contains 32 items, merge sort begins by creating 32 one-item lists. It merges these into two-item lists, then four-item lists, then eight-item lists, and so on. After five executions of step 3, merge sort will have produced a 32-item list, that is, a sorted list of the 32 original items.

The table tells us, then, exactly what we wanted to know. It says that step 3

---

[4] Again, this is an overestimate. Actually, as we have seen, the merging algorithm calls for at most seven comparisons in this case.

Number of times step 3 has been carried out	Number of items in each list
1	2
2	4
3	8
4	16
5	32
6	64

Figure 7.24 Effect of step 3 on the length of the merged lists.

of merge sort will be carried out five times in sorting a list of 32 items, six times in sorting a list of 64 items, and so on.

The pattern of the table is even clearer if we convert the right-hand column to binary. The result is shown in Figure 7.25. Every time step 3 is executed, one binary digit is added to the length of the lists it is working with. When this number is the same as the total number of items, all the items are contained in a single sorted list.

Number of times step 3 has been carried out	Number of items in each list (in binary)
1	10
2	100
3	1000
4	10000
5	100000
6	1000000

Figure 7.25 Effect of step 3 on the length of the merged lists.

The upshot is that the number of times step 3 is carried out grows as slowly as the *logarithm* of the length of the original list.

Now we can say how many comparisons merge sort makes. Each time step 3 is executed, merge sort makes as many comparisons as the total number of items to be sorted. Step 3 is carried out a number of times approximately equal to the logarithm of this same number of items.

Thus, the total number of comparisons is the number of items times the logarithm of the number of items. If we use n to stand for the number of items, this is

$$n \cdot \text{logarithm of } n$$

As a result, computer scientists call merge sort an **n-log-n** algorithm.

*   *   *   *   *

Now think back, one last time, to the telephone number list. The list contained 100 million items. The logarithm of this number is how many digits it takes to write it in binary: 27. Therefore, to sort this list, merge sort must do approximately 100 million times 27, or 2,700 million, comparisons.

At 1 million comparisons per second, this is 2,700 seconds, or three-quarters of an hour.

If we leave the list unsorted, we have to use linear search to look up numbers. In this case, we can check fewer than 1,000 in a 24-hour day. On the other hand, if we are willing to spend three-quarters of an hour just once, then for the rest of eternity we can look up numbers at the rate of about 40,000 a second.

Sorting and searching, it turns out, go hand in hand. They are partners in efficiency.

7.13 TAKING STOCK

In this chapter, we have cut two of the most important problems of computer science down to size. We sliced searching down from linear to logarithmic and sorting from *n*-squared to *n*-log-*n*.

In doing so, we have maintained a remarkably high level of abstraction. In our analysis, even the abstract picture of a computer memory did not come into play. We have gone beyond computers to think generally about efficient procedures for solving problems.

Our results show that this kind of abstract thinking can make an enormous difference in solving practical problems.

However, anyone who tries to translate our algorithm outlines into programs will run into trouble very quickly. We have taken for granted that list items can be removed and added and that lists themselves can be created, split, and organized into rows.

In fact, of course, all we have to work with is a computer memory that is a single long list of numbers. It is a tricky problem to organize those numbers so that the steps of efficient algorithms can be carried out. This is our next order of business.

EXERCISES

7.1. How many comparisons would binary search make in looking through an ordered list of 200,000,000 items? An ordered list of 800,000,000 items? An ordered list of 1,600,000,000 items? Assume that the searched-for item is not in the list. (*Hint*: Figure 7.2 should help.)

7.2. Suppose we limit binary search to ten comparisons. What is the longest ordered list that can still be searched? Be sure that binary search can find any given item in the list and also discover whether a given item is *not* in the list. (*Hint*: Figure 7.5 should help.)

7.3. The table in Figure 7.5 shows the number of comparisons binary search makes in the worst case. How would the table look if the second column showed the number of comparisons in the *best case*?

7.4. How would the table of Figure 7.5 look if the second column showed the number of comparisons necessary to find the smallest item in the list?

7.5. How would the table of Figure 7.5 look if the second column showed the number of comparisons necessary to find the second-largest item in the list?

7.6. Find the approximate logarithm of 50, 500, and 5,000.

7.7. Using diagrams like the ones in Figure 7.7, show how binary search looks for 17 in the following list: 1, 2, 4, 8, 16, 32, 64.

7.8. Using diagrams like the ones in Figure 7.7, show how binary search finds 84 in the following list: 30, 50, 55, 56, 57, 58, 59, 62, 69, 70, 84, 85, 86, 94, 100.

7.9. In making up the table in Figure 7.8, we assumed that each comparison step in binary search takes 100 times as long as a comparison step in linear search. What would this factor have to be for the two algorithms to take an equal amount of time processing a list of 4,095 items? A list of 1,000,000 items? A list of 100,000,000 items?

7.10. Suppose step 4 of the binary search algorithm in Section 7.5 was changed to read:

    4(b) If it is smaller, move **Low** to the number marked by **Middle** and go on to step 5.

    4(c) If it is larger, move **High** to the number marked by **Middle** and go on to step 5.

Which of the numbers in the list (3, 7, 10, 13, 15, 19, 20) would the algorithm still be able to find? What would happen if we used the modified algorithm to look for 9?

7.11.

    (a) Is it possible to use the "pile method" explained in Section 7.7 to sort a list of numbers? If so, say how; otherwise, explain why not.

    (b) Can the pile method be used to sort a list of words by length (for example, *zoo* goes before *anteater* because it is shorter)? If so, say how; otherwise, explain why not.

7.12. Continue Figure 7.10 to show the fifth and sixth pairs of **Old** and **New** lists.

7.13. How many comparisons will selection sort make to sort a list of 5 items? 10 items? 500 items?

7.14. Calculate the following sums:

    (a) $1 + 2 + 3 + \cdots + 898 + 899 + 900$

    (b) $100 + 101 + 102 + \cdots + 998 + 999 + 1,000$

    (c) $2 + 4 + 6 + \cdots + 96 + 98 + 100$

7.15. LR, LG, and SQ are three algorithms that process lists. They all lead to the same results, so we simply want to know which takes the least time. The number of steps carried out by LR is the same as the number of items in the list it is processing, and each step takes 20 units of time. The number of steps carried out by LG is equal to the approximate logarithm of the number of items, and each step takes 100 units of time. The number of steps carried out by SQ is equal to the square of the number of items, and each step takes 5 units of time.

    (a) Suppose LR and LG process a certain list in roughly the same amount of time. How many items must be in the list? You are expected to use guesswork to figure this out, but apply algebra or use a calculator if you find it useful.

    (b) How many items must be in a list if LR and SQ process it in roughly the same amount of time?

(c) How many items must be in a list if LG and SQ process it in roughly the same amount of time?

(d) For each of the three list lengths you have found and any two others, calculate how long LG, LR, and SQ will take to run. Compile your results in a table.

7.16. How many comparisons would the split-into-two sorting method of Section 7.10 take to sort a list of 10 items? A list of 20 items?

7.17. In Section 7.10, we claimed that the split-into-four sorting method would take 22 comparisons to sort a list of eight items. Explain how we arrived at this figure. (*Hints*: Note that this is the worst case, the *most* comparisons that might be made. Also, remember that, while it takes three comparisons to find the largest of four items, it only takes two to find the largest of three, one to find the largest of two, and so on.)

7.18. In the worst case, how many comparisons would it take split-into-four to sort a list of 16 items?

7.19. Figure 7.15 shows two steps toward merging a pair of lists. Show the next two steps.

7.20. Using diagrams like the ones in Figures 7.19 to 7.22, show how merge sort would order the following list of names: Bob, Arnold, Carol, Ralph, Ed, Sue, Ann, Stephen.

7.21. As given in Section 7.12, merge sort has four steps. Carry out all four steps twice on the following list and show the result: apple, grape, grapefruit, blueberry, banana, plum, cantaloupe, mango, pear, orange, strawberry, raspberry, nectarine, apricot, lemon, peach.

7.22. In Exercise 7.21, a total of eight steps were carried out. Exactly how many comparisons were made in each step?

7.23. Apply the approximate analysis method of Section 7.12 to find out how many comparisons merge sort makes in sorting a list of

(a) 8 items

(b) 16 items

(c) 64 items

(d) 1,024 items

In each case, how many comparisons will be made during step 3 of the algorithm?

7.24. Write an algorithm for finding the smallest number in an unordered list. How many comparisons will your algorithm make in processing a list of seven items?

7.25. Write an algorithm for finding the second-largest number in an unordered list. How many comparisons will your algorithm make in processing a list of seven items?

7.26. Write an algorithm for finding the median number in a list, that is, the one which is bigger than half the numbers and smaller than the other half. How many comparisons will your algorithm make in processing a list of seven items?

8 Data Structures

8.1 THE PRIORITY PROBLEM

For some time, we have been discussing algorithms in a very abstract way. The computer, with which these algorithms might be carried out, has faded quietly into the background. Now it is time to bring the computer back to the fore.

The advantage of the abstract approach is that it allows us to weed out inherently inefficient procedures, those which call for too much work no matter who or what follows them.

But, as we have pointed out, efficient procedures for *handling* information depend on good schemes for *organizing* information. It is no good to have a streamlined billing procedure if the files are so disorganized that it takes all day to look up a charge.

In the case of the computer, our options for storing information are particularly limited. All we have to work with is a long row of memory positions, each of which holds a single number.

In this chapter, we will concentrate on a few ways of getting the most out of this limited storage system. To get started, we will pose a kind of scheduling problem. As we will see, it is quite easy to find an efficient algorithm to solve the problem. But when we consider the details of how to carry out the algorithm on a computer, we will run into difficulties—difficulties we can resolve only with better storage schemes.

As it turns out, looking into these storage schemes, or **data structures**, will also give us some insight into the algorithms developed in Chapter 7.

* * * * *

In Chapter 7, we spent a good deal of time considering how to put a list of items in order. As we saw, one advantage of sorting a list is that it makes things easy to find. The largest item, for one, is always at the bottom of the list.

This last fact leads to extreme efficiency in solving certain problems.

For example, suppose we have a long list of projects, each of which is assigned a number to indicate how important it is. The higher the number, the more important the project. If we sort the list, according to these priority numbers, the most important project will end up at the bottom.

Consider the problem of scheduling the projects, once the list has been sorted. Since we want to tackle the most important project first, the next-most important project second, and so on, we can use the following algorithm:

1. Complete the project at the bottom of the list.
2. Erase it from the list.
3. If there are any projects left on the list, go back to step 1; otherwise, stop.

The beauty of this scheduling algorithm is that it does not require any searching. In step 1, no comparisons are used to find the most important project. In fact, if comparisons were the only measure of work, we could say that it takes no work at all to carry out the steps of the algorithm.

Of course, we are saying nothing about how much work the projects themselves might take. Our claim concerns the executive work—the work it takes to *direct* the projects.

Also, we are sweeping a good deal of this executive work under the rug by assuming that the list of projects has already been sorted. In fact, for the problem we have stated, ignoring this work makes no sense at all.

But consider a slightly more realistic variation of the scheduling problem. In this version, as each project is completed, another one is added to the list. The question of how to schedule projects efficiently in this case is called the **priority problem**.

Notice that the work of the priority problem is unending. New projects are added just as fast as old ones are completed. This is why it is reasonable to ignore the cost of sorting in our solution. Of course, the original list will have to be put in order, but from then on it is simply a matter of *keeping* it in order.

No matter how much work is involved in the initial sorting, this maintenance work will eventually overshadow it. This is something like buying a car and driving it for many years. In the long run, it will be more important if the car is inexpensive to keep up than if it was cheap to buy.

We will assume, then, that the original list of projects is given to us in sorted form. The question is what to do with the list.

8.2 A DECEPTIVE SOLUTION

At first glance, the priority problem seems no more difficult than our original scheduling problem. Here is the outline of an algorithm to solve it:

1. Complete the project at the bottom of the list.

2. Erase it from the list.

3. Add a new project to the list, at the proper position.

4. Go back to step 1.

Figure 8.1 shows the algorithm in action.

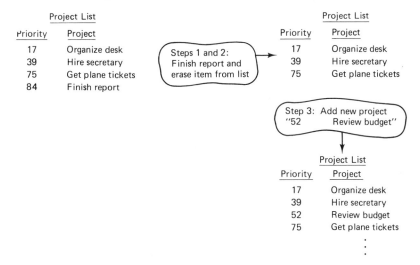

Figure 8.1 Following an algorithm for the priority problem.

As we hinted earlier, the algorithm hinges on *keeping* the sorted list in order. In particular, the key is step 3, where the algorithm calls for a new project to be added *at the proper position.* As the figure shows, if the project is added at the right place, the list stays in order. This is crucial, since step 1 presumes that the most important project is always at the bottom of the list.

Naturally, with the four-item list in the figure, the easiest way to find the proper place to add a new project is just to scan down the column of priority numbers, one by one.

With a much longer list, however, it would take too much work to look at all of the priority numbers. But, this is not necessary. To see why, consider the sorted list of names found in an ordinary telephone book. To add a new name in the proper place, do we need to look one by one through all the names in the book?

On the contrary, since the names are already in order, we can use binary search. For example, if we want to add a number for Kevin Lyver, we search for his name, even though we know it will not be found. Binary search will cut the list in half over and over until eventually only two entries are left to be searched:

Lytwyn Alvin	94 Edison Road	362-456-1414
Lyzcen Nancy	24 Ardsaw Lane	182-987-1095

At this point we can say immediately that Kevin's number should go between Alvin's and Nancy's.

Apparently, we have a logarithmic procedure for step 3 of our priority problem algorithm. The other steps require practically no work at all. Is the problem solved?

It is not, and the reason is that, although we can very quickly find where to add a new project, we cannot actually make the addition, in any reasonable amount of time. Furthermore, when we devise an easy way to add items to a list, one result will be that we can no longer find *where* to add them using binary search.

The upshot is that we cannot carry out step 3 efficiently. But to see why, we will have to say more precisely what we mean by a list.

8.3 REPRESENTING A LIST

When we first considered searching a list, in Chapter 6, we pictured it as a series of numbers stored next to each other in memory. Here is an example:

	17	44	51	65	77	0	
• • •	100	101	102	103	104	105	• • •

We agreed that the list would begin at Position 100. Also, we used the number 0 as an endmarker. This list, then, contains the numbers 17, 44, 51, 65, and 77. Notice that the numbers are sorted. They might be priority numbers for projects to be scheduled.

But consider using our priority problem algorithm on this list. Only one of three steps referring to the list can be carried out easily. This is step 2, which calls for the last item on the list to be erased. To "erase" it, we simply put an endmarker in its place. In our example, this amounts to putting a 0 in Position 104:

	17	44	51	65	0	0	
• • •	100	101	102	103	104	105	• • •

The list now contains 17, 44, 51, and 65—the 77 has been eliminated. Notice that the 0 in Position 105 is no longer of any significance.

As we said, step 2 is easy to carry out. Step 1, on the other hand, requires us to find the last item in the list. In the short example we have been looking at, this is no great hardship. But where is the largest item in the following list?

	17	44	51	65	79	84	
• • •	100	101	102	103	104	105	• • •

Without checking more numbers to the right, we cannot tell where the last item will be. The list might contain six items or 600. As things stand, the only way to find the end of the list is to search it item by item until reaching an endmarker.

We have said it takes no comparisons to find the largest item. Now it appears we might need to make hundreds.

This problem is easily resolved, however, if we slightly change the way we represent a list. Instead of an endmarker, we can use a *pointer* to indicate the position of the last item. In particular, we might store this pointer just before the list, in Position 99. Here is our original example, using this new representation:

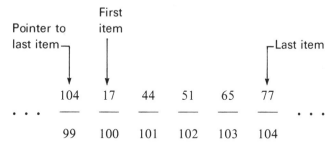

Notice that the first number in the list is still in Position 100. No endmarker is needed, since the number in Position 99 tells us where the list ends—in this case, at Position 104.

Now, as we claimed, it takes no comparisons to find the largest number in the list. The largest number is the last one, the one at the position number stored in Position 99.

Of course, with this new representation, we cannot erase the last item in the list by replacing it with 0. But we can still carry out step 2 of our algorithm easily. To erase the last item, we need only to subtract 1 from the pointer.

For example, if we decrease the pointer in our example to 103, we have the following:

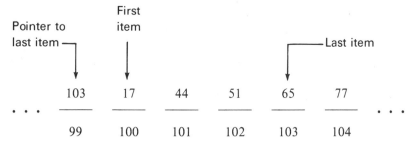

The list now runs from the number at Position 100 to the number at Position 103. The 77 stored at Position 104 is not part of the list, just as the numbers stored at Positions 105, 106, and higher are not part of the list. In effect, the 77 has been erased, even though it has not been removed from the memory.

8.4 SEARCHING

We are beginning to see why it matters how the numbers in the computer's memory are organized. A simple change in the way a list is represented cuts the work in step 1 of our algorithm from hundreds of comparisons or more to none at all. The new representation also allows step 2 to be carried out easily.

Since step 4 of the algorithm does not refer to the list, we need only to check whether it is possible to carry out the two parts of step 3: finding the proper position for a new priority number and adding it to the list.

As we have seen, the first part depends on binary search. For this part, our list representation is perfectly suited.

To perform a binary search we need only to be able to (1) remember the beginning of the part of the list to be searched, (2) remember the end of the part of the list to be searched, and (3) find the number midway between these points.

In the algorithm of Chapter 7, we used the markers **High** and **Low** to help us remember the beginning and end of the part of the list remaining to be searched. In a computer, we would use pointers for the same purpose. We might store these pointers in Positions 97 and 98. Here is an example:

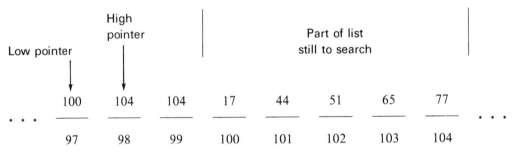

Here, we are searching the part of the list stored in Positions 100 through 104—in fact, the whole list. Apparently, the search has just begun.

The first step of a binary search is to find the number in the middle of the list. Notice that this is also easy with the list representation we are using. If we are looking between Positions 100 and 104, the middle number must be stored at the position halfway between these two. We can find it by taking the average: (100 + 104) ÷ 2 = 102. Thus, the first number to check is the one in Position 102.

Suppose we are searching for the number 31, in order to decide where to add it. Since 31 is lower than the middle number, the one at Position 102, we change the **High** pointer:

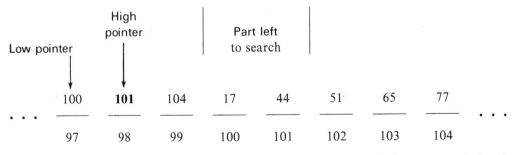

Now, just as in the telephone book example, binary search has narrowed the list down to two entries. The number 31 ought to be added just between them.

8.5 ADDING AND REMOVING ITEMS

Unfortunately, as we have hinted, this is no easy matter. The problem is that there is no memory position between Positions 100 and 101.

The natural solution is to make room for the new number by moving others out of the way. If we slide the numbers 44 through 77 one position to the right, the memory will look like this:[1]

	105	17		44	51	65	77	
• • •	───	───	───	───	───	───	───	• • •
	99	100	101	102	103	104	105	

This maneuver leaves room for the 31 in its proper position between 17 and 44. The question is, How much work have we done to squeeze the new number in?

Of course, by our usual measure of work, we have used only the few comparisons necessary for a binary search. But this is a clear example of why other measures may be necessary.

We originally agreed to count comparisons because, at least in some cases, the number of comparisons was closely related to the total amount of work. In those cases, we expected that an algorithm using 20 comparisons would require about 10 times as much work as an algorithm using two comparisons.

This new method for adding a number to a list is quite different. Most of the work is in moving other numbers out of the way, and this has nothing to do with how many comparisons are made.

In a list of 100 million numbers, it will take at most 27 comparisons to see where a new number should be added. But if the new number must go into the very first position, it will be necessary to move all 100 million numbers one position to the right.

This example points the way to a simple worst-case analysis. If we are unlucky, the number to be added will be smaller than all of the numbers already in the list. In this case, the new number must go in Position 100 and *all* the other numbers must be moved out of the way. In the worst case, then, the amount of work to add a number grows as quickly as the length of the list—our make-space procedure for adding numbers is linear.

Of course, a linear algorithm is not too bad if we want to use it only a few times. But we are planning to add items over and over, each time we come to step 3 of the priority problem algorithm.

Think back to our original linear algorithm for looking up telephone numbers. The problem was that it could not keep up with how fast new phone numbers need to be checked. Likewise, if projects are scheduled and completed at a very high rate, as they are in certain practical cases, our linear make-space algorithm will be left in the dust.

---

[1] Notice that we have also changed the end pointer stored at Position 99 to show that the end of the list has moved to the right.

The prime example is when a computer is used to schedule computer programs. Often, a computer's memory contains many different programs at the same time. Each program is assigned a priority number according to its importance, and one main program uses these numbers to decide which program to carry out.

In effect, our procedure for adding to a list calls for the whole list to be copied for each new item. This system will work, of course, but it is hardly efficient. We need a better idea.

*   *   *   *   *

Incidentally, the priority problem algorithm removes items from the *end* of the list, and we have seen that this is only a matter of changing the end pointer. But what if our representation of a list were to be used for the selection sort algorithm? In that procedure, items are frequently removed from the *middle* of a list. In order to fill up the hole, items to the right of the one removed would all have to be moved over.

In analyzing selection sort, we counted only the number of comparisons made to find the next largest item. Apparently, it might be necessary to *move* items even more than to compare them.

8.6 LINKED LISTS

For both selection sort and the priority problem algorithm, we need a way of representing lists that allows items to be added and removed easily.

We have claimed that computers can do any information processing work that people can do by using a step-by-step method. Surely it does not take any special powers to add items to a list and cross them off. Why not have the computer work just as a person would?

The answer, surprising as it may seem, is that the method most people use for adding items to a list and removing them is no more efficient than the make-space procedure we have been discussing.

Suppose we begin with the following list:

345
358
490
501
513
555
561
701
724
797

If we add a few numbers and cross a few off, the list might end up looking like this:

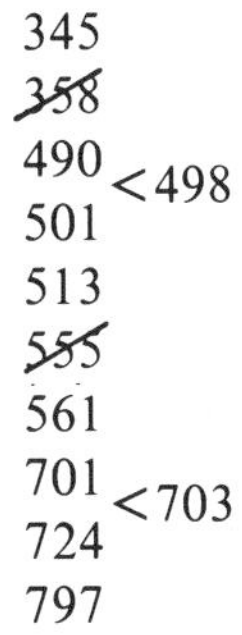

345
~~358~~
490 <498
501
513
~~555~~
561
701 <703
724
797

So far, we have avoided the moving that made our algorithms so inefficient. But how will the list look after more numbers are added and removed? Figure 8.2 shows the answer.

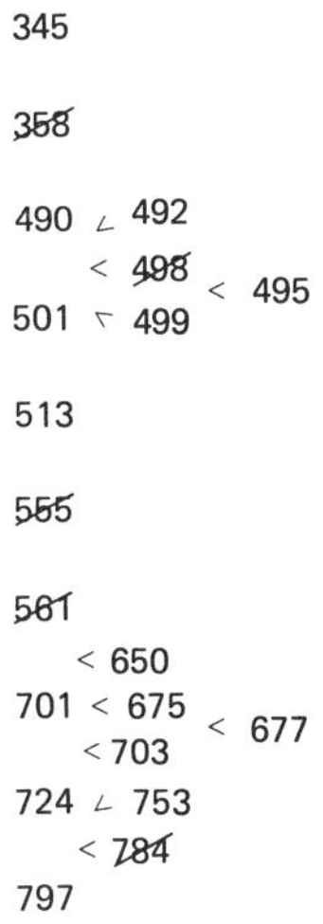

345

~~358~~

490 ∠ 492
       < ~~498~~ < 495
501 ⌐ 499

513

~~555~~

~~561~~
       < 650
701 < 675 < 677
       < 703
724 ∠ 753
       < ~~784~~
797

Figure 8.2 The list after many additions and deletions.

Sooner or later a person using a list like this will need to copy it. This is not just a matter of neatness. The picture in the figure barely represents a list—that is, we can hardly use it to determine the order of the items. If the list is not copied, it will eventually be *impossible* to see any order and the picture will be useless.

But copying numbers means moving them to a new location. It seems people rely on moving numbers just as our computer algorithm did.

*   *   *   *   *

If we want to avoid copying, the key is to find a way to keep the order of the items clear. As Figure 8.3 begins to show, one solution is to use arrows.

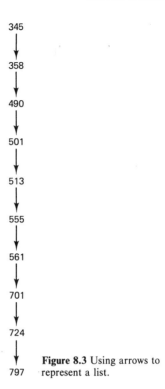

Figure 8.3 Using arrows to represent a list.

Of course, if the numbers are lined up in a neat column, the arrows are hardly necessary. They come in handy if the numbers are scattered over the page as in Figure 8.4. Notice that we can still follow the arrows from number to number to determine the order of the items.

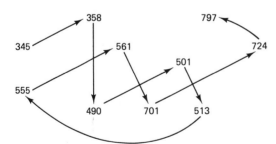

Figure 8.4 The same list.

The advantage of this system is that we can add or remove items without moving any of the others. Only arrows are redrawn.

As an example, consider adding 498 between the existing items 490 and 501. As the picture stands, an arrow shows that 501 comes immediately after 490. After the new item is added, this is no longer the case, so we erase this arrow. At the same time, we add new arrows to show that 498 now follows 490 and that 501 now follows 498. The result is shown in Figure 8.5.

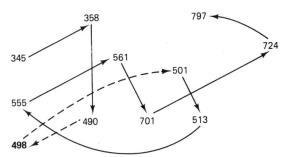

Figure 8.5 Adding a number to the list.

Notice that it does not matter where we write 498. The arrows suffice to show how it fits into the list.

*   *   *   *   *

To remove a number is even easier. We simply change the arrow that points to it so that it points instead to the following number. In our list, for example, 345 points to 358, which in turn points to 490. To remove 358, we just let 345 point directly to 490, as in Figure 8.6.

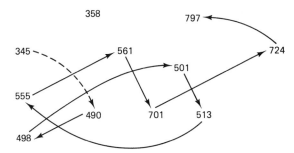

Figure 8.6 Removing a number from the list.

This leaves 358 in the picture, but not in the list. We will never come to it by starting at the first list item and following arrows.

*   *   *   *   *

This arrow system may seem complicated, but it allows us to add or remove a number by changing at most three arrows—that is, in no more than three steps. The work required does not increase as the list grows longer. By contrast, with our simpler way of representing a list, we may need as many steps as there are items in the list, one step to move each item out of the way.

We have discovered the best possible kind of algorithm. *N*-squared, linear, and logarithmic procedures all use more work for a larger problem. With the arrow representation, our method of adding items to a list and removing them requires only a fixed, or constant, amount of work, no matter how long the list. We call it a **constant-time** procedure.

Luckily, the arrow system also translates neatly into a way of representing lists in a computer memory. Instead of arrows, we use pointers.

To begin, we put the first item of the list in Position 100 and the others *anywhere* at all in the memory. This is like writing the numbers in random positions on the page. The result is shown in Figure 8.7.

. . .	345		. . .	490		. . .
	100	101		103	104	

. . .	561		724		. . .
	150	151	152	153	

. . .	555		. . .	701		. . .
	227	228		234	235	

. . .	358		513		. . .
	734	735	736	737	

. . .	797		501		. . .
	802	803	804	805	

Figure 8.7 First step toward representing the list in memory.

Of course, as it stands, this is like an arrow representation without the arrows. Since the first number in the list will always be stored in Position 100, we know the list begins with 345. But what comes next?

The next number after 345 is the 358 stored in Position 734. To indicate that fact, we add a pointer in Position 101, as shown in Figure 8.8.

Then we add a pointer after 358 to show where to find the *next* number. If we add in pointers after each number, we get the final representation shown in Figure 8.9. Notice that the pointer after 797, the last item in the list, is -1. This serves as an endmarker, so that we will not continue looking for more list items.

To interpret this diagram, we begin at Position 100. The number 345 here is the first item in the list. The following number, 734, tells us where to look for the next item.

Looking in Position 734, we find 358, the second item in the list. The following number, 103, tells us where to look for the third item.

Continuing in this way, we can find all the list items. The representation is a little difficult to get used to at first, but the order of the items is always perfectly clear. A step-by-step method is all it takes to find the next number.

The representation we have invented is usually called a **linked list**, because the items are linked together with pointers. Each item tells us where to find the next one.

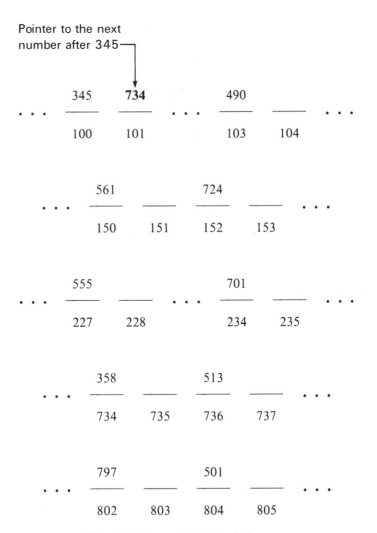

Figure 8.8 Using a pointer instead of an arrow.

345	734		490	804	
100	101		103	104	

561	234	724	802	
150	151	152	153	

555	150		701	152	
227	228		234	235	

358	103	513	227	
734	735	736	737	

797	−1	501	736	
802	803	804	805	

Figure 8.9 The final representation.

8.7 LINKED LIST OPERATIONS

With a linked list, adding or removing items is only a matter of changing pointers. We proceed just as when we added and erased arrows.

For example, look at the first four numbers in our list:

345	734		490	804	
100	101		103	104	

358	103		501	736	
734	735		804	805	

To us, these numbers mean the same as the following diagram.

$$345 \rightarrow 358 \rightarrow 490 \rightarrow 501 \rightarrow \cdots$$

To add the number 498 in its proper position, we store it at any random position in memory with a pointer leading to the next number, 501. Then we add a pointer from 490 to the new number, 498. This new pointer takes the place of the old one from 490 to 501, so there is no need to do any additional erasing.

Here is the result:

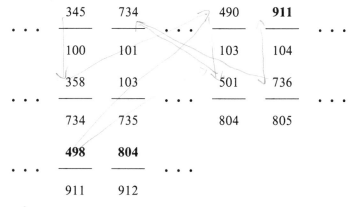

or, in picture form,

$$345 \rightarrow 358 \rightarrow 490 \rightarrow 498 \rightarrow 501 \rightarrow \cdots$$

As promised, we added a number to the list without moving any of the existing items. In fact, we did not even need to include the second half of the list in our diagrams. It was not affected.

*   *   *   *   *

Removing a number from the list is even easier. For example, to get rid of 358, we need only to change one pointer—the one indicating the next number after 345. If we change this to skip 358 and point to 490, the numbers in memory will be:

345	**103**		490	911	
100	101		103	104	
358	103		501	736	
734	735		804	805	
498	804				
911	912				

A picture of this would show 358 still pointing to 490:

$$345 \quad \rightarrow \quad 490 \quad \rightarrow \quad 498 \quad \rightarrow \quad 501 \quad \rightarrow \quad \cdots$$
$$\uparrow$$
$$358$$

But if we begin at 345, the first item in the list, and follow the pointers forward, we will never come to 358. It is effectively off the list.

8.8 SEARCHING A LINKED LIST

The linked list representation solves our problem with selection sort. We can remove an item from the middle of a list without moving any of the others.

For the priority problem, however, linked lists are no bargain.

Think back to step 3 of our algorithm for the priority problem. In this step, we are supposed to add a new project at the proper position in a list, according to its priority number. Binary search gave us a logarithmic way to find this proper position. But, because of our original way of representing lists, actually adding the project required a tedious, linear procedure—moving all the other projects out of the way.

Now we have found a painless way to add items to a list. No matter how long the list is, we need only to change a few pointers. The key to this method is the linked list representation we have worked so hard to develop. Unfortunately, this representation throws a monkey wrench into the workings of binary search.

With a linked list, we can add new items in a flash. But it leaves us no easy way to find out *where* to add them.

Binary search depends on our ability to find the number midway between two other numbers in a list. With our original list representation, this was simple, since the list items were stored in an unbroken sequence. If the first number in a list was stored at Position 100 and the last one at Position 500, we could say immediately that the number midway between them was at Position 300.

In a linked list, however, numbers are scattered all through the memory. If one number is stored at Position 100 and another at Position 500, there is no simple way to find the one midway between.

The only method is to start at Position 100 and follow pointers from number to number. If we pass through 44 numbers before coming to the last one, the middle number must be the one 22 steps away from the beginning.

But if we have to look through the whole list of numbers to find the middle number, the very first step of binary search will take as long as a complete linear search.

With a linked list, binary search is worse than linear.

8.9 A TOURNAMENT SOLUTION

Think again of a sorted list containing 100 million items. If we store the list using our original representation, binary search will tell us where to add a new item with just 27 comparisons. But actually adding the item may require us to move 100 million numbers out of the way.

If we use a linked list representation, we can add the item just by changing a few pointers. But to find where to add it may require us to look through all 100 million existing items.

Either way of organizing the data leads to a linear procedure or worse for step 3 of the priority problem algorithm. To improve efficiency, it appears we need an entirely new system of organization.

In fact, we are about to take a new approach, not just to step 3, but to the whole priority problem. The essence of the problem is our interest in the most important of a group of projects. Likewise, in many sports, the essence of the interest is in finding the best of a group of competitors. One approach to the priority problem, then, is to hold a tournament.

Figure 8.10 represents the results of a tennis tournament. Along the bottom row are the eight competitors. These eight are paired off for the first round of the tournament. The winners of the first round are listed on the next higher row, where they are again paired off to play in the second round, and so on.

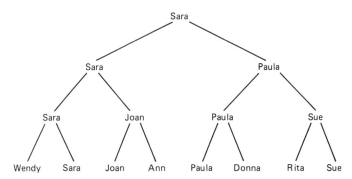

Figure 8.10 Results of a women's tennis tournament.

The figure, called a **tournament tree**, shows that Joan defeated Ann in the first round, but lost to Sara in the second round. Sara went on to defeat Paula in the next round to win the tournament.

Notice, incidentally, that seven matches were played to determine the champion. This is not surprising, in light of our earlier argument that it takes seven comparisons to find the largest of eight items. In this case, we are looking for the largest degree of tennis-playing skill.

The tournament approach does not save matches, then, in the original tournament. It begins to pay off if Sara leaves the competition and a new player named Alice steps in.

Figure 8.11 shows that it is not necessary to replay the entire tournament to find the new champion. The players in the four right-hand matches are the same as before, so we may as well assume that the outcomes will be the same. Only Sara's three matches need to be replayed. If Alice defeats Wendy and Joan and loses to Paula, as shown in Figure 8.12, this is enough to make Paula the new champion.

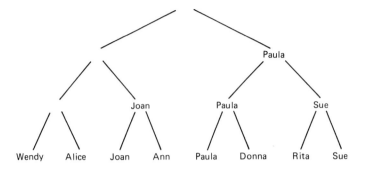

Figure 8.11 The players in most matches are the same.

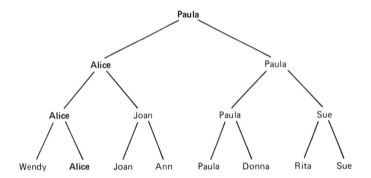

Figure 8.12 Three matches determine the new champion.

Notice that we have removed one player and added another with a minimum number of new matches. In fact, for a larger tournament, we will see that this number is small in comparison with the total number of players.

The upshot is that we have the key to a good algorithm for the priority problem. The competitors in a tournament might just as well be projects which win matches on the basis of their importance. In this case, the winner of the tournament would be the project which should be scheduled first.

If this project is completed and another is added, the tournament tree will give us a better way than linear of finding the new champion—the next project to be scheduled.

*   *   *   *   *

Before we analyze the algorithm, however, we may improve on the tournament tree slightly. Figure 8.13 shows a new way of representing the results of a tournament. Notice that this is definitely *not* an ordinary tournament tree.

In this new kind of diagram, each player is listed just above two players he can defeat. For example, we can tell from the figure that John is a better player than both Tom and Mike.

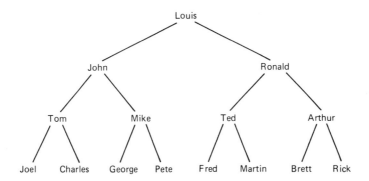

Figure 8.13 Results of a men's tennis tournament.

A diagram organized this way is called a **heap**. In the case of a tennis tournament, the person at the top of the heap is the best player.

A heap is better than a tournament tree for our purposes because more players can be listed in the same space. Compare the number of women in the tournament tree we discussed with the number of men shown here in the same-sized heap. A heap is a more compact way of representing the information we want.

8.10 REMOVING AND ADDING WITH A HEAP

Of course, for a heap to serve our purposes, we need a fast way of removing the champion and adding a new player. The obvious method with a tournament tree was to replay the champion's matches.

But look back at the heap for the men's tournament. We cannot tell whom the champion played.

Suppose, then, that the champion, Louis, is removed and a new player named Ralph steps in. Our approach will be to start Ralph at the top of the heap and let him sink, stage by stage, to his true level.

The new heap begins as in Figure 8.14.

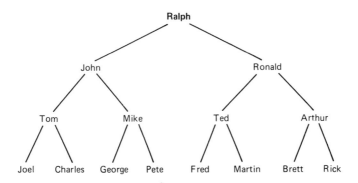

Figure 8.14 Finding the new champion: step 1.

Notice that most of the information in this heap is correct. It is still the case that John is better than Tom and Mike, that Ted is better than Fred and Martin, and so on. The only part of the heap that may be wrong is the very top, which tells us that Ralph is better than John and Ronald.

To see whether this part of the heap *is* wrong, we pit Ralph, John, and Ronald against each other in a minitournament to see who is best. Notice that this takes just two matches. The winner of the first match takes on the third player for the championship. In our example, if Ralph beats John and then loses to Ronald, Ronald is the best player of the three.

In this case, we can fix the top part of the heap by switching Ralph and Ronald, as in Figure 8.15. Notice that Ralph has fallen one level.

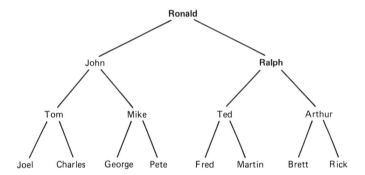

Figure 8.15 Finding the new champion: step 2.

Now the top part of the heap is correct: Ronald is better than Ralph and John. Most of the rest of the heap is correct, since it has not changed. We still do not know, however, whether Ralph is better than Ted and Arthur. This calls for another minitournament.

If Ralph wins this minitournament, the heap is correct as it stands. In this case, Ralph is better than Ted and Arthur and these two are already known to be better than the players below.

If Ralph does not win, he will switch places with the winner and sink another level.

There is a simple limit, however, to how many minitournaments will be played. Each one Ralph loses causes him to sink a level in the heap. In our heap, if Ralph sinks three levels, he will be on the bottom row with nowhere lower to go. At most, three minitournaments will be played. Since each requires two matches, it takes at most six matches to determine the new champion, even though the heap contains 15 players.

*   *   *   *   *

If we use a heap to store priority numbers instead of tennis players, the same method applies. Figure 8.16 shows a heap of 31 numbers.

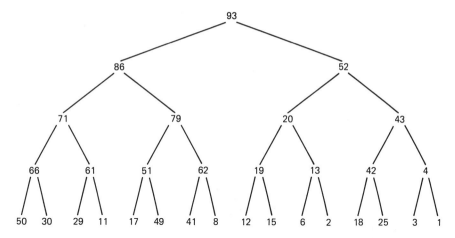

Figure 8.16 A heap of numbers.

If we complete the project with priority 93 and add a new one with priority 69, we will need to revise the heap. As a first step, we put 69 at the top of the heap, as in Figure 8.17. Then we let it sink to the appropriate level. We conduct a minitournament among 69, 86, and 52. That is, we find the largest of the three. This uses two comparisons.

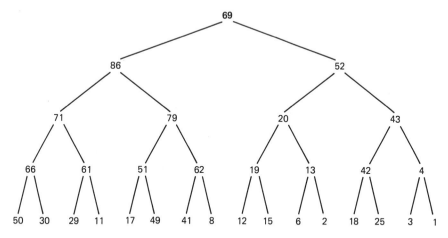

Figure 8.17 Finding the new largest priority number: step 1.

Since 86 is the largest, 69 and 86 trade places, as shown in Figure 8.18. The new number sinks one level.

Next, we hold a second minitournament among 69, 71, and 79. Since 79 wins, it trades places with 69, as shown in Figure 8.19. The new number sinks down another level.

In a third minitournament, 69 is found to be the largest of 69, 51, and 62. This means the heap is correct as it stands—each number is larger than the two

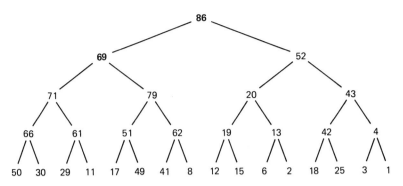

Figure 8.18 Finding the new largest priority number: step 2.

directly below. In all, we conducted three minitournaments, each using two comparisons. Adding the new number uses just six comparisons.

In fact, in this heap it is only possible for a number to sink four levels. At worst, eight comparisons will be made to add a number.

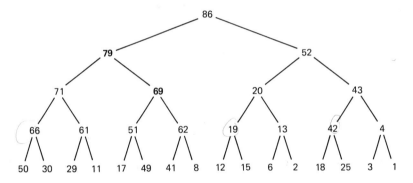

Figure 8.19 Finding the new largest priority number: step 3.

Notice, incidentally, that each minitournament also involves moving at most two items. Since the number of moves and comparisons is about the same, the number of comparisons is a good measure of total work in this case.

*   *   *   *   *

To add an item to a heap of 15 takes at most six comparisons; to add one to a heap of 31 items takes at most eight comparisons. In these small examples, our algorithm works well. But how efficient is it in general?

The answer is easy, once we see a good way to count the items in a heap.

At the top level of a heap is a single item. The next level contains two items; the following one, four. Each level contains twice as many items as the one above, since there are two items below each one on the higher level.

A heap with three levels, then, contains $1 + 2 + 4$ items. A heap with four levels contains $1 + 2 + 4 + 8$ items. These sums are precisely what we mean when we write the binary numbers 111 and 1111.

Thus, if a heap has 111111 items—63 in base ten—it must have six levels, the same as the number of digits in the binary number. The number of levels is the *logarithm* of the total number of items in the heap, the number of binary digits it takes to write the number of items.

We already know how compact the binary system is in representing numbers. Even a huge number like 100 million can be written with just 27 digits. Likewise, a heap containing 100 million items must have only 27 levels.

In a heap with 27 levels, a new number can only sink 26 levels. Each level it sinks requires two comparisons. The maximum number of comparisons to add a number to this enormous heap, then, is just 52.

In the worst case, adding to a heap uses twice as many comparisons as the logarithm of the total number of items. However, the factor of 2 is only a matter of percentages. Our algorithm for adding to a heap is essentially logarithmic.

8.11 A HEAP IN MEMORY

With a heap, we can find the largest item without searching—it is at the top. We can remove this item and add a new one using a logarithmic algorithm. We have an efficient solution to the priority problem, then, if only we can find a way to represent the heap in computer memory.

Luckily, this is quite easy.

As a first step, we number the items in a heap from top to bottom and from left to right, as shown in Figure 8.20.

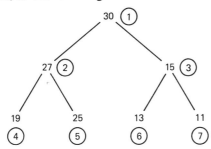

Figure 8.20 Numbering the items in a heap.

Suppose, now, that we store the items in memory *using these numbers as positions.* Here is the result:

	30	27	15	19	25	13	11	
...	—	—	—	—	—	—	—	...
	1	2	3	4	5	6	7	

Of course, in our computer, these first positions in the memory are normally reserved for a program. In a moment, we will see why this is not important.

For now concentrate instead on an even more serious problem. The *structure* of the heap appears to have been lost when we flattened it out to be stored in memory. How can we tell, for example, which number is above 15 or which two numbers are below?

A very natural impulse, at this point, is to think of adding pointers to show the relations between all the stored numbers. Amazingly enough, pointers are not necessary. All the relations we need are preserved in the memory position numbers.

To see how, look back at the original heap. The item numbered 6 is just below and to the left of the item numbered 3. The item numbered 4 is just below and to the left of the item numbered 2.

In both cases, the item below and to the left of any other item is numbered twice as high. This relationship holds in any heap, so long as the items are numbered from top to bottom and from left to right. Therefore, if the number 15 is stored in Position 3 in the memory, the item which is below and to the left of it in the heap is in Position 6.

Naturally, the item below and to the *right* is numbered 1 higher than the item below and to the left. If the item below and to the left of 15 is in Position 6, the item below and to the right must be in Position 7.

It is possible then, to figure out which two items are below any given item without the use of pointers.

Likewise, we can find the item above. Moving down, we double the position number or double it and add 1. Moving up, we halve the position number (if it is even) or halve it and ignore the remainder (if it is odd).

For example, 27 is in Position 2. Halving this gives us 1, the position where the number above 27 in the heap is stored. If we look for the number above 15 we will get the same answer. We know that 15 is stored in Position 3. Halving 3 gives us 1 with a remainder of 1. Ignoring the remainder, we find that the number above 15 is in Position 1.

This is correct. The 30 stored in Position 1 is above both 27 and 15.

When we draw a heap as in Figure 8.20, the information about its structure is contained in the lines that connect numbers. This structure is what allows us to use our logarithmic algorithm for removing and adding items.

Now we have a way to represent the heap in a computer memory system without using lines. Simple arithmetic is enough to tell us which number is above or below any other number.

Incidentally, this is why it does not matter where in memory the numbers are stored. Suppose our heap begins in Position 101, as follows:

	30	27	15	19	25	13	11	
. . .	——	——	——	——	——	——	——	. . .
	101	102	103	104	105	106	107	

Another simple piece of arithmetic will turn these new position numbers into the ones that explain the structure—we need only to subtract 100.

A heap may be stored anywhere in memory, then. If we use it to store priority numbers, it takes virtually no work to find the most important project. The largest priority number is always in the first position. And when this project is completed, adding a new one takes an amount of work which grows only as quickly as the *logarithm* of the number of projects.

Finally, we have a truly efficient solution to the priority problem.

8.12 HEAP SORT

We introduced the heap to help us with a scheduling problem. It is useful in general, however, whenever we have a group of items and need a quick way both to find the largest item and to remove and add items.

For example, the basic idea of selection sort was to remove the largest item repeatedly from a group. Using a heap, we can make selection sort as efficient as merge sort.

Suppose we begin with the same heap we pictured in the last section. It is shown again in Figure 8.21.

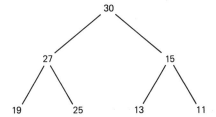

Figure 8.21 A heap of numbers to be sorted.

This heap contains seven numbers. To put them in order, we use the largest number—the one at the top of the heap—to start a list. We put a zero in its place and allow it to sink to its proper level, as we have described. Figure 8.22 shows the result.

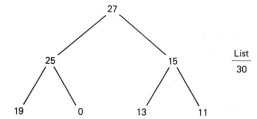

Figure 8.22 The same heap after 0 replaces the largest number.

Next, we remove the largest number remaining in the heap, put it on top of the list, and replace it with a zero. Figure 8.23 shows the result, after this second zero has sunk to its proper level.

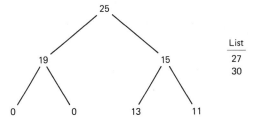

Figure 8.23 The same heap after 0 replaces the second largest number.

Continuing this way, we will eventually end up with a heap full of zeros and an ordered list of the original seven elements.

For each number we remove from the list, we add a zero and let it sink down. As we have seen, this takes an amount of work that depends on the logarithm of the original number of items in the heap—logarithm of n if there are n items.

We perform this work once for each item, as it is removed. If there are seven items, we do seven times the work. If there are n items we do n times the work—that is, n times logarithm of n. Selection sort using a heap is an n-log-n algorithm, then, just the same as merge sort.[2] Together, the combined algorithm and data structure are called **heap sort**.

Using a heap with selection sort is about as efficient a method as computer scientists have discovered for putting items in order. In fact, it can be proved that no algorithm is more than a percentage amount better. In particular, there is no possibility of finding a linear comparison-based algorithm for sorting. N-log-n is the best we can do.

8.13 OTHER SCHEDULING STRUCTURES

When we call the heap a data structure, we mean that it is a way of organizing information in a computer memory, the computer equivalent of an office filing system.

Ordinary lists and linked lists are other examples of data structures.

We study algorithms because they may be reused. Since sorting is a basic task, arising in many different cases, it pays to spend time finding an efficient way to approach it. Once we discover merge sort or heap sort, we save time with each new problem that depends on sorting.

Likewise, a good data structure is widely useful. Each is especially suited for certain tasks that arise in many varied situations. An ordinary list is useful because it allows a binary search. A linked list allows items to be added or removed efficiently. A heap is useful when we need to find the largest item and to add or remove items.

To complete the work of this chapter, we will look at two additional data structures—powerful and general ways of organizing information in a computer. Like the heap, both are related to scheduling problems.

A **queue**[3] is just another name for a line—the kind of line students wait in to register for classes. A key point about queues is that nothing happens to anyone except the person at the front. This person takes care of his or her business and then leaves the queue. Newcomers must join at the rear.

A queue is a way of scheduling people. It is a system often summed up in the phrase *first come, first served*.

---

[2] Of course, we have left out the work it takes to organize the numbers into a heap to begin with. However, this only adds a percentage to the total number of comparisons, so it does not affect our conclusion. To set up the heap, we would first put huge numbers in each position, numbers much larger than the real ones we plan to use. Then we would repeatedly remove one of these huge numbers, replace it with one of the numbers we really want to use and let this number sink down. When all the huge numbers have been replaced, we are left with a correctly organized heap of the numbers we want.

[3] Queue is pronounced the same as cue.

A **stack** is the opposite of a queue. It might be summed up, in contrast, by the phrase *first come, last served*. Newcomers join the line at the front, ahead of people who have waited longer. For example, if the class registration line looks like this:

> John   Susan   Mary   Pat   <REGISTRATION COUNTER>

then Pat is about to register. But suppose two new students arrive before she reaches the registration counter. If the registration line is a stack, they will join the line ahead of her like this:

John   Susan   Mary   Pat   Terry   Fran   <REGISTRATION COUNTER>

In this case, Fran and Terry will both register before Pat.

This is a strange way to schedule students for registration, but it makes sense in other cases. Suppose a store clerk is helping a customer when the phone rings. She goes to the phone and begins to give the caller directions to the store. But before she can finish, her boss calls her loudly from another room.

Probably the clerk will find out what her boss wants, then finish giving directions on the phone, and finally attend to her customer. The waiting line for her attention grows like this:

Customer   <CLERK'S ATTENTION>

↓

Customer   Caller   <CLERK'S ATTENTION>

↓

Customer   Caller   Boss   <CLERK'S ATTENTION>

Each person who interrupts the clerk joins the line at the front—ahead of the people already waiting. In other words, the clerk schedules her attention like a stack.

*   *   *   *   *

Incidentally, the stack takes its name from the usual way of scheduling trays in a cafeteria. As trays are washed, they are placed on a stack at the beginning of the cafeteria line. The last tray to be placed on the stack is the first one which will be picked up by a customer.

In our class registration example, it is as if the registrar were making a stack of the names of students in line. At first, Pat's name is at the top of the stack, as in Figure 8.24. She is about to be called to register. Then Terry and Fran arrive. Their names are placed on the top of the stack, just like two freshly washed trays. Figure 8.25 shows that Fran will now be the first called to register.

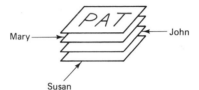

Mary ⟶   ⟵ John

Susan

Figure 8.24 A stack of student names.

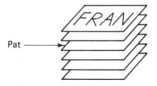

Pat ⟶

Figure 8.25 The same stack after two names are added.

In fact, it is almost always better to picture a stack as a pile rather than as a first come, last served line. When the boss calls our poor store clerk, then, her mental stack looks something like this:

Boss
Caller
Customer

At the top of the stack is her boss, the first person who will receive attention.

8.14 REPRESENTING THE STACK

Regardless of how we picture the queue and stack, however, they are of no use to us unless we can represent them with numbers stored in a computer's memory. As soon as we have done so, we will see that both structures can be used for much more than scheduling.

As we have already said, the queue and stack are essentially lists with special rules about adding and removing items. In a queue, items must be added at one end of the list and removed at the other. In a stack, items must be added to and removed from the same end.

Suppose, then, that we have a stack of numbers like this, with 76 at the top:

76
134
11
936

We can represent this stack with a simple list, so long as we include a pointer to the end of the list:

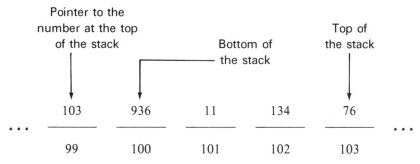

Notice that the numbers have been listed from bottom to top. Since the top of a stack is the only place we are allowed to add or remove items, the right-hand end of the list is the key to our representation.

To add an item, we increase the top pointer by 1, so that it points to an unused position, and then put the new item at this new top position. For example, if we add 660 to the stack, we get the following:

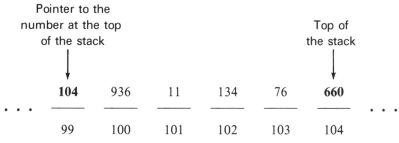

To remove the top item of the stack, we just decrease the top pointer by 1, like this:

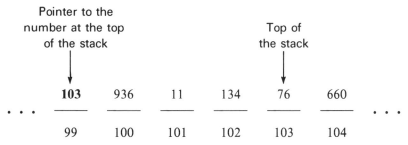

Now the 76 in Position 103 is at the top of the stack. The number 660 is still stored in the memory, but the top pointer tells us it is no longer part of the stack.

8.15 REPRESENTING THE QUEUE

The stack is so easy to represent as a list that it is natural to think of using the same idea for a queue. Suppose we have a queue of numbers, with 17 at the front of the line and 45 at the back, like this:

45   8   12   17   <FRONT>

Nothing can stop us from storing the numbers in memory as follows:

45	8	12	17
100	101	102	103

· · ·   _____ _____ _____ _____   · · ·

The problem is that newcomers are supposed to join a queue at the rear and we have not left much space at the rear of this one. The first number added would be stored in Position 99; the next one, in Position 98 and so on. But this means that only 100 items can be added, since this is the total number of memory positions to the left of where the 45 is stored.

One solution, of course, is to add each incoming number at Position 100, shifting the other numbers to the right to make room. We have seen, however, how much work it may take to make room in this way. It would be better if we could avoid moving the numbers.

A second solution is to store the line backward, like this:

17	12	8	45
100	101	102	103

In this case, the first number added at the rear of the queue would go into Position 104, the next would go into Position 105, and so on. Apparently, we can add as many items as the memory will hold. Unfortunately, this representation leads to a different sort of problem.

Suppose we add 77 to the back of the queue and remove 17 from the front. Here is the result:

12	8	45	77
101	102	103	104

We began with a queue of four items running from Position 100 to Position 103. After adding a number and removing one, we again have a four-item queue. Now, however, it runs between Positions 101 and 104. In fact, each time we add and remove a number, the queue will shift one position to the right. If our computer has a limited memory, the queue will eventually run past the last position, even if it never contains more than four items. It would be better to keep the queue in one place, as much as possible.

The best solution is to abandon the idea of storing the queue in consecutive positions in the memory and, instead, to use a linked list. The advantage, as we have seen, is that a linked list representation allows us to add and remove items while keeping the rest of the list fixed in place.

Since the numbers in a linked list are stored in a random order, we need a pair of extra pointers to tell us where to find the numbers at the front and back of the queue. Otherwise, however, the linked list works just as it did earlier. Here is an example:

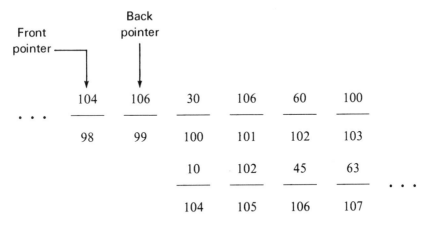

Although it is not immediately clear, this is a queue containing four numbers. To interpret it, we begin with the front and back pointers. These tell us that the number at the front of the queue is stored in Position 104 and the number at the back is stored in Position 106. Our initial picture of the queue, then, looks like this:

```
45     · · ·      10      <FRONT>
↑                 ↑
back             front
        ·
```

To fill in the rest of the queue, we begin at the front and follow pointers. The pointer after 10 is 102. This means that the number stored at Position 102 is the next one after 10 in the queue. Since this number is 60, we have the following picture:

```
45     · · ·   60←10      <FRONT>
↑               ↑
back           front
```

The pointer after 60 is 100, and so the number stored at Position 100 is next in the queue after 60. This number is 30.

Finally, the pointer after 30 is 106. But we already know that the number in Position 106 is the last item in the queue. Now we can draw a complete picture of the queue:

$$45 \leftarrow 30 \leftarrow 60 \leftarrow 10 \qquad <\text{FRONT}>$$

```
↑             ↑
back          front
```

Notice that the pointers lead *backward* from the front. To see why, imagine a line of students waiting to register for classes. Each memorizes the name of the person next in line and then the line breaks up. The students wait without standing in any particular order.

Even without a line, however, the students can easily register in order. Suppose Ann is originally the first in line. After she registers, she calls the name she remembers—the next person in line. Suppose this is Dan. After Dan registers, he calls the name *he* remembers.

In essence, each student points *backward* to the next student in line.

This example also shows us how to remove an item from the front of our queue. All we need to do is change the front pointer to the item that the item currently at the front is pointing to. In picture form, here is the result:

$$45 \leftarrow 30 \leftarrow 60 \qquad <\text{FRONT}>$$

```
↑        ↑
back     front
```

In memory, the same change looks like this:

New front
pointer ┐
        │
        ▼
102	106	30	106	60	100

· · ·

	98	99	100	101	102	103
			10	102	45	63
			104	105	106	107

· · ·

Notice that it is not necessary to remove the number 10 or the pointer following it from Positions 104 and 105. If we begin at the front of the modified queue and follow pointers to the back, we will never come to the number 10 or use the pointer in Position 105. They are no more a part of the queue than the numbers stored at, say, Positions 108 and 109.

This means we can now put Positions 104 and 105 to other uses. In particular, suppose we want to add the number 35 at the back of the queue. We can store it in Position 104.

Of course, we also need to change some pointers. The back pointer must be changed to show that the last number in the queue is now stored at Position 104. Also, until now the pointer following 45 has been irrelevant. As the last number in the list, 45 had nothing to point back to. Now, however, 35 follows 45, and so 45 must point back to the position where 35 is stored.

Here is the result:

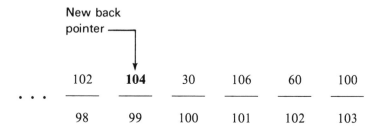

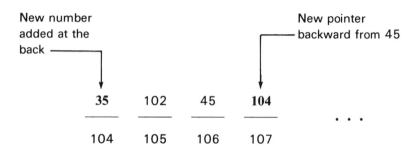

Notice that we have added a number to the queue and removed one without affecting where the queue is stored in memory. So long as we alternate removing and adding items, this queue will always remain between Positions 98 and 107.

8.16 APPLYING THE QUEUE

Now that we have shown how to represent stacks and queues, it is time to back up our claim that the structures are useful, beyond the obvious applications to scheduling. As a first example, we will show how the queue may be used to coordinate merge sort.

Suppose we have an eight-item list to sort. To begin, we line the eight items up into a queue. As we will see, it is important to think of each separate item in the queue as, itself, a list. We start, then with a queue of eight one-item lists:

$$113 \leftarrow 59 \leftarrow 276 \leftarrow 91 \leftarrow 80 \leftarrow 784 \leftarrow 900 \leftarrow 30 \ \text{<FRONT>}$$

We want, somehow, to end up with a queue containing a single, sorted eight-item list. Here is the algorithm we will follow:

QUEUE-BASED MERGE SORT

1. Remove the two lists at the front of the queue, merge them, and add the result at the back of the queue.

2. If there is just one list now in the queue, stop; otherwise, go back to step 1.

To apply the algorithm to our example, we begin by removing the two one-item lists from the front of the queue. If we merge these into a single two-item list and add it at the back of the queue, we get the following picture:

$$\begin{matrix} 30 \\ 900 \end{matrix} \leftarrow 113 \leftarrow 59 \leftarrow 276 \leftarrow 91 \leftarrow 80 \leftarrow 784 \quad \text{<FRONT>}$$

Since the queue does not contain just one list, step 2 sends us back to step 1. Again, we remove a pair of one-item lists from the front of the queue, merge them and add the resulting two-item list at the back of the queue. Here is the result:

$$\begin{matrix} 80 \\ 784 \end{matrix} \leftarrow \begin{matrix} 30 \\ 900 \end{matrix} \leftarrow 113 \leftarrow 59 \leftarrow 276 \leftarrow 91 \quad \text{<FRONT>}$$

After step 1 is carried out two more times, the queue will contain four two-item lists:

$$\begin{matrix} 59 \\ 113 \end{matrix} \leftarrow \begin{matrix} 91 \\ 276 \end{matrix} \leftarrow \begin{matrix} 80 \\ 784 \end{matrix} \leftarrow \begin{matrix} 30 \\ 900 \end{matrix} \quad \text{<FRONT>}$$

Since the queue still does not contain only a single list, the algorithm continues. The two two-item lists at the front of the queue are merged into a four-item list, and this is added at the back:

$$\begin{matrix} 30 \\ 80 \\ 784 \\ 900 \end{matrix} \leftarrow \begin{matrix} 59 \\ 113 \end{matrix} \leftarrow \begin{matrix} 91 \\ 276 \end{matrix} \quad \text{<FRONT>}$$

By now, it should be clear how the process will end. After the next execution of step 1, the queue will contain two four-item lists. When these are removed, to be merged, they leave an empty queue. The result of this last merge is a sorted eight-item list of the original numbers. This is added at the back of the empty queue. Since the queue now contains exactly one list, the algorithm stops in step 2.

*   *   *   *   *

A second use of the queue is easiest to explain through an example.

Suppose it is our responsibility to issue identification badges to everyone in an advertising agency. One way to make sure all the employees get a badge is to contact each one individually. If the agency is very large, however, this may call for an unreasonable amount of telephoning and knocking on doors.

For us, a much more attractive idea is to contact just a *few* employees. Then, after these have been issued a badge, we ask them to contact others. When the second batch of employees come to get a badge, we have them contact a third group, and so on. If we are lucky, everyone in the agency will be told to get a badge without our having to contact more than a handful directly.

The problem with this random, word-of-mouth system is that if we are *not* lucky, some employees may never be contacted. At the same time, others will be told to get a badge over and over, by various well-meaning colleagues.

The solution is to use a queue, taking advantage of the natural organization of the agency. We start by asking the president to form a line by himself at the badge-issuing desk, like this:

Pres. Mark Goodheart   <Badge Desk>

Then we carry out the following procedure:

1. Issue the person at the front of the line a badge.
2. Have that person tell all the people directly under his or her supervision to join the line at the back.
3. If there is anyone left in line, go back to step 1; otherwise, stop.

The president will get his badge and then ask all the people who work directly for him to join the line. These are the vice-presidents. Now the line looks like this:

Vice Pres. John Smith   Vice Pres. Jane Worthing   <Badge Desk>

After Jane Worthing gets her badge, she will ask all the account executives who work for her to join the line. The line will then stretch off the left side of the page, like this:

• • • Acct. Exec. Meg Asp Acct. Exec. Ed Carney VP John Smith <Badge Desk>

Next, John Smith will ask *his* account executives to join the line. And after Account Executive Ed Carney gets his badge, he will ask all of his *assistants* to line up.

Under this system, everyone in the company will get a badge and no one will be contacted twice. Notice, also, that we have contacted only one person directly: the president of the company.

*   *   *   *   *

This system works because the ad agency of our example is a **hierarchy**. That is, it is organized into levels, with employees at each level supervising employees at the next lower level. For companies, the usual way to represent a hierarchy is with an **organizational chart**, as in Figure 8.26.

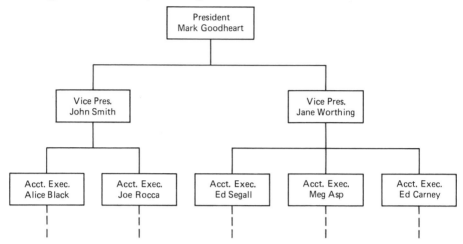

Figure 8.26 Organization chart for the advertising agency.

An organizational chart, however, is just one example of what computer scientists call a **tree**, a general way of representing a hierarchy. The most familiar example is a family tree, as pictured in Figure 8.27.

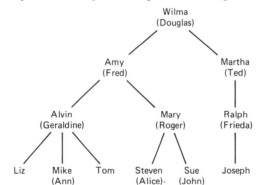

Figure 8.27 A family tree (spouses are listed in parentheses).

We can use a queue to contact all the people in this family, just as we used one to contact employees of the advertising agency. To begin, great-grandmother Wilma forms a line by herself. As she leaves the line, she asks all of her children to line up at the rear. The person now at the front leaves the line and asks *her* children to join the line at the rear.

If we continue in this way, each of Wilma's descendants will be asked to join the line, and none of them will be asked twice.[4] Again, if we are responsible for organizing this system, Wilma is the only person we will have to contact directly.

These examples we have given are only a hint of how often hierarchies arise in practical situations. In fact, hierarchies are so common that the trees which represent them are also a fundamental data structure of computer science. A major use of queues, then, is in looking systematically through the items in a tree.

---

[4] Spouses will never join the line. It includes only blood relatives.

8.17 TAKING STOCK

We have been looking, in this chapter, at how the organization of information affects the way it is handled. It turns out that this organization is often a crucial factor in performance. A good data structure turns a snail-paced algorithm like selection sort into a speed demon. A poor one slows even binary search down to a crawl.

Lists, linked lists, heaps, trees, stacks, and queues are among the most commonly used data structures. We have looked into how most of these may be represented in a computer's memory and how they are applied to practical problems.

We have not, however, fulfilled our promise to show what a stack is good for.

Of course, we have pointed out that a stack helps in dealing with interruptions. A harried sales clerk, or anyone else whose attention is often distracted, uses a mental version of a stack almost instinctively. But it may come as a surprise to learn that this problem of handling interruptions is of major importance in computer science.

In part, the reason is what we hinted at early in this chapter: A computer's memory often contains more than one program at a time. Sometimes, important programs may need to interrupt the computer to be carried out immediately. It may even happen that the interrupting program is itself interrupted by an even more important program.

Somehow, the computer must keep track of what it is doing, and for this purpose, the stack comes in handy.

But even if computers were never used by more than one programmer at a time, interruptions would still be a major topic. The reason is a peculiar one. As we will see in Chapter 9, programs spend a good deal of time interrupting themselves.

EXERCISES

8.1. Continue the example shown in Figure 8.1. Here are the next three projects and priority numbers: Call fire department (100); get a cup of coffee (20); meet with boss (70).

8.2. The memory pictured below is set for a binary search as described in Section 8.4.
   (a) How many numbers are in the list?
   (b) What is the significance of the number in Position 99?
   (c) What is the significance of the number in Position 98?
   (d) What is the significance of the number in Position 103?

	100	102	102	100	102	103	105	
...	97	98	99	100	101	102	103	...

8.3. Suppose, in Exercise 8.2, that binary search is used to look for 105. Will it be found? Show how the memory will look after the first comparison and any ensuing adjustments have been made.

8.4. The following ordered list is represented as in Section 8.4. Add 31 to the list and show the result. Then remove 20 and show the result. How many numbers are moved in each case?

	125	10	20	30	40	50	
· · ·	——	——	——	——	——	——	· · ·
	99	100	101	102	103	104	

8.5. Copy Figure 8.4 and then make all of the additions and deletions indicated in Figure 8.2. Do *not* erase any arrows or numbers. Mark any arrows not in use with an X.

8.6. Copy Figure 8.9 and then modify it as necessary to add 650 to the list.

8.7. Copy Figure 8.9 and then modify it as necessary to remove 724 from the list.

8.8. Copy Figure 8.9 and then modify it as necessary to remove 797 from the list.

8.9. Copy Figure 8.9 and then modify it as necessary to remove 345 from the list.

8.10. Draw a tournament tree for the following players: Pat, Sue, Carole, Fran, Mary, Martha, Barbara, Wendy. In each match, the winner is the one with the prior name in an alphabetical ordering. For example, Barbara would beat Fran.

8.11. Suppose Barbara leaves the tournament described in Exercise 8.10 and is replaced by Kate. Draw a revised tree marking the matches that must be played to determine the new champion. Is the number of matches played the same as in Figure 8.12?

8.12. Convert the tree of Exercise 8.10 into a heap.

8.13. Barbara leaves the tournament of the previous exercise and is replaced by Kate. Using diagrams like the ones in Figures 8.14 and 8.15, show how the new champion will be determined. Also, give a complete, ordered list of matches—who plays in the first match, who plays in the second match, and so on.

8.14. (a) Construct a heap with the following numbers: 10, 55, 30, 15, 20, 35, 60.
   (b) Remove 60 from the heap, replace it with 5, and show step by step how the heap is reorganized.
   (c) Remove 55, replace it with 70, and show step by step how the heap is reorganized.

8.15. How many comparisons will be made in a "minitournament" in a heap of 15 items? In a heap of 31 items? In a heap of 63 items?

8.16. The fourth level of a heap always has eight items. Say in one sentence how to determine the number of items on any other level.

8.17. How many levels will a 1,023-item heap have?

8.18. Draw a diagram of this heap:

100	95	60	90	85	30	29	82
1	2	3	4	5	6	7	8

80	83	5	20	25	26	27
9	10	11	12	13	14	15

8.19. What is wrong with this heap?

9	5	8	2	6	4	7
1	2	3	4	5	6	7

8.20. A heap of 1,023 items is stored in memory beginning at Position 1. Consider the item stored in Position 364. Give the position of the item
(a) Above it
(b) Below it to the left
(c) Below it to the right
(d) Two levels above it

8.21. Repeat Exercise 8.20 assuming the heap is stored beginning in Position 4.

8.22. Figures 8.21 to 8.23 show a heap used for sorting. Continue the example until a final, ordered list has been constructed.

8.23. The first three students to arrive at a registration counter are—in this order—Meg, John, and Alan. The registrar registers two of them. Then Alice arrives. The registrar registers the two remaining students. Show the order in which the four students register assuming
(a) The registrar treats the line as a queue.
(b) The registrar treats the line as a stack.

8.24. (a) Represent the stack shown below as described in Section 8.14.
(b) Show how the numbers in memory will change when the top item is removed.
(c) Show how they will change if 62 is then added to the stack.

$$
\begin{array}{c}
74 \\
101 \\
300 \\
\underline{95}
\end{array}
$$

8.25. (a) Represent the following queue in memory as a linked list. Use exactly 12 memory positions.

$$90 \quad 60 \quad 80 \quad 70 \quad 50 \quad <FRONT>$$

(b) Show how the memory will look if the number at the front of the queue is removed.

(c) Show how the memory will look if 40 is then added to the queue. *Do not use any memory positions other than the original 12.*

8.26. Use the two-step merging algorithm of Section 8.16 to put the following list of words into alphabetical order: pencil, eraser, paper, staples, glue, notebook, typewriter, ink. Show how the queue will look after each execution of step 1 of the algorithm.

8.27. Show how the advertising agency queue will look after John Smith calls his subordinates to join it.

8.28. We have given several examples of how trees are used in everyday life to organize information. Give at least one more.

9 Stacks, Subroutines, and Recursion

9.1 POWER OF EXPRESSION

Back in Chapter 6, we pointed out that computer programs are written in a kind of language. Of course, a program is only a list of numbers, but this is like saying that a book is only a list of letters. These lists have meaning, so long as we know how to interpret them.

The language we developed for our model computer is based on 15 number-coded instructions. We call it a **machine language**, because the machine we have built understands it directly. *We* need to interpret the program; for the computer, numbers translate directly into actions.

In a sense, the numbers flowing through a computer are like nerve impulses in our bodies. These, too, translate directly into actions.

Machine language is used in computers because it is simple, precise, and general. Considering the tens of thousands of words we use in English, the frequency with which we misunderstand one another, and the difficulty of explaining even such easy procedures as how to drive from one town to the next or how to roast a chicken, machine language is something of a miracle.

With a machine language of just 15 instructions, we can program *anything* it is possible for a computer to carry out and there is never any chance of misunderstanding. Each instruction is absolutely clear.

Despite these advantages, however, we do not generally use machine language to describe what a computer does. With such a simple language, it takes too long to say anything meaningful.

Machine language is general, in the sense that it can be used to write a tremendous variety of step-by-step procedures. It is weak in expression, however, just like a person with a small vocabulary. Our goal, in this chapter and the next, is to find ways of creating computer languages with a greater power of expression. That is, we want languages which make it easy to express important meanings.

As we hinted at the end of Chapter 8, a large role is played by interruptions and the use of stacks to cope with them.

9.2 SUBROUTINES AGAIN

A major drawback of machine language is its tiny vocabulary. Fortunately, we already know one solution to this problem. Instead of using instructions one at a time, we can group them together into program components—subroutines.

Although our model computer understands only 15 instructions, we can write an infinite number of subroutines. These subroutines, then, will make up the "words" of a much more powerful alternative to machine language—a mode of expression better suited to our own understanding.

In Section 6.4, for example, we introduced subroutines to store a number in the memory, to add 1 to a memory position, and to jump to a new part of the program if a comparison shows that two stored numbers are the same. Suppose we call these subroutines STORE, ADD-ONE, and JUMP-IF-NUMBERS-ARE-SAME. Then we can write a program that counts to 128 as follows:

1. STORE 128 in Position 100

2. ADD-ONE to Position 99

3. JUMP-IF-NUMBERS-ARE-SAME in Positions 99 and 100 to **Step 5**

4. JUMP-TO-POSITION **Step 2**

5. STOP

Notice that this program is not yet written entirely with subroutines. Steps 4 and 5 are ordinary instructions. The subroutines we *have* used, however, make it much easier to understand what the program does. It increases the number in Position 99 repeatedly until reaching 128.

Furthermore, this way of writing the program is still perfectly precise. If we want, we can copy the instructions that go into each subroutine from Section 6.4, translate to numbers, and load the result into our model computer.

As far as *we* are concerned, however, the program is best left as it is. As a way of describing a computer procedure, this is far better than a list of machine instructions. Subroutine names are more expressive.

Of course, the three small subroutines we have used are not far from simple machine instructions; a program using them is still difficult to understand. Our language of subroutines would include more sophisticated examples.

Here is the count-to-128 program again, using one of these sophisticated subroutines.

1. ADD-ONE to Position 99.

2. REPEATEDLY-UNTIL the number in Position 99 is 128 (if not yet, go back to **Step 1**).

Now the program is practically written in English. It means "add 1 to Position 99 repeatedly until the number in that Position is 128."

Easy as it is to understand, however, the program has not lost the precision of unembellished machine language. Each line refers to a definite subroutine, which in turn is made up of machine instructions.

Although REPEATEDLY-UNTIL appears to be plain English, in fact it is just a name. The subroutine to which it refers checks a memory position to see whether it contains a certain number. If it does not, the subroutine jumps to a different part of the program, in this case back to step 1. If it does contain the given number, the subroutine ends.

Here is an outline for the subroutine:

LOAD-TOP-FROM-POSITION **Memory-Position-to-Check**
LOAD-BOTTOM **Number-It-Might-Contain**
SUBTRACT
JUMP-IF-ZERO-TO-POSITION **Position-of-STOP-Instruction-**
                         at-End-of-This-Subroutine
JUMP-TO-POSITION **Beginning-of-Loop**
STOP

9.3 TWO PROBLEMS

Subroutines make programs easier to understand and compose. The more they hide the details of what the computer is doing, the more we can concentrate on the *abstract* procedure.

Unfortunately, as we have described them, subroutines have two serious shortcomings.

The first is that, although program outlines using subroutines are clear and precise, computers cannot understand them. Translating from subroutine names to lists of machine instructions which a computer can use is a simple, straightforward task—it amounts to copying predesigned outlines. But few people would undertake the job. A moderately large program might contain a million instructions, each of which must be copied correctly for the program to function.

Of course, since translating from outlines to programs is such a mechanical job, it seems reasonable to expect that computers themselves might be able to do it. In fact, this is why we have stressed the precision and clarity of our subroutine names. It does not take any intuition or understanding to work with them. We should be able to boil the work of translation down to step-by-step rules.

This question of automatic translation is a major subject, however, one we must postpone until Chapter 10. For now, we need to look into a second serious problem with our idea of building a language from subroutines.

*   *   *   *   *

For the sake of simplicity, we have looked only at very short programs in this book. Also, until now, we have tended to ignore the fact that real computers are built with only a limited amount of memory.

As a result of these simplifications, we have concentrated our attention on using algorithms and data structures to save *time*.

In practice, however, a fast algorithm is worthless if it uses more memory space than is available in our computer. In particular, if we translate an algorithm into a program so long that it does not fit in the computer's memory system, we have wasted our work.

We have considered subroutines as patterns to be copied as often as needed. In theory, this is perfectly reasonable; in practice, it would use far too much space.

For example, any computer that does not have a machine instruction to multiply two numbers will need a subroutine for the job. In a computer with as few instructions as ours, each copy of a multiplication subroutine would fill more than 100 memory positions.

In a program using 1,000 multiplications, say, to calculate formulas for an engineer, 100,000 memory locations would be filled just by the instructions for the multiplications.

If the engineer is using a small computer, a program written this way might leave no room for the data—the numbers the program is supposed to multiply. If the engineer is using a larger computer, he or she is probably sharing memory space with other programmers. If each programmer writes long programs, only a few people will be able to use the computer at one time.

In either case, it is important to keep programs short.

9.4 SHARING SUBROUTINES

In practice, then, long subroutines are rarely copied several times within a program. Instead, a single copy is shared by different parts of the program.

This sharing is tricky to arrange, however.

Suppose our collection of subroutines includes one called MULTIPLY that multiplies the numbers in Positions 399 and 400 and puts the answer back in Position 400. We want to use this subroutine to compute 3 times 4 times 5. Since there are two multiplications, we will have to use the subroutine twice.

Here is an outline for a program that gets the answer by multiplying 3 by 4 and then multiplying the answer by 5:

1. STORE 3 in Position 399
2. STORE 4 in Position 400
3. MULTIPLY
4. STORE 5 in Position 399
5. MULTIPLY
6. STOP

As we know from Section 6.4, machine-language instructions for the STORE subroutine fill exactly seven memory positions. Since it is so short, we will assume this subroutine may simply be copied three times in writing the program. The MULTIPLY subroutine, on the other hand, is quite long. As we have said, we would like to use just one copy.

To make the example concrete, let us suppose that MULTIPLY happens to fill exactly 100 memory positions. In this case, here is where the instructions of each part of the program would be stored in the memory:

   0   First STORE subroutine (to put 3 in Position 399)
   7   Second STORE subroutine (to put 4 in Position 400)
  14   MULTIPLY subroutine
114   Third STORE subroutine (to put 5 in Position 399)
121   *Instructions to use the* MULTIPLY *subroutine again*
???   STOP

The left-hand column shows where each set of instructions *begins*. For example, instructions for the first copy of the STORE subroutine, which puts 3 in Position 399, are stored beginning in Position 0. As we have said, this subroutine fills seven memory positions: Positions 0, 1, 2, 3, 4, 5, and 6. The single copy of the MULTIPLY subroutine fills 100 memory positions: Positions 14 through 113.

The main focus of our attention is the set of instructions beginning at Position 121. These are supposed to cause the second multiplication to be carried out. Since we are allowing ourselves just a single copy of the MULTIPLY subroutine, these instructions must somehow make use of this copy.

Consider what happens when the computer carries out the instructions in this program. As usual, it begins with the instruction in Position 0 and moves forward through the memory. The first three sets of instructions cause the computer to multiply 3 by 4 and store the product in Position 400. The fourth set stores 5 in Position 399. Here is how the memory will look after the first four instruction sets have been completed.

$$\cdots \quad \frac{5}{399} \quad \frac{12}{400} \quad \cdots$$

At this point, we only need to multiply the numbers in Positions 399 and 400 to get the final answer. Since the MULTIPLY subroutine does exactly this, we are almost at the point of having what we want. The instructions of the MULTIPLY subroutine, however, are stored beginning at Position 14 and the computer is currently about to carry out the instruction stored in Position 121.

The question is, What should we put at Position 121 to cause the computer to go back to Position 14?

Perhaps it seems obvious that we should just use a JUMP-TO-POSITION instruction, like this:

   0   First STORE subroutine (to put 3 in Position 399)
   7   Second STORE subroutine (to put 4 in Position 400)
  14   MULTIPLY subroutine
114   Third STORE subroutine (to put 5 in Position 399)
121   JUMP-TO-POSITION 14
123   STOP

But what if we do? The computer will go back to Position 14, of course, and perform the multiplication. However, having completed the instructions in memory positions 14 through 113, it will continue with the instruction at Position 114. That is, it will again store 5 in Position 399.

Next, it will go on to the instruction in Position 121. But this instruction is JUMP-TO-POSITION 14. The computer will go back to Position 14 and begin a third multiplication.

In fact, we have created an endless loop. As the program stands, it will go on multiplying by 5 over and over, with no end in sight unless someone turns off the power.

*   *   *   *   *

Actually, the never-ending loop we have created is quite easy to correct, in this case. We want the computer to stop after it has performed exactly two multiplications. After the second, we know there will be a 5 stored in Position 399. Therefore we need only to insert a few instructions after the MULTIPLY subroutine to check this position. If a 5 is found, the computer should jump immediately to a STOP instruction.

This solution, however, is a little like patching a flat tire with bubble gum. It might work in some cases, but it is not a good, general method.

Consider, for example, what would happen if we tried to write a program involving *one hundred* multiplications, each carried out by the same copy of the MULTIPLY subroutine. The program might look like this:

0	Miscellaneous instructions
94	Instructions to store 36 in Position 399
	and 45 in Position 400
108	JUMP-TO-POSITION 5555
110	Miscellaneous instructions
417	Instructions to store 81 in Position 399
	and 14 in Position 400
431	JUMP-TO-POSITION 5555
433	Miscellaneous instructions
	.
	.
	.
5555	MULTIPLY subroutine
5655	???

The MULTIPLY subroutine is first used here to multiply 36 by 45. A little later it is used to multiply 81 by 14. Since the subroutine is stored beginning at Position 5555, we can carry out a multiplication just by jumping to that position. The question is how to get back afterward to the right place in the program.

For example, after the first multiplication, we want the computer to continue with the instruction in Position 110. After the second, it should continue with the instruction in Position 433.

Of course, we can use the same method that worked before. After the MULTIPLY subroutine we can include instructions to use the number in Position 399 to decide where to go. The instructions would begin like this:

> 5655   If the number in Position 399 is 36, JUMP-TO-POSITION 110
> If the number in Position 399 is 81, JUMP-TO-POSITION 433
>
> .
> .
> .

But with 100 multiplications, we would need 100 of these compare-and-jump tests. Certainly this is not the neatest solution to our problem.

Furthermore, in some cases it is not a solution at all. We have been assuming that each multiplication stores a different number in Position 399 and that we will *know* these numbers while we are writing the program. What would we do if two multiplications involve the same numbers? Or if the numbers to be multiplied are not known beforehand because they are calculated within the program?

The number stored in Position 399 gives a kind of hint about where to go when the MULTIPLY subroutine is completed. But why rely on a hint? Why not simply provide a way to tell the subroutine directly where to go when it is finished?

In fact, this leads to a much more reliable, general solution to the problem of using subroutines. In the case of our example, we can use Position 9999 as a kind of clearinghouse. Before any part of the program jumps to the MULTIPLY subroutine, it stores the memory position where MULTIPLY should return in Position 9999. Each time MULTIPLY finishes, it checks Position 9999 to see where to go.

This leads to the following revised version of our program:

> 0   Miscellaneous instructions
> 94   Instructions to store 36 in Position 399
>   and 45 in Position 400
> 108   Instructions to store 117 in Position 9999
> 115   JUMP-TO-POSITION 5555
> 117   Miscellaneous instructions
> 417   Instructions to store 81 in Position 399
>   and 14 in Position 400
> 431   Instructions to store 440 in Position 9999
> 438   JUMP-TO-POSITION 5555
> 440   Miscellaneous instructions
>
> .
> .
> .
>
> 5555   MULTIPLY subroutine
> 5655   Instructions to jump to the position stored in Position 9999

After the first multiplication, MULTIPLY will find 117 stored in Position 9999, so it will continue with the instructions beginning in Position 117. After the second multiplication, it will find 440 and jump to that position.

*   *   *   *   *

At the end of Chapter 8, we said that programs spend a good deal of time interrupting themselves. Now it is easy to see why.

The program we have been discussing runs through a list of instructions, interrupting itself every so often to carry out a multiplication. As we have shown, the program must be careful to remember *where* it has been interrupted by storing a *return position* in Position 9999. After the interruption—to carry out instructions of the MULTIPLY subroutine—the number stored in Position 9999 shows where to continue.

In fact, every subroutine used in a long program is treated as an interruption in the same way. Each is stored just once in the memory. To use it, the computer jumps to where the subroutine is stored. But before jumping, it stores a return position. When the subroutine is finished, it uses this return position to jump back to the interrupted part of the program.

9.5 INTERRUPTED INTERRUPTIONS

So far, we have seen how to deal with a main program which interrupts itself occasionally to execute subroutines. A single position in memory—say, Position 9999—can be used to store the correct return position.

Unfortunately, programs and subroutines often form a much more disorderly tangle. As we are about to see, interruptions may themselves be interrupted. In this case, it is not enough to remember a single return position.

Think back to the harried store clerk of Chapter 8. She is talking to a customer when the phone rings. Suppose that, as she answers the phone, she uses the mental equivalent of our Position 9999 to remember to get back to the customer after the interruption. We might picture her memory this way:

Customer

• • •   ——————   • • •

"9999"

If nothing were to happen until the end of the phone conversation, the clerk would check this position in her memory and return to helping the customer.

Problems arise, however, when her boss interrupts the telephone call. To remember to get back to the phone call after this interruption, she stores the new "return position" in her memory as follows:

Phone

• • •   ———   • • •

"9999"

But now the poor customer is completely forgotten.

The solution, of course, is for her to use a stack. When the phone rings, she puts the customer on the stack:

Customer
_____

When her boss calls, she puts the phone on the stack:

Phone

Customer
_____

After finishing with her boss, she removes the top item from the stack to see what she should get back to—in this case, the interrupted phone call. When she finishes the phone call, she will find the customer on the stack, waiting to be served.

*   *   *   *   *

Precisely the same approach allows programs to cope with subroutines which interrupt other subroutines.

As an example, consider a subroutine called DIVIDE that uses the ordinary grade-school method for division. This method calls for a good deal of multiplication. Therefore, DIVIDE will need to interrupt itself sometimes to use the MULTIPLY subroutine.

Now suppose we write a program called MAIN which, among other calculations, uses DIVIDE to perform several divisions. When MAIN is running, it will interupt itself to use DIVIDE, which in turn will interrupt itself to use MULTIPLY.

A stack keeps track of all this quite easily.

When MAIN begins, the stack is empty. Instructions of MAIN are carried out until the first division is required. At this point, MAIN stores a return position on the stack and jumps to the beginning of DIVIDE. The stack looks like this:

Position to return to in MAIN
_____

Incidentally, this stored position is not the _beginning_ of MAIN. It is the part of MAIN just after the first division—the correct place to _continue_.

As we have said, after some instructions of DIVIDE have been carried out, a multiplication will be required. DIVIDE stores a return position on the stack and jumps to MULTIPLY. Now the stack looks like this:

Position to return to in DIVIDE

Position to return to in MAIN
_____

When MULTIPLY is finished with its work, it will remove the position number on the top of the stack and use it to jump back to continue at just the point where the DIVIDE subroutine has been interrupted. This leaves just one return position on the stack:

Position to return to in MAIN

This position will not be used immediately, however, since DIVIDE calls for more than just one multiplication. For each one, DIVIDE will store a return position on the stack and jump to MULTIPLY. Each time MULTIPLY finishes it will remove this position and use it to continue at the right place in DIVIDE.

Eventually, however, the work of division will be completed. DIVIDE will remove the last position number from the stack and jump back to continue at the correct position in MAIN.

Of course, this whole process will be repeated for the next division MAIN requires, but we do not need to consider the details. They are just the same as in the case we have already described.

*   *   *   *   *

This abstract approach is easily put into practice. Instead of using Position 9999 to hold a single return position, we could use it as the top pointer of a stack, represented as we described in Chapter 8. The items in the stack would just be return positions—numbers—and these would be stored in positions following Position 9999.

This is a final solution to coping with the interrupted interruptions caused by subroutines. In fact, it is the way subroutines are actually handled by most computers.

9.6 A HIERARCHY OF SUBROUTINES

We began this chapter with the goal of creating powerfully expressive computer languages. After so many pages concerned with how to save space by sharing copies of subroutines, it may seem that this goal has been forgotten. In fact, the stack method leads to two new ways of achieving it.

The first point to notice is that subroutines give us more than we bargained for.

Our original purpose in using subroutines was to create a second level of vocabulary for the computer. The first level—the machine language the computer understands directly—is tedious and confusing. Our idea was to use machine instructions just once, to write a large collection of subroutines. From then on, instead of writing a program as a list of instructions, we could write it as a list of subroutine names.

The two-level vocabulary system we set out to construct might be pictured as in Figure 9.1.

This is a long step forward toward an expressive computer language, because subroutines carry out substantial units of work—units people can easily understand. It is clearer to say that a computer uses a subroutine to compare two numbers than to say that it loads two numbers into the arithmetic-logic unit's **Top** and **Bottom** registers, subtracts them, and checks to see whether the result is zero.

Subroutines allow us to think on a higher level.

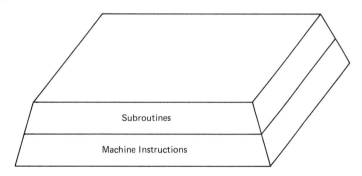

Figure 9.1 Two-level hierarchy of languages.

Our original idea, however, provided for only two levels: machine instructions, and subroutines written with machine instructions. With the stack method we have invented, we can do infinitely better. We can use subroutines as components of still more powerful subroutines to create levels as high as we like.

Figure 9.2 pictures the hierarchy we are considering. Notice that the components at every level above the bottom are called subroutines. They are still just pieces which we can use to design complete routines, or programs.

At the bottom level of this diagram are machine instructions like ADD, LOAD-TOP, and JUMP-IF-ZERO-TO-POSITION. These are used to write second-level subroutines like ADD-ONE, JUMP-IF-NUMBERS-ARE-SAME, and MULTIPLY.

At the third level is our DIVIDE subroutine, which is written using the lower-level MULTIPLY subroutine. And above the DIVIDE subroutine, we might find a subroutine to find square roots, since these are calculated using division.[1]

Of course, we can continue upward as far as we like. But stop for a moment to consider what will happen if a statistician who wants to calculate formulas writes a program using the SQUARE ROOT subroutine. When the program is run, then, it will be interrupted at some point for a square root to be computed. The SQUARE ROOT subroutine that carries out this work will itself be interrupted every time it requires a division. And the DIVISION subroutine will be interrupted repeatedly for multiplications.

With the stack method, however, all this is handled neatly. When each multiplication is completed, the DIVIDE subroutine it has interrupted is continued. When divisions are completed, the SQUARE ROOT subroutine continues. And when a square root has been calculated, the computer continues working on the main program, which is what has called for the square root to be calculated in the first place.

Moreover, the statistician never needs to know about all these interrupted interruptions. As far as he or she is concerned, the program simply asks for a square root to be calculated.

---

[1] The square root of 9 is 3, because 3 squared is 9. In general, the square root of any number is what we have to square to get that number.

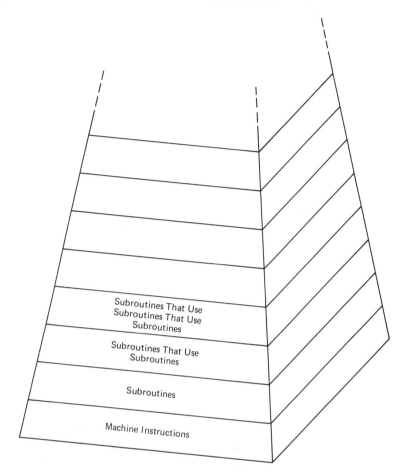

Figure 9.2 Infinite-level hierarchy of languages.

In fact, the statistician's new program may, in turn, be used as a subroutine by someone who knows little about statistics. An executive who wants to analyze sales might write a program which uses that statistics program as a subroutine to estimate how fast sales are growing.

The statistician relies on lower-level subroutines to calculate square roots and divide numbers, without knowing the details of how these subroutines are written. Likewise, the executive may rely on subroutines the statistician has written, free from concerns regarding the statistical procedures involved.

In general, the higher the level of the subroutine, the farther it is from the details of what the computer is doing and the closer it is to our own way of thinking about a problem. That is, the higher the level, the greater the power of expression.

Using machine instructions to write simple subroutines gave us a new language. The stacking method allows us to construct a *hierarchy* of languages—each level a little closer to our own.

9.7 SUBROUTINES AND DEFINITIONS

At the beginning of Section 9.6, we said that the stacking method of handling subroutines helps in *two* new ways with the problem of expressing algorithms to a computer.

As we have already seen, one advantage of the stacking method is that it allows subroutines to use other subroutines. This leads to the hierarchy we have just considered. But the stacking method also allows something we know to be both powerful and dangerous—self-reference.

There is nothing to stop a subroutine from using *itself* as a building block.

Before we investigate the power of self-referential subroutines, however, it is a good idea to get acquainted with the danger. The best place to start is with the reason self-reference is avoided in dictionaries.

*   *   *   *   *

In general, a dictionary is useful because it explains difficult words in terms of words we already know. We might use it to find out that purslane is a kind of weed sometimes used in salads.

Of course, sometimes we may not know even the words in the definition. If the dictionary tells us that a cuttlefish is a kind of mollusk that secretes an inky fluid, this is no help if we do not know what a mollusk is. Luckily, we can use the dictionary to find out. It will tell us that a mollusk is a soft-bodied creature with a shell, like a snail, an oyster, or an octopus.

This example brings up two key points.

The first is that using definitions to explain other definitions is very much like writing subroutines with other subroutines. The definition of *cuttlefish* uses the word *mollusk* just as the DIVIDE subroutine uses MULTIPLY.

The second point is that a dictionary is useless unless its definitions or its definitions of words used in other definitions, and so on, eventually lead us to words we already know. If a dictionary tells us that a lek is 100 qintars and that a qintar is roughly equivalent to 30 zlotys, it is no help at all.

Although we do not usually think of it this way, a dictionary is a hierarchical system, as pictured in Figure 9.3. At the lowest level are easy, familiar words like *soft, shell,* and *body.* These are used to define a second level of vocabulary, including words like *mollusk.* At the third level are words whose definitions use the second-level vocabulary, and so on.

The key here is the bottom level—the words we do not need a definition to understand. Without it the dictionary never really tells us anything.

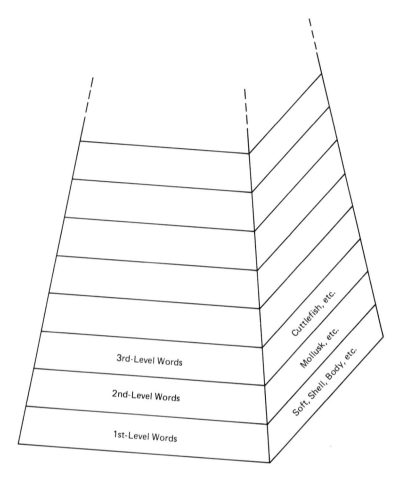

Figure 9.3 Hierarchy of words in a dictionary.

Likewise, the key to our hierarchy of subroutines is the base level—the machine instructions which a computer understands directly. If subroutines were described only in terms of other subroutines, we could never translate them into a program for the computer to carry out.

9.8 CIRCULARITY

To be of use, then, a dictionary must have a bottom level. But how is it possible *not* to have a bottom level? If we define a lek in terms of qintars and qintars in terms of zlotys, and so on, it seems we must eventually come to words we know.

Unfortunately, this is not so. Suppose the dictionary contains the following definitions:

Lek: 100 qintars.
Qintar: Roughly 30 zlotys.
Zloty: About 1/3000th of a lek.

These three entries create a never-ending loop or circle of references. When definitions lead back to the word being defined, as in this case, a dictionary is said to suffer from **circularity**.

It does not take three definitions to create circularity, however. Suppose a dictionary tells us that a cuttlefish is a kind of mollusk and that a mollusk is any animal closely related to the cuttlefish. If we look up *cuttlefish,* we will have to interrupt ourselves to find out what a mollusk is. While reading *that* definition, we will come to the word *cuttlefish* and interrupt ourselves to look it up.

Of course, we can go on this way forever. The definitions never lead to a bottom level.

In fact, the clearest example of circularity is when a definition refers directly to the word defined, as in the following entry:

Gnu: Any offspring of the female gnu.

There is nothing incorrect about this definition. It is simply of no use if we do not already know what a gnu is.

This is why self-reference in definitions is dangerous. In general, it leads to circularity—that is, it keeps us from getting to a bottom level. On principle, then, dictionary definitions are expected not to refer to the word being defined.

*   *   *   *   *

It would seem that the same reasoning should rule out self-reference in subroutines. For example, consider the following two-step description of a division subroutine:

NEW-DIVIDE SUBROUTINE

1. Divide using the subroutine NEW-DIVIDE

2. STOP

This is the computer equivalent of our gnu definition.

Suppose we try to use it. The computer begins with step 1, which calls for it to use a certain subroutine. It carefully stores the correct return position on the stack and then jumps to this subroutine.

But the subroutine it jumps to is NEW-DIVIDE, and so the computer begins to carry out the steps of NEW-DIVIDE for a second time. Of course, it gets only as far as step 1, which calls for it to use a certain subroutine. The computer carefully stores a second return position on the stack and then jumps to this subroutine.

Of course, no division will ever be carried out. Circularity has prevented the computer from ever reaching a bottom level of instructions that explain how to perform a division.

9.9 RECURSION

Surprisingly, however, it is possible for both definitions and subroutines to use self-reference without causing circularity. Here is an example:

> The *p*-value of a number: Twice the *p*-value of the next smaller number,
> except that the *p*-value of 1 is 1.

This definition certainly *seems* circular. It tells us, for example, that the *p*-value of 344 is twice the *p*-value of 343. Since we do not already know what a *p*-value is, this is not much help.

But notice that the ends of the circle do not quite meet. The definition does not tell us that the *p*-value of 344 is the *p*-value of 344. It defines the *p*-value of 344 in terms of something else, the *p*-value of 343.

This definition is not circular, because it *does* eventually lead to a bottom level. Figure 9.4 shows how:

The *p*-value of 344 is twice the *p*-value of 343
The *p*-value of 343 is twice the *p*-value of 342
The *p*-value of 342 is twice the *p*-value of 341
  .
  .
  .

The *p*-value of 3 is twice the *p*-value of 2
The *p*-value of 2 is twice the *p*-value of 1
The *p*-value of 1 is 1   **Figure 9.4** Using the definition of *p*-values.

The bottom-level statement, given in the definition, is that the *p*-value of 1 is 1. From this, we can work our way up to any higher level:

> The *p*-value of 2 is twice the *p*-value of 1: 2·1, or 2.
> The *p*-value of 3 is twice the *p*-value of 2: 2·2, or 4.
> The *p*-value of 4 is twice the *p*-value of 3: 2·4, or 8.

If we continue on this way, we will eventually get the *p*-value of 344.

Apparently, our definition of *p*-value is not circular at all. Perhaps it would be best to call it "spiral," since it spirals down toward a base-level fact—in this case, the fact that the *p*-value of 1 is 1. Usually, however, this kind of definition is called **recursive**.

*   *   *   *   *

In a moment, we will show how our recursive definition of *p*-values may be translated into a recursive subroutine, one that uses self-reference. First, however, take a moment to look at the first few *p*-values, which are collected in Figure 9.5.

	p-value of
Number	the number
1	1
2	2
3	4
4	8
5	16

Figure 9.5 *p*-values.

P-values, it turns out, are just the place values of the binary number system. In binary, the third place from the right has the value 4, the same as the *p*-value of 3; the fifth place from the right has the value 16, the same as the *p*-value of 5; and so on.

In essence, we have given the definition of binary place values in the following form:

Binary place values: Every binary place value is twice the place value on its right, except for the rightmost place value, which is 1.

This definition is self-referential, since it explains place values in terms of place values. But it is recursive, not circular. The definition includes a bottom level by giving us the place value of the rightmost position.

9.10 A RECURSIVE SUBROUTINE

Since *p*-values are binary place values, they are of practical importance. If we can translate our dictionary definition into a subroutine, we will have a way of calculating these important values.

The following is just an outline of what we want, but it shows all the essential points. A subroutine designed according to this outline will calculate the *p*-value of the number stored in Position 500 and put the result in Position 501.

P-VALUE SUBROUTINE

1. If the number in Position 500 is 1, jump to step 6.
2. Subtract 1 from Position 500 and store the answer back in Position 500.
3. Use the P-VALUE subroutine to calculate the *p*-value of the number in Position 500 and store the answer in Position 501.
4. Multiply the number in Position 501 by 2 and store the answer back in Position 501.
5. Return.
6. Store 1 in Position 501.
7. Return.

The first point to notice about this subroutine is that it is self-referential. Step 3 calls for it to use itself. Despite the seeming paradox of this idea, however, the subroutine will work correctly, as we will soon show.

A second important point about the subroutine is how it ends. If the computer gets to either step 5 or step 7, it will use the top item on the stack of return positions to decide where to go next. In either case, the subroutine is finished. Whatever instructions it has interrupted should continue.

*   *   *   *   *

Suppose, now, that we want to use the subroutine P-VALUE to calculate the p-value of a number. All we need is a start-up program that stores this number in Position 500, stores the position of a STOP instruction on the return stack, and then jumps to the beginning of P-VALUE.

If P-VALUE works correctly, it will store the p-value we want in Position 501. Then, when it is finished, the subroutine will check the stack to find out where to go next. But the instruction stored at the return position on the stack is a STOP. Therefore when P-VALUE is finished, processing will halt.

As a first test, we will assume that the start-up program has been written to store a 1 in Position 500. Hopefully, when the computer stops, the p-value of 1 will be stored in Position 501.

After the start-up program stores 1 in Position 500, it puts the position of a STOP instruction on the stack and jumps to the beginning of P-VALUE. In step 1, P-VALUE checks the number in Position 500. Since this number is 1, it jumps to step 6. In step 6, it stores 1 in Position 501. In step 7, it checks the stack to see where to go next. The stack sends it to a STOP instruction, and when it executes this instruction, it stops.

At this point, Position 501 contains 1. This is the correct p-value for 1.

*   *   *   *   *

In this case, we have used only the bottom-level part of the subroutine. To test out the recursive part, suppose we modify the start-up program so that it stores 2 in Position 500.

What we hope is that, when the computer stops, the p-value of 2 will be stored in Position 501. Note also that to get the p-value of 2, according to the definition, the computer should first calculate the p-value of 1 and then multiply the answer by 2. In fact, this is exactly how it proceeds.

Here, then, is the analysis. After the start-up program stores 2 in Position 500, it puts the position of a STOP instruction on the stack and jumps to the beginning of P-VALUE. In step 1, P-VALUE checks the number in Position 500, but since this is not 1, P-VALUE goes on to step 2.

In step 2, P-VALUE subtracts 1 from the number 2 stored in Position 500 and puts the result, 1, back in Position 500. Notice that, with 1 stored in Position 500, the computer is set to use P-VALUE to calculate the p-value of 1—the first step in calculating the p-value of 2. Step 3 does just this. But take time to consider the details.

Step 3 calls for P-VALUE to interrupt itself to carry out a subroutine. After this interruption, the computer should continue with step 4 of P-VALUE. Thus, before doing anything else, P-VALUE must store this return position on the stack, as follows:

Position of P-VALUE's step 4
Position of a STOP instruction

Next, still as part of its step 3, P-VALUE jumps to the beginning of the interrupting subroutine. But in this case, the interrupting subroutine is P-VALUE itself.

Fortunately, we already know exactly what P-VALUE will do if we jump to it with 1 stored in Position 500. We analyzed this case just a moment ago. It will store 1, the p-value of 1, in Position 501 and then jump to the position indicated by the top item on the return stack.

The position indicated at the top of the stack is P-VALUE's own step 4. Therefore, after removing this from the stack, the computer continues with step 4. Notice that, as a result of step 3, the number in Position 501 is now the p-value of 1. In step 4, P-VALUE multiplies this by 2, to get the p-value of 2, and stores the result, 2, back in Position 501.

Finally, in step 5, P-VALUE checks the stack to see what to do next. But the stack now looks like this:

Position of a STOP instruction

P-VALUE jumps to the STOP instruction and halts. As we hoped, the p-value of 2 is stored in Position 501.

*   *   *   *   *

We have analyzed these first two cases in detail to show how large a part the return stack plays in handling a recursive subroutine. Imagine, for example, testing P-VALUE beginning with 344 stored in Position 500. Interruptions would interrupt interruptions so many times that it would be almost impossible for us to trace the computer's steps.

Fortunately, the stack keeps track for us. And if we want to see that the computer will get the right answer, we can analyze the subroutine much more simply.

Since the number 344 is not 1, step 1 of the subroutine has no effect. Step 2 prepares to calculate the p-value of the next lower number by subtracting 1 from the 344 in Position 500. This leaves 343 in that position.

In step 3, the p-value of 343 is calculated by the P-VALUE subroutine and stored in Position 501. Step 4 finds the correct p-value for 344 by doubling the one found for 343. It stores the answer in Position 501, just as we want.

Of course, we have left a hole in this argument. We are assuming that P-VALUE can correctly calculate the *p*-value of 343. But to check this, we would use exactly the same kind of reasoning. Clearly, to get the *p*-value of 343, the subroutine will subtract 1, use P-VALUE to calculate the *p*-value of 342, and then double the answer.

But this still leaves open the question of whether P-VALUE correctly calculates the *p*-value of 342. This in turn will lead to the question of whether it correctly calculates the *p*-value of 341, and so on. The point is, eventually everything will depend on whether P-VALUE correctly calculates the *p*-value of 1, and this, we have already seen, it does.

Since it calculates the *p*-value of 1 correctly, it must also be correct for the *p*-value of 2. Since this is so, it must be correct for the *p*-value of 3, and so on, up to 344 or higher.

9.11 APPLYING RECURSION

Most people learning for the first time about recursion consider it a kind of interesting trick—a clever way to calculate place values.

The trick, however, appears to be quite specialized.

After all, place values are especially suited to recursion. Since each is twice the value on its right, it is natural to think of calculating the fifth place value using the fourth, the fourth using the third, and so on.

But what other problems have the same structure? Can we find anything useful other than place values that may be defined and computed recursively?

The answer to this question is a little hard to believe. Instead of giving it immediately, we will simply provide three examples of what recursion is good for.

Multiplication. Consider the fact that 5 · 344 is 1,720 and 5 · 343 is 1,715. Is it any surprise that the first answer is 5 more than the second? In the first case, we are adding up 344 fives; in the second, 343 fives. One more 5 added up gives an answer that is larger by 5.

In general, we may say that 5 times any number gives an answer 5 more than 5 times the next smaller number. This leads to a recursive definition for multiplying by 5:

Five times a number: Five more than 5 times the next smaller number,
                           except that 5 times 1 is 5.

Suppose we use this to calculate 5 · 3. The definition tells us that the answer is 5 more than 5 · 2. This, in turn, is 5 more than 5 · 1.

The definition tells us directly that 5 · 1 is 5. Therefore, 5 · 2 is 5 more than this, or 10. And 5 · 3 is 5 more than this, or 15.

Our recursive definition translates to the following recursive subroutine, which multiplies the number in memory position 500 by 5 and puts the answer in Position 501.

MULTIPLY-BY-FIVE SUBROUTINE

1. If the number in Position 500 is 1, jump to step 6.

2. Subtract 1 from Position 500 and store the result back in Position 500.

3. Use MULTIPLY-BY-FIVE to multiply the number in Position 500 by 5 and put the answer in Position 501.

4. Add 5 to Position 501 and store the result back in Position 501.

5. Return.

6. Store 5 in Position 501.

7. Return.

If the number to be multiplied by 5 is 1, the computer will jump immediately to step 6. This stores the correct answer, 5, in Position 501. If the number to be multiplied is larger than 1, steps 2, 3, and 4 use MULTIPLY-BY-FIVE to calculate the answer for the next lower number and then add 5.

Incidentally, it would be easy to modify the MULTIPLY-BY-FIVE subroutine to calculate 6 times or 7 times any number. In fact, with only slightly more work, we may write a general, recursive subroutine for multiplying any two numbers.

Finding the Largest Number in a List. Finding the largest number in a list of 15 items boils down to finding the largest number out of the first 14 and then comparing this with the fifteenth number. Likewise, we can find the largest number out of the first 14 by finding the largest number out of the first 13 and then comparing this with the fourteenth number. Also, in a list of just one item, that single item must be the largest.

This suggests a recursive definition:

> **Largest number in a list**:   Whichever is larger, the last number
> or the largest number in the rest of the list,
> except that in a list containing just one
> number, that number is automatically the
> largest

To see how this definition applies, suppose we begin with the list in Figure 9.6. The definition tells us that the largest number in this list is the larger of two numbers: the last number in the list, 19; and the largest number in the rest of the list. We can see that this will give us the correct answer. The largest number in the rest of the list is 12. Comparing 12 and 19 will show, correctly, that 19 is the largest in the list.

```
12
7
19
```

Figure 9.6 A list of three numbers.

But how does the *definition* tell us the largest number in "the rest of the list"? The answer is that "the rest of the list" is itself a list, as shown in Figure 9.7. To find the largest number in this list, the definition tells us to compare the last number, 7, with the largest number in the rest of this shorter list.

Figure 9.7 "The rest of the list" is a list of two numbers.

Again, we can use our insight to see that the largest number in the rest of the list is 12—it is the *only* number in the rest of the list. That means we will be comparing 7 and 12 to find the largest in the two-number list.

But we may use the definition, instead of relying on insight. After we remove the last item from the two-number list, "the rest of the list" is just the number 12. If we consider this to be a list containing one item, the definition tells us directly that this item is the largest.

To find the largest in a three-number list, the definition tells us first to find the largest number in a two-number list, the top two numbers. To find the largest item in the two-number list, it tells us first to look for the largest item in a one-number list. Finally, however, it tells us directly that the single item in this list is certainly the largest.

This is the bottom level, and it allows us to work back up to find the largest item in the original three-number list.

9.12 APPLYING RECURSION: THE TOWER OF HANOI

As a last example, we will show how recursion solves a kind of puzzle called the **tower of Hanoi**. The puzzle is shown in Figure 9.8. It uses a board with three pegs and a number of circular disks, each with a hole in the middle.

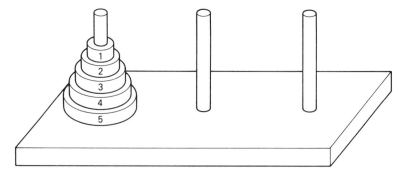

Figure 9.8 The tower of Hanoi puzzle.

As the figure shows, all the disks start on the leftmost peg. The disks are all different sizes and they are stacked up in size order with the largest on the bottom to form a kind of tower.

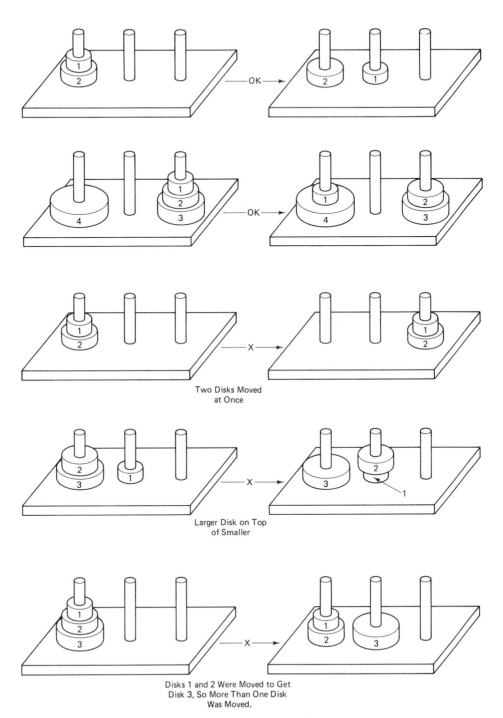

Figure 9.9 Legal and illegal moves in the tower of Hanoi puzzle.

The idea of the puzzle is to move the tower to the middle peg, while obeying two rules:

> Rule 1. Only one disk may be moved at a time.
>
> Rule 2. A larger disk may not be placed on top of a smaller one.

Figure 9.9 shows a few legal and illegal moves.

An important point about the tower of Hanoi puzzle is that it is really a series of puzzles—one with a tower of two disks, one with a tower of three disks, and so on. As Figure 9.10 shows, it is easy to solve the puzzle for a tower of two disks.

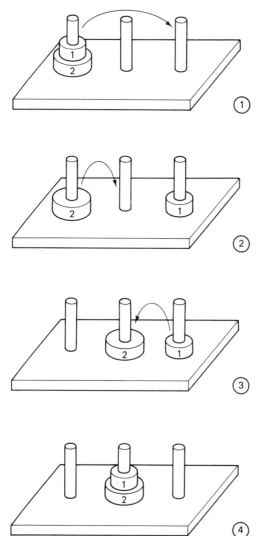

Figure 9.10 Solving the two-disk puzzle.

But what about moving a five-disk tower, or a 50-disk tower or a 1,000-disk tower? The solution is a little complicated even for a three-disk tower, as Figure 9.11 demonstrates. Luckily, recursion gives us the solution for a tower of *any* size.

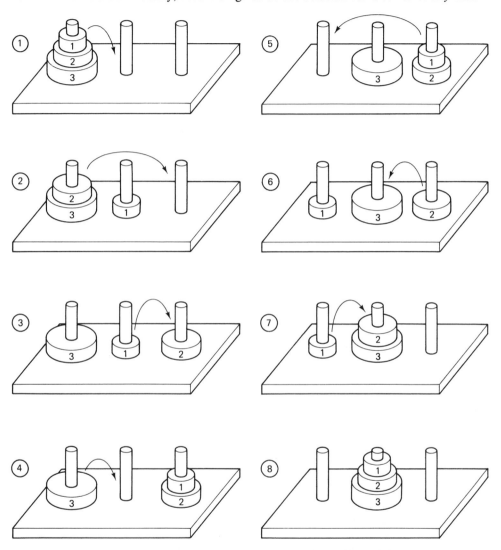

Figure 9.11 Solving the three-disk puzzle.

The key, as we have already pointed out, is that the tower of Hanoi is really a *series* of related puzzles. Recursion works by reducing hard problems down to simpler ones. For example, we reduced the problem of multiplying 344 by 5 down to the slightly simpler one of multiplying 343 by 5. Likewise, as we are about to see, a hard tower of Hanoi puzzle may be reduced to a simpler one.

Take the six-disk tower shown in Figure 9.12 as an example. We would like to move this tower to the center peg.

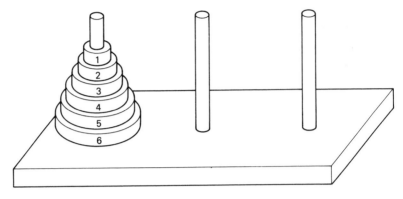

Figure 9.12 A six-disk puzzle.

Here is an idea for a solution: If we only knew how to move a *five*-disk tower from one peg to another, we could solve the six-disk puzzle. The answer, shown in Figure 9.13, is nearly identical to the solution we showed for the tower of two disks.

Of course, this is not really a solution. We have not shown a legal way to move the five-disk tower in steps 1 and 3. However, the problem of moving a five-disk tower would be easy, if only we knew how to move a *four*-disk tower. Figure 9.14 shows a three-step method.

By now, it should be obvious how we can get a solution. To move a six-disk tower, all we need to know is how to move a five-disk tower. To move a five-disk tower, we just need to know how to move a four-disk tower.

Continuing this way, we will eventually need to know how to move a one-disk tower. But this is easy. A one-disk tower is just a disk. The rules permit us simply to pick it up and move it.

                   *   *   *   *   *

We can use these observations to write a single, compact solution to all of the tower of Hanoi puzzles. For clarity, the solution uses special names for the three pegs: **tower** peg for the one on which the tower begins, **target** peg for the one to which we want to move the tower, and **other** for the remaining peg. Also, in any tower, we will call the bottom disk the **base** and the rest of the tower the **peak**. Figure 9.15 illustrates these definitions.

Here, now, is the recursive solution:

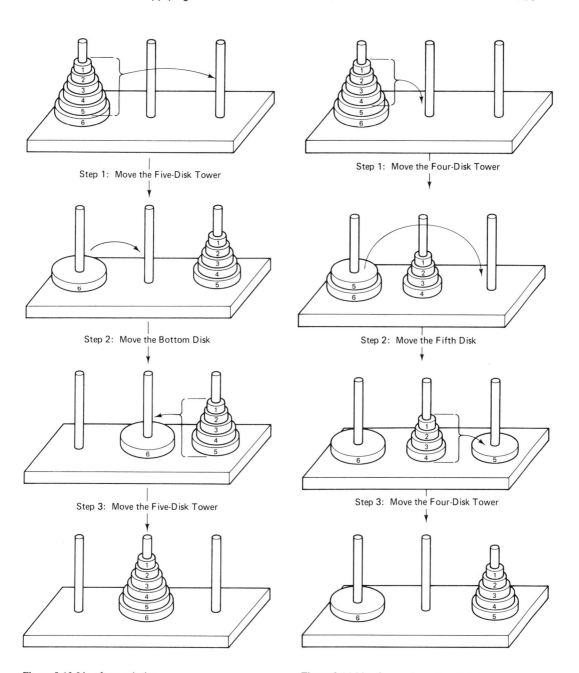

Figure 9.13 Idea for a solution.

Figure 9.14 Idea for moving a five-disk tower.

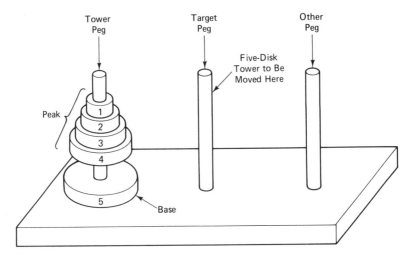

Figure 9.15 The tower, target, and other pegs; the peak; and the base.

TOWER-OF-HANOI-SOLUTION

1. If the tower to be moved contains just one disk, move it to the target peg. In this case, this is the end of the solution.

2. Otherwise, use the TOWER-OF-HANOI-SOLUTION to move the peak to the other peg.

3. Move the base to the target peg.

4. Use TOWER-OF-HANOI-SOLUTION to move the peak from the other peg to the target peg.

Notice that this solution does not refer to the size of the tower. It works as well for a three-disk tower as for a 1,000-disk one.

The solution breaks the problem of moving a tower down to simpler problems —moving the peak and the base. The base is a single disk, so the rules permit us to move it directly. Moving the peak is, in general, a complicated task, but it is easier than moving the whole tower.

Figure 9.16 shows the solution at work on a 500-disk tower. As the solution proceeds, it calls on itself twice to show how to move a 499-disk tower. If there is any question that the solution indeed shows how this is possible, Figure 9.17 settles the matter. It shows the solution at work moving the 499-disk tower to the right-most peg.[2]

---

[2] Notice that, in this case, the names of the pegs have changed temporarily.

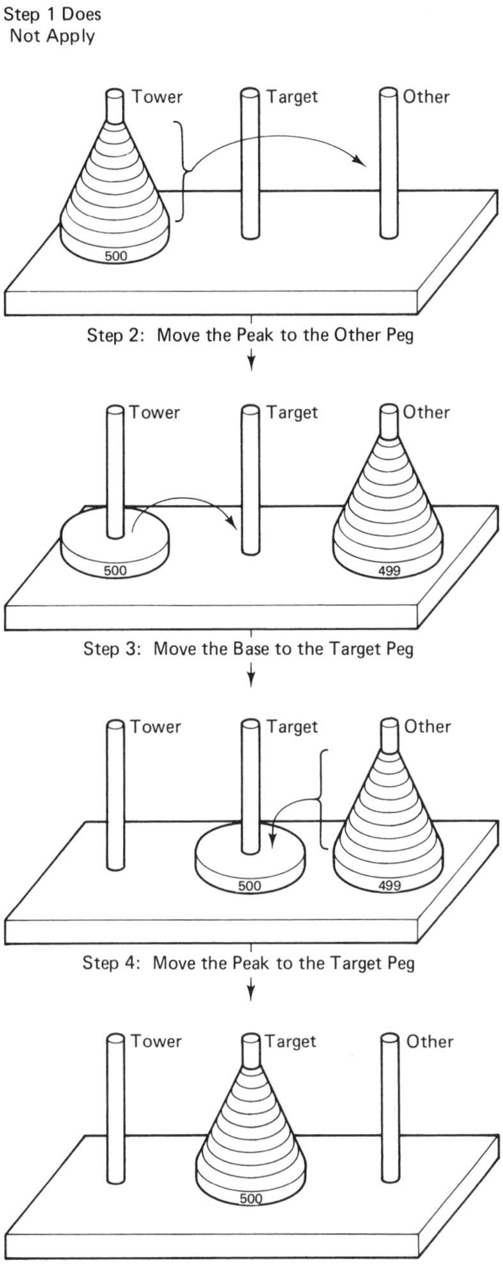
Step 1 Does
Not Apply
Tower
Target
Other
500
Step 2: Move the Peak to the Other Peg
Tower
Target
Other
500
499
Step 3: Move the Base to the Target Peg
Tower
Target
Other
500
499
Step 4: Move the Peak to the Target Peg
Tower
Target
Other
500

Figure 9.16 Applying the recursive solution to a 500-disk tower.

Step 1 Does
Not Apply

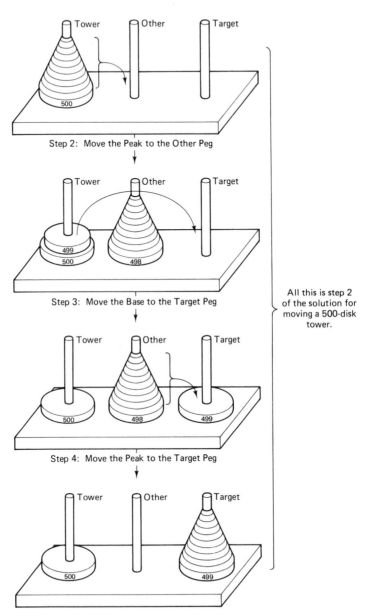

Figure 9.17 Applying the recursive solution to a 499-disk tower.

Of course, even this diagram leaves open the question of whether the solution really shows how to move a 498-disk stack. But, by now, it should be clear that, with enough diagrams, we could prove the solution really does provide all the details.

9.13 TAKING STOCK

Recursion appears at first to be a trick. After a little study, however, we have seen that it applies in quite a wide variety of cases: in arithmetic, list processing, and puzzle solving. By now it is reasonable to wonder about the limits of this approach.

That is, exactly what problems have a recursive solution?

The answer is strange: *All* problems have a recursive solution, so long as they have any algorithmic solution at all. If a computer can solve it, it can be done with recursion. On the other hand, questions like the halting problem that are too tricky for algorithms are also beyond the scope of recursion.

Of course, these claims are quite vague. We have never even carefully defined what we mean by recursion. But the claims *can* be made perfectly precise. In fact, they are essentially mathematical.

We have seen that computers simply manipulate numbers. A program is a way of specifying what manipulations are to be performed—how the computer should turn the ordered list of numbers filling its memory into another ordered list.

Recursion may be defined as another way of specifying how numbers should be manipulated. Our recursive definition for multiplying by 5 is a good example.

The point is that these specification methods are equally powerful. Any manipulation which may be specified by one may also be specified by the other.

This, however, is a theoretical point. For us, the key information is that recursion is not a trick at all. It may be applied to any problem.

Of course, the fact that it *may* be applied is not always a good reason for applying it. Our recursive multiplication subroutine would take a huge number of steps to calculate 5 · 344. The grade-school method of multiplication is much simpler, in this case.

Sometimes, however, as with the tower of Hanoi puzzle, a recursive solution is by far the neatest. It gives us a powerful, compact way to express a method of solving the puzzle. And, most important, the mode of expression is perfectly suited to a computer.

To deal with subroutine interruptions, all the computer needs is a stack, even if subroutines interrupt themselves.

*   *   *   *   *

We have come a long way, then, toward our goal of developing expressive languages for computers. The stack makes possible an infinite hierarchy of subroutines reaching up toward our own natural ways of thinking and talking. At the same time, it also handles recursion—a completely new and general way of expressing algorithms.

With all this progress, however, our computer still understands only programs written with numbers. Whether we describe a calculation by giving the names of high-level subroutines or by writing a recursive solution, the computer is still powerless to act unless the description is translated to machine language.

If we could only make this translation itself a kind of automatic computation, we would be in a far better position to communicate with the machine. Is it possible?

Chapter 10 will tell.

E X E R C I S E S

9.1. Translate the first counting program of Section 9.2 to machine language, using the subroutines introduced in Section 6.4.

9.2. Translate the second counting program of Section 9.2 to machine language.

9.3. Suppose we want to write a machine-language program to store 1,000 numbers in various positions in memory. If we use a different copy of the storing subroutine of Section 6.4 to store each number, how much memory space will the program take up? If, instead, we do everything possible to make the storing instructions compact, how *few* memory positions will we use.

9.4. Where would the program MAIN of Section 9.5 be in the hierarchy of Figure 9.2? What about the counting programs of Section 9.2?

9.5. Consider the statistician's program of Section 9.6. At which level would this be in the hierarchy of Figure 9.2? What about the executive's program described in the same section?

9.6. Consider the following program:

0	A.	Miscellaneous instructions	⎫
20	B.	Instructions to use subroutine I	⎪
39	C.	Miscellaneous instructions	⎬ Main Program
48	D.	Instructions to use subroutine II	⎪
67	E.	STOP	⎭
68	I-A.	Miscellaneous instructions	⎫
95	I-B.	Miscellaneous instructions	⎬ Subroutine I
100	I-C.	Instructions to use subroutine II	⎪
119	I-D.	Instructions to return	⎭
131	II-A.	Miscellaneous instructions	⎫
194	II-B.	Miscellaneous instructions	⎬ Subroutine II
236	II-C.	Instructions to return	⎭

As usual, the left-hand column gives the memory position of the first instruction of each instruction set. Also, we have given each set of instructions an identifying label. For example, the instructions stored in Positions 95 through 99 are labelled I-B.

(a) Using these labels, give the order in which the instruction sets will be executed.

(b) What will be on the top of the return stack when set I-A is executing? What will be on top of the stack when set II-A is executing for the first time? For the second time?

(c) At most, how many items will be stored on the stack? What instruction set will be executing when this many items are stored? Give a picture of the stack.

9.7. Look up *glebe* in a dictionary. If necessary, look up any words in the definition that are still unclear. Copy all of the definitions you have looked up (just the relevant parts) and give a single definition of *glebe* in your own words. For you, at which level is *glebe* in the hierarchy of Figure 9.3?

9.8. Find an example of circularity in a real dictionary. Document it by giving the name of the dictionary along with the relevant definitions. (*Examples*: Many dictionaries use the word *a* in defining *a*; some define *dog* using the word *canine* and *canine* using the word *dog*. Another popular ruse is to define *love* in terms of *affection*, *affection* as a kind of *fondness*, and *fond* using the word *loving*.)

9.9. Consider the following definition:

> **The *d*-value of a number**:   Two more than the *d*-value of the next smaller number, except that the *d*-value of 0 is 0.

(a) Use the definition to calculate the *d*-values of 0, 2, and 5.

(b) What is the *d*-value of 2,679?

9.10. Consider the following definition:

> **The *r*-value of a number**:   The same as the *r*-value of a number smaller by 4, except that the *r*-value of 1 is 0, the *r*-value of 2 is 1, the *r*-value of 3 is 2, and the *r*-value of 4 is 3.

(a) Use the definition to calculate the *r*-values of 3, 7, 15, 16, 17, 18, 19, 20, and 1,000,000,001.

(b) Give a nonrecursive definition of *r*-values.

9.11. In a list of words, we sometimes call the first word the **head** of the list and the rest of the list the **tail**. For example, in the list *apple berry pear pineapple*, the head is *apple* and the tail is the shorter list *berry pear pineapple*.

Consider the following definition:

The *m*-value of a list: The *m*-value of a list is itself a list.
To get it, add the head of the original
list at the *end* of the *m*-value of
the tail of the list, except if the
original list has no tail. In this
case, the *m*-value of the list is the
list itself.

(a) Use the definition to compute the *m*-value of the one-item list *Harry*. Notice that this list has no tail.

(b) Use the definition and the result of part (a) to find the *m*-value of the two-item list *Sue Harry*.

(c) Use the definition and the result of part (b) to find the *m*-value of the three-item list *John Sue Harry*.

(d) Explain in simple English what the *m*-value of a list is. Use just one sentence.

9.12. Is it possible for two definitions to refer to each other without circularity? If so, give an example; otherwise, explain why circularity must always arise.

9.13. In Section 9.9, we gave a recursive definition of binary place values. Modify the definition so that it defines base ten place values. Then modify the *p*-value subroutine of Section 9.10 correspondingly.

9.14. Suppose step 1 of the P-VALUE subroutine in Section 9.10 is changed to read as follows:

1.   If the number in Position 500 is 2, jump to step 6.

What will the modified subroutine calculate for the *p*-values of 2, 3, 4, and 5? What will happen if it is used to calculate the *p*-value of 1?

9.15. Modify the subroutine MULTIPLY-BY-FIVE so that it multiplies by 6.

9.16. Suppose step 6 of MULTIPLY-BY-FIVE is changed to read as follows:

6.   Store 3 in Position 501.

What will the modified subroutine calculate if it begins with 1 stored in Position 500? With 2 stored in Position 500? With 3 stored in Position 500? In general, what does the modified subroutine do?

9.17. Suppose step 2 of MULTIPLY-BY-FIVE is changed to read as follows:

2.   Subtract 2 from Position 500 and store
the result back in Position 500.

What will the modified subroutine calculate if it begins with 1 stored in Position 500? With 3 stored in Position 500? With 5 stored in Position 500? In general, what does the modified subroutine do?

9.18. As given in the chapter, the subroutine MULTIPLY-BY-FIVE cannot calculate 5 · 0. This may be remedied by changing just two numbers used in the subroutine. Which two and to what should they be changed?

9.19. Explain how the definition of the largest number in a list given in Section

9.11 can be used to find the largest number in the following list: 7, 8, 4, 10, 2.

9.20. A girl playing with the tower of Hanoi puzzle has figured out how to move a four-disk tower between any two pegs. Give her step-by-step instructions for moving a six-disk tower from the left peg to the middle peg.

Your task will be simplified if you consider the disks to be numbered from 1 to 6 and refer to the left, middle, and right pegs as L, M, and R. Instructions may then be given in the following form:

> Move 5 from L to R.

Notice that since the girl has already figured out how to move four-disk towers, the following is an acceptable instruction:

> Move four-disk tower from M to R.

9.21. Repeat Exercise 9.20, but give instructions for moving a 106-disk tower from the left peg to the middle peg. Assume the girl has already figured out how to move a 104-disk tower. Use the abbreviated form for instructions described in Exercise 9.20.

9.22. The following instructions are given in the abbreviated form described in Exercise 9.20. They explain how to move a four-disk tower from the left peg to the middle peg, assuming someone already knows how to move three-disk towers.

> Move three-disk tower from L to R.
> Move 4 from L to M.
> Move three-disk tower from R to M.

(a) Modify these instructions by including details of how to move three-disk towers. In particular, in place of the instructions calling for three-disk towers to be moved, substitute instructions calling only for two-disk towers or single disks to be moved.

(b) Modify the instructions developed in part (a) by including details of how to move two-disk towers. In place of instructions calling for two-disk towers to be moved, use only instructions for moving single disks.

The result in part (b) should be a complete set of one-disk-at-a-time instructions for moving a four-disk tower.

9.23. The game of nim is played in many variations. In one simple version, two players remove pebbles from a large pile. Each player, in turn, may take one, two, or three pebbles. The player who takes the last pebble loses.

We may begin to analyze the game as follows: If one pebble remains in the pile when it comes to our turn, we have lost.

If five pebbles remain, our position is no better. No matter what we do, our opponent can leave us with the last pebble. If we take one pebble, our opponent will take three and leave us one. If we take two pebbles, our opponent will take two, again leaving us one. Finally, if we take three, he or she will take one and leave us one.

If nine pebbles remain, no matter how many pebbles we take, our opponent will leave us with five. We have just seen that this means we will lose. If 13 pebbles remain, no matter how many we take, our opponent will leave us with nine.

Thus, if we are left with 1, 5, 9, 13, or some similar number of pebbles, we will lose. Naturally, we would like to turn the tables and leave our *opponent* with 1, 5, 9, or 13 pebbles.

Use these hints to develop a recursive procedure for calculating how many pebbles to take. If it is correct, this procedure should calculate that if 100 pebbles are left in the pile, we should take three.

10 Translation

10.1 BOOTSTRAPPING

If a nineteenth-century American man was down and out, he was likely to be advised to "pick himself up by the bootstraps." The expression means, roughly, to take oneself in hand or make something of oneself, but the force of it comes from an image most people today do not easily call to mind.

The fact is, the nineteenth-century American man wore boots, and since they were notoriously hard to pull on, his boots were often equipped with loops of leather at the top. In the morning, he slipped his fingers through these bootstraps and pulled, straining and swearing, until the boots were where he wanted them.

Naturally, once his boots were on, it would have been pointless for him to go on pulling. No amount of straining or swearing was likely to result in his rising any distance into the air.

Despite the impossibility, however, the image of a man lifting himself up by his own bootstraps conveyed a powerful message of self-reliance: If a man could not raise himself up physically without relying on outside support, nineteenth-century Americans believed he could at least do so economically and socially.

In fact, the force of the image has propelled the expression far beyond its historical context. It remains in use today, more than half a century after most Americans exchanged boots for shoes.

Moreover, the notion of **bootstrapping**, of raising something up by its own power, has proven quite versatile.

For example, consider a poor country which exports cheaply made manufactured goods. These are inexpensive to produce because citizens of a poor country are willing to work for low wages. But cheaply made products bring in little money. The country stays poor and wages remain low.

This cycle of poverty may sometimes be broken, however. If the government uses money received from exports to buy manufacturing equipment, to build roads and communication lines, and to send students abroad to study, a nation may sometimes bootstrap itself to prosperity.

Of course, these efforts are likely to have little *immediate* effect. Manufacturing equipment will be of no use until citizens are educated to use and maintain it. Roads are necessary for transporting goods, but they bring little benefit until production is in full swing.

Moreover, the income from exports will be small at first. Despite good intentions, the government will be constrained by its budget.

At some point, however, investments will pay off. Industry will begin to produce. Students returning from abroad will train younger students. Taxes from increased exports will pay for more roads and other improvements, and these, in turn, will spur industry.

Once this kind of effort is properly begun, the economy will continue to expand, bolstered by its own production, lifted, we might say, by its own bootstraps.

Bootstrapping is equally important in evolution. Just as a country may build a thriving economy on the poorest foundation, an animal may develop spectacular traits on the basis of the most unexceptional beginnings.

Consider the porcupine, for example. Biologists tell us that the animal developed its quills over many generations through natural selection. Porcupines with soft hair were caught by wolves and eaten. Only the prickliest lived to reproduce.

But this explanation is incomplete. Why did the porcupine develop quills and not speed, like the antelope, or camouflage, like the chameleon?

Part of the answer is simply that the porcupine's ancestors chose to meet danger rather than flee from it. If they had been disposed to run, natural selection would have favored those who were swiftest. After many generations, porcupines might have developed long legs.

Once porcupines began to face up to danger, however, prickliness determined survival. At that point, the trend was set. Natural selection tended to make the porcupine pricklier, and the pricklier it got, the less likely it was to run from danger.

In a sense, the porcupine picked itself up by the bootstraps and developed quills.

Note again that, after a certain point, change promotes further change. Bootstrapping is a kind of self-reinforcing feedback. Productive industry brings in money for investment in industry. Quills lead to sharper quills.

*   *   *   *   *

Perhaps the most striking example of evolutionary bootstrapping is our own—the phenomenal rate at which we developed a powerful brain as a result of the invention of language.

Language gave a competitive edge to those who used it. But also, the more we depended on language, the more important intelligence became for survival. Natural selection led to an increase in brain size, which in turn promoted the use of language.

Intelligence, it seems, is also a bootstrapping operation. It builds on itself.

*   *   *   *   *

As a technical term, *bootstrapping* is actually quite modern. It was coined to describe the process of bringing a computer up from its minimal base of understanding to a higher, more practical level.

As we have hinted, this process uses the computer as a tool for making the computer itself more powerful.

We are about to look at bootstrapping, in this narrower sense. Keep the larger meaning in mind, however. Eventually we will want to ask how far the computer may raise itself and whether the bootstrapping operation will "catch on" as our own intelligence has.

10.2 A PROGRAM TO TRANSLATE

In Chapter 5, when we introduced machine-language programs, we pointed out that they are difficult to read. Here is an example:

0	0	1	1	5	13	1	11	0	
0	1	2	3	4	5	6	7	8	. . .

Although we studied this program carefully in Chapter 5, it may well be hard to recognize. As we pointed out then, for human use it is much better to write the program as follows:

```
0    LOAD-TOP 0
2    LOAD-BOTTOM 1
4    ADD
5    STORE-IN-POSITION 1
7    JUMP-TO-POSITION 0
```

Perhaps now it will be clear that this is our first counting program.

To review how it works, recall that the left-hand column gives the memory position of the instruction on its right. The LOAD-TOP instruction is in Position 0. The LOAD-BOTTOM instruction is in Position 2.

Also, although we are not told directly, we can see that the 0 of LOAD-TOP 0 is in Position 1—it is in the next position after the LOAD-TOP instruction.

The effect of the first four instructions, then, is to add the numbers in Positions 1 and 3 and store the result back in Position 1. The last instruction sends the computer back to the beginning, so the first four instructions will simply be executed over and over. Since the number in Position 3 is always 1, the effect is to add 1 repeatedly to Position 1, that is, to make the computer count.

As this example shows, it is much easier for us to understand a program written with words. Unfortunately, in this form it is meaningless to the computer. The machine understands only programs consisting of a list of numbers. The solution, as we have suggested several times, is to use the computer as an automatic translator.

*   *   *   *   *

To ease the burden on such a translator, we will begin by introducing three-letter abbreviations for each of our 15 machine instructions, as shown in Figure 10.1.

Machine instruction	Three-Letter code	Instruction
0	LTP	LOAD-TOP
1	LBT	LOAD-BOTTOM
2	SBR	SHIFT-BOTTOM-RIGHT
3	STL	SHIFT-TOP-LEFT
4	SUB	SUBTRACT
5	ADD	ADD
6	AND	AND
7	ORX	OR
8	CLR	CLEAR
9	LTF	LOAD-TOP-FROM-POSITION
10	LBF	LOAD-BOTTOM-FROM-POSITION
11	JTP	JUMP-TO-POSITION
12	JIZ	JUMP-IF-ZERO-TO-POSITION
13	SIP	STORE-IN-POSITION
14	STP	STOP

Figure 10.1 Three-letter codes for machine instructions.

A program written with these abbreviations is not nearly as clear as one with the instructions written out in full. On the other hand, the abbreviations are still much better than an unvarying string of numbers. Our counting program, for example, is not too hard to decipher in the following form:

```
0    LTP  0
2    LBT  1
4    ADD
5    SIP  1
7    JTP  0
```

What we have in mind, now, is to put the program into the computer's memory system *in this form*. Naturally, it will be of no immediate use there, since the computer does not understand three-letter abbreviations. We can bridge the communication gap, however, with a second program. This program—the vaunted **translator**—will be designed to convert strings of abbreviations and numbers into ordinary machine language. With it, we can turn the first program into one the computer can carry out.

To begin, then, we enter the untranslated counting program at, say, Position 501.

	L	T	P	0	L	B	T
. . .	501	502	503	504	505	506	507

1	A	D	D	S	I	P	1
508	509	510	511	512	513	514	515

J	T	P	0	−1	
516	517	518	519	520	. . .

Note that we have pictured letters stored in memory positions. As we have pointed out several times, memory chunks actually store patterns of voltage, which we are free to interpret as we like. In this case, some patterns which would normally be considered as numbers are interpreted as letters, according to the table given in Figure 6.1.

Deciding which voltage patterns to treat as numbers and which to treat as letters is easy, mainly because all of our instruction abbreviations use exactly three letters. Since our program begins in Position 501, the patterns in this position and the next two should be considered as *letters* making up a three-letter instruction code. Since the code is LTP, or LOAD-TOP, we know the next position in memory must be interpreted as a *number* to be placed in **Top**. The following three must again be interpreted as letters of an abbreviated instruction, and so on.

A few other points about the memory picture are also worth noting.

First, we have added an endmarker to our program. The −1 in Position 520 will warn the translator that it has come to the end of the program. Otherwise it would go on forever, interpreting stored voltage patterns as numbers and three-letter codes.

Also, this picture of our untranslated program leaves out the numbers in the left-hand column, which were used to remind us where the various instructions would be stored in the memory. In fact, these are unnecessary. The first instruction must automatically go in Position 0. The rest simply follow in order.

As a last point, notice that we have completely sidestepped the question of how to get numbers and letters into the memory. It is all very well for us to show an L in Position 501. But how did it get there?

Of course, we have talked before of storing voltage patterns manually. All we need is a voltage source to hook up to input wires of the memory system. But this method is clearly impractical. Furthermore, anyone willing to translate letters into voltage patterns is probably also willing to work directly in machine language. This is not the person for whom the translator is designed.

The answer, as anyone who has seen a computer knows, is that numbers and letters are entered into a computer using a typewriter-style keyboard. Some consequences of this fact are considered later in this chapter, and the full details of the process are given in Chapter 12.

For now, however, we want to concentrate on the question of translation. We will assume that the untranslated program *has* been stored in the memory somehow and we will look into what our translator will need to do with it.

10.3 AN IDENTIFICATION KEY

When the translator goes to work on the counting program, it will begin by looking at the first instruction, letter by letter. A *person* reading the same program would normally look at the first three letters as a group, since together they make up a single abbreviation. Suppose, however, that we are forced to look at the letters one by one, as the computer does.

As soon as we see that the first letter is L, we can be sure that the instruction is either LBF, LBT, LTF, or LTP. After looking at the second letter, T, we may narrow the list down to just LTF and LTP. Finally, the third letter, P, shows that the instruction is LTP. We know this means LOAD-TOP.

Each letter we look at narrows down the possibilities. Of course, this narrowing-down process may seem too simple to be worth describing. But how can a computer "narrow down possibilities"? To get an answer, we do need to describe the process step by step.

*   *   *   *   *

Our approach will be based on a kind of book, sometimes called an **identification key**. This key will be divided up into sections, one to help us identify instructions beginning with an A, one for instructions beginning with a C, and so on, one section for each first letter.

Our 15 instructions use only six different initial letters—A, C, J, L, O, and S—and so the identification key will be divided into six sections. As Figure 10.2 shows, page 1 of the key is an index to the sections.

Suppose, again, that we are attempting to identify LTP. This index tells us we should turn to page 10 for information about all instructions beginning with L. This page is shown in Figure 10.3.

```
┌─────────────────────────────────┐
│            — Page 1 —           │
│                                 │
│       Check the First Letter.   │
│                                 │
│   If it is A, Turn to Page 2    │
│             C, Turn to Page 5   │
│             J, Turn to Page 7   │
│             L, Turn to Page 10  │
│             O, Turn to Page 13  │
│             S, Turn to Page 15  │
│          other, ERROR           │
└─────────────────────────────────┘
```

Figure 10.2 Page 1 of the
identification key.

```
┌─────────────────────────────────┐
│            — Page 10 —          │
│                                 │
│      Check the Second Letter.   │
│                                 │
│   If it is B, Turn to Page 11   │
│             T, Turn to Page 12  │
│          other, ERROR           │
└─────────────────────────────────┘
```

Figure 10.3 Page 10 of the
identification key.

Page 10 is an index to the L section of the key. This section is made up of smaller sections, one for each possible letter that might *follow* an L. In particular, for information about instructions beginning with LT, the index tells us to turn to page 12.

As shown in Figure 10.4, page 12 shows us how to use the third letter to identify the instruction. In our example, the third letter is P, so the instruction must be LOAD-TOP.

```
┌─────────────────────────────────┐
│            — Page 12 —          │
│                                 │
│      Check the Third Letter.    │
│                                 │
│   If it is F, the Instruction is│
│            LOAD-TOP-FROM-POSITION│
│             P, the Instruction is│
│            LOAD-TOP             │
│          other, ERROR           │
└─────────────────────────────────┘
```

Figure 10.4 Page 12 of the
identification key.

The complete key is shown in Figure 10.5. Notice that the key will not accept any three-letter code other than the 15 we are using. For example, suppose we attempt to use it on XYZ. The index on page 1 tells us that any code beginning with a letter other than A, C, J, L, O, or S is erroneous.

Clearly, once this 19-page key is written, it is easy to describe a step-by-step procedure for using it to identify instructions. In fact, in a moment we will show how to turn the key into a subroutine. But first, how was the key itself constructed?

— Page 1 —

Check the First Letter.

If it is A, Turn to Page 2
C, Turn to Page 5
J, Turn to Page 7
L, Turn to Page 10
O, Turn to Page 13
S, Turn to Page 15
other, ERROR

— Page 2 —

Check the Second Letter.

If it is D, Turn to Page 3
N, Turn to Page 4
other, ERROR

— Page 3 —

Check the Third Letter.

If it is D, the Instruction is
ADD
other, ERROR

— Page 4 —

Check the Third Letter.

If it is D, the Instruction is
AND
other, ERROR

— Page 5 —

Check the Second Letter.

If it is L, Turn to Page 6
other, ERROR

— Page 6 —

Check the Third Letter.

If it is R, the Instruction is
CLEAR
other, ERROR

— Page 7 —

Check the Second Letter.

If it is I, Turn to Page 8
T, Turn to Page 9
other, ERROR

— Page 8 —

Check the Third Letter.

If it is Z, the Instruction is
JUMP-IF-ZERO-TO-POSITION
other, ERROR

— Page 9 —

Check the Third Letter.

If it is P, the Instruction is
JUMP-TO-POSITION
other, ERROR

— Page 10 —

Check the Second Letter.

If it is B, Turn to Page 11
T, Turn to Page 12
other, ERROR

— Page 11 —

Check the Third Letter.

If it is F, the Instruction is
LOAD-BOTTOM-FROM-POSITION
T, the Instruction is
LOAD-BOTTOM
other, ERROR

— Page 12 —

Check the Third Letter.

If it is F, the Instruction is
LOAD-TOP-FROM-POSITION
P, the Instruction is
LOAD-TOP
other, ERROR

— Page 13 —

Check the Second Letter.

If it is R, Turn to Page 14
other, ERROR

— Page 14 —

Check the Third Letter.

If it is X, the Instruction is
OR
other, ERROR

— Page 15 —

Check the Second Letter.

If it is I, Turn to Page 16
T, Turn to Page 17
U, Turn to Page 18
B, Turn to Page 19
other, ERROR

— Page 16 —

Check the Third Letter.

If it is P, the Instruction is
STORE-IN-POSITION
other, ERROR

— Page 17 —

Check the Third Letter.

If it is L, the Instruction is
SHIFT-TOP-LEFT
P, the Instruction is
STOP
other, ERROR

— Page 18 —

Check the Third Letter.

If it is B, the Instruction is
SUBTRACT
other, ERROR

— Page 19 —

Check the Third Letter.

If it is R, the Instruction is
SHIFT-BOTTOM-RIGHT
other, ERROR

Figure 10.5 The identification key.

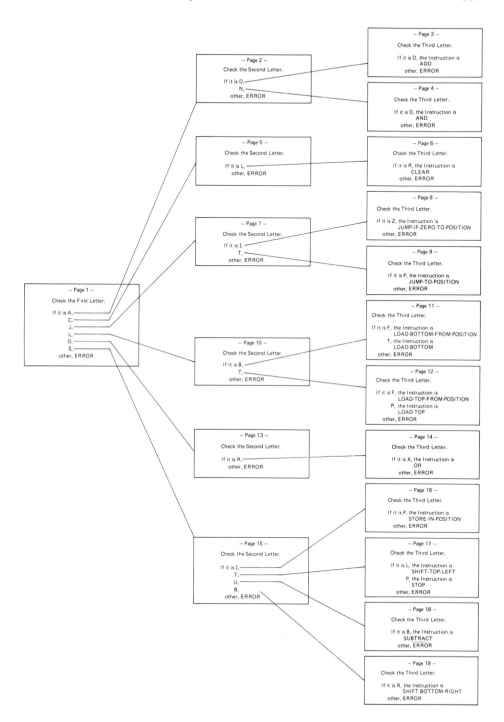

Figure 10.6 The identification key reorganized.

As a first step toward the answer, consider Figure 10.6. Here, the pages of the key have been arranged into columns. The first column contains the page that asks us to look at the first letter of the instruction we are identifying. The second column contains all pages that ask us to look at the second letter, and the third column shows pages that ask us to look at the third letter. Notice, also, that connecting lines have replaced page references. If we are identifying LTP, for example, one of these lines takes us from page 1 to page 10.

Now, if we strip down the diagram and tip it on its side, we get something familiar. Figure 10.7 shows that an identification key is just a kind of tree.

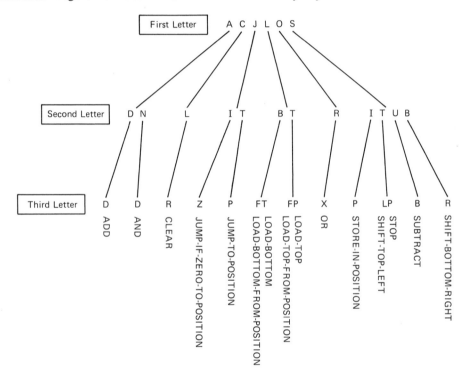

Figure 10.7 The identification key is a tree.

This is further evidence that certain data structures are fundamental ways of organizing information. But also, it gives us a straightforward way of *constructing* an identification key: Simply draw a tree and work backward.

To design an identification key for our 15 instruction codes, we use the six possible first letters to form the highest branching point of a tree. Under each letter, we write a list of the letters that might possibly follow it. These lists form a second level of branching points. Finally, under each letter in this second level, we write a list of all the possible third letters, along with the instructions they identify.

This gives us a tree like the one shown in Figure 10.7. It is easy to tip this tree on its side and add boxes so that the branching points look like pages. To make the tipped-over diagram just the same as Figure 10.6, we need only to add a page number at the top of each page.

We may number the pages any way we like, so long as the main index—the first branching point—becomes page 1. In our example, page numbers were chosen to divide the key neatly into sections, one for each first letter. This makes the key easier to understand, but it is not essential to its working.

Once we have reconstructed Figure 10.6 by adding page numbers, we can work back to Figure 10.5 just by replacing connecting lines with page references. If a line runs from the main index to page 10, we replace it with a note in the main index reading "Turn to page 10."

Finally, we put the pages in order and stack them up. At this point, our identification key is ready to use.

10.4 A SUBROUTINE FOR THE KEY

Given a tree, we have shown how it is possible to construct an identification key. But why go to this extra trouble? The tree itself may be used to identify instructions: simply start at the top and let the letters in the three-letter code determine which branches to follow.

The point, however, is that we want to design a program, a translator which will convert a string of numbers and three-letter codes into machine language. Identifying three-letter codes is a part of the work this program will undertake.

We use an identification key, rather than a tree, simply because it is already very close to a program. In fact, the identification part of our translator will be a 19-part subroutine, each part modeled on one page in our key. The outline for part 1, for example, is based on our main index of page 1:

IDENTIFICATION SUBROUTINE - PART 1

1. Read the first letter of the three-letter code.

2. Jump to part 2 if the letter is A.

3. Jump to part 5 if the letter is C.

4. Jump to part 7 if the letter is J.

5. Jump to part 10 if the letter is L.

6. Jump to part 13 if the letter is O.

7. Jump to part 15 if the letter is S.

8. Show that an error has been found.

9. STOP

Notice that if the first letter is, say, Z, the computer will not jump at all. Instead, it will reach step 8 of this part, indicate in some way that it has found an error, and stop at step 9.

On the other hand, so long as the first letter might be part of a recognizable three-letter code, the computer will jump to a new part of the program, just as we would follow instructions to turn to a new page.

If the three-letter code under consideration is LTP, these instructions will send the computer to part 10 of the program. The outline of that part is based on page 10 of our key:

IDENTIFICATION SUBROUTINE - PART 10

1. Read the next letter.

2. Jump to part 11 if the letter is B.

3. Jump to part 12 if the letter is T.

4. Show that an error has been found.

5. STOP.

If the computer is analyzing LTP, these instructions will cause it to jump to part 12. Here, the instruction will be identified.

*   *   *   *   *

Fortunately, identifying the instruction is the hardest part of translating it. For example, suppose the translator is working on our counting program, which begins like this:

	L	T	P	0	L	B	T	
. . .	501	502	503	504	505	506	507	. . .

When part 12 of the identification subroutine reads the P in Position 503, it will identify the first instruction as LOAD-TOP. At this point, translating the instruction into machine language is a matter of two steps.

First, LOAD-TOP itself translates to 0. This 0 must be stored at an appropriate place in the memory. Since the LTP under consideration is the first instruction in the program, the instruction number should be stored at the beginning of memory, in Position 0.

Second, every LOAD-TOP instruction is followed by a number. In this case, the full instruction is LOAD-TOP 0. This 0 must be copied from Position 504 to Position 1 so that it will follow the translation of LOAD-TOP.

In the following outline of part 12, this translation process is outlined in step 8. Notice that we have also shown, in step 6, how to translate LOAD-TOP-FROM-POSITION.

IDENTIFICATION SUBROUTINE - PART 12

1. Read the next letter.

2. Jump to step 6 if the letter is F.

3. Jump to step 8 if the letter is P.

4. Show that an error has been found.

5. STOP

6. Carry out steps for translating LOAD-TOP-FROM-POSITION.

   (a) Store 9 at the appropriate place in memory.

   (b) Read the next number from memory (the one just after LTF) and copy it into the following memory position.

7. Return to the main translator program.

8. Carry out steps for translating LOAD-TOP:
   (a) Store 0 at the appropriate place in memory.
   (b) Read the next number from memory (the one just after LTP) and copy it into the following memory position.

9. Return to the main translator program.

*   *   *   *   *

By now it should be clear that it is possible to design an identification subroutine very much like our identification key. In fact, the subroutine not only identifies three-letter codes; it translates them.

Of course, the outlines we have given leave out some important details. For example, as the subroutine looks through the untranslated program, it will need a pointer to keep its place. This pointer would start at 501 and the subroutine would need to increase it by 1 each time it "reads" the next letter.

Another pointer would be needed to keep track of where the translated instructions go. This pointer would start at 0, since the first translated instruction should go in Position 0, and the subroutine would increase it by 1 each time it adds an instruction code or other number to the machine-language program it is producing.

Also, in several places, we have called for the subroutine to signal an error. Since the only kind of signal our computer can send is a number, we might write the subroutine so that it stores 999 in Position 0 if it detects an error.

Details like these are crucial for a programmer actually writing the subroutine we have described. For our purposes, however, we have gone far enough. The essential point is only that our identification subroutine is not an impossible dream like the stop-analyzer. Given time, a programmer could turn our outlines into a working machine-language subroutine.

10.5 THE TRANSLATOR

Once written, this identification subroutine acts as a one-instruction translator. It reads a three-letter code and converts it to machine language, copying the number following the instruction, if necessary.

To complete our translator we only need a short program which uses this subroutine repeatedly while watching out for the endmarker. Here is an outline for this main program.

TRANSLATOR PROGRAM

1. If the next letter or number in the untranslated program is -1, stop.

2. Use the IDENTIFICATION subroutine.

3. Go back to step 1.

Suppose we write machine instructions for this program and execute it, with our counting program stored as before:

	L	T	P	0	L	B	T
• • •	501	502	503	504	505	506	507

1	A	D	D	S	I	P	1
508	509	510	511	512	513	514	515

J	T	P	0	−1	
516	517	518	519	520	• • •

Step 1 will check the L in Position 501 to see whether it is -1. Since it is not, step 2 will use the identification subroutine. We have already seen that this reads LTP 0 and stores the translation 0-0 using the first two memory positions. Step 3 sends the computer back to start again at step 1.

This time, step 1 checks the L in Position 505 to see whether it is -1. Since it is not, step 2 calls on the identification subroutine. This identifies LBT as LOAD-BOTTOM. It translates LBT 1 to 1-1 and stores these numbers in memory positions 2 and 3, just after the translation of LTP 0. Step 3 sends the computer back to step 1.

As the computer continues, three more instructions will be translated, the last being JTP 0. When the computer returns to step 1 for the sixth time, it checks the number in Position 520 to see whether it is -1. Since it is, the program stops.

The translator has done its work. Our counting program has been converted to a machine-language version stored in the computer beginning at Position 0. If we simply set the computer running again, it will count.

*   *   *   *   *

Take a moment now to put our progress in perspective.

The basic problem is that machine language does not come naturally to human programmers. Our solution is to use a translator program.

One point we have tended to ignore, however, is that the translator program itself must be written entirely in machine language. We have described the program in outline form, using English phrases like *show that an error has been found*. But our descriptions must eventually yield a list of numbers, machine-language instructions for the computer to execute.

It is important to keep in mind what a long, tedious project it would be to write this program. Our translator uses a 19-part subroutine, each part consisting of four to nine steps and each step requiring many machine-language instructions.

Of course, since the steps and parts are very similar, writing the subroutine is not intellectually demanding. But it would take a long time and the result would be a confusing list of well over a thousand numbers. These numbers would then have to be entered painstakingly into the computer's memory, one by one. Is the translator worth the effort?

Positively. Once the machine-language version of the translator program is written and stored in the computer's memory, *we will never again have to write a machine-language program.*

Instead, we may write programs using three-letter codes and let the translator turn these automatically into machine language.

$$* \qquad * \qquad * \qquad * \qquad *$$

Since the translator program will be used many times, it is best to store it in an out-of-the-way part of the memory. For example, we might design it to be stored beginning at memory position 10000.

Of course, our computer always begins by executing the instruction in Position 0. We may still use the translator, however, by storing a JUMP-TO-POSITION 10000 instruction in memory positions 0 and 1.

Suppose we do this and also store our untranslated counting program beginning at memory position 501. When we set the computer running, the first instruction it sees is JUMP-TO-POSITION 10000. This causes it to continue with the instruction stored in Position 10000, that is, with the translator program.

As we have seen, this program stores a machine-language version of the counting program beginning at Position 0. To execute this program, we simply wait until the translator stops and set the computer running again.

Notice that this process uses the translator program without changing it. After the translation, it remains, intact, in memory positions 10000 and following. To translate a new program written with three-letter codes, we just store this program beginning at Position 501, store a JUMP-TO-POSITION 10000 at the beginning of memory, and set the computer running.

In writing our translator, we have created a computer tool for making the computer more powerful. In a sense, once it contains a translator program, a computer *understands* three-letter codes, just as well as it understands machine language.

10.6 ASSEMBLY LANGUAGE

It seems that if someone gives us a new computer, our first project ought to be to write a translator. This single machine-language program frees us from any further machine-language programming.

Of course, using three-letter codes in place of the numerical instructions of machine-language eases the job of programming only very slightly. It is natural to think of writing a more powerful translator.

We are about to consider just such a project. But before we begin, it is important to see that we will not be starting from scratch. It is not necessary to write this new translator in machine language. Instead, we may write it using three-letter codes and use our first translator to convert it automatically to machine language.

Here is the essence of computer bootstrapping.

We begin with a computer that understands only machine instructions. Using those instructions, we write a primitive translator. Once this translator is installed, the computer effectively understands a new programming language, one slightly easier for us to use. In the case of our example, it is a language that uses three-letter codes in place of machine instructions.

With this new language, we may write a more sophisticated translator. This, in turn, defines another, still more convenient programming language.

Each new language paves the way to a better translator. Each improved translator yields a more expressive language. Computer power raises the computer to a higher level of understanding.

*   *   *   *   *

As a starting point for a second-level translator, consider the program we developed in Section 6.3 to add up a list of numbers. Recall that the list is stored beginning in Position 100 and that 0 is used as an endmarker.

1. CLEAR   {Start the running total at 0.}
    STORE-IN-POSITION **Position-of-Total**

2. LOAD-TOP 100   {Start the pointer at 100, the
    ADD   position of the first number
    STORE-IN-POSITION **Position-of-Pointer**   to be added.}

3. LOAD-TOP-FROM-POSITION pointer   {If the pointer now points
    LOAD-BOTTOM 0   to the number 0 then
    ADD   jump to a STOP instruction.}
    JUMP-IF-ZERO-TO-POSITION **Step 6**

4. LOAD-BOTTOM-FROM-POSITION **Position-of-Total**   {Otherwise,
    ADD   add the number to which it poin
    STORE-IN-POSITION **Position-of-Total**   to the running total and store
                                                         the sum back in memory as the
                                                         new running total.}

5. LOAD-TOP-FROM-POSITION **Position-of-Pointer**
    LOAD-BOTTOM 1   {Change the pointer so that it
    ADD   points to the next list item . . .}
    STORE-IN-POSITION **Position-of-Pointer**
    JUMP-TO-POSITION **Step 3**   {. . . and go back to add it.}

6. STOP

A distinctive feature of this program outline is its use of names in place of memory positions: **Step 3**, **Step 6**, and **Position-of-Pointer**. **Step 3** stands for the position where the first LOAD-TOP-FROM-POSITION instruction will be stored; **Step 6**, for the position where the STOP instruction will be stored; and **Position-of-Pointer**, for the location of a pointer that indicates which number in the list is next to be added.

For this version of the program, we have also introduced the name **Position-of-Total** for the place in memory where the running total of all numbers added so far will be stored. In Section 6.3, when we needed a memory position for the running total, we simply picked one: Position 99.

One reason to use names instead of position numbers is that they make the program clearer. It is simpler to remember that the running total is stored at a place called **Position-of-Total** than that it is stored at Position 99. This is the same reason we prefer three-letter abbreviations to instruction codes: People work more easily with words than with numbers.

Also, some of the names are a *necessary* part of the program, at least while we are developing it. When we are working out instructions for step 3 of the program, we have no way to know where the STOP instruction of step 6 will be stored. As a result, we cannot immediately say what position number should be used after the JUMP-IF-ZERO-TO-POSITION of step 3. We are forced to use a name for this position temporarily.

Even if we did know this position number, however, there would still be a good reason to use a name in its place: A program which uses only names may be translated to be stored *anywhere* in the memory.

When we discussed our first translator, for example, we said it would be a good idea to put it in an out-of-the-way part of the memory. We showed how it could be stored beginning in Position 10000 and used by starting with a JUMP-TO-POSITION 10000 at the beginning of the memory.

In fact, there is nothing to stop us from having *hundreds* of programs stored in the memory at the same time, each beginning at a different position. To use any particular program, all we need is to make the computer jump to the place in memory where it begins.

But to put this idea into practice, we should write programs so that they may be stored beginning at any position. If position numbers are used instead of names in jump instructions, this flexibility is lost. For example, if we write

JUMP-IF-ZERO-TO-POSITION 8

instead of

JUMP-IF-ZERO-TO-POSITION **Step 3**

then the instructions for step 3 *must* begin at Position 8. We are no longer free to store our program at other places in the memory.

For all of these reasons, then, it is convenient to use names in place of position numbers. If we combine this idea with our three-letter codes, the result is what is usually called an **assembly language**. A translator that converts from assembly language to machine language is thus termed an **assembler**.

*   *   *   *   *

When we turn our add-up-a-list program into assembly language, it looks quite unfamiliar at first. In fact, we have made a number of important changes, each for reasons which must be explained.

```
                                 CLR;
                                 SIP   TOTAL;
                                 LTP   100;
                                 ADD;
                                 SIP   +POINTER-AND-LOOPSTART;
POINTER-AND-LOOPSTART:           LTF   9999;
                                 LBT   0;
                                 ADD;
                                 JIZ   END;
                                 LBF   TOTAL;
                                 ADD;
                                 SIP   TOTAL;
                                 LTF   +POINTER-AND-LOOPSTART;
                                 LBT   1;
                                 ADD;
                                 SIP   +POINTER-AND-LOOPSTART;
                                 JTP   POINTER-AND-LOOPSTART;
        END:                     STP;
```

We are about to analyze the language used in this program point by point. But before we begin with the details, notice how the use of names makes the main *structure* clear. The general form of the program is as follows:

```
                                 ---
                                 ---
                                 ---
POINTER-AND-LOOPSTART:           ---
                                 ---                        ⎫
                                 ---                        ⎪  Main
                                 JIZ   END;                 ⎬ program
                                 ---                        ⎪  loop
                                 ---                        ⎪
                                 JTP   POINTER-AND-LOOPSTART; ⎭
        END:                     STP;
```

The main part of the program is a loop. It begins with the instruction which will be stored in a memory position called **POINTER-AND-LOOPSTART** and runs through the JTP (JUMP-TO-POSITION) instruction near the end of the program. This jump sends the computer back to the beginning of the loop.

The computer will be caught in a loop, then, executing the same set of instructions over and over. Fortunately, we have provided a means of escape. Each time through the loop, a test will be carried out and, depending on the result, the JIZ (JUMP-TO-POSITION-IF-ZERO) instruction may send the computer to the memory position called END. If so, the computer will halt, since a STP (STOP) instruction is stored at END.

All this corresponds nicely to our high-level understanding of what the computer is supposed to be doing. We want it to add numbers repeatedly to a running total, stopping when it comes to a zero.

10.7 AMBIGUITY

Now it is time to look at some of the details of our assembly language. As we do, keep in mind that the language is written to be read by a program—an assembler designed to convert it into machine language.

Notice that we begin the project of creating an assembler with a head start.

First, as we have pointed out, the assembler program itself does not have to be written in machine language. Instead, we may use three-letter codes and have our original translator convert it to machine language automatically.

Moreover, the outlines we developed for the translator's identification subroutine may be used to specify part of the assembler. After all, we have not changed our three-letter codes; the same process may be used to identify them.

Despite these advantages, however, designing an assembler is a tricky business.

One problem is **ambiguity**, the possibility that a program may have two different meanings. For example, suppose an assembly-language program contains the following instructions:

```
LTF     BULBF
ADD
```

From the way these letters are placed on the page, it is clear that we mean for the computer to load the **Top** register from a position called BULBF and then perform an addition. Unfortunately, the assembler will not be able to see the page we are looking at. In the memory, these two instructions will be stored as a continuous string, like this:

	L	T	F	B	U	
. . .	501	502	503	504	505	

	L	B	F	A	D	D	
	506	507	508	509	510	511	. . .

What is to stop the assembler from interpreting this as

```
LTF     BU
LBF     ADD
```

that is, as instructions to load the **Top** register from a memory position called BU and the **Bottom** register from one called ADD?

In fact, it might also interpret the string of letters as a single instruction:

```
LTF   BULBFLBFADD
```

In this case, the meaning is: Load the **Top** register from a memory position called BULBFLBFADD.

In fact, all three interpretations are equally correct. As it stands, the program is ambiguous.

The problem is that it is not always clear how to break a long string of letters into instruction lines. This explains our use of semicolons in our add-up-a-list program. Each semicolon marks the end of a line.

*   *   *   *   *

The colon, the other punctuation mark we used, serves a very similar purpose. For example, consider the following string of characters stored in the memory:

	L	T	F	S	I	P
· · ·	501	502	503	504	505	506

C	L	R	;	
507	508	509	510	· · ·

The semicolon shows that this is a single line of a program, but the line itself is ambiguous. It might be interpreted in any of three ways, as

```
LTFSIP   CLR;        or
LTF      SIP   CLR;  or
         LTF   SIPCLR;
```

The problem is that we have no way of telling how many of the first few letters, if any, form a name for the place in memory where the instruction is to be stored. In the first example, LTFSIP is the name of the memory position where a CLR instruction is stored; in the second, LTF is the name of the position where a SIP instruction is stored. In the third example, no name is given for the position of the LTF instruction.

To distinguish among the three possibilities, we use a colon, which breaks the line into two pieces. Anything to the left is a name. Of the letters on the right, the first three are the instruction. The others, if there are any, also form a name.

For example, if we modify the line we are considering as follows

	L	T	F	:	S	I
...	___	___	___	___	___	___
	501	502	503	504	505	506

P	C	L	R	;	
___	___	___	___	___	...
507	508	509	510	511	

then it *must* be interpreted as follows:

```
LTF:    SIP  CLR;
```

That is, it is a STORE-IN-POSITION instruction which places a number in the memory position called CLR. The STORE-IN-POSITION instruction itself is stored in a position called LTF.

Incidentally, if a line does not include a name at the left, it will have no colon. In this case, we interpret the line as if all the letters are to the right of a colon.

10.8 NUMBERS AND LETTERS

A third and more serious kind of ambiguity arises from the fact that numbers and letters are both stored in the memory system as voltage patterns. The pattern that means 12 may also be interpreted as an L.

But then how is the assembler to take the following string in memory?

	L	T	F	12/L	;	
...	___	___	___	___	___	...
	501	502	503	504	505	

Should the **Top** register be loaded with a number from Position 12 or with one from a position identified by the one-letter name L?

Before we answer this question, notice that there is no ambiguity in the voltage patterns stored at Positions 501 through 503. Since there is no colon in this line, the first three positions must contain *letters* forming an abbreviation for an instruction. The pattern stored in Position 501 might be interpreted as the number 12 in other circumstances, but here it is clearly meant as a letter.

As we have just seen, however, the pattern stored in Position 504 is another matter. Both interpretations make sense. Naturally, this will cause problems for our assembler.

The solution, oddly enough, is to spell out numbers just as we spell out names and three-letter abbreviations for instructions. Of course, we are not proposing to store the number 12 in six memory positions as t-w-e-l-v-e. Instead, just as we have voltage patterns for the 26 letters and several marks of punctuation, we will use a few more to stand for the ten digits 0, 1, 2, 3, 4, 5, 6, 7, 8, and 9. Then we will store 12 in two memory positions as 1-2.

This is a very peculiar idea, so we will look into it in detail. Figure 10.8 starts us off by expanding the list of character codes from Figure 6.1 to include codes for digit characters. Incidentally, we are using the word *character* here to mean, roughly, any single mark used in writing: a letter, a digit, or a punctuation mark. As we are learning, all of these are used in our assembly language.

0	Space	10	J	20	T	30	;	40	5
1	A	11	K	21	U	31	?	41	6
2	B	12	L	22	V	32	-	42	7
3	C	13	M	23	W	33	:	43	8
4	D	14	N	24	X	34	+	44	9
5	E	15	O	25	Y	35	0	•	•
6	F	16	P	26	Z	36	1	•	•
7	G	17	Q	27	.	37	2	•	•
8	H	18	R	28	,	38	3	999	Endmarker
9	I	19	S	29	"	39	4		

Figure 10.8 Character codes for letters and numbers.

To see how the digit codes will be used, the first point is to remember that the numbers 0 through 999 in the table are just a shorthand way of representing voltage patterns. When the table tells us that 12 is the code for L, this 12 is used in place of the binary number

$$0000000000001100.$$

And the binary number, in turn, is only meant to remind us that a chunk of 16 flip-flops is storing the following voltage pattern:

off-off-off-off-off-off-off-off-off-off-off-off-on-on-off-off

It is this pattern of voltages, really, which we are interpreting as the letter L. We use the decimal number 12 to refer to this pattern only as a matter of convenience.

Now consider the following pair of patterns:

off-off-off-off-off-off-off-off-off-off-off-off-off-off-off-on
off-off-off-off-off-off-off-off-off-off-on-off-off-on-off-off

The first pattern would mean 1, if it were interpreted as a binary number. But we are *not* interpreting it as a number. Instead, using the table of Figure 10.8, we can see it stands for the letter A.

Likewise, the second pattern would mean 36, if it were interpreted as a binary number. The table tells us, however, that it stands for the *character* 1.

To "spell out" the number 12 in the memory, then, we will store the voltage pattern for 36, followed by the voltage pattern for 37. Since this cannot be confused with the voltage pattern for 12, which stands for L, we have solved the ambiguity problem for our assembler.

Of course, with all these different interpretations, we are likely to get confused ourselves. To keep things straight, we will put quotation marks around digit characters in our memory pictures. Figure 10.9 shows three examples.

```
        L       T       F       L       ;
 · · ·  ―――     ―――     ―――     ―――     ―――      · · ·   = LTF L;
        501     502     503     504     505
```

```
        L       T       F      "1"     "2"      ;
 · · ·  ―――     ―――     ―――    ―――     ―――     ―――      · · ·   = LTF 12;
        501     502     503     504     505     506
```

```
        L       T       F       12      ;
 · · ·  ―――     ―――     ―――     ―――     ―――      · · ·   = LTF L;
        501     502     503     504     505
```

Figure 10.9 Letter, digit character, and number, in Position 504.

Notice that, in the last case, the voltage pattern stored in Position 504 is the one which means 12, if interpreted as a binary number. Now, however, we are considering every pattern to be a code for a character. This pattern, according to our table, stands for the letter L.

10.9 INTERPRETING A NUMBER

Apart from solving our ambiguity problem, spelling out numbers digit by digit brings us much closer to the workings of a real-life computer.

As we mentioned earlier, a typewriter-style keyboard is almost always used to get numbers into a computer's memory. The details are taken up in Chapter 12, but one point is obvious: A typewriter keyboard has no key for the number 12. Instead, we have to hit the "1" key and then the "2" key. We are *forced* to enter the number one digit character at a time.

If each key we hit places one character code in the memory, the result will look like this, just as we want:

```
           "1"     "2"
 · · ·     ―――     ―――     · · ·
           504     505
```

On the other hand, this creates a new problem for the assembler. If we want our computer to *use* the number 12, this pair of character codes will have to be converted into an ordinary binary number. Fortunately, this is not too hard to do.

To start, notice that it is easy to convert an individual character code for a digit into the corresponding binary number. The code for "1" is the binary pattern for 36, the code for "2"is the binary pattern for 37, and so on. Each code is 35 higher than the number it stands for. To convert it, we just need to subtract 35.

Using this way of converting digits, we can give the outline of a subroutine for converting *strings* of digits into a single binary number. Notice that the subroutine knows it has come to the end of the number to be converted when it reads a semicolon. This is because, in our assembly language, numbers are used only at the end of instruction lines.

NUMBER-CONVERSION SUBROUTINE

1. Start the **Answer** at zero.

2. Read the next character, and if it is a semicolon, report **Answer** and stop.

3. If it is not a semicolon, it must be a digit character. Convert it to binary by subtracting 35.

4. Multiply **Answer** by 10 and add in the new, converted digit.

5. Go back to step 2.

Suppose this subroutine is used to convert the following string of digits in the memory:

	"2"	"3"	"1"	;	
• • •	───	───	───	───	• • •
	504	505	506	507	

In step 1, **Answer** is set to zero. In steps 2 and 3, the digit character "2" is read and converted to the number 2. In step 4, **Answer** is multiplied by 10 and this 2 is added. Since **Answer** is 0, multiplying by 10 gives 0 again. After adding 2, **Answer** will be 2.

Notice that this is correct: after looking at just a single digit, the computer has seen the number 2. It is not done with its work, however. Step 5 sends it back to step 2.

This time, steps 2 and 3 read the digit character "3" and convert it to the number 3. In Step 4, **Answer** is first multiplied by 10, making it 20. Then 3 is added, to make the new **Answer** 23.

Notice that this is again correct: after looking at two digits, the computer has seen the number 23. In fact, although the subroutine is still not finished, we can see why it will work. The digits "23" mean the number 23, by themselves. But if we add another digit on the right, the same digits will mean 230—ten times as much. To include the third digit, we multiply by 10 and add it in.

In the case of our example, this makes the **Answer** 231. The next character to be read is a semicolon, which causes the subroutine to report this answer and stop.

The subroutine works correctly because it follows the rules of the base-10 number system. Each new digit changes the meaning of previous digits, since these must now be one place farther to the left. In this case, they count values 10 times as high.

*   *   *   *   *

In the discussion we have just concluded, it is important to realize that the computer is not calculating in base 10. In fact, as we know, the computer works only with binary numbers. When we speak of the number 23, or twenty-three, we mean that the computer is calculating with the binary number 0000000000010111. When it starts **Answer** at 0 or multiplies it by 10, these are binary operations. Of course, the final **Answer** is also in binary.

The upshot is that our assembler will be equipped with a way to convert a number given character by character in *decimal* to an equivalent number in *binary*.

This is a tremendously important point, so we will take a moment to emphasize it.

Until now we have very freely used decimal numbers in place of binary. We have referred to a memory chunk, for example, as Position 500 and we have considered loading the number 103 into the **Top** register. All of this was only for convenience in our discussion, however. Actually, the name of the memory chunk is a pattern of voltages corresponding to the binary number 0000000111110100, and the number to go in **Top** is 0000000001100111.

Likewise, in discussing the translator we designed at the beginning of this chapter, it was perfectly natural for us to *talk* about using an instruction like LTP 394 and to *picture* how it would look in the memory this way:

	L	T	P	394	
· · ·	——	——	——	——	· · ·
	501	502	503	504	

In fact, however, the number in Position 504 must be 0000000110001010.

To use the computer we designed, it is necessary for all numbers to be expressed in binary, and until now, the tedious work of figuring out how to represent all those binary numbers has rested entirely on our own shoulders.

Once we have completed our assembler, however, we will never again have to concern ourselves with binary. If we want to get the decimal number 394 into the **Top** register, we will need only to put the following seven characters into the memory:

	L	T	P	"3"	"9"	"4"	;	
· · ·	——	——	——	——	——	——	——	· · ·
	501	502	503	504	505	506	507	

The assembler will take care of the rest.

10.10 PARSING

We have said a great deal now about the details of our assembly language and how they affect the assembler that will translate it. After one last detail, we may return, finally, to the add-up-a-list program with which we began.

Consider the following line of assembly language:

```
PART-TWO:     LTF   394;
```

PART-TWO is used here as a name for the memory position where the LTF instruction is stored. If we want to return to this position later, all we need is the following JUMP-TO-POSITION instruction:

```
JTP   PART-TWO;
```

As we have made clear, this trick of using names in place of memory positions is one of the main advantages of our assembly language. By adding a string of letters and a colon at the beginning of any line of an assembly-language program, we can name the position where the instruction of that line will be stored.

The problem—the detail we must attend to—is that we have not yet said how to name the *next* position after the instruction. For example, after the program is translated, where will the number 394 following the LTF instruction be stored? Naturally, it will be in the position just after the one called PART-TWO. But suppose we want to refer to this position in the program. What will we call it?

The answer is that we will call it +PART-TWO, the plus sign standing for the phrase *the next position after*. Using this notation, we can change the number 394 in the line we are considering to zero with the following pair of instructions:

```
CLR
SIP   +PART-TWO;
```

*   *   *   *   *

As our first example of the use of assembly language, we gave a version of our add-up-a-list program. Now we are in a good position not only to understand it ourselves, but to see how the assembler will understand it.

As far as the assembler is concerned, the program begins simply as a long list of characters. Letters, digits, and punctuation are all stored in an unbroken sequence. We might picture it like this:

```
CLR;SIPTOTAL;LTP100;ADD;SIP+POINTER-AND-LOOPSTART;POINTER-A
ND-LOOPSTART:LTF9999;LBT0;ADD;JIZEND;LBFTOTAL;ADD;SIPTOTAL;
LTF+POINTER-AND-LOOPSTART;LBT1;ADD;SIP+POINTER-AND-LOOPSTAR
T;JTPPOINTER-AND-LOOPSTART;END:STP;
```

Let us see step by step how to make sense of this. The first step is to break the confusing mass of characters into separate lines, each ending with a semicolon. Here is the result:

```
C  L  R  ;
S  I  P  T  O  T  A  L  ;
L  T  P  " 1 "  " 0 "  " 0 "  ;
A  D  D  ;
S  I  P  +  P  O  I  N  T  E  R  -  A  N  D  -  L  O  O  P  S  T  A  R  T  ;
P  O  I  N  T  E  R  -  A  N  D  -  L  O  O  P  S  T  A  R  T  :  L  T  F  " 9 "  " 9 "  " 9 "  " 9 "  ;
L  B  T  " 0 "  ;
A  D  D  ;
J  I  Z  E  N  D  ;
L  B  F  T  O  T  A  L  ;
A  D  D  ;
S  I  P  T  O  T  A  L  ;
L  T  F  +  P  O  I  N  T  E  R  -  A  N  D  -  L  O  O  P  S  T  A  R  T  ;
L  B  T  " 1 "  ;
A  D  D  ;
S  I  P  +  P  O  I  N  T  E  R  -  A  N  D  -  L  O  O  P  S  T  A  R  T  ;
J  T  P  P  O  I  N  T  E  R  -  A  N  D  -  L  O  O  P  S  T  A  R  T  ;
E  N  D  :  S  T  P  ;
```

Notice that we have left spaces between all the characters to emphasize that we have not yet decided how to group them into names and three-letter codes.

The next step is to analyze each line. If it includes a colon, any letters to the left form a name and the first three letters to the right are an instruction abbreviation. If the line does not include a colon, the very first three letters should be grouped as an instruction. Now we have the following:

```
                          CLR;
                          SIP    T  O  T  A  L  ;
                          LTP    " 1 "  " 0 "  " 0 "  ;
                          ADD;
                          SIP    +  P  O  I  N  T  E  R  -  A  N  D  -  L  O  O  P  S  T  A  R  T  ;
POINTER-AND-LOOPSTART:    LTF    " 9 "  " 9 "  " 9 "  " 9 "  ;
                          LBT    " 0 "  ;
                          ADD;
                          JIZ    E  N  D  ;
                          LBF    T  O  T  A  L  ;
                          ADD;
                          SIP    T  O  T  A  L  ;
                          LTF    +  P  O  I  N  T  E  R  -  A  N  D  -  L  O  O  P  S  T  A  R  T  ;
                          LBT    " 1 "  ;
                          ADD;
                          SIP    +  P  O  I  N  T  E  R  -  A  N  D  -  L  O  O  P  S  T  A  R  T  ;
                          JTP    P  O  I  N  T  E  R  -  A  N  D  -  L  O  O  P  S  T  A  R  T  ;
END:                      STP;
```

To analyze the characters to the right of the instruction, we need only to check the first one in each line. If it is a letter, the characters to the right should be grouped as a name. If it is a plus sign, the *following* characters should be grouped as a name. If it is a digit, the characters to the right should be interpreted as a decimal number.

The result is the program, as we originally gave it:

```
                              CLR;
                              SIP    TOTAL;
                              LTP    100;
                              ADD;
                              SIP    +POINTER-AND-LOOPSTART;
    POINTER-AND-LOOPSTART:    LTF    9999;
                              LBT    0;
                              ADD;
                              JIZ    END;
                              LBF    TOTAL;
                              ADD;
                              SIP    TOTAL;
                              LTF    +POINTER-AND-LOOPSTART;
                              LBT    1;
                              ADD;
                              SIP    +POINTER-AND-LOOPSTART;
                              JTP    POINTER-AND-LOOPSTART;
           END:               STP;
```

*   *   *   *   *

The analysis we have just completed depends on the fact that our assembly language follows certain strict rules. Here are a few examples:

1. Each line of a program must end with a semicolon.

2. Each line must contain exactly one instruction.

3. If the instruction is JIZ, JTP, LBF, LTP, or SIP, it must be followed by either a number or a name.

4. If the instruction is LBT or LTP, it must be followed by a number.

5. Any instruction may be preceded by a name and a colon.

6. A name preceding an instruction may be any string of characters, so long as the first one is a letter and none of the characters is a colon, a plus sign, or a semicolon.

7. A name following an instruction may be any of the names permitted by rule 6, or any of those names with a plus sign added at the beginning.

These rules limit what strings of letters, numbers, and punctuation we may form. For example, they do not permit us to begin a program with any of the following:

```
    A B C ;                        (violates rule 2)
    A B C : S I P ;                (violates rule 3)
    A B C : S I P : J T P ;        (violates rule 6)
```

At the same time, the rules give meaning to strings which they do permit. They tell us what the parts are and how they relate to each other.

In a sense, these rules are like the rules of English grammar. Just as our assembly-language rules tell us how to put together letters, numbers, and punctuation into meaningful program lines, grammatical rules tell us how to put words together to form meaningful sentences.

Grammar prohibits us from making statements like this one:

The lion the tiger bit.

At the same time, we depend on grammar to help us figure out the relationship between words in a sentence. In the lion-tiger example, it is impossible to decide which animal did the biting precisely because the rules of grammar are violated. However, consider another example:

The echidna bit the karakul.

In this case, the fact that the sentence is grammatical allows us to say definitely that the echidna did the biting, even if we have no idea what either an echidna or a karakul is.

Understanding an English sentence is partly a matter of identifying the role each word plays and the relationship between words, using the rules of grammar as a guide. This process is called **parsing**. In effect, parsing determines the *structure* of a statement, leaving us the problem of filling in the meaning.

Analyzing an assembly-language program to determine how it is divided into lines, which characters group together to form instructions, which should be interpreted as numbers—all this is also a kind of parsing. The work of this section has shown that the parsing of an assembly-language program can be reduced to an algorithm.

Since it is clear how to use semicolons to break a program up into lines, we will give the outline of a subroutine for the rest of the parsing work, that is, for analyzing a single line:

LINE-PARSING SUBROUTINE

1. Set a pointer to the first character in the line.

2. Using the pointer, read through all the characters in the line to see whether it contains a colon. Then set the pointer back to the first character again. If no colon was found, jump to step 4.

3. Using the pointer, read all the characters up to the colon. These form the name of a position where an instruction will be stored. Set the pointer to the next character after the colon.

4. Read three characters, beginning with the one to which the pointer is pointing. These should form an instruction abbreviation (which may be identified, if necessary, by our IDENTIFICATION subroutine). Set the pointer to the next character after these three.

5. Without moving the pointer, read this character.
   (a) If it is a semicolon, stop.
   (b) If it is a plus sign, jump to step 7.

(c) If it is a letter, jump to step 8.

(d) If it is a digit, continue with step 6.

6. The remaining characters, up to the semicolon, are the digits of a decimal number (which may be converted to binary if necessary by our NUMBER-CONVERSION subroutine). Stop after processing these characters.

7. Move the pointer to the next character.

8. The remaining characters, up to the semicolon, form the name of a position where an instruction or number will be stored. Stop after processing these characters.

Of course, this is still only an outline. One major fault is that it does not include steps to check the line it is parsing for possible errors. For example, in step 5a, the subroutine stops because it has encountered a semicolon just after an instruction. But this does not always make sense, as the following line shows:

SIP;

The SIP (STORE-IN-POSITION) instruction *must* be followed by a name or number, as stated by our rule 3. Before stopping in step 5a, our subroutine should make sure that the line is permitted.

This is just one of many kinds of error checks our line parser would need to perform. But now that we have given the main steps in parsing a line, we will consider error checking as a kind of detail and move on to the remaining work of the assembler.

10.11 AN ALGORITHM FOR THE ASSEMBLER

This work, of course, is to translate a program from assembly language to machine language. To see what this entails, consider the add-up-a-list program one last time:

```
                                CLR;
                                SIP     TOTAL;
                                LTP     100;
                                ADD;
                                SIP     +POINTER-AND-LOOPSTART;
POINTER-AND-LOOPSTART:          LTF     9999;
                                LBT     0;
                                ADD;
                                JIZ     END;
                                LBF     TOTAL;
                                ADD;
                                SIP     TOTAL;
                                LTF     +POINTER-AND-LOOPSTART;
                                LBT     1;
                                ADD;
                                SIP     +POINTER-AND-LOOPSTART;
                                JTP     POINTER-AND-LOOPSTART;
END:                            STP;
```

We have already shown how numbers and three-letter codes can be translated to machine-language form using the NUMBER-CONVERSION and IDENTIFICATION subroutines. The main question, then, is what to do about the names.

Notice that there are really two kinds of names. TOTAL is an example of the first kind. It is used to identify a position *outside* the program which will be used to store a number—in this case, the running total of the numbers added so far.

We will call this kind of name a **variable**, since the position it stands for may be used to store any number, just as a variable in algebra may stand for any number.

END and POINTER-AND-LOOPSTART are examples of the second kind of name. These are used to identify positions *within* the program. In fact, as the name suggests, POINTER-AND-LOOPSTART identifies *two* such positions. By itself, it is the position of the LTF instruction at the start of the main program loop. With a plus sign added at the beginning, it is the position of the pointer used to indicate the number in the list which is next to be added.[1]

We will use the term **label** for names of the second kind.

Fortunately, it is easy to distinguish labels from variables. Labels must appear at least once in the left-hand column of the program, that is, at the beginning of a line, followed by a colon. Thus, we can identify them while parsing. Any remaining names must be variables.

*   *   *   *   *

The question, again, is what to do about names. Since all names stand for memory position numbers, the answer is, Use the numbers they stand for.

Consider labels first. Since these stand for positions within a program, we cannot translate them to numbers without knowing where in the memory the program will be stored. Once this is specified, however, the rest is only a matter of counting.

Suppose, for example, that our add-up-a-list program will be stored beginning in Position 8000. Then the first instruction, CLR, will go in that position. The second instruction, SIP, fills two positions—one for the STORE-IN-POSITION instruction and one for the position number where something will be stored. The two positions are, of course, 8001 and 8002. If we continue counting, in this way, we will find that the first LTF instruction is stored in Position 8008. This, then, must be what POINTER-AND-LOOPSTART stands for.

We can find the position number for which END stands in just the same way. It will be Position 8029.

Determining position numbers named by a label, then, amounts to counting work. For *variables*, we can use any memory positions we like, so long as they are not otherwise employed. The safest approach is to use positions just after the end of the program. If we do so, TOTAL will be Position 8030.

---

[1] Incidentally, the program shows an initial pointer value of 9999. This is irrelevant, however, since the fifth instruction of the program sets the pointer to 100, the beginning position of the list of numbers.

Together, these names and position numbers form a kind of dictionary:

```
END                        8029
POINTER-AND-LOOPSTART      8008
TOTAL                      8030
```

Since we have shown step by step how to compile this kind of dictionary, we can write instructions for a subroutine to carry out the work. And with the use of this DICTIONARY subroutine, we can, at last, give an outline for our assembler:

1. Run once through the program to compile a dictionary listing position numbers for each of the names. This step relies on the LINE-PARSING and DICTIONARY subroutines to:
   (a) Identify the names in each line.
   (b) Distinguish labels from variables.
   (c) Count, to determine position numbers for labels.
   (d) Assign position numbers after the end of the program to variables.

2. Run through the program again, translating each line according to the following procedure:
   (a) Parse the line using the LINE-PARSING subroutine.
   (b) Ignore any label to the left of a colon.
   (c) Use the IDENTIFICATION subroutine to translate the three-letter code into a machine-language instruction.
   (d) If there is a number following the instruction, calculate the equivalent in binary using the NUMBER-CONVERSION subroutine.
   (e) If there is a name following the instruction, translate it to a position number using the dictionary compiled in step 1. Add 1 to the number in the dictionary entry if the name begins with a plus sign.

Of course, this outline is only the roughest suggestion of how the assembler would operate. A full specification might run to a hundred pages. It would include details of the data structure to be used in the dictionary and efficient procedures for looking names up in it, kinds of grammatical errors the assembler should look for and what to do about them, conventions for telling the assembler where to store the translated program, and much, much more.

In fact, designing even the simple kind of assembler we have been discussing is quite a daunting project. The rough ideas we have laid out should make it clear, however, that the difficulties are not insurmountable.

With this point in mind, it is time to move on to a related topic.

10.12 TAKING STOCK

In Chapter 9, our main concern was to increase the expressive power of our programs. Through subroutines and recursion, we suggested it would be possible to bring the computer closer to our own way of thinking and talking.

In a sense, however, this suggestion may have been misleading. No matter how sophisticated our subroutines or recursive algorithms, the *computer* remained as simple-minded as ever. We could *think* about a program as a collection of powerful subroutines, but in reality it was still just a list of numbers.

In this chapter, on the contrary, we have presented the outline of a method for actually increasing the power of the computer. As we have put it several times, a translator or assembler program raises the computer to a higher level of understanding.

Of course, in this kind of statement the word *understanding* has a very narrow meaning.

A computer understands machine language in the sense that it responds properly to machine-language statements. If we tell a dog to roll over and it does so, we say it understands. Likewise, if we tell our computer to 0-12, and it responds by loading 12 into the arithmetic-logic unit's **Top** register, we may say it understands.

In this sense, we truly increase our computer's understanding when we write a translator for it. With an assembler in its memory, a computer may be said to understand assembly language.

The fact that this is possible makes the computer unique among machines. Others, whether mechanical or electronic, come with certain built-in capabilities.

A radio "understands," in a sense, how to respond when we turn the volume and tuning knobs. But the only way to change what it understands is to modify it physically—to attach new circuits with additional knobs.

By contrast, we may increase a computer's understanding without adding any parts. This is such a peculiar fact that we have taken a full chapter to look at the details of how it is possible.

Now, however, we intend to leave the details behind. As we have said, a new translator gives us a new language. Since we know translation is possible, it is time to draw up a wish list. What kind of language would we *like* the computer to understand?

In Chapter 11, we propose an answer to this question.

E X E R C I S E S

10.1. Give an example of bootstrapping other than the ones discussed in the chapter.

10.2. What is meant by the phrase "catch on" in the last sentence of Section 10.1?

10.3. Define "bootstrapping" in the general sense.

10.4. What will be stored in memory position 0 after each of the following programs is executed?

(a)	0	LTP 4	(c)	0	LTP 1
	2	LBT 3		2	STL
	4	SUB		3	LBT 2
	5	SIP 0		5	SUB
	7	STP		6	JIZ 10
				8	SIP 0
(b)	0	LTP 1		10	STP
	2	LBF 4		11	ADD
	4	ADD		12	SIP 0
	5	SIP 0		14	STP
	7	STP			

10.5. Suppose the program in Exercise 10.4a is stored in memory untranslated, as described in Section 10.2. How many memory positions will the program fill? Show the contents of the first four memory positions. If the program is translated and then stored, how many positions will it fill?

10.6. Which pages of the key in Figure 10.5 will be used in identifying the instruction SHIFT-BOTTOM-RIGHT?

10.7. Suppose the three-letter code for SHIFT-TOP-LEFT is changed to LTS. What changes will need to be made in the key in Figure 10.5? Give a complete picture of all modified pages.

10.8. Write a key to identify the following animals: antelope, bear, crocodile, dog, frog, goat, hippopotamus, jackal, kangaroo, llama, monkey, octopus, parakeet, quail, zebra. The first page might look like this:

> If it flies, turn to page 4.
> If it sometimes goes in the water, turn to page 7.
> Otherwise, turn to page 11.

Try to use as few pages as possible.

10.9. Give an outline for part 2 of the identification subroutine discussed in Section 10.4.

10.10. In the example of Section 10.5, the translator program translates a counting program. How many times is step 2 of the translator executed?

10.11. The counting program introduced at the beginning of Section 10.2 was shown stored beginning at Position 0. If it is copied as is, beginning in Position 10000, and a JUMP-TO-POSITION 10000 instruction is stored at Position 0, the counting program will not work correctly. Why not? What can be done to correct it?

10.12. Convert the counting program given in Section 10.2 to the assembly-language form described in Section 10.6.

10.13. The following string of letters is the beginning of an assembly-language program: SIPSTLBFADD. Since punctuation has been omitted, the fragment is ambiguous. Show all the ways it might be interpreted.

10.14. For each possible interpretation in Exercise 10.13, show how the string of letters should be punctuated.

10.15. Copy the assembly-language program given at the end of Section 10.6 and indicate which names are labels and which are variables.

10.16. Parse the following. That is, show what assembly-language program it represents.

```
CLR;SIPTOTAL;LTP5;ADD;LBF:SIPJIZSUB;LTFJIZSUB;LBFTOTAL;
ADD;SIPTOTAL;LBT1;SUB;JIZSTR;JTPLBF;STR:STP;
```

10.17. Translate the program given in Exercise 10.16 into machine language. Assume it is to be stored beginning at Position 0 in memory.

10.18. Translate the following program into machine language, assuming it will be stored beginning in Position 0. Note that the distinction between variables and labels has been blurred here. Our assembler would need to be able to handle this problem.

```
                LTP 5;
        ODDEND: LBT 9;
                ADD;
                SIP ODDEND;
                JTP ODDEND;
```

What will this program do? Does it contain a never-ending loop?

10.19. In Section 10.10, we gave seven rules of assembly-language "grammar." Give two more.

10.20. The statement *The lion the tiger bit* is ungrammatical in English. Make up a rule that would prohibit this sentence, but be careful that the rule does not also prohibit any grammatical sentences.

10.21. If the add-up-a-list program were stored beginning at Position 3107, how would the variable-label dictionary look?

10.22. If the program of Exercise 10.16 were stored beginning at Position 1000, how would the variable-label dictionary look?

10.23. What are the main differences between our three-letter code language and our assembly language?

10.24. Which would take up more space in memory: an assembly-language program, the same program written in our three-letter code language, or the same program translated into machine language?

11 An Algorithmic Language

11.1 WHY NOT ENGLISH?

In Chapter 10, we discussed many details of translation, but our main point was that, despite the difficulties involved, it is possible for us to teach our computer a new language.

Now let us suppose we have a battalion of first-rate programmers at our disposal. All we need to do is specify a language and the programmers will set to work developing a translator to turn it into machine instructions.

What kind of language would we like the computer to understand?

A natural first response is that we would like the computer to understand English. Then, if we wanted it to add up some numbers or put a list in order, we could simply tell it so, just as we would tell a friend or co-worker.

Clearly, this is a goal worth attaining. For several reasons, however, English is not the best choice for a computer language.

First, instructions in English are most often given in a form we will call **nonprocedural**. That is, they do not explain *how* to carry out the required task. No procedure is specified. If we ask someone to put a list of names into alphabetical order, we rely on his or her ability to figure out a way to do it.

Also, informal instructions of the kind we give in English assume a general understanding of the world, what we often call **common sense**. For example, we would expect someone to use family names, rather than given names, in alphabetizing a list.

It is not unreasonable to think of writing a translator program that takes all this into account. The problem is simply that such a program, if it is possible at all, would be extremely difficult to write. In fact, as we will discuss in detail in Chapter 13, battalions of first-rate programmers *have* been working on English translators—for more than 30 years—with remarkably little success.

Moreover, even if we had such a translator, the nonprocedural nature of ordinary English would be a serious drawback. Often, as in the case of sorting a list, procedure is crucial.

Suppose a translator converts the English instruction *put this list in order* into a program using the selection sort algorithm with a linked list. The translation may be correct, in a sense, but for a long list it is useless. In general, we want to maintain control over procedure. That is, we want our computer language to describe not tasks, but algorithms.

This suggests another reason why English is a poor choice for a computer language. It is not well suited to describing algorithms.

Imagine, for example, trying to explain long division to someone over the telephone. Or imagine how our explanation of sorting algorithms in Chapter 7 would read if there were no illustrations.

English lacks the precision and specialized vocabulary to explain these procedures clearly.

11.2 AN ALGORITHMIC LANGUAGE

English is nonprocedural, complex, and vague. We want a language which is just the opposite: simple, precise, and designed expressly for describing algorithms.

This is not the end of our list of requirements, however.

It is also essential that our algorithmic language capture the full potential of the computer. That is, we must be able to use it to express *any* algorithm a computer is capable of following.

Our model machine language is versatile in just this way. Using only programs written with the 15 basic instructions, our computer can carry out any information processing work possible for a computer to perform.

What we are asking of our algorithmic language, then, is that it should be *no less* versatile than machine language. If an algorithm may be expressed in machine language, we should also be able to describe it with our algorithmic language.

As a last requirement, we would like our language to lead to concise, clear programs. It is one thing to express an algorithm and quite another to express it in a way people find easy to understand. To keep our programs readable, it is best to make them short. If a program must be long, it will be clearer if it is written as a collection of easy-to-understand parts. Our algorithmic language should promote the use of this kind of structure.

*   *   *   *   *

In the next section, we will begin to describe exactly this kind of language. But before we do, take a moment to consider two additional points.

First, although we have already discussed three languages—machine language, machine language written with three-letter codes, and assembly language—these three are very similar in one respect. All of them require us to say precisely which machine instructions are to be executed.

Moreover, most of these instructions depend more on the organization of the computer than on what we are trying to use it for. For example, to add two numbers, we need to use the instructions LOAD-TOP, LOAD-BOTTOM, and ADD. Of these, only ADD describes what we are trying to do.

By contrast, the algorithmic language we are about to consider will make no direct reference to machine instructions. Instead, the language will be based on tasks we might want the computer to perform.

Adding is one such task. To make the computer add, say, 3 and 4, we will write simply:

$$3 + 4$$

Naturally, the translator may translate this as

```
LOAD-TOP 3
LOAD-BOTTOM 4
ADD
```

But it might just as well translate it as

```
LOAD-BOTTOM 3
LOAD-TOP 4
ADD
```

As far as we are concerned, the difference is irrelevant.

The first point about our algorithmic language, then, is that it will consist of units of useful work, rather than machine instructions.

The second point is closely related. Since it shields us from machine-language considerations, the algorithmic language we are discussing gives us an abstract way of thinking about the computer. When we write

$$3 + 4$$

we are simply calling on the computer's ability to add. The details of how the addition will be carried out have been abstracted away.

The tremendous significance of this abstract conception is that it applies equally to other computers than our model. So long as a computer can add, it makes sense to think of giving it the instruction

$$3 + 4$$

By contrast, the instruction LOAD-TOP makes sense only for *our* computer, because it happens to have a register called **Top**.

Imagine, for example, a computer with only one register, called **Main**. With this computer, we might use the following instructions to add 3 and 4:

```
LOAD-MAIN 3
ADD-TO-MAIN 4
```

Programming in this computer's machine language, it seems, would be extremely different from programming in our familiar machine language. With our algorithmic language, however, the *same* program will work just as well on either computer, so long as both are equipped with appropriate translators.

The second point about our algorithmic language, then, is that it is computer-independent. With machine language, each computer is different. Learning to program a new computer may be a formidable task. With our algorithmic language, however, there is nothing new about a different computer, from the programmer's point of view. The same abstract conception and programming skills apply.

11.3 LOOPS

We are about to describe an algorithmic language called AL. The best place to begin is with this question: What are the fundamental elements of a computer algorithm?

One, certainly, is the ability to repeat actions. To count, we programmed the computer to add 1 repeatedly. Selection sort repeatedly selected the largest remaining item in a list. Even our three-letter-code translator worked by repeatedly applying the IDENTIFICATION subroutine.

In fact, it is fair to say that the computer draws much of its power from an ability to repeat simple manipulations. That is, its power is based on the use of loops.

In AL, loops are indicated plainly by the word LOOP. The action to be repeated in the loop will be marked off with square brackets. Also, each loop will have a name, given just after the word LOOP. Here is an example:

```
LOOP   SAMPLE   [action to be repeated]
```

The name of the loop—SAMPLE, in this case—is a variable. Variables are more powerful in AL than they were in our assembly language, but the idea is much the same. A variable is the name of a place in the computer's memory where something may be stored.

In the case of a loop name, the computer stores 1 in the variable just before it carries out the action between square brackets for the first time. It stores 2 before it carries out the action a second time and so on.

Incidentally, we have said nothing about stopping the loop. In fact, the loop called SAMPLE would never stop. It would go on repeating the action between square brackets forever.

If we want a loop that stops, we need to add a **stopping condition**. This goes between the name and the square brackets. Here is an example:

LOOP   COUNTER   COUNTER = 3   [*action to be repeated*]

The stopping condition in this case is the statement COUNTER = 3, that is, that the number stored in the variable COUNTER is 3. When this condition is met, the loop stops.

Each time through the loop, the computer (1) checks the stopping condition, (2) changes the number stored in COUNTER, and (3) carries out the action between square brackets. Also, before the loop begins, it starts COUNTER at 0.

Here is what happens, then, when the computer executes the loop called COUNTER:

1. The computer stores 0 in COUNTER.

2. It checks the stopping condition, but since the number in COUNTER is not 3, it continues.

3. It stores 1 in COUNTER and carries out whatever is specified between the square brackets for the first time.

4. It checks the stopping condition again, but the number in COUNTER is 1, not 3, so it continues.

5. It stores 2 in COUNTER and carries out the specified action a second time.

6. Again, it checks the stopping condition, but the number in COUNTER is 2, not 3, so it continues.

7. It stores 3 in COUNTER and carries out the action between square brackets for a third time.

8. When it checks the stopping condition again, however, it will find that the number in COUNTER is indeed 3. At this point, it stops.

Notice that the stopping condition COUNTER = 3 causes the computer to repeat the given action three times. If we wanted the same action repeated 1 million times, we would simply change the stopping condition to COUNTER = 1000000.

*   *   *   *   *

In Section 5.7, we considered using a program loop to calculate how much money we would get if we left $100 in the bank at 7 percent interest for 150 years. The answer was a staggering $2.5 million.

But in 150 years, the money is not likely to do us much good. How long would we have to wait to have a balance of just $1 million?

An AL program to calculate the answer would use the following loop:

LOOP   YEARS   BALANCE > 1000000   [*instructions to multiply the*
                                         number in BALANCE *by 1.07 and*
                                         store the result back in BALANCE   ]

The stopping condition here uses the symbol $>$, which means "greater than." The name BALANCE is simply another variable. It is used to store the amount of money we have in the bank at any time. The stopping condition, then, amounts to this statement: Stop if the amount of money in the bank is more than 1 million dollars.

Of course, this is not a complete program. For one thing, we need to start the balance off at $100. But suppose that the number 100 *has* been stored in BALANCE somehow. Here is how the loop will operate:

1. The computer checks the stopping condition, but the number in BALANCE is 100, which is not greater than 1,000,000. So the computer continues.

2. It stores 1 in the variable YEARS and carries out the action between square brackets. In this case, that is to increase the number in BALANCE by 7 percent.

   {*Notice that* YEARS *now contains 1 and* BALANCE *contains 107. That is, after 1 year, the bank balance will be $107.*}

3. The computer checks the stopping condition, but 107 is not greater than 1,000,000, so it continues.

4. It stores 2 in YEARS and increases the number stored in BALANCE by 7 percent.

   {*Now* YEARS *contains 2 and* BALANCE *contains the bank balance after 2 years: $114.49.*}

   .
   .
   .

271. The computer checks the stopping condition, but the number stored in BALANCE is approximately 991,274, still not greater than 1,000,000. Therefore the computer continues.

272. It stores 136 in YEARS and increases the number in BALANCE by 7 percent.

   {*Now* YEARS *contains 136 and* BALANCE *contains the bank balance after 136 years: about $1,060,660.*}

273. The computer checks the stopping condition one last time, but now the number in BALANCE *is* greater than 1,000,000, so the computer stops.

Each time through the loop, the number in BALANCE is changed just as the actual bank balance would change. YEARS counts the number of times the loop is executed, and the stopping condition causes the loop to stop when we have a balance of more than 1 million dollars.

The result is that, when the loop stops, YEARS will contain the answer to our question: It takes 136 years for 100 dollars to grow to 1 million at 7 percent interest.

Incidentally, compare this one-line loop statement with an assembly-language loop. Figure 11.1 shows a *simpler* loop than the one we have been considering. It just repeats some set of instructions 136 times.

```
                         CLR;
                         LTP 1;
                         ADD;
         LOOPSTART:      SIP COUNTER;
                              .
                              .
         {instructions to be repeated}
                              .
                              .
                         LTF COUNTER;
                         LBT 136;
                         SUB;
                         JIZ END;
                         LBT 1;
                         ADD;
                         JTP LOOPSTART;
         END:            STP;
```

Figure 11.1 An assembly-language loop.

11.4 DATA MANIPULATION

We began the previous section by asking about the fundamental elements of a computer algorithm. We have demonstrated the power of repetition. But what actions will we want to repeat?

As the bank example shows, calculation is one extremely useful kind of action. In AL, we use the usual symbols to call for addition and subtraction. For example, to instruct the computer to add or subtract 7 and 5, we will write simply

$$7 + 5$$

or

$$7 - 5$$

For multiplication and division, the symbols we choose are less familiar. Instead of writing

$$7 \cdot 5$$

and

$$7 \div 5$$

we write

$$7 * 5$$

and

$$7 / 5$$

The reason, as we mentioned in Chapter 10, is that most computers use a typewriter-style keyboard as a way of putting information into the memory. We prefer to use only symbols commonly found on such a keyboard.

Incidentally, in AL it makes perfectly good sense to use variables, as well as numbers, in calculations. If we write

$$1.07 * \text{BALANCE}$$

it means we want the computer to calculate the product of two numbers: 1.07 and the number stored in the variable BALANCE.

Note that this calculation does not change the number in BALANCE. We have not yet said how we will instruct the computer to put numbers into variables. This is an important and somewhat subtle point, so we will take a moment to be sure it is clear.

The number stored in BALANCE is like a balance printed in a savings account passbook. If you are earning 7 percent interest, you might like to multiply that balance by 1.07 to see how much money you will have next year. But performing this calculation does not affect the number printed in the passbook. You are using the number without changing it.

Likewise, the computer may calculate

$$1.07 * \text{BALANCE}$$

without affecting the number stored in the variable.

*   *   *   *   *

Another important point to note about calculations is that, if we are not careful, they may be ambiguous. For example, what should be the computer's answer in the following calculation:

$$5 + 3 * 2?$$

If it adds first, it will get 8 times 2, or 16. If it multiplies first, it will get 5 plus 6, or 11.

It is essential to have an unambiguous way of specifying calculations, if we want to have accurate control of the computer. The solution in AL is to use parentheses to show the computer which operations to do first.

For example, here are the two calculations we have just been discussing:

$$(5 + 3) * 2$$
$$5 + (3 * 2)$$

The answer is 16 in the first case, 11 in the second.

Of course, if the order of operations is unimportant, we may leave out the parentheses. In this case, the computer will carry out the operations from left to right. For example, if we write

$$1 + 2 + 6 + 8$$

the computer will begin by adding 1 and 2. Then it will add 6 to the answer, and so on. But this order is irrelevant, since the final answer does not depend on it.

*   *   *   *   *

Calculation is one important way to manipulate the information stored in a computer. Equally important are the logical manipulations represented in our machine language by the instructions AND and OR. AL includes these instructions and, in addition, the logical NOT.

One use of these **logical operators** is in constructing stopping conditions for loops. For example, consider the following:

```
LOOP  YEARS  (BALANCE>1000) OR (BALANCE<50)
          [     instructions to multiply the
                number in BALANCE by 1.07, subtract
                8, and then store the answer back
                in BALANCE                              ]
```

The idea here is that someone earns 7 percent interest but takes 8 dollars out of the bank each year. He or she wants to know how many years it will be before the balance either rises above 1,000 dollars or sinks below 50.

The loop will proceed, changing the balance as specified, until one *or* the other condition arises.

In checking the stopping condition, the computer first compares the number in BALANCE with 1,000. If it is larger, the first part of the stopping condition is **true**. Otherwise it is **false**. Then it checks the second part and gets a second logical answer: **true** or **false**. Finally, it uses the OR operation to put these two logical values together.

If the answer is **true**, one *or* the other of the conditions must have been met, so the loop stops.

For example, if the number in BALANCE is 49, the statement BALANCE>1000 is **false**. The statement BALANCE<50 is **true**. Finally, **false** OR **true** is the same as **true**, and so the loop stops.

*   *   *   *   *

We have noted that variables are more powerful in AL than in assembly language. One good example of this is that AL variables may be used to store a whole *string* of letters or other characters—a word, a sentence, or even a whole paragraph of text. Of course, the computer's memory still stores just one character per position. What we are saying is that a variable in AL may refer to a group of memory positions, instead of just one.

To manipulate these **string variables**, AL will use four special operations: JOIN, FIRST, LAST, and LENGTH.

To see how these work, suppose we have two string variables, WORDA and WORDB. WORDA contains the string of letters "ant"; WORDB contains "eater."

JOIN instructs the computer to put two strings together. For example, if we give the computer the AL instruction

                    WORDA JOIN WORDB

the computer will arrive at the result "anteater."[1]

FIRST instructs the computer to separate off the first part of a string. Just how much to separate off is specified with a number. For example, if we write

                    WORDB FIRST 3

the computer will separate off the first three characters of what is stored in WORDB. The result is the string "eat."

LAST works just the same as FIRST except that it causes the computer to separate off the last part of a string of characters. For example,

                    WORDB LAST 4

produces the result "ater."

Incidentally, we may use FIRST and LAST together to get some middle part of a string. Consider the instruction

                (WORDB LAST 4) FIRST 3

In executing this, the computer begins with what is inside parentheses. We have already said that this—WORDB LAST 4—gives the result "ater." The computer continues, then, with the following manipulation:

                    "ater" FIRST 3.

The result is "ate," the first three of the last four letters of "eater."

The last of our string operators is LENGTH, which is used to determine the number of characters in a string. For example,

                    WORDA LENGTH

gives a result of 3, since the string "ant" contains three letters.

                *   *   *   *   *

---

[1] Notice, again, that this does not change what is stored in the variables. WORDA still contains "ant" and WORDB still contains "eater."

In summary, AL provides ways to manipulate three kinds of information, or data. Numbers may be manipulated with arithmetic operations: addition, subtraction, multiplication, and division. Logical values may be ANDed, ORed, or NOTed. Finally, strings of characters may be joined with the JOIN operator, measured with the LENGTH operator, or broken into parts with FIRST and LAST.

We can demonstrate the power of all these manipulations by combining them in a single instruction. Consider the following example:

```
LOOP MIRROR  NOT ((WORD FIRST ((WORD LENGTH) / 2))=
                   (WORD LAST ((WORD LENGTH) / 2)))

        [    instructions to change the string
             stored in WORD to the next item in
             a list of words                              ]
```

Notice that, as we have pictured it, this instruction runs on for several lines. Of course, when we store the instruction in memory, it will be just a long list. The L from LOOP will be stored in one memory position, followed by O in the next position and so on through to the closing bracket at the end of the instruction.

When we show the instruction on paper, however, it is helpful to clearly separate the main parts. In this case, although the instruction is quite complicated, the parts are easy to identify. We are considering a LOOP instruction called MIRROR. It has the stopping condition

```
NOT ((WORD FIRST ((WORD LENGTH) / 2))=(WORD LAST ((WORD LENGTH) / 2)))
```

and the action to be repeated is one which changes the string stored in the variable WORD.

Now, look carefully at the stopping condition. It includes not only parentheses, but parentheses within parentheses. The innermost pair contains the instruction

```
WORD LENGTH
```

This asks the computer to determine how many characters are in the string stored in the variable WORD. Suppose, for now, that WORD contains the string "couscous." Then the computer will get the answer 8.

The stopping condition, then, is this:

```
NOT ((WORD FIRST (8 / 2))=(WORD LAST (8 / 2)))
```

The computer works next on the innermost pair of parentheses remaining. This time it contains 8 / 2. The computer divides 8 by 2 and gets four as an answer. In effect, it has computed half the length of the string "couscous."

The condition now looks like this:

```
NOT ((WORD FIRST 4)=(WORD LAST 4))
```

At this point, we may practically read it in English. It says that the loop should stop if the first four letters in WORD are *not* the same as the last four letters. But in the string "couscous," the first four and last four letters *are* the same. So the loop will not stop.

Instead, it will carry out the action in square brackets, which is to take a new string from a list and put it in WORD.

Then the stopping condition will be checked again. Each time it is checked, the computer will first calculate half the length of the string. Then it will use this number to get the first half and the last half of the string. If they are *not* the same, it will stop.

If the computer puts strings into WORD from the following list:

couscous

bonbon

echidnas

aa

woofwoof

it will stop when it comes to "echidnas."

11.5 VARIABLES AND DATA TYPES

It should be clear by now that variables are a central feature of AL. We have already shown how to use information stored in them. But how did the information get there in the first place?

The simple answer is that AL includes a STORE instruction. Actually, it might be better to call it a STORE-IN instruction, as the following example shows:

```
STORE 100 IN BALANCE
```

This puts the number 100 into the variable BALANCE. If BALANCE has been storing another number, this original number will be lost.

In executing this instruction, the computer works from left to right. That is, it first figures out *what* to store—in this case, the number 100—and then puts it in the memory location named by the variable.

This order is important, because it means we may use what is stored in a variable to determine what should be stored *next* in that same variable. Consider this example:

```
STORE   BALANCE * 1.07   IN BALANCE
```

Suppose BALANCE contains the number 100 when the computer comes to this instruction. To execute the instruction it:

1. Figures out what to store by carrying out the calculation BALANCE * 1.07. This gives 107 as a result.

2. Stores this number, 107, in BALANCE.

The first step *uses* the number stored in BALANCE. The second step *changes* it.

The STORE statement may be used just as well to put information into string variables. For example, consider this instruction:

STORE VOWELS IN LETTERS

This takes whatever string is already stored in the variable called VOWELS and puts it in the variable called LETTERS. If VOWELS happens to contain the string "aeiou," then the effect of this instruction is to store "aeiou" in LETTERS.[2]

This example raises an important question. Suppose we want to store the *string* "VOWELS" in LETTERS. That is, we would like LETTERS to contain a string of capital letters: V, O, W, E, L, and S. Obviously,

STORE VOWELS IN LETTERS

will not do the trick.

Actually, the previous paragraphs contain a good hint to the answer. To stress that we mean a string of letters, we put "aeiou" and "VOWELS" in quotation marks. In the same way, AL uses quotation marks to distinguish variables and strings. To store the letters V, O, W, E, L, and S in LETTERS, we write

STORE "VOWELS" IN LETTERS

*   *   *   *   *

We have already introduced the term **string variable** for the kind of variable in AL that may store a string of characters. Actually, AL use four kinds of variables. Two of these are used to store different kinds of numbers.

Integers are numbers with no fractional part, numbers like 0, 1, 2, and 371 or negative numbers like -1, -2 and $-1,004$. As we said in Chapter 4, these may be represented with a single string of binary digits.[3]

Real numbers are *all* numbers corresponding to points on a number line, those which include a fractional part, like 7.6, $\frac{1}{3}$, $-72\frac{1}{2}$, and those that do not, like 0, 1, 2, 371, -1, -2, and $-1,004$. In Chapter 4, we suggested using *two* strings of binary digits to represent real numbers, one for the actual digits and another to show where to put the binary point.

The upshot is that real numbers and integers are represented differently and may even require different amounts of memory storage space. For this reason, AL uses different kinds of variables to store them: **real variables** and **integer variables**.

The same reason accounts for the fourth kind of variable, which is used to store logical values. The best way to represent these values is with a single bit of memory, voltage on for **true** and voltage off for **false**.

---

[2] Notice, again, that the variable VOWELS is unaffected. It contains "aeiou" both before and after the instruction is executed.

[3] Of course, we must be satisfied with representing only numbers within some given limit. See Section 4.6.

A chunk of memory large enough to hold a single integer will have quite a number of bits—16 in our model computer, for example. This memory space is enough to hold 16 logical values.

*   *   *   *   *

In essence, as far as AL is concerned, information is of four different kinds: real, integer, logical, and string. These **data types** are treated differently by the translator. For example, it will accept instructions for logical operations only on logical variables.

The instruction

```
STORE ITISSNOWING OR ITISRAINING IN WEATHERISBAD
```

makes no sense unless all three variables are of the logical type. Likewise, the instruction

```
STORE "hamburger" IN FOOD
```

makes sense only if FOOD is a string variable.

With numerical calculations, the situation is slightly trickier. Integers may be combined only with integers and reals may be combined only with reals. But numbers written out in the program will be interpreted whichever way makes sense.

For example, in the instruction

```
STORE COST + MARKUP IN PRICE
```

all three variables must be of the same type. The instruction makes sense if they are all integers or if they are all reals, but not if the types are mixed.

On the other hand, the instruction

```
STORE 100 IN BALANCE
```

makes sense whether BALANCE is a real or an integer variable. The only difference is in how the number 100 will be represented in the computer's memory.

*   *   *   *   *

We have been talking about data types, but we have not yet said how we will specify them in a program. For example, how is the computer to know that FOOD is a string variable?

In fact, for each variable we use in an AL program, we must also have an instruction to set aside space for it. Since the four data types are used differently, are represented differently, and may require different amounts of space, this instruction must give the data type. Here are three examples:

```
VARIABLE ITISSNOWING LOGICAL;
VARIABLE BALANCE REAL;
VARIABLE COUNTER INTEGER
```

These instructions set aside memory storage space for the variables ITISSNOW-ING, BALANCE and COUNTER, which are of the data types logical, real, and integer. VARIABLE instructions must always be given before a variable is used. The easiest approach will just be to put them all together at the beginning of the program.

Incidentally, this example also introduces the use of the semicolon in AL as punctuation. If a program has more than one instruction, semicolons mark the separation between instructions.

One last, important point about the VARIABLE instruction is that it is slightly different for string variables.

An integer variable always uses a certain set amount of storage. The same is true of real and logical variables. A string variable, however, needs one chunk of memory for each character. It needs more space if it is storing a long string than if it is storing a short one. The VARIABLE instruction for a string variable, then, must include a number showing the maximum length of the string. For example, the instruction

```
VARIABLE WORDA STRING 10
```

calls on the computer to set aside memory space sufficient to store 10 characters and call this space WORDA.

*   *   *   *   *

At this point, we have introduced enough of AL to write a complete program. It calculates how long it takes for $100 to grow to $1 million at 7 percent interest:

```
VARIABLE BALANCE REAL;
VARIABLE YEARS INTEGER;
STORE 100 IN BALANCE;
LOOP YEARS BALANCE>1000000 [STORE BALANCE * 1.07 IN BALANCE];
STOP
```

Notice that the program includes a STOP instruction. We will see in the section after the next why this is necessary.

11.6 CONDITIONALS

We have identified repetition and data manipulation as two essential elements of computer algorithms. A third is choice.

Several of our algorithms in previous chapters, for example, have relied on the computer's ability to compare two numbers and use the result to decide what to do next. In essence, we asked the computer to carry out an action only under certain conditions.

AL includes a straightforward way of specifying such **conditional** instructions. Consider the following example:

```
IF BALANCE>500 THEN [STORE 1.07 * BALANCE IN BALANCE] OTHERWISE []
```

IF indicates that the instruction is conditional. BALANCE>500 is the condition. The rest of the instruction is broken up into two parts: what to do if the condition statement is true and what to do if it is not. In the example, if the condition holds, BALANCE should be increased by 7 percent. If not, nothing at all should be done.

This instruction is meant to reflect the policy of many banks, which give customers interest only if they maintain a minimum balance. We might translate the instruction into English this way: *If* the balance is more than $500, *then* increase it by 7 percent; *otherwise* do nothing.

Notice that square brackets are again used to enclose an action. This is a good time to mention that such an action may consist of more than one instruction, so long as the instructions are separated by semicolons.

For example, suppose a company offers its employees an option. Each employee may either take a 5 percent raise and have $1,000 added to a retirement plan or take a 2 percent raise and have $5,000 added. Here is an instruction translating this option:

```
IF WANTFIVEPERCENT=TRUE THEN [STORE SALARY * 1.05 IN SALARY;
                             STORE 1000 + RETIREPLAN IN RETIREPLAN]
            OTHERWISE [STORE SALARY * 1.02 IN SALARY;
                             STORE 5000 + RETIREPLAN IN RETIREPLAN]
```

11.7 SUBROUTINES

With the data manipulation, repetition, and conditional instructions we have discussed, AL programs may be written for any information processing task computers can perform. This does not mean, however, that the language already meets all of our requirements.

Most important, as the language stands, it would be difficult to keep AL programs readable.

The solution is to use subroutines to break a program up into understandable units. As we saw in Chapter 9, subroutines can be used to build more powerful subroutines in a never-ending hierarchy. But, if each level in the hierarchy is only slightly higher than the one below, subroutines can be kept simple.

To specify a subroutine in AL, we use the word SUBROUTINE, followed by a name and an action, between square brackets as usual. Here is an example:

```
SUBROUTINE NEWEMPLOYEE [STORE 15000 IN SALARY;
                        STORE 0 IN RETIREPLAN]
```

This subroutine sets up financial records for a new employee at our hypothetical company. It assigns the employee a starting salary of $15,000 and notes that no money has yet been invested for the employee in the retirement plan.

Incidentally, the subroutine name NEWEMPLOYEE is not a variable. It is used only to refer to the subroutine when we want these instructions executed. To use the subroutine, we write just

```
USE NEWEMPLOYEE
```

Suppose we put the company's raise-and-retirement-plan option in another subroutine, like this:

```
SUBROUTINE ENDOFYEARADJUSTMENTS
   [IF WANTFIVEPERCENT=TRUE THEN [STORE SALARY * 1.05 IN SALARY;
                                 STORE 1000 + RETIREPLAN IN RETIREPLAN]
                     OTHERWISE [STORE SALARY * 1.02 IN SALARY;
                                 STORE 5000 + RETIREPLAN IN RETIREPLAN]]
```

Then the following instructions will calculate how much an employee will be earning and how much he or she will have in the retirement plan after 25 years, assuming the 2 percent option is chosen:

```
USE NEWEMPLOYEE;
STORE FALSE IN WANTFIVEPERCENT;
LOOP YEARS YEARS=25 [USE ENDOFYEARADJUSTMENTS]
```

The point of using subroutines here is to make the program easy to read. These three lines tell us that the program is setting up records for a new employee, noting that he or she does not want the 5 percent raise option, and making necessary end-of-year changes to the records 25 times.

This outline of the action abstracts away the details of what records are kept and what end-of-year adjustments are necessary. Abstraction makes it clearer.

Of course, these three lines are not a complete program. A complete program is shown in Figure 11.2.

Notice that the program divides neatly into sections; the first part defining the variables; the second, giving the main outline of the program; and the third, filling in the details of the outline by defining subroutines. The STOP instruction separates the main program from the subroutines.

We have said that this way of writing programs makes them easy to read. It also helps if we want to make a change. If the company wants to start new employees at a higher salary, it is not necessary to rethink the whole program. The place to make changes is in the NEWEMPLOYEE subroutine.

```
VARIABLE WANTFIVEPERCENT LOGICAL;
VARIABLE YEARS INTEGER;
VARIABLE SALARY REAL;
VARIABLE RETIREPLAN REAL;

USE NEWEMPLOYEE;
STORE FALSE IN WANTFIVEPERCENT;
LOOP YEARS YEARS = 25 [USE ENDOFYEARADJUSTMENTS];
STOP;

SUBROUTINE NEWEMPLOYEE [STORE 15000 IN SALARY;
                        STORE 0 IN RETIREPLAN];

SUBROUTINE ENDOFYEARADJUSTMENTS
   [IF WANTFIVEPERCENT = TRUE THEN [STORE SALARY * 1.05 IN SALARY;
                                   STORE 1000 + RETIREPLAN IN RETIREPLAN]
                        OTHERWISE [STORE SALARY * 1.02 IN SALARY;
                                   STORE 5000 + RETIREPLAN IN RETIREPLAN]]
```

Figure 11.2 Salary and retirement program.

11.8 NUMBERING VARIABLES

One last feature of AL variables will complete our introduction to the language. This feature is based on the fact that we often have many pieces of the same kind of information: grades for each of a hundred students, names of all the books in a library, and so on.

In cases like these, we would like to have just one variable name refer to the whole list of items.

To see why, consider the company offering its employees a salary and retirement option. Till now, we have used the variable SALARY to store an employee's rate of pay. In reality, of course, if the company has hundreds of employees, we will need a different variable for each salary.

One idea is to use variables like these:

```
JOETURNERSSALARY
MARIAGONZALEZSSALARY
EDWHITMANSSALARY
```

The problem, however, is that names of this kind make automatic processing impossible.

Suppose we want to increase each employee's salary by 5 percent. The only possibility is to write instructions as follows:

```
STORE JOETURNERSSALARY * 1.05 IN JOETURNERSSALARY;
STORE MARIAGONZALEZSSALARY * 1.05 IN MARIAGONZALEZSSALARY;
STORE EDWHITMANSSALARY * 1.05 IN EDWHITMANSSALARY;
                                    .
                                    .
                                    .
```

If the company has 382 employees, we will need 382 instructions to repeat this simple manipulation 382 times. Since the work of the manipulation is the same in each case, however, we ought to be able to use a loop to repeat it.

What we have in mind is this: The first time the action of the loop is carried out, Joe's salary is raised 5 percent; the second time, Maria's is raised; the third time, Ed's; and so on. The loop would look something like this:

```
LOOP EMPLOYEE EMPLOYEE=382 [ STORE someone's-salary * 1.05
                                  IN someone's-salary        ]
```

For this to work, however, the variable we have indicated by *someone's-salary* must automatically *change* each time the STORE instruction is executed. It should be the variable storing Joe's salary when EMPLOYEE is 1—that is, the first time the STORE instruction is carried out. It should be the variable storing Maria's salary when EMPLOYEE is 2, and so on.

The solution, in AL, is to use just one variable name, SALARY, and number it. SALARY.1 will store Joe's salary, SALARY.2 will store Maria's salary, and so on, through to SALARY.382.

With this numbered variable, we may write a single loop instruction to raise all the salaries:

```
LOOP EMPLOYEE EMPLOYEE=382 [ STORE SALARY.EMPLOYEE * 1.05
                                 IN SALARY.EMPLOYEE    ]
```

The first time the action between square brackets is carried out, 1 will be stored in EMPLOYEE. Therefore, the computer will

```
STORE SALARY.1 * 1.05 IN SALARY.1
```

That is, it will increase the number stored in SALARY.1 by 5 percent.

The second time the action between square brackets is carried out, 2 will be stored in EMPLOYEE and the number in SALARY.2 will be increased. The third time, SALARY.3 will be increased, and so on.

* * * * *

Of course, a numbered variable needs more memory space than an ordinary one. Our numbered SALARY variable, for example, needs 382 times as much space as an ordinary real variable, since it holds 382 numbers.

To warn the computer about the extra space required, we need to include a kind of note in our VARIABLE instruction. It would be written this way:

VARIABLE SALARY.382 REAL

We may number string variables as well, as in the following example:

VARIABLE LASTNAME.35 STRING 12

Here, we have asked the translator to set aside memory space for 35 strings, each of which may be up to 12 letters long.

*   *   *   *   *

A last point about this subject is a little tricky: Numbered variables may themselves be numbered.

Suppose a professor has grades for 30 students. We have seen that it is a good idea for her to assign the students numbers and then use a numbered variable, say, GRADE.1 through GRADE.30. GRADE.1 will hold the grade of student 1, GRADE.2 will hold the grade of student 2, and so on.

But what if the professor also has three classes? The best solution is for her to number the numbered variables.

Take GRADE.1. This stores the grade of student 1. But now there is a student 1 in each of three classes. To hold their grades she may use GRADE.1.1, GRADE.1.2, and GRADE.1.3.

With this system, GRADE.7.2 will contain the grade of student 7 in class 2.

Again, using numbered variables makes automatic processing easy. For example, suppose the professor can devise a set of instructions to calculate the class average in class 1. The instructions will make use of the numbers stored in GRADE.1.1 through GRADE.30.1.

But once she has these instructions, she may just as easily calculate averages for all three classes, using a loop:

LOOP CLASSNUMBER CLASSNUMBER = 3   [*instructions to calculate the*
                                      class average using numbers
                                      stored in GRADE.1.CLASSNUMBER
                                      through GRADE.30.CLASSNUMBER]

When the loop action is first carried out, CLASSNUMBER will contain 1 and the average-figuring instructions will use numbers stored in GRADE.1.1 through GRADE.30.1. That is, it will use grades from the first class to calculate an average.

The second time, CLASSNUMBER will hold 2. The averaging will use numbers stored in GRADE.1.2 through GRADE.30.2. That is, it will use grades from the second class.

The third time, the average for the third class will be computed.

11.9 SORTING IN AL

At the beginning of this chapter, we asked what language we would like our computer to understand. Now we have proposed an answer. It may be easy to think of improvements to AL, but as it stands, the language is quite powerful.

To demonstrate, we will write an AL program to sort a list of 1,000 numbers using selection sort.

The first point to notice is that AL makes it easy to create such a list. We will simply use the instruction

```
VARIABLE ITEM.1000 INTEGER
```

to create a numbered variable capable of holding 1,000 numbers.

The next point is that the *essence* of selection sort is a simple repeated action. To sort a list, we repeatedly remove the largest remaining item and add it to the sorted list we are creating. If the list contains 1,000 items, this step must be repeated 1,000 times.

Our main program, then, will be just the following instruction:[4]

```
LOOP MAIN MAIN=1000 [USE SELECTIONSTEP]
```

The subroutine SELECTIONSTEP, which we are about to design, carries out the main work. It looks through all the remaining list items, picks out the largest, and transfers it to the sorted list.

At this point, it appears that we had better have a variable to hold the sorted list. We will use the numbered variable SORTEDITEMS, created with the following instruction:

```
VARIABLE SORTEDITEMS.1000 INTEGER
```

After the list is sorted, SORTEDITEMS.1 will contain the smallest number in the list, SORTEDITEMS.2 will contain the next larger number, and so on up to the largest number, which will be stored in SORTEDITEMS.1000.

Our job now is to design the subroutine SELECTIONSTEP. As we have said, this subroutine finds the largest remaining item and transfers it from ITEM to SORTEDITEMS. Here, then, is what we will write for the subroutine:

```
SUBROUTINE SELECTIONSTEP [USE FIND;
                          USE TRANSFER]
```

Of course, all we have really done here is break a hard job into two pieces. Now we need to roll up our sleeves and get to work.

*   *   *   *   *

---

[4] Actually, the main program will also include one other instruction, as we will see. This instruction does not, however, relate directly to the sorting process.

FIND locates the largest number remaining in the original list, ITEM. TRANSFER stores this number at the proper position in the new list, SORTED-ITEMS.

Consider TRANSFER first. To do its job correctly, it needs to know only what number FIND has found and where in SORTEDITEMS to put it.

To solve the first problem, we will design FIND so that it stores the largest number, once it is found, in a variable called LARGEST.

For the second, we can begin by noting that the first number TRANSFER stores in SORTEDITEMS will be the largest of all the 1,000 numbers. Naturally, it belongs at the bottom of the list, in SORTEDITEMS.1000. The next number transferred is the largest *remaining* number—the second largest number of the original 1,000. This belongs in SORTEDITEMS.999.

As each number is transferred, it goes in the next lower-numbered slot within the SORTEDITEMS variable.

Our solution, then, is this: (1) TRANSFER will use a variable called SLOT to remember which slot to use next; (2) SLOT must originally contain the number 1,000; and (3) each time TRANSFER stores a number, it must decrease the number in SLOT by 1.

Here, then, is our TRANSFER subroutine:

```
SUBROUTINE TRANSFER [ STORE LARGEST IN SORTEDITEMS.SLOT;
                  STORE SLOT  ─  1 IN SLOT ]
```

Notice that this does *not* include any instructions to start SLOT out at 1,000. We will attend to this point in a moment. Otherwise, the subroutine does just what we want: it puts the number stored in LARGEST into the correct slot of SORTED-ITEMS and decreases the SLOT number by 1.

Figure 11.3 shows an example in which the third-largest number in the original list is about to be transferred to SORTEDITEMS.

```
ITEMS.1      6301      SLOT   998        SORTEDITEMS.1      ---
ITEMS.2         4      LARGEST 7761      SORTEDITEMS.2      ---
ITEMS.3       777                        SORTEDITEMS.3      ---
    .                                          .
    .                                          .
ITEMS.634    7761                              .
    .                                          .
    .                                          .
ITEMS.998      97                        SORTEDITEMS.998    ---
ITEMS.999     104                        SORTEDITEMS.999   8560
ITEMS.1000     41                        SORTEDITEMS.1000  8771
```

Figure 11.3 As TRANSFER goes into action.

FIND has located the largest number remaining in the original list, 7,761, and stored it temporarily in the variable called LARGEST. The variable called SLOT shows that this should go into the 998th slot in SORTEDITEMS. Notice that the largest and second-largest numbers have already been stored in higher-numbered slots of SORTEDITEMS.[5]

All TRANSFER does then, is store 7,761 in SORTEDITEMS.998 and change the number in SLOT to 997.

*   *   *   *   *

Our last main design task is to write a subroutine for FIND.

As we saw in Chapter 7, finding the largest item in a list is only a matter of looking through all the items, remembering all the time which item is the largest so far. When all the items have been considered, the largest so far is the largest in the whole list.

For reasons which will soon be clear, it is important to remember *where* this item has been found as well as what it is. We propose, then, to use the variable LARGESTSLOT to remember the slot number of the largest number in ITEM. If the largest number is stored in ITEM.634, as in Figure 11.3, LARGESTSLOT should contain the number 634.

To find the largest item, we will begin by storing 1 in LARGESTSLOT. This indicates that before we look at any other numbers, the one stored in ITEM.1 is the largest so far.

Then we will use a loop to look at each of the numbers in ITEM. Here is an outline:

```
LOOP NEXTSLOT NEXTSLOT = 1000 [ instructions to check the
                                number stored in ITEM.NEXTSLOT ]
```

The action enclosed here in square brackets will be repeated 1,000 times. The first time, NEXTSLOT will contain 1 and the computer will check the number in ITEM.1. That is, it will look at it to see whether it is larger than the largest number so far. The second time, NEXTSLOT will contain 2 and the number in ITEM.2 will be compared with the largest number so far.

By the time the loop has finished, each of the 1,000 numbers will have been checked.

What do we mean by "checking" a number? In fact, we simply want the computer to compare the number under consideration with the largest so far, the one in ITEM.LARGESTSLOT. If it is larger than the largest number so far, *it* is now the largest number and its slot number, NEXTSLOT, should be stored in LARGESTSLOT. Otherwise, no work is necessary.

This translates to a conditional instruction, as follows:

---

[5] We have not shown the numbers stored in SORTEDITEMS.1 through SORTEDITEMS.998, since these are irrelevant and would make the picture confusing. There *are* numbers stored in those variables, but they will be lost when TRANSFER moves the rest of the 1,000 numbers into SORTED-ITEMS.

```
IF ITEM.NEXTSLOT>ITEM.LARGESTSLOT
                      THEN [STORE NEXTSLOT IN LARGESTSLOT]
                      OTHERWISE []
```

If we use this instruction inside the square brackets of our NEXTSLOT loop, we will nearly have completed the FIND subroutine. Here is how it looks so far:

```
SUBROUTINE FIND [   LOOP NEXTSLOT NEXTSLOT=1000
                    [  IF ITEM.NEXTSLOT>ITEM.LARGESTSLOT
                                  THEN [STORE NEXTSLOT IN LARGESTSLOT]
                                  OTHERWISE []
                    ]
              ]
```

Figure 11.4 catches FIND in the middle of its work, looking for the largest number in ITEMS.

```
ITEMS.1    6301          LARGESTSLOT   1
ITEMS.2       4          NEXTSLOT 3
ITEMS.3     777
ITEMS.4    6984
            .
            .                          Figure 11.4 As FIND looks for the largest
            .                          number in ITEM.
```

As we can tell from NEXTSLOT, the computer is about to carry out the action of the LOOP in FIND for the third time. It has already checked the first two slots of ITEMS, and so far, the largest number it has seen is the 6,301 in slot 1. This information is indicated by the 1 stored in LARGESTSLOT.

When it carries out the LOOP action for the third time, the computer checks to see whether ITEMS.3 is larger than ITEMS.1, the current largest. Since it is not, nothing happens.

Before carrying out the LOOP action for a fourth time, the computer stores 4 in NEXTSLOT. When it carries out the action, it checks to see whether ITEMS.4 is larger than ITEMS.1. Since it *is*, the number 4 is stored in LARGESTSLOT. This indicates that ITEMS.4 is the largest of the numbers checked so far.

*   *   *   *   *

A moment ago, we said we had *nearly* completed the FIND subroutine. To finish it, we only need to attend to a pair of important details. First, it is the job of the FIND subroutine to put the largest number into LARGEST, once it has been found. This is easily accomplished with the following instruction:

```
STORE ITEM.LARGESTSLOT IN LARGEST
```

Of course, this instruction must be used after the NEXTSLOT loop has finished—
that is, after the largest number has been found.

The second point is that FIND is meant to be used 1,000 times. As it stands,
it will find the same number over and over again. The largest number in the list
the first time it looks will also be the largest the second time it looks and the third
and so on.

Somehow, each largest item must be removed as it is found, so that the following search will locate the *next*-largest item.

We know, of course, that it is a tricky business to remove numbers from a
sequential list like the one we are using. To keep the program simple, we will
assume that it is to be used only with numbers larger than zero. In this case, as
each largest remaining number is found, we can "remove" it by storing a zero in its
place. The next search will compare this zero with some number, and since it will
certainly not be larger, it will have no effect.

To carry out this plan, we will wait until the largest number has been found
and stored in LARGEST and then use the following instruction:

```
STORE 0 IN ITEM.LARGESTSLOT
```

This instruction puts the finishing touch on our FIND subroutine. Here is the
result:

```
SUBROUTINE FIND
    [    LOOP NEXTSLOT NEXTSLOT=1000
            [   IF ITEM.NEXTSLOT>ITEM.LARGESTSLOT
                    THEN [STORE NEXTSLOT IN LARGESTSLOT]
                    OTHERWISE []
            ];
        STORE ITEM.LARGESTSLOT IN LARGEST;
        STORE 0 IN ITEM.LARGESTSLOT
    ]
```

All the square brackets makes this subroutine a little daunting at first, but a closer
look should be reassuring. FIND consists of three instructions, a LOOP and two
STOREs. The LOOP instruction repeatedly checks numbers in ITEMS to find the
largest. The first STORE puts this number into LARGEST, so that TRANSFER
can use it; and the second STORE erases it from ITEMS by storing a zero in its
place.

To complete our sorting program, we need only instructions for two setup
tasks. Before the main processing can begin, the computer must store 1,000 in
SLOT. Also, the list of numbers to be sorted must be stored in ITEM. We will
combine these tasks into a subroutine called SETUP.

Figure 11.5 shows the final completed program.

Incidentally, this is a perfect example of how we can create a hierarchy of
subroutines as discussed in Chapter 9. Our main program makes use of the sub-

routine SELECTIONSTEP, which is composed of the lower-level subroutines
FIND and TRANSFER. These in turn are written with the base-level instructions
provided by AL.

```
VARIABLE MAIN INTEGER;
VARIABLE SLOT INTEGER;
VARIABLE LARGEST INTEGER;
VARIABLE NEXTSLOT INTEGER;
VARIABLE LARGESTSLOT INTEGER;
VARIABLE ITEM.1000 INTEGER;
VARIABLE SORTEDITEMS.1000 INTEGER;

USE SETUP;
LOOP MAIN MAIN=1000 [USE SELECTIONSTEP];
STOP;

SUBROUTINE SELECTIONSTEP [USE FIND;
                          USE TRANSFER];

SUBROUTINE FIND
   [    LOOP NEXTSLOT NEXTSLOT=1000
            [  IF ITEM.NEXTSLOT>ITEM.LARGESTSLOT
                     THEN [STORE NEXTSLOT IN LARGESTSLOT]
                     OTHERWISE []
            ];
        STORE ITEM.LARGESTSLOT IN LARGEST;
        STORE 0 IN ITEM.LARGESTSLOT
   ];

SUBROUTINE TRANSFER [ STORE LARGEST IN SORTEDITEMS.SLOT;
                      STORE SLOT — 1 IN SLOT ];

SUBROUTINE SETUP [  STORE 1000 IN SLOT;
                    STORE 452 IN ITEM.1;
                    STORE 710 IN ITEM.2;
                    STORE  17 IN ITEM.3;
                              .
                              .
                              .
                    STORE  86 IN ITEM.1000 ]
```

Figure 11.5 AL program to sort a list.

11.10 OTHER LANGUAGES

In fairness, we must now admit that AL is a fiction. To date, no one has written a
translator for any computer to turn AL programs into machine language.

This is not to say, however, that such a translator would be difficult to design. AL is an extremely simple, straightforward language. In fact, it is a scaled-down version of languages like Basic, Pascal, Fortran, and Cobol, for which translators were written decades ago.[6]

All of these languages give us ways to express the basic elements of computer algorithms: repetition, data manipulation, conditional action, and subroutines.

Fortran takes its name from the phrase *formula translation*. It was designed to make scientific algorithms—many of which rely on complicated calculations and formulas—easy to express.

Basic is a somewhat simpler version of Fortran, especially designed for the beginning programmer. As with AL, its instructions are given with ordinary English words to make them easy to understand.

The last three letters in Cobol stand for *business-oriented language*. It is tailored to the needs of business-related information processing. Our salary and retirement calculation is one example of the kind of work Cobol is designed to make easy.

Finally, the newest of the four, Pascal, was developed as a teaching language, but is also popular for general problem solving. It has special facilities for developing data structures. Also, the rules of the language are especially strict, making it somewhat more difficult to write an incorrect program.

There is a great deal to say about these languages, and the hundreds of others which are less well known. But the two most important points are these: First, all of the languages are equally versatile. That is, if we can write instructions in one to express a certain algorithm, we may express the same algorithm in all of the others as well. Second, each language makes some algorithms and data structures easier to express and others more difficult. Scientific calculations are awkward in Cobol. It is easier to create a linked list in Pascal than in Fortran.

A third point is that, despite their differences, these languages have a great deal in common. Consider, for example, the program we developed in Section 11.7 to determine an employee's salary and retirement plan savings after 25 years. Figures 11.6 and 11.7 show the same program in Basic and Pascal.[7]

By comparing these with the AL program shown in Figure 11.2, we may see something about how the languages operate. Here are a few observations:

Data Typing. Basic and Pascal use very different approaches to data types, with AL representing a kind of compromise between the two.

---

[6] Of course, for practical reasons, the rules for writing programs in these languages are more complicated than the ones we have given for AL. We have used a hypothetical language to focus on the *essence* of an algorithmic language, which the details of syntax, or program grammar, tend to obscure.

[7] Incidentally, Basic and Pascal are used in many slightly differing versions. In some versions these programs would require minor changes.

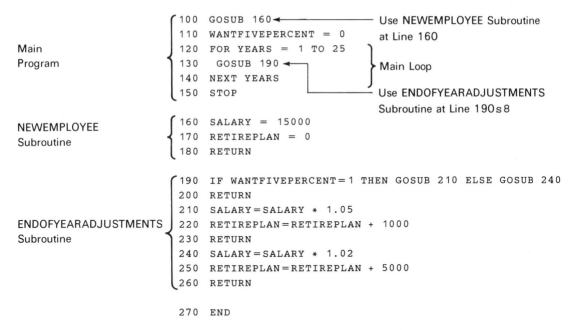

Figure 11.6 The salary and retirement program in Basic.

Basic has only two data types, corresponding closely to AL's real and string variables. The WANTFIVEPERCENT variable in the Basic program holds a number, rather than a logical value. We store 1 in the variable to mean **true** and 0 to mean **false**.

Incidentally, this example begins to show how it is possible for different languages to span exactly the same range of information processing tasks. Although Basic does not have AL's built-in facility for using logical information, logical values can still be represented using stored 1s and 0s. No versatility is lost by omitting the logical data type.

In fact, as we have seen many times, binary digits are all we need to represent *every* kind of information that can be stored in a computer memory. So long as a language allows us to manipulate 1s and 0s in a few simple ways, other data types serve only as a convenience.

In contrast with the limited options of Basic, Pascal provides a wide variety of data types—all those offered in AL and more. Of particular interest is a **pointer** type, which makes it easy in Pascal to create linked lists, queues, and other pointer-based data structures. In fact, since Pascal allows the programmer to define *new* data types on the basis of the given ones, linked lists and queues may themselves be data types.

The VAR instruction is used in Pascal as AL uses VARIABLE.

```
PROGRAM SALARYRETIRE

VAR WANTFIVEPERCENT : BOOLEAN;
SALARY, RETIREPLAN : REAL;
YEARS : INTEGER;
```

NEWEMPLOYEE
Subroutine

```
PROCEDURE NEWEMPLOYEE;
  BEGIN
    SALARY := 15000;
    RETIREPLAN := 0
  END;
```

ENDOFYEARADJUSTMENTS
Subroutine

Begin and End Act
As Brackets

```
PROCEDURE ENDOFYEARADJUSTMENTS;
  BEGIN
    IF WANTFIVEPERCENT
      THEN BEGIN
        SALARY := SALARY * 1.05;
        RETIREPLAN := RETIREPLAN + 1000
        END
      ELSE BEGIN
        SALARY := SALARY * 1.02;
        RETIREPLAN := RETIREPLAN + 5000
          END
  END;
```

The Name of a Subroutine
Means to Use the Subroutine

Main
Program

```
BEGIN
  NEWEMPLOYEE;
  WANTFIVEPERCENT := FALSE;
  FOR YEARS := 1 TO 25 DO ENDOFYEARADJUSTMENTS
END;
```

Figure 11.7 The salary and retirement program in Pascal.

Assigning Values. Basic and Pascal both use what may seem like an odd notation in place of AL's STORE instruction. In Basic, the instruction

```
SALARY = 15000
```

causes the computer to store 15000 in the variable SALARY. In Pascal, the equivalent instruction is

```
SALARY := 15000;
```

In both cases, the computer first looks on the right side of a symbol to see *what* should be stored. Then it looks on the left to see *where* to store it.

The advantage of this notation is that it is extremely concise. For practical programming work, it would be a nuisance to have to use the words *store* and *in* in place of the symbol = or := ("colon equals"). On the other hand, since the equals sign has another meaning entirely in mathematics, the notation often confuses beginning programmers. The common Basic instruction

$$X = X + 1$$

is an inconsistent statement, if interpreted according to the rules of algebra. In a program, however, it just means to increase the number stored in X by 1.[8]

Loops and Brackets. In Basic, loops are indicated by the pair of instructions FOR and NEXT, which serve to bracket the action of the loop. The FOR instruction gives the loop name, which is a variable, as in AL. It also gives both starting and stopping conditions for the variable. In our sample program, YEARS begins at 1 and increases to 25, at which point it causes the loop to stop.

In general, Pascal uses the words BEGIN and END as brackets. In Figure 11.7, however, the loop action is just a single instruction, so no brackets are used.

Subroutines. The best place to see Pascal's use of brackets in our example is in the ENDOFYEARADJUSTMENTS subroutine. Here, the first BEGIN and the last END serve just the same purpose as the square brackets in AL's SUBROU-TINE instruction. As in the AL program, this subroutine consists entirely of a conditional instruction, and within this instruction, two additional BEGIN-END pairs again take the place of AL's brackets.

In Pascal, instructions are separated by semicolons, just as in AL. In Basic, by contrast, each instruction is given on a separate numbered line. These line numbers lead to a quite different way of handling subroutines. Instead of naming subroutines, Basic depends on line numbers to distinguish them. The instruction

GOSUB 160

means "go to the subroutine which begins at line number 160 and execute it." Each subroutine must end with the instruction RETURN, which sends the computer back to continue with the work the subroutine has interrupted.[9]

*   *   *   *   *

[8] Remember, the statement must be interpreted from *right* to *left*. First get the value in X and add 1. Then put the answer back into X.

[9] Notice, incidentally, that the ENDOFYEARADJUSTMENTS subroutine of our Basic program is really a two-level hierarchy of subroutines. The main subroutine begins on line 190. Depending on the option an employee chooses, however, this subroutine cause one of two second-level subroutines to be carried out. These begin at lines 210 and 240.

Despite these points, and many others which might be added, it should be clear that Basic, Pascal, and AL translate algorithms in much the same way. Fortran and Cobol are also closely related to these three languages.

Although the differences between these languages are significant, all are built on a foundation of repetition, conditionals, subroutines, and data manipulation. They are related in much the same way as the Romance languages: Spanish, French, Italian, Portuguese, and Romanian.

Some computer languages, however, are as different from Basic and Pascal as Chinese is from Italian.

One radically different group of languages is founded on the use of recursion, as suggested in Chapter 9. Lisp is the most popular example of this type.

To find the biggest number in a list using Lisp, we would issue an instruction to compare the first item with the biggest item in the *rest* of the list. Of course, we would have to include a note in our instruction to the effect that the biggest item in a one-item list is just that single item.

This way of approaching the problem is not impossible in, say, Pascal, but it would be relatively awkward. Likewise, in Lisp it is more awkward, though not impossible, to find the largest item in a list using the loop approach we developed earlier in this chapter.

In fact, some versions of Lisp do not include any kind of loop instruction.

Another language radically different from Basic, Pascal, and AL is Smalltalk. Rather than writing a single list of instructions, a Smalltalk programmer creates a world of programmed "objects." Each object controls a small part of the computer's memory and is equipped with instructions for what to do when certain messages are received.

For example, one object might be a stack. This kind of object would respond to two kinds of messages. One would instruct it to add an item to the top of the stack. Another would request it to take the top item off the stack and send it back in a return message.

Once objects like these are created, tasks are carried out by sending them messages . . . and having them send each other messages.

*   *   *   *   *

Again, it is important to stress that these other language types are no more or less powerful than Basic, Pascal, or AL. They do not extend the capabilities of the computer; they just make it easier to *express* certain kinds of procedures.

Of course, this is not a minor point. Ever since we introduced Boolean algebra in Chapter 1, we have been pointing out how important expression is in thinking and problem solving.

It does, however, explain part of the reason we introduced AL in this chapter and not Basic, Lisp, Cobol, Smalltalk, or Fortran.

In its simple way, AL captures the essence of all these **high-level** languages. It demonstrates how we may boil the power of the computer down to a handful of expressive instructions—and then build these up to yield clear, precise procedures for processing information.

11.11 TAKING STOCK

Now consider, one last time, the upward path which we have been treading.

A computer fresh from the factory understands only certain obscure machine instructions. We use these to write a translator, which allows us to program using three-letter instruction codes instead of numbers.

This eases our next task—writing an assembler to translate programs written with base-ten numbers, variables, and labels. With this assembly language, in turn, we write a much more ambitious, third translator. Finally, this last translator allows us to write algorithms for the computer in a convenient, high-level language like AL.

At this point, we have in our possession a very different machine from the one shipped from the factory. In three steps it has been bootstrapped to an incredibly high degree of understanding.

And yet, the computer still has nothing of the intelligent thinking power of a human infant. It does not create instructions for itself to carry out. As it stands, it may follow an algorithm, not design one.

Is it possible that bootstrapping may raise the computer to an even higher level? Is it possible for a computer to exhibit intelligence? To program itself?

We intend to take these questions up in earnest in Chapter 13, but two points are in order now.

First, most computers *today* are controlled with high-level languages like Basic and Pascal. This is not to say that most people who use computers are programmers. On the contrary, executives, airline reservationists, writers, teachers, and other computer users simply call on the computer to use programs others have written.

Of course, the instructions they use to control these programs might be considered a kind of higher-level language. But in nearly all cases, these new languages are severely restricted. They are not general ways of expressing work for the computer to do.

Our first point, then, is that most computers have not *yet* been bootstrapped beyond high-level languages.

The second point is that bootstrapping is an extremely important force in a way we have not yet considered: As computers stand, they are already a tremendous aid in producing new, improved computers.

Computers today help design the massive, complex circuits we discussed in the first chapters of this book. They automatically test new designs. In fact, they are routinely used to control the manufacture of new computers.

The more powerful computers become, the more help they are in designing and manufacturing ever more powerful computers. The upshot is that computer improvements tend to lead to further improvements.

This takes us back to a question posed at the beginning of Chapter 10. Will computer bootstrapping "catch on"? That is, will computers eventually be powerful enough to design and build better computers *on their own*? If so, computer power might increase as our own intelligence did, lifted by its own force.

These are points we must consider in depth.

Before we do, however, we have cause for a kind of celebration. We have considered a tremendous range of computer-related topics from transistors to translators. It is as if we have been climbing up a long, steep mountain. Now we have come to the top and we are about to be rewarded with a view.

The view is of the computer as most of us know it, not as a conglomeration of heaps, algorithms, and logic gates, but as a glowing screen and neatly designed keyboard. It awaits us in Chapter 12.

EXERCISES

11.1. A cookbook recipe is both procedural and nonprocedural. Explain.

11.2. Consider the following AL instruction:

        LOOP   TEST   TEST>4 [*action to be repeated*]

  (a) What is the name of the loop?
  (b) In one sentence, explain the stopping condition.
  (c) What will be stored in TEST after the instruction is completed?
  (d) How many times will the action in square brackets be repeated?

11.3. The YEARS loop in Section 11.3 is used to calculate how many years it takes for $100 to grow to $1,000,000 at 7 percent interest.
  (a) How should the instruction be modified to calculate how many years it takes for $100 to grow to $1,000,000 at 8 percent interest?
  (b) How should the instruction be modified to calculate how many years it takes for $100 to grow to $100,000 at 7 percent interest?
  (c) Will the changes suggested in parts (a) and (b) affect the number of times the action in square brackets is repeated?
  (d) What would happen if the stopping condition were changed to read BALANCE = 1000000?

11.4. How many times will the action in square brackets be repeated in the following loop?

        LOOP   QUICK   QUICK = 0   [STORE QUICK + 1 IN BALANCE]

11.5. What answer will the computer get in performing the following calculations?
  (a) 4 * 3
  (b) 4 / 3
  (c) 5 - 3 - 2
  (d) 8 / 2 / 2
  (e) 8 + 2 * 4

11.6. Add parentheses to the following expression so that the computer will get 10 as its answer: $16 - 8 - 4 - 2$.

11.7. Suppose 5 is stored in YEARS. What answer will the computer get in each of the following calculations?

(a) YEARS * 3

(b) YEARS / YEARS + 1

(c) YEARS − YEARS − YEARS

In each case, what will be stored in YEARS after the calculation is completed?

11.8. Change the YEARS loop of Section 11.4 so that it stops when

  (a) The balance is between 50 and 60 dollars.

  (b) Either the balance is less than 30 dollars or 50 years have passed, whichever comes first.

  (c) The balance is less than or equal to 40 dollars. Note that AL does not use the symbol < =. Instead, find a way to combine <, =, and OR.

11.9. Suppose WORDA contains "ant" and WORDB contains "eater." What will the computer get as a result of the following calculations?

  (a) WORDA FIRST 2

  (b) (WORDA LAST 1) JOIN (WORDA FIRST 2)

  (c) WORDB FIRST (WORDA LENGTH)

11.10. Say in one sentence when the MIRROR loop in Section 11.4 will stop if the NOT is removed from its stopping condition.

11.11. Consider the following AL instructions:

```
STORE 100 IN X;
STORE X/10 IN Y
```

After the instructions are executed, what will be stored in X? What will be stored in Y?

Suppose a third instruction is added as follows:

```
STORE Y/10 IN X
```

After all three instructions are executed, what will be stored in X and Y?

11.12. Change the program given at the end of Section 11.5 so that it calculates

  (a) How much money $100 would grow to in 50 years at 7 percent interest.

  (b) How many years it would take for 1 dollar to grow to $1,000,000 at 10 percent interest.

  (c) How many years it would take $100 to grow to $1,000,000 at 7 percent interest if 5 dollars is withdrawn each year.

11.13. Write a conditional statement to

  (a) Cut the price of an item 25 percent if its original price is more than 10 dollars.

  (b) Compare the words stored in WORDA and WORDB and store the longer one in WORDL. (*Hint*: If the one in WORDA is longer, *then* store it in WORDL; *otherwise* store the other word in WORDL.)

11.14. Write a conditional instruction that adds 5 percent to a bank balance below $500, 6 percent to a balance between $500 and $1,000, and 7 percent to a balance over $1,000. (*Hint*: As usual, the conditional includes two pairs of square brackets with instructions inside. The trick here is to put a second conditional inside one of these pairs.)

11.15. Show how to modify the program in Figure 11.2 if
  (a) Employees get a starting salary of $20,000.
  (b) We want to see what happens if an employee does decide to take the 5-percent option.
  (c) Employees who choose the 5-percent salary raise get no contribution to the retirement plan.

11.16. At Joe's Grocery Store, Joe buys food items for a certain cost. He adds a 20 percent markup to get the selling price. Finally, he adds 6 percent tax to the selling price to get the final price.

Using the variables COST, MARKUP, SELLINGPRICE, TAX, and FINALPRICE, write AL subroutines to:
  (a) Calculate the selling price, assuming a number has already been stored in COST.
  (b) Calculate the final price, assuming the selling price has already been stored in SELLINGPRICE.

Finally, use these subroutines in a complete program to calculate the final price of an item that costs Joe 5 dollars. The main part of your program should have just three lines.

11.17. What program might the following loop be part of? What does the loop do?

```
LOOP  ITEM  ITEM=67  [STORE COST.ITEM * .75 IN COST.ITEM]
```

11.18. What program might the following loop be part of? What does the loop do?

```
LOOP  ITEM  ITEM=67  [STORE COST.ITEM + TOTAL IN TOTAL]
```

11.19. Write a loop using numbered variables to convert a list of words to a list of initial letters. For example, the list DOG, CAT, MOUSE would be converted to D, C, M.

11.20. The sorting program of Section 11.9 uses three subroutines. In a single sentence, explain the function of each subroutine.

11.21. Briefly explain the function of the following variables in the sorting program of Section 11.9: SLOT, LARGESTSLOT, SORTEDITEMS, LARGEST.

11.22. Will the sorting program of Section 11.9 work correctly if
  (a) The original list contains some repeated numbers?
  (b) ITEM is made a real variable instead of an integer one?
  (c) The subroutine called SETUP begins by storing 999 in SLOT?

11.23. Suppose line 120 of the Basic program in Figure 11.6 were changed to read as follows:

```
120 FOR YEARS = 1 TO 10
```

Say in one sentence what the modified program would calculate.

11.24. Suppose line 110 of the Basic program in Figure 11.6 were changed to read as follows:

```
110 WANTFIVEPERCENT = 1
```

Say in one sentence what the modified program would calculate.

11.25. What effect would it have if the main part of the Pascal program shown in Figure 11.7 were changed to read

(a) ```
BEGIN
    WANTFIVEPERCENT: = FALSE;
    NEWEMPLOYEE;
    FOR YEARS: = 1 to 25 DO ENDOFYEARADJUSTMENTS
END
```

(b) ```
BEGIN
    NEWEMPLOYEE;
    NEWEMPLOYEE;
    WANTFIVEPERCENT: = FALSE;
    FOR YEARS: = 1 to 25 DO ENDOFYEARADJUSTMENTS
END
```

(c) ```
BEGIN
    NEWEMPLOYEE;
    WANTFIVEPERCENT: = FALSE;
    FOR YEARS: = 1 to 25 DO ENDOFYEARADJUSTMENTS;
    FOR YEARS: = 1 to 25 DO ENDOFYEARADJUSTMENTS
END
```
```

12 Practicalities

12.1 REAL COMPUTERS

Through 11 chapters, we have been focusing on the *idea* of a computer. Now we will take a look at the reality.

A real computer, at the heart of it, is very much like the machine we have been discussing. Most people, however, never get to see more than the surface, and this surface makes it seem extremely different from our model computer.

We may sum up the difference this way: A real computer includes features that make it more comfortable and practical to use. To recall an analogy from Chapter 5, it is as if we have been studying a stripped-down model of a car to see how it operates. Now we are going to put in the seats and air conditioning.

12.2 EXTERNAL MEMORY

The first point on our list of practicalities is a matter of economics. From a technical point of view, it is possible and even desirable to build a computer with only a transistor memory. Such computers exist, but they are extremely expensive.

Instead, most computers use two kinds of memory. These are usually called **internal memory** and **external memory**, for the simple reason that the first is packaged inside the same box as the main computer and the second is packaged outside, in a separate box.

The internal memory is just the kind we studied in Chapter 2. It is made with transistors or other exclusively electronic parts and is used for most of the actual work of the computer, just as we have explained.

This kind of memory has the advantage of being fast. We may store or read a number in somewhere between a millionth and a billionth of a second.[1]

This speed is extremely important, because it limits the general operating speed of the computer. Remember that every instruction to be carried out is stored as a number in the memory. This means the computer must read at least one number from memory for each instruction: the instruction number itself.

A controller circuit designed to carry out a billion instructions per second is of no use if it is connected to a memory unit which allows only one number to be read per second. The result would be a computer running at *less* than one instruction per second, since many instructions require more than one number to be read from memory.[2]

A computer operating at high speed is like a stockbroker operating at high speed. The stockbroker must have telephone numbers, prices, prospectuses—all kinds of working information—laid out on a desk for immediate use.

On the other hand, a desk is an expensive kind of storage unit. If *all* the stockbroker's records and books were spread out on desktops, they might fill an office the size of a football field.

Instead, of course, the majority of these records are likely to be stored in a filing cabinet. The information there is not as easily accessible, but it is also used much less frequently.

In just the same way, a computer uses its external memory as a huge filing cabinet for storing information which is not immediately needed. Like a filing cabinet, external memory is relatively economical and slow.

The two premier examples of external memory are **disks** and **tapes**. Both of these use magnetic materials rather than transistors to store information.

Computer tape is exactly the same kind of tape as is used in cassettes for recording music. In fact, ordinary cassette tapes have been used by some small computers as external storage. This **magnetic tape** is just what the name would suggest: plastic tape with iron compounds mixed in so that it may be magnetized. A key point is that each small segment of the tape may be magnetized separately.

When music is recorded, a magnetic tape ends up with each section along its length magnetized to a different intensity. These varying intensities record the varying air pressures that we perceive as music.

For storing computer data, however, the principle is much simpler. Magnets have two ends, or poles, which we usually call north and south. These correspond neatly to the 1s and 0s of computer memory.

---

[1] Of course, all figures of this sort change rapidly as technology progresses. The access times may be substantially different now from what they were when this book was written.

[2] The LOAD-TOP-FROM-POSITION instruction, for example, required three numbers to be read from memory: the instruction number, the *position* of the number to be loaded into TOP, and the number itself.

To store data on tape, then, we simply divide the tape up into equal lengths and magnetize each segment to represent one bit. We might let a piece of tape with the north pole up represent a 1 and a piece with the south pole up represent a 0.

Figure 12.1 illustrates this with an example.

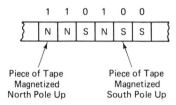

Piece of Tape
Magnetized
North Pole Up

Piece of Tape
Magnetized
South Pole Up

Figure 12.1 Section of magnetic tape storing a representation of the binary number 110100.

Magnets make convenient computer storage for three reasons. First, as we have said, they have two states: north pole up and south pole up. These correspond neatly to the 1s and 0s of computer data.

Second, magnetization may be changed. Magnets create a magnetic field, just as the earth creates a gravitational field. Gravity pulls objects down toward the earth. Magnetic fields pull iron objects toward a magnet.

The essential point, though, is this: If we put a magnet in a strong field from another magnet, the first magnet may be remagnetized in a different direction.

Figure 12.2 shows a north-pole-up magnet being remagnetized into a south-pole-up magnet. It is important to understand that the small magnet has not been turned upside-down in this picture. The field from the large magnet has changed how the particles *inside* the small magnet are lined up, and this, in turn, affects the direction of its magnetization.

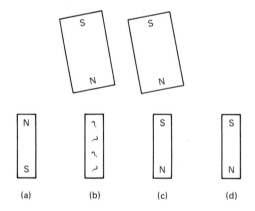

(a)   (b)   (c)   (d)

Figure 12.2 Changing the direction of magnetization in a magnet.

The upshot is that the pieces of a strip of magnetic tape may be magnetized into a pattern of north-pole-up's and south-pole-up's to store certain information and then, later, may be changed to a different pattern to store new information.

The third convenient fact about magnetism is that it is closely related to electricity. Strangely enough, electricity running through a wire creates a magnetic field, and likewise, a magnet passing through a circle of wire causes electricity to flow.

The reason is something for physicists to explain, but the fact is of great practical importance. A strip of magnetized magnetic tape running by a loop of wire produces electrical pulses. This means the north-pole-ups and south-pole-ups may be converted into voltages for a computer to use.

Likewise, the computer may be hooked up to an electronic device which creates magnetic fields on demand. This means the computer may magnetize pieces of magnetic tape to store information.

Together, these three points make magnetic tape a convenient, inexpensive place for computers to store and read information.

Tapes have an unfortunate disadvantage for computers, however, just as they do for the music lover. If you want to hear the last song on a tape, you must wait while the tape winds forward. If you want to hear the first song next, you must wait while it rewinds.

A tape is called a **sequential** storage medium, because the stored information is laid out in a long, continuous sequence. The only way to get from one part of the sequence to another is to pass through all the parts in between.

The obvious solution to this problem is to use a record player. It allows us to play any song immediately. This kind of medium offers what is called **random access**.

The computer equivalent of a record player is a **disk drive**. The **disk** it spins is made of the same kind of magnetic material that goes into magnetic tape. Instead of a needle, it has a recording and sensing head like a tape recorder's. This means it may *store* information by magnetizing parts of the disk, as well as *read* information by checking the magnetization in various parts.

The information on a phonograph record is stored in a long spiral groove that the needle follows. On a computer disk, it is organized into circular **tracks**, each of which is divided into arcs or **sectors**. Figure 12.3 illustrates this organization. The disk drive spins the disk at high speed and accepts instructions from the computer to move its head back and forth over the tracks. Once the head is positioned over a track, the computer must wait until the desired sector spins into position underneath it.

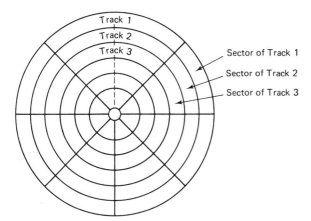

Figure 12.3 Tracks and sectors in a computer disk.

To read what is in that sector, the computer uses the electrical pulses that the magnets there cause as they whirl by the disk drive's head. To write new information into the sector, the computer causes the head to produce magnetic fields. These create a pattern of tiny magnetized regions in the sector.

Incidentally, this explanation points up two key differences between transistor memory and the disk and tape memories we have been considering.

First, as we pointed out in Chapter 1, transistor circuits are **solid-state** devices. That is, they have no moving parts; there is nothing to wear out. By contrast, disk drives and tape units contain motors which physically move the magnetic material.

Second, an advantage of magnetic memories is that stored information stays stored when we turn the power off. The music on a cassette tape, for example, does not disappear when we unplug the tape recorder. Memory with this property is termed **nonvolatile**.

By contrast, the kind of transistor memories we described in Chapter 2 *are* volatile—they depend on a power supply. If we cut it off, all the flip-flops put out no voltage and the stored information is lost.[3]

A last point to consider in comparing transistor and magnetic memories is that both are based on two-state devices. They store information the same way, coded as 1s and 0s or T's and F's. For this reason, their capacity is measured in the same units.

It would be reasonable to measure a memory unit's capacity by the number of two-state devices that go into making it—that is, the number of bits, or binary digits, which the unit can store. A more common unit, however, is the **byte**. A byte is normally 8 bits, enough to store one letter or other character.[4] A chapter of this book uses about 60,000 characters, so it would fill roughly 60,000 bytes of computer memory.

Most computer memories are large enough these days that it is easier to measure memory capacity in thousands or even millions of bytes. The corresponding units are **kilobytes** and **megabytes**, often abbreviated to just K and M.

Thus, this entire book would fill about 900K of memory.

*   *   *   *   *

To summarize, nearly all real computers use a small solid-state electronic memory for working with information that must be read and changed quickly and, for extra storage, a larger, slower, cheaper memory relying on magnetic materials.

The reason is simply that solid-state memory costs too much to use it for all purposes. Also, practically speaking, a computer user ordinarily works with only a

---

[3] It is possible to build nonvolatile solid-state memories, but these are more costly.

[4] As we have explained several times, letters are represented in the computer as numbers or, equivalently, as voltage patterns. When we say that 8 bits are enough to store one letter, we really mean that the most *commonly* used codes for representing letters use that amount of memory space.

small fraction of the information stored in a computer. Imagine, for example, a woman writing a novel: She may have stored 10 chapters, but she is unlikely to edit more than one chapter at a time.

12.3 INPUT AND OUTPUT

The division of memory into internal and external parts is one way real computers differ from our model. A second feature of practical, working computers is that they provide easy ways to get information into and out of the memory.

Since Chapter 5, we have been discussing projects which would require us to store long lists of numbers in the cells of our computer's memory system. It is possible, as we said from the beginning, to do all this storing just by hooking up voltage supplies to the memory system's input wires.

Actually, it would not be necessary for us to repeatedly hook up voltage supplies and detach them. Instead, we could use voltage supplies with on-off switches. If one such voltage supply is permanently attached to each memory system input, we can get the correct voltage on each wire just by flipping switches.

This scheme is not only theoretically possible. It was used in some of the earlier small computers. In our computer, however, the memory system has 16 data inputs, another 16 inputs for a name, and two control inputs. Imagine having to flip more than 30 switches for every letter we want to store in the memory. For many purposes, this method would be impractically slow.

Instead, as we have already mentioned, most computers are equipped with **input devices** that make it convenient to get information into the memory. By far the most common of these is a typewriterlike **keyboard**.

The details of how a keyboard works with a computer vary substantially from machine to machine. But we can use our model computer to demonstrate at least one of the possibilities. We begin by noting that the keys on a keyboard are simply push-button switches, like the button of a doorbell. When a key is pressed, power goes on in a circuit. We can use the keys, then, to control the voltages supplied as inputs to a logic circuit.

When we press the A key, voltage will be supplied at one input. When we press the B key, voltage will be supplied at another input, and so on.

The logic circuit, then, takes input from all of the various keys. It uses these to determine voltages on output wires running directly to a chunk of flip-flops within the memory system. We might use, say, the flip-flops that make up memory position 15000. All this is pictured in Figure 12.4.

Now, here is what happens if we press the A key. First, voltage is supplied to an input of the logic circuit. Second, on the basis of this input, the logic circuit puts out voltages to the inputs of the flip-flops in memory position 15000. Third, these voltages cause an A to be stored in the memory position.

The obvious problem with this scheme is that, as things stand, the keyboard may be used for storing letters in only one particular memory position: Position 15000. This is not as great a limitation as it might appear, however.

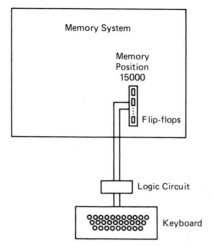

Figure 12.4 Using a keyboard as an input device.

For example, suppose we write a simple machine-language program based on the following outline:

1. Start a pointer at 501 and store 999 in Position 15000.
2. If the number in Position 15000 is 999, go back to step 2.
3. Take the number from Position 15000 and store it in the memory position indicated by the pointer.
4. Increase the pointer by 1 and store 999 in Position 15000.
5. Go back to step 2.

The heart of this program is step 2, which forms a loop all in itself. If the number stored in Position 15000 happens to be 999, step 2 will simply repeat without stopping.

Since step 1 stores 999 in Position 15000, this is exactly what happens. The computer checks the number in Position 15000 over and over. Each time, it discovers that the number stored there is 999, and this causes it to continue with step 2, checking the number yet again.

At some point, however, while the program is running, someone may happen to push the A key on the keyboard. This immediately stores the number corresponding to A—say, 1—in Position 15000.

Now, the computer hops into action. The number in Position 15000 is not 999, and so the computer goes on to step 3. It takes the number 1 in Position 15000 and stores it in Position 501, since this is the position stored in the pointer.

Next, it stores 999 in Position 15000, increases the pointer to 502, and goes back to step 2.

At this point, the computer is stuck in a loop again. So long as no one touches the keyboard, it will repeat step 2 indefinitely. But if the D key is pressed, the computer will go on to step 3 and store the number representing D in Position 502.

Each time a key is pressed, it has the effect of storing a letter in the next memory position. The 999 is used as a kind of signal to the computer that no new key has yet been pressed on the keyboard.

Of course, this program is a simplified example. But it does show how we can use a keyboard. The keys struck in our example might well be the first steps toward storing the assembly-language instruction ADD in the memory, beginning at memory position 501. Note that this is possible even though the keyboard affects only Position 15000 directly.

Apparently, however, using a keyboard in this way depends on having a machine-language program already stored in the memory. This leaves us with a kind of chicken-and-egg paradox: The keyboard cannot function until the program is already in place, but we depend on the keyboard to put in the program. We will show, in Section 12.4, how this paradox is resolved.

For now, it is more important to note that a keyboard is not the only input device we might think to hook up to the memory system. Any device that puts out voltages may be used to get information into a computer in roughly the same manner.

If we are studying weather patterns, we might use an electronic thermometer that gives the temperature in binary as a pattern of voltages on wires. If we combine this thermometer with an electronic clock and a logic circuit, we can design an input device that stores the current temperature in memory position 15000 once an hour.

If we leave this input device connected and use the machine-language program we just described, the computer's memory will automatically be filled with a list of hourly temperatures.

Likewise, we might get input from machinery in a factory, so that the computer's memory is automatically filled with production figures. Or we might use the device found in automatic bank teller machines that reads a number stored on a piece of magnetic tape on the back of a plastic identification card. Or we might use the device found in grocery stores, that reads patterns of black bars printed on packaged goods and turns them into voltages for computer input.

All of these give us a way to get useful numbers into the computer memory, without the inconvenience of working the memory system's controls manually.

*   *   *   *   *

The input system we have described uses memory position 15000 as an **interface**, or connection, with the world outside the computer. Through this narrow window the computer may learn what key is being pressed on a keyboard, what the temperature is, who is using a bank machine—virtually anything.

Naturally, we expect that this information will be processed in some way by a program. Temperatures might be averaged. A customer's bank balance will be adjusted. An AL program entered with a keyboard will be converted to machine language by a translator and then executed.

Eventually, in all these cases, the computer will have computed something which we, in the outside world, would like to know. Here is another serious inconvenience of our model computer: The only way to get information out of it is to check voltages on the memory system's output wires.

Naturally, if we are typing information into the computer in the form of letters and numbers, we would like to get answers back in the same convenient form. For this, we need an **output device**.

Perhaps the simplest solution is to use an electric typewriter. First, however, we need another interface. We might use the chunk of flip-flops in memory position 15001. Then, as shown in Figure 12.5, we could connect the output wires of these flip-flops, through a logic circuit, to the typewriter.

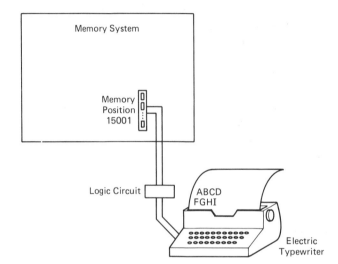

Figure 12.5 Using a typewriter as an output device.

In the figure, when a computer program stores an A in Position 15001, the pattern of voltages corresponding to an A goes out from the flip-flops to the logic circuit. Given this input, the logic circuit puts out voltage over the A wire. This has the same effect as hitting the A key on the typewriter—power is supplied to make the A bar strike.

For the computer to type out an answer, then, all it needs to do is store the letters of the answer, one at a time, in Position 15001.

*   *   *   *   *

This plan is very nearly a good one, but it is faulty in one important respect. If the computer stores an A in Position 15001, the logic circuit will send out voltage on the A wire until something else is stored. This means that the typewriter will produce an endless *series* of A's, instead of just one.

What we need is a signal, like the 999 signal used for input.

One solution is to rig the typewriter up so that as soon as a letter is typed, voltage goes out briefly over a wire leading back to the computer. This voltage would be used to store 999 in Position 15001. In this way, each letter would cancel itself from the memory just after being typed. Of course, we also need to make sure the logic circuit between the memory and typewriter does not send out any voltage when it gets an input of 999.

In addition to keeping the typewriter from repeating letters, this use of the 999 signal is vital in another way. Since a 999 in Position 15001 means that the typewriter has typed one letter and is ready for another, it acts as a signal to the computer to store the next letter.

Without such a signal, the computer might store new letters in Position 15001 at the rate of thousands or millions per second. The poor typewriter would never be able to keep up.

*   *   *   *   *

Typing machines meant to be used with a computer are called **printers**. They come in many types, from inexpensive **dot-matrix printers**, which create letters with patterns of dots, to **laser printers**, which draw with lasers on a light-sensitive printing drum.

The key point, however, is that all of these are controlled with voltage patterns leading into a logic circuit. And just as the computer may receive input in the form of voltage patterns from many different devices, it may also put out voltage patterns to control many kinds of devices.

The most common of these output devices is a **visual display unit**, or **VDU**, which shows letters and sometimes pictures on a television-style screen.[5]

At the back of such a screen is a kind of gun, which shoots electrons. The screen itself is coated with a special material that glows briefly if an electron strikes it. The gun sweeps across the screen, aiming at all the parts in turn, and fires from time to time.

The result is a pattern of glowing dots on the screen. By controlling when the gun fires, it is possible to make these dots form letters.

The letters will disappear in a fraction of a second, however, if the gun does not repeat the same pattern of firings over and over. Thus, the VDU contains a block of memory to store information about which places on the screen should be kept glowing. It uses this information to control when the gun fires.

Inside, then, a VDU is quite complex. Fortunately, from the outside, it may be controlled with simple voltage patterns.

If the computer puts out a pattern of voltages representing an A, the VDU uses these to do all the rest. It stores a new series of dot positions in its memory and then, each time its gun sweeps over these positions, it fires. The result is a glowing A on the screen.

Output voltages from a computer may also be used to control a **plotter**, a kind of drawing machine. In this case, the voltages usually do not represent letters, but

---

[5] This kind of screen is technically a *cathode-ray tube*, which has inspired some people to use the name CRT in place of VDU.

rather commands, for example, for the plotter to lift the pen from the paper, put the pen down on the paper to get ready to draw, move the pen a little to the right, and so on.

As a last example, we might use the computer's output voltages to control machinery in a factory. In fact, it is easy to create a feedback loop. With such a loop, the machine sends information about itself to the computer. The computer processes the information and, according to programmed rules, sends back voltages which affect the operation of the machine.

If the computer sees that the temperature of the machine is too high, it slows it down. If it receives information that a vital part is cracked, it shuts the machine off.

*   *   *   *   *

One last, extremely significant point is this: We have created interfaces in our computer with the idea of allowing *people* to put information in and get it out conveniently. But the interfaces may just as well allow computers to communicate with other computers.

Consider two computers connected as shown in Figure 12.6. When the computer on the left stores a voltage pattern in memory position 15000, the computer on the right receives this same pattern in its memory position 15001. Likewise, the computer on the right may send a pattern to the one on the left.

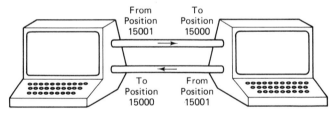

Figure 12.6 Computers communicating.

Moreover, it is not necessary for the two computers to be connected directly, as shown in the figure. A much more common practice is to use ordinary telephone lines for communication.

In this case, one computer puts out a voltage pattern, through its output interface. The pattern is fed into a device called a **modem**,[6] which converts the pattern to a series of tones. It might use a high tone for voltage on and a low one for voltage off. These tones go out over a telephone line, just as they would if a person was singing into the handset.

At the other end of the line, possibly even in a different city or country, a second modem hears these tones and converts them back to a pattern of voltages. These voltages then serve as input to a second computer, through its input interface.

[6] *Modem* is an abbreviation of the term *modulator-demodulator*.

This second computer, of course, may send information back to the first one in exactly the same manner.

Computer communication of this sort makes it possible to distribute computing power over a wide physical area. It is one important reason why so many businesses now use many smaller, **personal computers** in place of a single, larger **mainframe** computer.

12.4 THE OPERATING SYSTEM

A computer with input and output devices connected and with memory divided between internal and external parts is much more complex than our simple model.

As we have seen, we will need a program to check the input interface continuously to see whether a new key has been typed and, if so, to store the corresponding pattern. But the simple program we outlined in the last section only begins to do the job. For example, as the program is written, it just goes on storing one letter at a time forever. If we are typing in a program written in AL, eventually we will want it to be translated and executed.

Somehow, the letter-storing program must be extended so that it understands some string of typed letters as a **command** to run the AL program which has been entered.

A second point is that the program will very likely produce answers which ought to appear on our VDU screen. The computer must have a program to control this output, so that it does not send voltage patterns to the VDU faster than it can store and display them.

A third point to consider is that we will probably want to save the AL program by storing it on a disk, after we have finished typing it in. This, too, requires a great deal of work on the computer's part.

For one thing, we will indicate that the program is to be stored on the disk by typing another command on our keyboard. The letter-storing program must again be extended to recognize this command.

To make use of the disk drive, the computer needs to keep a directory showing what is stored in each track and sector. Before it can store the program we have written, it must check the directory to find unused disk space.

If there is not enough free space left to store our program, the computer must notify us, by sending a message to the VDU. If free space *is* available, the computer must issue a complex series of commands to the disk drive to get the recording head positioned over the correct track and then to make it store the letters and numbers that make up the program.

Finally, it must add an entry to the disk directory with the name of this new program and its location on the disk.

All this brings up a fourth consideration. The disk directory itself is something we may need to work with. We ought to be able to issue a command from the keyboard for the computer to give us the names of all the programs stored on the disk, as shown in the directory. Naturally, this would be displayed on our VDU.

Another command should be available to erase programs, by removing them from the directory.

Other commands would be convenient, if not essential. We would like to be able to rename stored programs, to copy them, to inquire about the amount of free space left on the disk, and so on.

*   *   *   *   *

By now, two points should be clear.

First, we need a collection of programs for dealing with the ordinary house-keeping chores of computing: getting information in, getting it out, and moving it between internal and external memory.

Second, we need a kind of command language for telling the computer what chores to do, along with an interpreter for identifying those commands.

Together, the programs and command interpreter form what is usually called an **operating system**. The operating system performs much the same function as the controller circuit does at a lower level: It regulates the flow of information within the computer.

Note that the operating system is itself a machine-language program. Before it is stored in the computer's memory and set running, no commands can be issued from the keyboard and nothing will appear on the VDU screen.

Again, we are faced with a seeming paradox. How is it possible to get the operating system into the memory if it cannot be typed in through the keyboard? The answer, as the next section will show, depends on bootstrapping.

12.5 A COMPUTER SESSION

Throughout this book, we have been explaining parts and aspects of the computer. Now we are poised to put the last parts together. It is time to look at a real computer in action.

We will consider the case of the novelist. She has written a ten-chapter book using a computer and now she wants to edit the first chapter.

Her machine is a small one, a personal computer. It is equipped with a keyboard and a television-style screen and it has a disk drive built into the main unit where the actual computer—the internal memory and controller circuits—are stored.[7]

She also has an inexpensive dot-matrix printer.

In the morning, when she sits down to work, the computer is off. If we could look through the packaging into the controller circuits, we would notice, first, that the controller is much more sophisticated than the one we designed in Chapter 4. It understands a machine language consisting of more than 100 instructions.

---

[7] Notice that, although the disk drive is packaged together with the main computer in this case, it is still considered external memory. If we look *inside* the box containing the drive and the internal memory, we will still find that they are very separate.

On the other hand, what is more important is that the machine has not yet been bootstrapped to understand any higher-level language, not even assembly language.

To bootstrap the machine, the novelist puts a disk in the disk drive and turns the machine on. In less than a minute, the computer is fully bootstrapped. A message appears on her screen indicating that the computer is ready for the day's work. At this point, the computer's internal memory contains not only an operating system program, which has sent her this message, but a translator for the high-level language Pascal.

How did all this get there?

The answer, first of all, is that the computer is built with a small amount of nonvolatile memory. This memory is the kind that stores information even when the power is off. The computer is wired so that it automatically begins executing the machine instructions stored in this part of the memory as soon as the power switch is flipped on.

The nonvolatile memory contains a simple start-up program. All this program does is bring information from the disk into the internal memory. In fact, it does not even look through a directory to find the information. Instead, it assumes that what it wants is stored in a certain fixed place on the disk.

Assuming the novelist has used the correct disk, this copied information will be the operating system and Pascal **compiler** or translator.

The start-up program, then, loads the operating system into the internal memory. This operating system, as we have said, is just a machine-language program. The last instruction of the start-up program causes a jump to the first instruction of the operating system. That is, it sets the operating system running.

The operating system, as we have already seen, then issues a general "all is well" message and awaits the novelist's commands. Keep in mind that she has set off this flurry of activity with just two easy actions: popping a disk into the disk drive and flipping the power switch.

Incidentally, the process is an example of bootstrapping because the computer uses a simple program, the start-up loader, to read in a more sophisticated program, the operating system. Its own power and resources allow it to acquire more of the same.

*   *   *   *   *

Once the computer has been "booted," it will accept and carry out any commands included in the operating system's command language. Our novelist begins by removing the "system" disk she has used to get the computer going and inserting another that she believes contains the first chapter of her novel.

To check, she types DIRECTORY.

The operating system program has been running quietly all this time, waiting for something to be typed. When the novelist types her command, the operating system stores the letters—D, I, R, and so on—in an unused part of the internal memory. When she hits the RETURN key on her keyboard, it knows she has finished a command and it goes to work interpreting and carrying it out.

The directory the novelist has requested to see is stored on the disk itself, in a fixed position. The operating system program copies the directory information into internal memory and then puts it out, one character at a time, to the VDU.

Here is what the novelist sees on her screen:

```
           * DIRECTORY *

           DAVID.LETTER
           HEARTBREAK.ONE
           HEARTBREAK.TWO
           TAX.INFO
```

Apparently, this disk contains four **files**: two chapters from her book *Heartbreak*, a letter to her friend David, and some information about her taxes.

Now that she knows for sure that this disk contains the file she wants, she takes it out and replaces it with one labeled WORDHANDLER. This is a commercially-designed **word processing** program.[8]

With this disk in the disk drive, she types

```
           RUN WORDHANDLER
```

Notice that, although she is about to use the word processing program, what she has just typed is a command for the operating system. To carry out the command, the operating system:

1. Checks the directory on this new disk to see where the file called WORDHANDLER is stored.
2. Copies this file, which happens to be a list of machine instructions, into an unused part of the internal memory.
3. Jumps to the beginning of these instructions.

This last step sets the new program running. At this point, the operating system program is still stored in the internal memory, but it no longer controls the computer. The word processing program has taken over.

A word processing program is one designed to ease the task of writing and editing. Although each such program has different capabilities, all start from a common base. They allow us to type text from a keyboard, make insertions in the middle of a passage, erase parts, move parts, and search through the text for a pattern of letters, replacing it if necessary.

A word processing program, then, must begin with text to process. WORD-HANDLER attempts to get this by sending the following message to the screen:

```
      Insert disk and type name of file:
```

Our novelist puts the disk containing her first chapter back into the disk drive and types CHAPTER.ONE.

WORDHANDLER then checks the disk directory to make sure the file is

---

[8] The name is fictitious, although the program is like many real ones.

there. If not, it would create a new file for a new piece of text. But since CHAPTER.ONE *is* on the disk, WORDHANDLER loads it into an empty part of the internal memory.

Once the text is in the internal memory, the program goes on to display the first 20 lines of it on the novelist's screen. At this point it stops to await her editing commands.

The screen the novelist sees is filled with the first words of her chapter, and the letter in the upper left-hand corner of her screen is flashing. This flashing spot is called a **cursor**. It indicates what part of the text is about to be edited.

As it happens, there is nothing the matter with the first word, which contains the flashing letter. Farther along, however, in the third line, a word is misspelled. To correct this mistake, the novelist must first move the cursor to the misspelled word. To do so, she hits the ↓ key on her keyboard twice. Each time she hits that key, the cursor moves down one line.

Of course, although it appears that the key is affecting the screen directly, the connection is actually much more roundabout.

When the novelist presses the ↓ key, a voltage pattern is sent to the computer and stored. The WORDHANDLER program, which has been waiting for something to be typed, interprets this as a command. It changes stored numbers indicating the position of the cursor and also sends voltage patterns to the VDU to change the appearance of the screen accordingly.

The novelist continues by pressing the → key repeatedly to move the cursor rightward to the misspelled word. Then, she types the word correctly. As she types each letter, it appears on the screen. The misspelled word and all the words after it simply move over and down to make room.

Again, of course, the word processing program is the mediator. It makes changes in the copy of her chapter stored in the internal memory and then changes the display.

Afterward, to erase the misspelled word, she holds down a key marked CONTROL on her keyboard and repeatedly presses the E key. Each time she presses E, the letter under the cursor disappears and the letters and words on the right move over to fill the space.

The CONTROL key is used here to change the code sent from the keyboard to the computer. If an ordinary E code were sent, WORDHANDLER would insert a letter E in the text. Pressing CONTROL and E together sends a different code, which WORDHANDLER interprets as a command to erase.

The novelist continues editing in this way. By pressing the control key with various other keys, she can send WORDHANDLER commands to display the next 20 lines of her chapter, to change the heroine's name from Jane to Monique everywhere it appears in the text, to reorder paragraphs, and so on.

At last, when she is satisfied with the chapter, she will send a command that asks WORDHANDLER to store the modified chapter on the disk. This is a vital step, because, so far, all of her changes have affected only the version of her chapter which WORDHANDLER has copied into the internal memory. The original disk version has remained unchanged.

Incidentally, this fits in perfectly with our description of the difference between internal and external memory. While the novelist is working on the chapter, it is stored in the internal memory, where it may quickly be read or modified. For long-term storage, it goes back onto the disk.

Once WORDHANDLER has stored the edited version of CHAPTER.ONE in place of the original version, our novelist issues one last command to the program by pressing CONTROL and X. This means "exit."

But WORDHANDLER does not simply stop when it receives this command. Instead, it jumps back to an instruction of the operating system program so as to start that program running. The upshot is that, as WORDHANDLER finishes, the operating sytem takes over.

This is a crucial point, because, without some program running, the computer has no way to understand commands issued from the keyboard. In fact, it will do nothing at all with the codes it receives.

From the moment the novelist turns on the power, some program is controlling the computer. First it is the start-up program, which reads in the operating system program. The start-up program passes control to the operating system, which in turn passes control to WORDHANDLER. When WORDHANDLER is told to stop, it passes control back to the operating system.

At this point, the novelist may run other programs, check disk directories, and so on. When she is finished for the day, she simply switches the machine off.

With the power off, all the information in the volatile, internal memory—including the operating system program—is lost. Once again, the computer understands only machine language.

But everything necessary for the next day's work is safely stored in permanent, external memory. The operating system is on the system disk ready to be loaded again, and the new version of Chapter 1, also in magnetic form, is ready to be mailed to the publisher.

12.6 TAKING STOCK

In this chapter, we have focused on the workaday computer. We have completed a grand tour of the computer and we have fulfilled the promise made in our first pages: we have explained how it works.

In fact, we have done a good deal more than explain computer circuits. As we have seen, a major part of the computer's power comes not from **hardware**, the actual wires and transistors used to build it, but from **software**, the layers of programs and interpreters we add to the physical machine. These, also, we have looked into.

Finally, now, we have seen how hardware and software combine to produce the information processing workhorse which is the crowning achievement and hallmark of the information age. Although we have left out many details and simplified our story in places, the sketch we have given of the computer is reasonably accurate and complete, at least as computers now stand.

The main question we have left open is this: What will computers become?

This is not a question to be answered in definite terms, except by oracles. But it is one we have promised to address, at least in part. In our last chapter, we will tackle one aspect of the question—the possibility that computers may someday be intelligent.

EXERCISES

12.1. Is a book a sequential or a random-access storage medium? What about a scroll? Explain your answer.

12.2. Imagine a tape like the one in Figure 12.1 with millions of 1s stored on it and just a few hundred 0s. In some places, there might be thousands of 1s in a row. This would make it difficult to read the tape accurately. Why? How might the problem be resolved?

12.3. About how many bytes of computer memory would a 15-page typed, double-spaced term paper fill? Show your calculations.

12.4. How many bits are there in 4M of memory? How many kilobytes?

12.5. Is a keyboard solid-state? Explain your answer.

12.6. Why is the logic circuit necessary in Figure 12.4? That is, why is it not possible to connect wires directly from each keyboard key to some of the flip-flop inputs?

12.7. In Section 12.3, we gave the outline of a program to accept input from a keyboard. Expand the outline so that, if someone types a diagonal (/) on the keyboard, the program will jump to Position 10000. Assume that 45 is the code for a diagonal.

12.8. In Section 12.3, we gave the outline of a program to accept input from a keyboard. Translate the outline into a machine-language program to be stored beginning in Position 0.

12.9. Is the memory in a VDU volatile?

12.10. Can a computer operate without an operating system? Explain your answer. Can it operate without any means of input? Without any means of output?

12.11. Suppose the novelist of Section 12.5 is editing a chapter of her novel when a jolt of static electricity completely changes the contents of her computer's internal memory. Exactly why is this a problem for her? What should she do next?

12.12. We have pointed out that a disk needs a directory to say where each file is stored. Would a tape also need a directory? Explain why or why not.

12.13. The novelist of Section 12.5 stores chapters of her novel on disks instead of in the computer's internal memory. Why?

12.14. What language is the novelist's operating system written in? The WORD-HANDLER program? The HEARTBREAK.ONE file?

12.15. The SHOW command causes the novelist's operating system to display a disk file. If she types SHOW DAVID.LETTER, the letter will appear on her screen. Describe in detail how this happens.

12.16. What would happen if the novelist used the SHOW command described in Exercise 12.15 as follows: SHOW WORDHANDLER?

12.17. Is a disk hardware or software? What about a disk drive? A roll of magnetic tape? An operating system? A Pascal translator?

13 Machine Intelligence

13.1 FALLACIES

Is it possible for a machine to be intelligent? Perhaps the oddest fact about this question is that almost everyone is sure about the answer—some people are sure machines can never be intelligent, others are just as sure they can and will be.

Moreover, it is extremely hard to predict which side of the question a person will fall on. It is not simply a matter of training. Psychologists, philosophers, computer scientists, and members of the general public are all divided into two camps.

Knowing a great deal about computers or intelligence does not seem to settle the point. Likewise, ignorance about both apparently does not inhibit anyone from forming a strong opinion.

In the few pages remaining here, we certainly do not expect or intend to lay this question to rest. It is, however, the place of a textbook to alleviate ignorance, and we will begin by debunking some of the fallacious arguments put forward on both sides.

Our discussion, naturally, will focus on the possibility of programming *computers* for intelligence. But keep in mind that machine intelligence in general is the real question. As we have pointed out several times, anything a computer can do is also within the scope of a machine built with motors, gears, and rods.

The Shifting Target Fallacy. The field of **artificial intelligence**—the part of computer science concerned with programming computers to think—has had some striking successes and failures in its first 30 years. We will be talking about some of these in detail later.

For now, we only want to note a peculiar fact about the successes: Skeptics often point to some particular thinking task as a defining example of what human intelligence can accomplish that machines never will. When artificial intelligence researchers respond, however, with programs that do handle these tasks at human levels of competence, skeptics do not change their minds. Instead, they change their definitions.

Chess playing is a case in point, since there was a time when skeptics and artificial intelligence researchers agreed that it takes intelligence to play a good game of chess.

To someone who has never played chess, this agreement may seem strange. After all, chess is just a game with rules. Is it not possible simply to feed the rules into a computer, have it calculate all the possibilities, and then put out a list of the moves necessary to play a perfect game?

Certainly this is true of a game like tic-tac-toe. Why should chess be any different, in principle?

In fact, in principle it *is* possible to have a computer work through all the possible moves that might ever be made in a chess game and pick out the ones which lead to a win. The problem, in practice, is that there are too many possibilities to consider—more than the number of atoms in the universe.

It is safe to say that there will *never* be a computer powerful enough to analyze a chess game this way, even given centuries of working time.

Lacking the capacity and computation power to check all the possibilities, both human and computer chess players resort to strategies and rules of thumb. They try to "get control of the middle of the board," "force the opponent into unprofitable trades," and so on. Until recently skeptics and boosters alike agreed that this approach would require intelligence.

Of course, now it is possible to buy a good chess-playing computer for less than $100, and the best computer programs play at a very high level, defeating all but the most brilliant human players.

We might add that, in other games, computers have fared even better. Checker-playing programs are matched about equally with the very best human players, and in backgammon, the world's best player, bar none, is a computer.

What do the skeptics say to the demonstrations? They now agree that these games do not require intelligence, in the true sense of the word.

Intelligence is hard to pin down, of course, but many people seem to define it as "whatever it is we can do that computers can't." Naturally, by this definition, computers will never be intelligent. But it is the definition, not the computer, which is at fault.

The Intelligence-Genius Fallacy. Another problem for artificial intelligence researchers is that many people confuse notions of intelligence and genius.

Here, again, chess is a good illustration. Detractors argue that really good chess playing is creative in a way computers cannot match. After all, people can still defeat even the best programs. In this sense, they say, computers are not intelligent even in the narrow realm of the game.

The problem with this argument is that it works just as well to prove that most *people* are not intelligent. After all, nearly all of us would be defeated in a game of chess by the same grandmasters who can beat the computer. Apparently, we do not have the creativity it takes to play a "really good game of chess."

The point, of course, is that the superior ability which distinguishes human grandmasters from computers is evidence not of intelligence, but of genius.

Whatever definition we choose for intelligence, we had better not rule ourselves out. If a computer program designed to come up with new mathematical theorems only produces results which are less than earthshaking, this does not prove it is unintelligent. The same is true of most working mathematicians.

In fact, most of us, most of the time, do nothing that is not done better by someone else. Still, we like to consider that our abilities, such as they are, as evidence of intelligence. If a computer can match average abilities, like ours, we must be ready to concede that it, too, is intelligent.

The Determinism Fallacy. A slightly more sophisticated argument against the possibility of computer intelligence begins with a simple fact: Computers do nothing but follow instructions.

This *is* a fact, of course, as 12 chapters of this book have shown. A computer's actions are completely determined by the program controlling it. It does not follow, however, as many skeptics would have it, that

1. Computers cannot perform creatively and that

2. A computer cannot be smarter than its programmer.

The paradox of the creative machine, perhaps more than anything else, has been a barrier to clear thinking about artificial intelligence. No matter how we define intelligence, creativity seems to be at the crux of it. At the same time, creativity implies creation. A creative thinker produces something completely new. By contrast, we know that a computer only reorganizes and processes information. It cannot make something from nothing.

The problem with this line of reasoning is that it rests on a shaky premise, not about computers, but about people. It is *possible*, of course, that we get our new ideas by applying some special kind of power—a power we get from something other than the gray matter in our brains. Some people believe intuition is such a power. It is equally possible, however, that we get our ideas the same way computers do: by rearranging information.

In fact, if people think exclusively with their brains, that is, if all thinking is the result of signals sent between brain cells, then new ideas *must* be formed in this way, for we have every indication that brain cells work according to simple, fixed rules, just like logic gates in a computer. In this case, *we* are creative machines.[1]

In fact, it is not hard to see how at least some kinds of creativity might boil down to mechanical processes.

Take the example we gave earlier of a program to generate mathematical theorems—proven mathematical truths. If we confine ourselves to Boolean algebra, all we need is the list of axioms from Chapter 1 and a set of rules for putting them together.

---

[1] We are not saying here that people *do* think exclusively with their brains, only that *if* they do, then thinking is a mechanical, albeit highly complex, process.

A computer program that applies these rules to the axioms will produce new logical statements. These new statements may then be combined, according to the same rules, to get still more statements. In fact, by following this process, the computer can produce any number of new logical equalities.

Programs of this sort are not only possible in theory; they have been written and tested. The main conclusion researchers have drawn is that, for anything approaching human creativity, more sophisticated techniques are necessary. But, if the programs are failures in one sense, they are successes in another. Theorem-generating programs are creative.

These programs are also a good counterexample to the idea that computers can never surpass their programmers. The Boolean algebra program might be written by a woman who is a logic professor, a genius in her field, and yet, if the program runs long enough, it will eventually state some logical truth the professor never conceived.

Moreover, although the professor created the program and knows every instruction the computer will carry out in executing it, she *cannot* know all the theorems the program will produce. She may mentally trace the computer's actions to determine the first theorem it will state. She may even work out on paper the first thousand theorems it will state. But the program must eventually come to theorems the professor did not forsee.[2]

A programmer and a creative program are like a professor and student. A man may teach a young woman the laws of physics. He may teach her how to design experiments and how to search through data for patterns. At some point, however, she will begin to apply what he has taught her and, when she does, he is powerless to say what she may discover.

She may be lucky and stumble across an important insight he missed. She may gain new insights by working harder than he does. Finally, she may combine his teachings with those of another professor to yield ideas neither would have invented individually.

In every case, the student goes beyond her mentors simply by applying what she has been taught. A program, in just the same ways, may create knowledge inconceivable to its programmer, even if it does nothing more than follow the programmer's instructions.

The Uncomputability Fallacy. Perhaps the most sophisticated argument skeptics have concocted against artificial intelligence is based on the facts of uncomputability, as described in Chapter 6.

The disturbing truth, as we know, is that there are some simple tasks computers cannot perform. In particular, self-analysis of many kinds is impossible for a programmed computer.

The importance of this fact is not overstated by the skeptics. As they point out, human intelligence rests on a basis of consciousness or self-knowledge. When we think about a problem, we think about *how* we are thinking about it at the same

---

[2] In fact, we have already given a much simpler example of a program that behaves in a manner unpredictable to its programmer. Think back to the program we outlined in Section 6.8 to look for perfect numbers. Unless we happen to know whether there are perfect numbers larger than 28, we cannot say whether the program will stop.

time. Often, this self-analysis is the germ of a creative solution. We see that our method of attack is faulty and we invent a new one.

If the computer lacks our abilities of self-analysis, the skeptics say, it will never attain human levels of intelligence.

Again, the fallacy here is in misperceiving not computers, but people. The halting problem proof is quite definite in its implications about the limits of computing. The question is whether it does not apply as well to human reason.

We know a program cannot be written to tell infallibly whether other programs will stop. But is a human programmer up to the task? If human thinking is entirely a matter of signals between brain cells, then the answer is—positively no.

In this case, the programmer's own method of analyzing programs can be captured in an algorithm, and this algorithm, in turn, can be used to write a program he or she will analyze incorrectly.

If people think with their brains, and not with some extraphysical ability, then human powers of analysis and self-analysis are limited just as the computer's are. The halting problem proves it.

But then the halting problem does not point up any essential difference between people and computers, as the skeptics would have it. Programs might well harness the insights of human-style, *partial* self-analysis.

*   *   *   *   *

We have been firing off potshots at the skeptics now for several pages. It is time to take aim at the believers.

In fairness, however, we must start by saying that most computer scientists have been humbled by the results of the first 30 years of artificial intelligence research. In 1960, it would have been easy to find boosters ready to bet that thinking computers would soon be commonplace. Now it would be hard to find any expecting comprehensive machine intelligence within decades.

The Projection Fallacy. Surprisingly, while researchers have toned down their optimism, many outside the field believe that artificial intelligence is already an achieved fact.

What is even stranger is that this misguided opinion is not new. People have persistently attributed intelligence to computers since they were invented in the 1940s.

These first computers were lumbering monsters, often filling huge rooms and working for hours to carry out simple calculations. The most modest of today's desktop computers can perform the same tasks in minutes.

In the public eyes, however, calculation was a kind of thinking. An enthusiastic press dubbed the new machines "giant electronic brains," and many people took the phrase literally. Manufacturers were forced to reassure the public that these "brains" they produced were not likely to think up a takeover plot during off hours.

In retrospect, it is easy to see that people were straining to understand computers in terms of themselves. Learning that the machine could calculate, they projected other human qualities onto it—understanding, creativity, and even a thirst for power.

This tendency to project qualities onto the computer—to explain their actions in human terms—only increased as computers grew more sophisticated.

In the 1960s, Joseph Weizenbaum at the Massachusetts Institute of Technology created a conversation program called Eliza. People could type messages to Eliza in English and Eliza would respond by typing back answers.

To devise each answer, Eliza used a "script"— a set of rules. One particular script caused the program to act something like a psychiatrist. It began by directing Eliza to ask the patient about his or her problems.

Weizenbaum's results with Eliza and the psychiatrist script were astounding. His own secretary, after a few exchanges with the computer, asked him to leave the room so she could converse more intimately with Eliza. Other people, apparently, also discussed intimate subjects with the computer. When Weizenbaum casually suggested "bugging" the program so that he could record what people were saying to Eliza, he was accused of invasion of privacy.

In fact, some professional psychiatrists went so far as to publish articles suggesting that Eliza might be used for practical therapy in busy hospitals.

The reason these results are so astounding is that Eliza had absolutely no comprehension of English, let alone of psychology or human emotions. The rules in the program's script were extremely simple, most of them based on key emotional words.

For example, if the patient typed in a sentence containing the word *mother*, the program would automatically respond with a related sentence that Weizenbaum had concocted. One of these sentences was *Tell me more about your family*.

Other rules in the script simply converted statements into questions. For example, Eliza might change *I* to *you* and *am* to *are* and add a *Why do you think* at the beginning. Here is the result:

Patient: I can't help being depressed all the time.

Eliza: Why do you think you can't help being depressed all the time?

Patient: I am a bad person.

Eliza: Why do you think you are a bad person?

Patient: I hate my mother.

Eliza: Tell me more about your family.

With a few more tricks of this kind, Eliza convinced many people that an intelligent computer had been built and programmed. They observed a humanlike surface and assumed the computer was humanlike below—that it had the kind of in-depth understanding we bring to conversation.

Again, the machine exhibited a few human qualities; human observers projected the rest.[3]

---

[3] Incidentally, no one was more mortified by this than Weizenbaum himself. He wrote the popular book *Computer Power and Human Reason* (New York: W.H. Freeman & Company Publishers, 1976) to set the record straight.

As a last example, consider the **expert system** programs developed in the 1970s and popularized in the early 1980s. These programs attempted to capture the thinking of a human expert in a specialized field.

Expert systems marked a major turning point in artificial intelligence research. Earlier researchers had aimed to give computers a broad, general kind of intelligence—the ability to learn, generalize from examples, formulate plans, and so on. With expert systems, they concentrated instead on building a huge base of information about a single, technical subject along with methods for applying the information.

This concentration paid off. Expert systems were developed to diagnose diseases, to identify chemicals from precise measurements of their colors, and to analyze geological data to decide where to prospect for valuable minerals. In these tasks, and many others, the programs performed at or near human levels.

For the first time, computers were used to solve important practical problems having more to do with reasoning than with calculation. Medical diagnosis programs, for example, proceeded logically, as a doctor would. They used symptoms to identify possible diseases and asked careful questions to narrow the possibilities still further.

Also, as effective tools for solving practical problems, expert systems were marketable. After decades of producing chess players and toy psychiatrists, artificial intelligence researchers finally had something to sell. The business community sat up to take notice and the media had a field day.

Unfortunately, the public was misled, again, into thinking that the problems of artificial intelligence had been solved.

In fact, expert systems are extremely unintelligent, in most senses of the word. An expert system for medical diagnosis cannot invent a new diagnostic technique. It does not even improve with experience.[4]

Also, unlike the human expert, a medical diagnosis program cannot leave medicine behind and take up chemical analysis. It has no general reasoning abilities, only techniques specifically suited to one field.

Finally, despite the expertise captured in an expert system, the program lacks common sense. If you complain to a human doctor about the rainy weather, the doctor may wonder whether you have been out in it catching a cold. A medical expert system has no understanding of the world, beyond its store of diagnosis rules. It cannot make this kind of connection.

If an expert system can solve problems bright people must study years before tackling, it is tempting to think that it must be generally intelligent. The fallacy, once again, is projection.

The Theory-Practice Fallacy. If the lay public has been over-hasty in attributing intelligence to computers, researchers have often been too quick to assume that programming this intelligence is only a matter of time.

There are two quite separate reasons why computers might *never* be intelligent, the first being that our own intelligence may not be up to the challenge of programming them.

---

[4] Often related programs are designed to learn new rules from experience, but these programs are separate from the expert system, per se.

Tasks that a child manages easily—learning a language or recognizing faces, for example—are beyond today's computers precisely because we have not been able to understand *how* the child manages them.

Nor is there any assurance that we someday *will* understand. All of our research so far into human intelligence indicates that it is immensely complex.

It may be that artificial intelligence is possible in theory, but not in practice. Human thinking may follow a completely algorithmic pattern, and yet we may never discover the algorithm. In fact, it may be that certain circuits and programs would yield intelligence far superior to our own and yet our own limitations might keep us from finding the right combination.

The point here is simple, although it is not widely considered: Even granting that intelligence is a matter of mechanics, people may never succeed in mechanizing it.[5]

The Philosophic Fallacy. The second reason computers may never be intelligent is that it is possible that intelligence is not a matter of mechanics.

The problem here is not confined to artificial intelligence research. It is equally inherent in other scientific fields. In fact, it is fair to say that all of science is founded on the dangerous ground of an unprovable assumption.

The assumption is simply that the natural world is governed by consistent laws and that we may discover these laws through careful observation of nature.

In the case of artificial intelligence, researchers assume that thinking takes place in the brain and that the brain is a physical object subject to the laws of chemistry and physics. This does not mean they intend to explain thinking by considering the brain atom by atom. It does mean, however, that they believe there is nothing "unexplainable" about thinking, no mystic power of intuition transcending physics.

From a pragmatic point of view, the scientific assumption has been dramatically successful. To it we owe modern medicine, architecture, communications, transportation, agriculture—virtually every material comfort of our civilization.

With centuries of success built upon this assumption, it is natural for many people to regard it now as an established fact. The fact is, however, that science cannot prove or disprove its own philosophical underpinnings.

Science has not turned up any evidence to suggest that unmeasurable forces are at work in human thinking. Nor will it. By professional definition, a scientist studies only what is measurable. If thinking *is* the result of mystical powers, scientists will never discover the fact.

All this is certainly not to say that the scientific assumption is false, in artificial intelligence research or in any other field. But until an intelligent computer is built and programmed, we are forced to admit that the project *may* be impossible, even in theory.

---

[5] Incidentally, we have made a strong case for the power of bootstrapping and have gone so far as to suggest that computers may someday design more powerful versions of themselves. This does not contradict the alternative possibility that intelligent computers may never exist. The bootstrapping effort may simply not get off the ground. That is, human ingenuity may never produce a computer capable of designing a better one.

13.2 INTELLIGENCE

As some of the foregoing arguments illustrate, intelligence is tricky to define. We must have some definition, however, for the sake of discussion. With apologies for circularity, then, we propose the following:

> **Intelligence**:   The ability to act in ways that would be considered evidence of *human* intelligence.

Despite the obvious failings of this definition, it introduces an important and useful idea. In judging the intelligence of a machine, we will look not to its mechanism, but to its actions. If it behaves intelligently, we will call it intelligent.

This definition is designed with the target-shifting skeptic in mind. It is only natural that intelligent behavior should lose its mystery after it is captured in a program. But mystery should not be a necessary feature of intelligence. If a certain kind of behavior is agreed to demonstrate intelligence before it is explained, it ought to be considered intelligent afterward as well.

Before the advent of computers, chess-playing and medical diagnostic skills were held to be marks of intelligence. By our definition, then, chess-playing programs and medical expert systems are also intelligent.

Two points are immediately in order, before we put this definition to work. First, when we say that a chess-playing program is intelligent, by our definition, we clearly do not mean it is so in all ways. We mean simply that it plays chess intelligently. The definition recognizes *partial* intelligence.

Second, the definition is extremely lenient. Since adding and subtracting numbers was thought to require intelligence before machines were designed for the purpose, our definition forces us to say that computers calculate intelligently.

In mitigation of these points, we should add that nothing in the definition prevents us from making personal judgments about the *value* of various intelligent behaviors. We may well feel that the kind of intelligence involved in medical diagnosis is more important and interesting than the kind involved in addition.

*   *   *   *   *

If we want computers to be intelligent, what must they do? By our definition, the answer is that they must do whatever people do that demonstrates intelligence.

When we begin to analyze intelligent human actions, however, we find that they often have a great deal in common. Chess and checker playing, for example, both involve strategy and planning. Game playing in general depends on some of the same intellectual faculties used in other kinds of problem solving. An intelligent player learns from mistakes, invents useful rules of thumb, and so on.

One approach to understanding and creating intelligence, then, is to investigate these common elements of intelligent human behavior. We will do so, and to emphasize that we are looking into everyday intelligence and not, say, mathematical genius, we will choose a homely example for our investigation.

Consider, then, Jeff and Joanna, who are moving house. Their immediate problem is simply to load furniture and packed belongings into a truck they have rented.

On the face of it, this problem is so ordinary that it may be hard to see how intelligence is involved at all. In fact, as we are about to see, the difficulties are imposing.

To start, the truck may not be packed haphazardly. One reason is that the couple's belongings will not fit in the truck unless space is used carefully. Another is that Joanna's collection of porcelain sculptures is not likely to fare well if, say, a dresser is placed on top of it.

Before they begin any physical work, then, Jeff and Joanna need a plan. After a few minutes to think it over, they will probably arrive at something like the following:

LOADING PLAN

Load all the furniture into the truck first.

Next, fill nooks and spaces with durable or crushable items.

Finally, lay fragile items on top.

Of course, this plan is only an outline. As the work progresses, these major tasks will need to be divided into smaller ones, each requiring its own plan. For example, the couple will need a plan for loading the furniture: heavier items should be loaded before lighter ones.

Even moving an individual item may require a plan. The plan for a heavy dresser might be to remove the drawers and then roll it on a dolly.

Notice, also, that Jeff and Joanna's plans are flexible at every level of detail. When Jeff comes to a flight of stairs while rolling the dresser on a dolly, he must scrap the original plan and come up with a new one. When Joanna notices a safe place for her porcelain collection in the space under a chair, she will put it there, even though the main plan tells her to load fragile items last.

Evidently, both in planning and in carrying out plans, Jeff and Joanna must rely on common sense. When we analyze what we mean here by the phrase *common sense*, however, we will find that it is uncommonly complex.

First of all, loading the truck is not just a theoretical problem of fitting geometrical shapes into a fixed space. It is important to know that dollies do not roll down stairs, that fragile items may break if heavy ones are placed on top of them, that porcelain is fragile, and that dresser drawers may be removed. Knowing facts like these about physical objects is one part of common sense.

Another part is illustrated by Joanna's decision to put her sculpture collection under a chair. Possibly, of course, she might have found a good place for it after packing the rest of the truck. Her decision is guided by the common-sense notion that it is wise to take advantage of opportunities as they arise.

General rules of thumb like this one are called **heuristics**.

Having a large collection of useful facts and heuristics is essential for common sense, but it is not sufficient. For example, Jeff knows that the dolly is made of rough wood and that rough wood sometimes gives people splinters. He knows that wood burns. He knows that the dolly has wheels and that, if wheels squeak, it is a good idea to oil them.

When he comes to the stairs, however, he is likely to have an accident if he begins to turn all these points over in his mind. Instead, from his huge store of potentially relevant information, he must instantly recall the one essential fact—that wheels roll well only on smooth surfaces.

Common sense, then, is not only a matter of having useful information about the world and how to cope with it, but also of finding the right information at the right time. This, in turn, depends on two separate factors.

One reason Jeff gets the fact he needs so quickly is that his memory is phenomenally well organized. By contrast, consider looking through an encyclopedia for a sentence indicating that wheeled vehicles do not perform well on stairs. Would there be an article on wheels? If not, should we look under transportation? Or under specific uses of wheels like automobiles?

Finding the correct article is only part of the problem—the easier part, since encyclopedias arrange articles alphabetically. Even if we are lucky enough to find an article on wheels, we might be forced to read several pages of it before turning up the information we want.

Clearly, Jeff's store of common-sense facts is organized much more efficiently. He can check his memory to see if wheels are used in cars, if wheels are usually square, if there are any words that rhyme with wheel, and if there is ever any reason to have a wheel spinning horizontally, all in less time than it would take to reach for the W volume.

Organization is only half the story, however. The other half is knowing what to look up.

As Jeff rolls the dresser toward the stairs, all kind of relevant and irrelevant thoughts cross his mind. Some are touched off internally: he wonders, for example, how long it will take to pack the truck. Other thoughts are sparked by information arriving through his senses: he notices how hot it is; he sees the hallway light switch, the closet door,. . .the *stairs*.

Somehow this seemingly chaotic flow of thoughts must be controlled, however. In fact, it is directed with amazing efficiency so that, of all the possible paths Jeff's thoughts might take, the one that leads to a question about wheels and stairs is chosen in time to avert disaster.

*   *   *   *   *

Planning, heuristics, sophisticated memory organization, world knowledge— we have uncovered all of these in looking at the simple job of packing a truck. Moreover, we are far from finished. Consider the following sequence of events:

> Jeff and Joanna are straining to carry a heavy antique wooden table. As they pass through a doorway, one of the legs hits and cracks slightly. "Hold it," Joanna says. "Let's flip it over and roll it on the dolly like you did with the dresser." On the next trip out to the truck, they use the dolly to roll a heavy box of framed paintings instead of carrying it.

What elements of intelligence come into play here?

First, faced with a problem, Joanna solves it in a uniquely human way. The problem is how to move the antique table safely. Part of the trouble is that it is too heavy to maneuver easily. From this point in her reasoning, Joanna draws an **analogy**: The table is like the dresser in that both are heavy. With this comparison in mind, she considers rolling the table on the dolly and realizes this will make it easier to maneuver.

Notice that the key step in this line of reasoning is not a matter of applying logic. Joanna's insight is based on association. She solves a problem by thinking of another one *like* it.

This approach is not guaranteed to work. For example, Joanna might have noticed that the table is like her porcelain sculpture collection in that both are fragile. This might have made her think of putting it in a box with padding.

Also, most of the analogies Joanna might have made are as irrelevant to her problem as Jeff's stockpile of facts about wood and wheels. She needs some kind of control mechanism to make sure she keeps her comparisons to the point.

Despite its drawbacks, however, thinking by analogy is a primary source of human creativity. Surefire creation rules—like the ones used in the Boolean algebra theorem generator—appear to play an extremely minor role by comparison.

Associative thinking, then, is one element of intelligence evidenced in the moving scenario. Another is learning. After cracking the table leg, Jeff and Joanna do not make the mistake of trying to carry the box of paintings. Instead, they draw on experience.

This ability to learn is an obvious feature of human intelligence. Less obvious is the fact that it depends heavily on abstraction, of the kind we discussed in Chapter 5.

In abstracting, we move from particular examples to general classes. For example, after seeing a number of devices for turning things on and off, we develop the abstract notion of a switch.

The individual examples of switches, on which we base this notion, may differ widely in color, in design, and in the appliances they control. In abstracting to the general idea, we find what the examples have in common—power control—and filter out other details.

The important point is that general classes make general ideas possible. Having the notion of a switch, we may learn that switches are two-state devices. Without it, we are forced to note *separately* that the white, squarish, toggling unit in the hallway is a two-state device, the round, chrome, push-button unit on the television is a two-state device, and so on.

On a more mundane level, Joanna's experience with the table causes her to add a new heuristic to her store of common sense: Unwieldy, fragile items should be rolled, rather than carried. But the formation of this thought, in turn, depends on her ability to create the abstract category of unwieldy, fragile items.

Without abstraction, each slightly differing version of a problem would require a new solution. Experience would not be generally applicable, and thus, learning would be impossible.

*   *   *   *   *

One final bit of intelligent behavior in the moving scenario is so complex that it appears to rely on nearly all the elements we have identified so far. And yet, it is a basic element of human thinking.

We are referring to language, the production and interpretation of statements like Joanna's: "Hold it, let's flip it over and roll it on the dolly like you did with the dresser."

Leaving aside the question of how Joanna forms this statement, consider for a moment the task Jeff faces in understanding it.

In theory, this task may be divided into two parts: parsing the sentence to determine its structure, and extracting the meaning. In practice, however, these parts cannot be separated.

It is impossible to determine the meaning of *flip*, for example, without understanding what part it plays in the sentence. Taken alone, the word might be a noun meaning "an aerial somersault," or it might be a verb meaning "to turn over."

The same is true of *roll*, which would be edible in another context.

At the same time, it is impossible to determine the structure fully without taking meaning into account. Consider the phrase *like you did with the dresser*. Does Joanna mean to *roll* the table like the dresser or to flip *and* roll it like the dresser?

The answer is obvious to Jeff, because he remembers that the dresser did not require any flipping. But there is nothing inherent in the sentence that indicates this fact. In parsing, he uses meaning and context to determine that the phrase *like you did with the dresser* modifies only the verb *roll*.

There are other ambiguities in the sentence that might trip Jeff up. A dolly could be a kind of toy. A dresser could be a person who dresses. The word *it* in the phrases *flip it* and *roll it* refers to something not specified in the sentence.

Finally, the phrase *hold it* has perfectly sensible meanings other than the one Joanna intends. Jeff might think that she is reminding him to hold the dresser, or suggesting for him to hold the door as they pass through.

In fact, of course, Jeff avoids all these pitfalls and understands instantly that

1. *Dolly* here refers to a rolling device.
2. *Dresser* refers to the piece of furniture he is moving.
3. *It* in the phrases *flip it* and *roll it* refers to the dresser.
4. And *hold it* means simply to stop, with the word *it* referring to nothing at all.

Again understanding the context of the situation is what leads Jeff to correct interpretations. This ability to fit statements into a framework, or **frame**, is a central part of human language understanding and, apparently, a fundamental feature of our thinking.

*   *   *   *   *

By now, we have compiled quite a long list of elements of intelligent behavior. Without much trouble, we may also add a few from earlier chapters.

In Chapter 1, for example, we discussed **chunking**—the ability to think of many related elements as a single system. Chunking is the mental leap we take when we consider a group of people as a family, or a construction of wires, hammers, boards, and keys as a piano.

Without it, our world would be an unintelligible morass of sensations. It is impossible to have the notion of a "face," for example, without being able to chunk together the ideas of "eyes," "ears," "nose," and so on.

In fact, even these simpler ideas are chunked-together visual images. An eye is an oval shape with a dark, circular center and a curving brow above. Imagine having to think of each of these geometric parts separately to have the idea of "eye" in mind.

Actually, without chunking, it might be impossible to think of something as complex as an eye. Psychological investigations have shown that people normally can keep only five to nine ideas in mind at once. By chunking, however, a single one of those ideas may take the place of many. As we have remarked, chunking unclutters the mind.

In Chapter 1, we also looked into logical reasoning. George Boole may have been wrong in assuming that most human thought boils down to logical deduction, but a working grasp of at least some of his laws is essential in everyday life.

Leaving aside the work of mathematicians and other specialists, the logic people apply is often so simple that it goes unnoticed. If we see Jeff at a party, we are likely to look for Joanna. Unconsciously, we have constructed the following logical argument:

Jeff and Joanna usually go places together.

Jeff is here.

Therefore, Joanna is probably here too.

As a final item for our list, consider the kind of consciousness we discussed in Chapter 2 and, again, earlier in this chapter. We have defined it as a feedback loop making possible self-knowledge, and self-analysis.

We have already pointed out that consciousness is often at the bottom of creative problem solving. We observe ourselves thinking about a problem and adjust the method of attack as we proceed.

In fact, however, this system of thinking and thinking about thinking appears to have a great deal to do with creativity of other kinds.

Suppose a composer named Glenn Lieberman is writing his tenth trio sonata. He is likely to ask himself whether this new piece of music does not sound too much like the last nine. He will think not only about the music, but about his way of composing it. If he *is* in a rut, this self-analysis will help him break out of it—to compose creatively.

We have introduced this aspect of consciousness as a two-level system, but it may sometimes reach higher. Thinking about thinking about thinking might seem a waste of time, but consider the composer again.

In writing his tenth trio sonata, Lieberman may notice that his melodic themes are always roughly the same length, 10 to 15 notes long. Here he is thinking about his composing—thinking about thinking. The result might be that he experiments with longer or shorter themes.

A few trio sonatas later, the same level of self-analysis might lead Lieberman to discover that his themes are always beautifully harmonious. He might think to introduce intentional discord.

Eventually, however, he may begin to see patterns, not only in his composing, but in his analyses of it. For example, he may notice that every time he tries to break out of a musical rut, his solution is to change his approach to melody. This itself is a kind of rut. To break out of it, he might consider writing a trio sonata based primarily on rhythm, or one without fixed melodic themes.

In this case, Lieberman is analyzing his analysis of his composing—thinking about thinking about thinking.

This faculty of many-leveled self-analysis is what keeps the composer from mechanically churning out the same kind of music. In fact, it is at the core of human creativity. All of us notice the patterns in our own behavior and the patterns in how we break those patterns, and so on. The result is that we can change ourselves and our approaches to the many problems of living.

And yet, this many-leveled self-analysis is neither complete nor infinitely deep. All of us have patterns at many levels which we do not notice or cannot change. In a composer, these patterns amount to musical style. In the rest of us, they form the basis of personality.

13.3 MACHINE INTELLIGENCE

People organize masses of practical information about the world as well as masses of heuristics for how to deal with it. They make analogies, use frames, think logically, understand English, chunk, abstract, learn, plan. Moreover, they watch themselves doing all these things and profit from the self-analysis to act creatively.

What about computers?

Part of the answer is that researchers have programmed them to do all of these things. The other part is that they can do none of them nearly as well as we do.

The reason is as odd as it is simple: People cannot say how they do what they do.

The question of what goes on in people's minds is at least as old as ancient Greek philosophy. And for centuries, there have been scientific theories of the mind, both psychological and physiological.

The result of all this investigation, however, is almost embarrassing. After thousands of years, no one can even explain how people understand simple sentences, or how they remember so quickly not to roll dollies down stairs.

One reason so little progress has been made in all this time is that, until recently, theories were virtually untestable. Psychologists might have had ideas about how facts are organized in the human brain, but ethics prevented them from digging directly into someone's skull to check.

For the most part, psychological evidence about human intelligence was gathered secondhand, by observing performance on problem-solving and memory tests. The results were open to interpretation, and interpretations differed widely.

The advent of computers changed this dramatically. Given a computer, someone who has a theory about how facts are organized in human memory should be able to write a program that uses the same organization system. If the program does not perform as well as people do, the theory must be mistaken, or at least incomplete.

Of course, if the program is a success, this does not prove that the theory is correct. The computer may perform as well as humans using an entirely different approach.

As an acid test for proving theories wrong, however, the computer has been tremendously effective. In the space of 30 years, artificial intelligence research has virtually wiped out traditional ideas about how the mind functions. In trying to use these ideas to design programs, researchers have either turned up inconsistencies or found that essential details were left out.

It is as if people had argued for centuries about the theory of architecture and then, when they finally came down to building a house, no one could make a wall stand up.

*   *   *   *   *

By contrast, despite many setbacks, artificial intelligence researchers have laid a foundation and erected a framework. Progress in **natural language processing** illustrates what has been accomplished.

Natural languages are the ones people naturally use to communicate— English, Chinese, and so on—as opposed to invented languages like Fortran or the notation of Boolean algebra. From our discussion, in Chapter 11, it should be quite evident that, while Fortran may be parsed and interpreted with relative ease, understanding English is not nearly such a simple matter.

This was not evident, however, to early artificial intelligence researchers, who attempted to write programs to translate between Russian and English. They expected a quick success. Individual words would be translated using a dictionary. Grammatical rules compiled by linguists would be used to take care of chores like conjugating verbs and forming plurals.

The result?

Sheer disaster. In one test, researchers fed in the English phrase *The spirit is willing, but the flesh is weak*. The program translated it into Russian and the result was fed in to be translated back into English. The final output was a statement about bad meat and good vodka.

The problem, naturally, was that the program took the word *spirit* to mean an alcoholic beverage. Without a common-sense understanding of the world, translation is impossible.

Having learned this lesson, however, researchers went on to produce better programs. One famous example is Terry Winograd's SHRDLU program, designed to understand English statements about a simplified environment that came to be called "blocks world".

Blocks world was simply a table top with blocks scattered on it. The blocks were of different shapes and colors and might be stacked up to make piles, arches, towers, and so on.

Winograd began by giving SHRDLU a general understanding of this world, something like our own understanding of the real world. For example, the program might have access to "common-sense" facts like these:

1. Semicircle blocks have curved tops.

2. It is impossible to stack something on a block with a curved top.

3. To pick up a block with other blocks stacked on top of it, it is first necessary to take these other blocks off.

In addition, he gave it specific facts about the condition of blocks world. For the situation pictured in Figure 13.1, these might be as follows:

1. There is a small, yellow, semicircle block on top of a big, blue square block,

2. There is a small, blue, square block standing by itself,

and

3. There is a big, red, square block standing by itself.

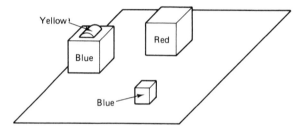

Figure 13.1 Blocks world.

Winograd then designed SHRDLU to use this information in interpreting English sentences. The result was a language processor with a much more human approach than the unsuccessful translators.

By typing messages back and forth, Winograd and SHRDLU could have conversations something like this one:

Winograd: Pick up the blue block.

SHRDLU: Do you mean the big one or the small one?

Winograd: The small one.

SHRDLU: OK.

Winograd: Put it on the red block.

SHRDLU: OK.

The program's understanding of the state of blocks world allows it to see that Winograd's first statement is ambiguous. It requests a clarification.

Understanding of context in conversation helps with the word *it* in Winograd's last statement. SHRDLU understands from previous statements that this refers to the small blue block.

Of course, SHRDLU had no understanding of the real world beyond the table top. In practical terms, it was useless. But in the early 1970s it was a striking success, a far cry from Eliza-like programs of the preceding decade.

Moreover, SHRDLU pointed the way to practical programs. Building on Winograd's work, researchers have gone far beyond blocks world. Today, programs can understand English in many real-world environments. Given a base of facts about major American companies, for example, programs can answer complicated questions like this one:

Which firms are the top five in earnings?

The best of today's natural language processors are still a long way from competing with human language skills, but they are also far from toys. Computers *now* cope with language intelligently.

*   *   *   *   *

Creative programs are also gradually becoming a force to be reckoned with.

Early attempts called for computers to place dots randomly on a page to create a "picture" or string notes together in simple patterns to compose "music." A little experimentation showed mainly that this kind of creativity is stultifyingly boring.

As with language processing, however, breakthroughs resulted when researchers narrowed the problem. One famous example is Douglas Lenat's AM program, which conducts original mathematical research.

Instead of just letting the program randomly put facts together to get new ones, Lenat introduced heuristics to give the computer a sense of which facts are of mathematical interest.

AM proceeds something like a real mathematician. It might start out, for example, by investigating division. At first, it just experiments, dividing numbers to see what happens. Eventually, however, Lenat's heuristics will lead the program to take a special interest in some of the results.

One heuristic, for example, suggests looking at extreme cases. AM might decide to look at numbers which have very few or very many divisors.[6] This leads it to narrow its experiments. It might check all the numbers from 1 to 100 to see how many divisors each has.

This turns up the fact that every number has at least two divisors: 1 and the number itself. AM uses this fact to create a new concept, numbers with only two divisors. This new kind of number—which human mathematicians call "prime"— then becomes a new research interest for the program. It goes on to conduct experiments concerning prime numbers.

When the AM program was first tested, more than 10 years ago, it turned up nothing people had not already discovered. It did, however, hit on subjects that professional mathematicians had considered worthy of attention. In particular, it invented at least one recognized mathematical concept that Lenat himself had never heard of.

*   *   *   *   *

---

[6] A divisor of a number is one which divides it evenly. For example, the number 12 has six divisors: 1, 2, 3, 4, 6, and 12 all divide it evenly.

As a last example of what intelligent programs are capable of, consider Ryszard Michalski's INDUCE program, which simulates a certain kind of learning.

Earlier in this chapter, we pointed out how important it is for people to form abstract classes like "switch." Very often, however, distinguishing between classes is difficult. For example, how can we tell an oak from a maple tree?

Of course, if a man does not know the difference, it is not necessary to tell him. If we show him a few examples of each, he will eventually learn that, say, the oak trees are the ones producing acorns. That is, he will create an identification rule.

This process is central to our ability to learn a language. Of the words we know, very few were carefully defined for us. We learn what *man, apple, truck*, and *tree* mean just by seeing plenty of examples.

Distinguishing between classes is also important in advanced fields of learning. For example, doctors need to develop identification rules to decide whether someone's symptoms mean heartburn or appendicitis.

This is where INDUCE comes in. Michalski developed the program using a series of puzzles. INDUCE was given information about, say, two groups of toy trains. Its problem was to form an identification rule explaining how to distinguish the groups.

When Michalski had written a good program for this job, however, he tested it on a real-world problem, diagnosing soybean diseases. He gave the program information about hundreds of already diagnosed plants and asked it to come up with ways to identify all the different diseases. Then he did the same with human experts.

INDUCE did as well as the best of the experts, and better than some.

13.4 TAKING STOCK OF OURSELVES

We have tried to be evenhanded in this chapter, considering both the successes and failures of artificial intelligence research. After the examples we have just given, however, it is hard not to feel as if intelligent computers are already nipping at our intellectual heels.

Keep in mind, too, that the examples we have been discussing are already out of date. Computers can do much more than we have said. And they will do still more tomorrow.

The growth of mechanical intelligence is disturbing to many people. It upsets our conception of ourselves as conscious beings. It makes us ask what we are and what it is important for us to be.

Are *we* computers?

This, finally, is the question that artificial intelligence poses, and poses ever more clearly as computers grow in power. The question is not about computers, but about ourselves.

Unfortunately, the answer is not given in these pages. It is written in the future, perhaps a future we will live to see. This much, however, we may say: Whatever the answer, computers will help us find it.

Index